Contents

53

102

Lisbon

www.timeout.com

Time Out Digital Ltd
4th Floor
125 Shaftesbury Avenue
London WC2H 8AD
United Kingdom
Tel: +44 (0)20 7813 3000
Fax: +44 (0)20 7813 6001
Email: guides@timeout.com
www.timeout.com

Published by Time Out Digital Ltd, a wholly owned subsidiary
of Time Out Group Ltd. Time Out and the Time Out logo are
trademarks of Time Out Group Ltd.

© Time Out Group Ltd 2015
Previous editions 1999, 2001, 2004, 2007, 2010.

10 9 8 7 6 5 4 3 2 1

This edition first published in Great Britain in 2015 by Ebury Publishing
20 Vauxhall Bridge Road, London SW1V 2SA

Ebury Publishing is part of the Penguin Random House group of companies
whose addresses can be found at global.penguinrandomhouse.com

Distributed in the US and Latin America by Publishers Group West
(1-510-809-3700)

For further distribution details, see www.timeout.com.

ISBN: 978-1-84670-332-4

A CIP catalogue record for this book is available from the British Library.

Printed and bound in China by Leo Paper Products Ltd.

While every effort has been made by the author(s) and the publisher to
ensure that the information contained in this guide is accurate and up to
date as at the date of publication, they accept no responsibility or liability
in contract, tort, negligence, breach of statutory duty or otherwise for any
inconvenience, loss, damage, costs or expenses of any nature whatsoever
incurred or suffered by anyone as a result of any advice or information
contained in this guide (except to the extent that such liability may not be
excluded or limited as a matter of law). Before travelling, it is advisable
to check all information locally, including without limitation, information
on transport, accommodation, shopping and eating out. Anyone using
this guide is entirely responsible for their own health, well-being and
belongings and care should always be exercised while travelling.

All rights reserved. No part of this publication may be reproduced, stored
in a retrieval system, or transmitted in any form or by any means, electronic,
mechanical, photocopying, recording or otherwise, without prior permission
from the copyright owners.

Penguin Random House is committed to a sustainable future for our
business, our readers and our planet. This book is made from Forest
Stewardship Council® certified paper.

MIX
Paper from
responsible sources
FSC® C018179
www.fsc.org

189

40

177

Time Out **Lisbon**

Editorial
Editor Alison Roberts
Copy Editor Dominic Earle
Listings Editor Alexandre Bezerra
Proofreader Marion Moisy

Editorial Director Sarah Guy
Group Finance Manager Margaret Wright

Design
Senior Designer Kei Ishimaru
Designer Rob Baalham
Group Commercial Senior Designer Jason Tansley

Picture Desk
Picture Editor Jael Marschner
Deputy Picture Editor Ben Rowe
Freelance Picture Researcher Lizzy Owen

Advertising
Managing Director St John Betteridge

Marketing
Senior Publishing Brand Manager Luthfa Begum
Head of Circulation Dan Collins

Production
Production Controller Katie Mulhern-Bhudia

Time Out Group
Chairman & Founder Tony Elliott
Chief Executive Officer Tim Arthur
Publisher Alex Batho
Group IT Director Simon Chappell
Group Marketing Director Carolyn Sims

Contributors
Lisbon's Top 20, Lisbon Today, Itineraries, Diary, Lisbon's Best, Film, Performing Arts, Escapes & Excursions Alison Roberts. **Explore** Brad Cherry, Alison Roberts (*Walk* Peter Wise). **Hotels** Alexandre Bezerra, Alison Roberts. **Children** Barry Hatton, Alison Roberts. **Gay & Lesbian** John Owens, Alison Roberts. **Nightlife** Alexandre Bezerra, Alison Roberts. **History** Brad Cherry, Alison Roberts. **Architecture** Dave Rimmer, Alison Roberts. **Essential Information** Alexandre Bezerra, Alison Roberts.

Maps JS Graphics Ltd (john@jsgraphics.co.uk)

Cover and pull-out map photography Masterfile

Back cover photography Clockwise from top left: LisbonLux; Giancana/Shutterstock.com; © Park Bar, Lisbon; Living Allowed; Steve Photography/Shutterstock.com

Photography pages 4 (top), 5 (bottom left), 12 (bottom), 13 (top), 40, 53, 62 saiko3p/Shutterstock.com; 4 (bottom), 10, 10/11, 11, 25 (top), 36/37, 42/43, 114/115, 116, 102, 159, 198/199, 204 StockPhotosArt/Shutterstock.com; 5 (top), 189 Marafona/Shutterstock.com; 5 (bottom right), 177 (bottom left) rui vale sousa/Shutterstock.com; 7, 205 Rosa Reis; 12 (top) JCphotography; 12 (middle) Benoit Daoust/Shutterstock.com; 13 (bottom), 203 Martin Lehmann/Shutterstock.com; 14, 104/105, 180 Giancana/Shutterstock.com; 14/15 LisbonLux.com - Mario Fernandes; 15 LisbonLux; 16/17 Rui Gomes/Shutterstock.com; 20 (top), 177 (top) Turismo de Lisboa; 21 (left) Clara Azevedo; 22 Sergey Peterman/Shutterstock.com; 22/23 (top) Plaats/Wikimedia Commons; 23, 182/183 Rob van Esch/ Shutterstock.com; 24/25 Bert Kaufmann/Wikimedia Commons; 25 (bottom), 31, 223 José Frade; 26/27 Alexander Silva; 30 ModaLisboa/Rui Vasco; 32 Gustavo Miguel Fernandes/Shutterstock.com; 36 (top) Paulo Barata; 36 (bottom) David Rato; 37, 157 Imagens de Luz; 38/39 Markus Mainka/Shutterstock.com; 49 Steve Photography/Shutterstock. com; 58 GVictoria/Shutterstock.com; 58/59 INTERPIXELS/Shutterstock.com; 66 anyaivanova/Shutterstock.com; 69 Paulo Seabra; 70 jiawangkun/Shutterstock.com; 70/71, 174 (top) nito/Shutterstock.com; 74 Paulo Barata; 80 Miguel Angelo Silva/Shutterstock.com; 83 Miguel Guedes Ramos; 90 Ricardo Junqueira; 90/91 ATGImages/Shutterstock. com; 101 Cortesia Atelier Joana Vasconcelos; 104, 166, 190 Luis Santos/Shutterstock.com; 106 (bottom) © António Jorge Silva/Atelier-Museu Júlio Pomar 2014; 111 Oliver Hoffmann/Shutterstock.com; 113, 203 Rob Wilson/ Shutterstock.com; 114 Christopher Poe/Shutterstock.com; 121 Ververidis Vasilis/Shutterstock.com; 126 © Galeria Filomena Soares; 128/129, 150 Paulo Vaz Henriques; 137 (right) Everett Collection/REX; 146 Pedro Janeiro; 153 Samuel Sequeira; 154 João Silveira Ramos; 156 Alipio Padilha; 160 Agathe Poupeney/Fedephoto; 161 © Abílio Leitão; 162 Joao Morgado; 164/165 Karol Kozlowski/Shutterstock.com; 167 karnizz/Shutterstock.com; 168 Marina Mikhaylova/Shutterstock.com; 169 Jorge Pereira/Shutterstock.com; 170 Sean Pavone/Shutterstock.com; 173 Luis Louro/Shutterstock.com; 174 (bottom) Luis Ferreira Alves; 175 © 2009 Casa das Histórias Paula Rego; 177 (bottom right), 200 Cantemir Olaru/Shutterstock.com; 178 ruzgar344/Shutterstock.com; 179 Anton_Ivanov/Shutterstock. com; 181, 240/241 Carlos Caetano/Shutterstock.com; 184/185, 186 Time Out Museum-Lisbon City Council; 187 Science Photo Library; 195 stick2target.com; 196 Jean-Claude Francolon/Gamma-Rapho/Getty Images; 201 Gary James Calder/Shutterstock.com; 202 Vlada Z/Shutterstock.com; 206/207, 222 PLANO FOCAL; 208, 212 Living Allowed; 213 Luis Aniceto; 215 José Manuel; 221 Artur Henriques

The following images were supplied by the featured establishments: 2, 20 (bottom), 21 (right), 22/23 (bottom), 24 (bottom), 27, 28/29, 40/41, 46, 54, 65, 79, 87, 88, 94, 97, 106 (top), 110, 130, 134, 135, 137 (left), 138, 139, 141, 142, 145, 171, 209, 210, 217, 218

About the Guide

GETTING AROUND

Each sightseeing chapter contains a street map of the area marked with the locations of sights and museums (❶), restaurants (❶), cafés and bars (❶) and shops (❶). There are also street maps of Lisbon at the back of the book, along with an overview map of the city. In addition, there is a detachable fold-out street map.

THE ESSENTIALS

For practical information, including visas, disabled access, emergency numbers, lost property, websites and local transport, see the Essential Information section. It begins on page 206.

THE LISTINGS

Addresses, phone numbers, websites, transport information, hours and prices are all included in our listings, as are selected other facilities. All were checked and correct at press time. However, business owners can alter their arrangements at any time, and fluctuating economic conditions can cause prices to change rapidly.

The very best venues in the city, the must-sees and must-dos in every category, have been marked with a red star (★). In the sightseeing chapters, we've also

marked venues with free admission with a FREE symbol.

THE LANGUAGE

Many Lisboetas speak a little English, but a few basic Portuguese phrases go a long way. You'll find a primer on page 233, along with some help with restaurants on page 234.

PHONE NUMBERS

Lisbon numbers start with 21 (this forms part of the number). To dial another part of Portugal from Lisbon, simply dial the number, which invariably starts with 2; there are no area codes. (If you have an old number together with an area code starting with zero, try replacing the zero with a 2.) From outside Portugal, dial your country's international access code (00 from the UK, 011 from the US) or a plus symbol, followed by the country code for Portugal (351). So, to reach the Museu Nacional de Arte Antiga, dial +351 21 391 2800. For more on phones, *see p231*.

FEEDBACK

We welcome feedback on this guide, both on the venues we've included and on any other locations that you'd like to see featured in future editions. Please email us at guides@ timeout.com.

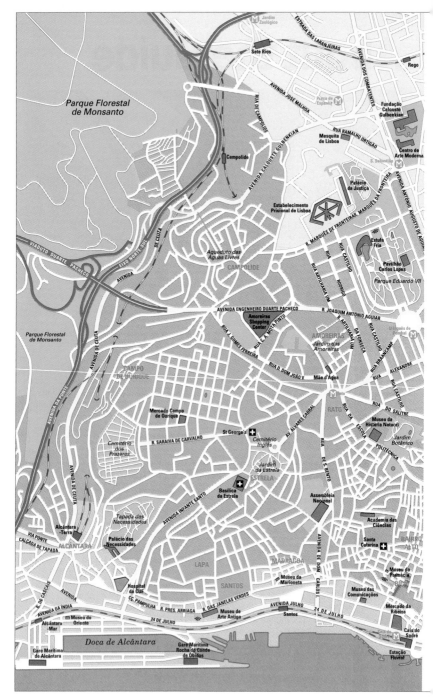

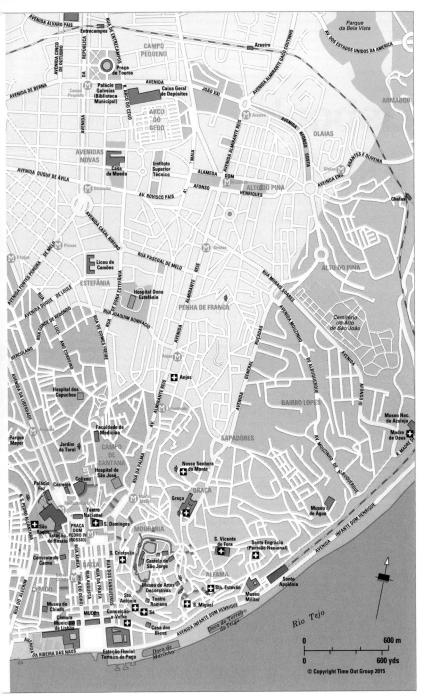

Lisbon's
Top 20

*From historical sights to
affordable food, drink and
fun, we count down the
city's top attractions.*

1 Castelo de São Jorge
(page 64)

St George's Castle is the place to head to
get a sense of Lisbon's history, from the
city's pre-Roman origins to the Christian
Reconquest. The mainly Moorish
structure standing today has been overly
renovated, but strolling around or sitting
on the ramparts will fill an atmospheric
hour or so. Above all, the location, on
top of one of Lisbon's highest hills,
makes this a great vantage point to
get a sense of the city's topography.

2 Baixa
(page 42)

Laid out in the wake of the devastating 1755 earthquake – which had a huge impact on European culture at the time – Lisbon's Baixa, or downtown, was intended and heralded as an exemplar of Enlightenment ideals of elegance and order. Construction was overseen by the chief minister of the time, known to posterity as the Marquês de Pombal (see also p190).

3 Alfama
(page 64)

There could hardly be a greater contrast with neighbouring Baixa than this jumble of houses, many of whose walls and foundations date back centuries. The lines traced out by streets and alleyways in this maze are largely inherited from Moorish times. Here, traditions such as fado music are also very much alive. The ideal way to get to know Alfama is to wander and get a little lost.

4 Azulejos
(page 202)

The most striking feature in architectural – and interior – decoration in Portugal, ceramic tiles have a history that stretches back to late medieval tines. The peak was reached much later, in the 17th and 18th centuries, when church and monastery cloisters and palaces were lined with wonderful panels. Today, many artists are again favouring *azulejos* as a medium.

5 Portuguese cuisine
(page 74)

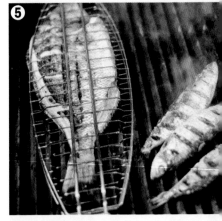

If there's anything the Portuguese think and talk about as much as football, it's food – invariably the traditional kind. Today a new generation of chefs such as José Avillez and Henrique Sá Pessoa are reinventing the old standards, by applying modern techniques to the best fresh seafood and other local ingredients. You'll find the price-quality relationship here amazingly good, if you take care to avoid tourist traps and head for places that are packed with locals tucking into authentic *cozinha portuguesa*.

6 Oceanário
(page 132)

The Oceanarium is one of the legacies of the 1998 Expo (World Fair), whose theme was the world's oceans. Its striking architecture contains a range of habitats that teem with species, both above and below water. Information for visitors is copious and excellent. For families, this is a highlight of any visit to Lisbon.

8 Monumental Belém
(page 98)

The Mosteiro dos Jerónimos and nearby Torre de Belém are prime examples of Manueline architecture, or Portuguese late Gothic, the flamboyant artistic product of an era of maritime expansion by a confident regime. Clustered nearby are a bevy of other historical sights, including antique boats and coaches.

9 Fado
(page 149)

Fado music is perhaps the leading cultural expression of the city in which it emerged, and also of the nation. Its lyrics and sound often express a very Portuguese *saudade* – an intense but vague yearning. Fado fell out of fashion after the 1974 Revolution, but the keepers of the flame sheltered it in *casas de fado* in Alfama and elsewhere, and it's now enjoying a revival, with younger singers frequently topping the national charts.

10 Miradouros
(pages 57, 67 & 89)

One of the disadvantages of Lisbon's hilly terrain is that sightseeing can be very tiring. One of its advantages is that walkers are regularly rewarded with fabulous views from various *miradouros* (lookout points), each of which gives a different perspective on the city. Most have a terrace and, in some cases, occasional live music.

7 Gulbenkian Foundation
(page 158)

Set in a delightfully leafy park, the privately owned Fundação Calouste Gulbenkian runs the capital's premier museum of fine and applied arts (Western and Oriental), a lively modern exhibition centre, and a packed season of classical music concerts with performers including the Gulbenkian's own orchestra and choir.

11 Trams & funiculars
(page 224)

You're sure to catch sight of – and probably take a picture of – one of the city's antique trams clanging through the streets, or an equally venerable funicular or elevator. But you have to step on board for an eyeful of their wooden interiors and carefully oiled antique machinery (made in now-disused factories in far-off places such as Glasgow) – though beware of pickpockets. Until the mid 1990s, routes were still being taken out of service; now there are not one but two tourist services, and they're pondering adding regular ones.

12 River Tagus
(page 90)

Lisbon is almost within skimming distance of the ocean and, although its shore is bathed by the Tagus rather than the Atlantic, the estuary is so broad that locals often refer to it as 'the sea'. Its reflective surface gives Lisbon a unique light. Lately, new riverside promenades have renewed the city's long-neglected acquaintance with the Tagus, while a river cruise – or just a simple ferry to Cacilhas – offers a splendid alternative city panorama.

13 Museu Nacional de Arte Antiga
(page 95)

This is the only place that offers a real sense of the course of Portuguese art through the centuries. The museum also harbours painting and statuary from across Europe, as well as ceramics and furniture produced in China and India for the Portuguese market. Among its icons are the *Painéis de São Vicente* (St Vincent Panels) and the recently restored *Custódia de Belém*, a Manueline-style monstrance that was the pinnacle of the goldsmith's art.

14 Coffee and cakes
(page 107)

The Portuguese know their coffee and are demanding enough to ensure you're unlikely to be faced with a poor excuse for the stuff. It's served in myriad ways, at the counter in scruffy *tascas* or on the terrace at sophisticated cafés – as often as not accompanied by a cake or pastry.

15 Funky souvenirs
(pages 55, 80 & 85)

A resurgence of local pride in Portuguese products has added prettily packaged vintage soaps and creams, ceramic

figurines and other charming items to an already long list of unusual souvenirs you can pick up in Lisbon. Other crafty buys include funkily painted versions of the traditional Barcelos cockerel, handbags and other elegant items made from cork, and, of course, *azulejos*.

16 Portuguese wine
(page 144)

An impressive three Portuguese wines in the top four in *Wine Spectator*'s 2014 list of Top Wines underscores the strides made in recent years in raising the global profile of this important product. The prices of the wines named immediately soared. Thankfully, many others remain astoundingly cheap. In Lisbon, there are ever more places to sample them too.

17 Outdoor nightlife
(pages 142-155)

A balmy climate and friendly locals make whiling away an hour or two drinking on the street (or beach) a pleasure. No weekend in Lisbon is complete without hitting a bar or two in the Bairro Alto or Cais do Sodré – and perhaps heading for a club afterwards. Despite tighter restrictions on opening hours these days, this is very much a late-night scene compared with most European cities.

18 Museu Colecção Berardo
(page 102)

The Berardo houses one of Europe's leading collections of modern art, with works by artists from Duchamp and Picasso, through Basquiat and Bacon, to locals such as Pedro Cabrita Reis and Joana Vasconcelos. And even better, it remains free to all. It's housed in the Centro Cultural Belém, which has lots more to offer in both the visual and the performing arts.

19 Urban art
(page 26)

Burgeoning local talent and a positive attitude from the local authorities have combined to establish Lisbon as a major centre for street art. Vhils (Alexandre Farto) is the best-known native exponent, but a range of big-name foreign artists have left their mark as well, along with a growing band of local talent.

20 Sintra
(page 176)

Yes, it's beyond the city limits but a trip to the world's first centre of Romantic architecture (according to UNESCO) should be included in any but the briefest visit to Lisbon. Today, this magical hill resort is Portugal's second most-visited destination, after the capital. You'll need a full day to get the most out of the place and soak up the unique atmosphere.

Lisbon Today

Recession and regeneration.

TEXT: ALISON ROBERTS

Lisbon dominates Portugal in much the way that London lords it over the UK and Paris bestrides France – as natives of the country's second city, Porto, will tell you, not without some resentment. Yet while the Greater Lisbon region is home to well over two million people (more than one fifth of the national total) and accounts for well over one third of the nation's GDP, the population of the city proper is barely half a million.

For decades, there was a steady outflow of families from the crowded traditional *bairros* to roomier accommodation in ugly but patently more modern suburbs and satellite towns. Those left behind, often in dilapidated rent-controlled flats, were on average older and poorer.

Yet the city never lost its power as a cultural magnet – the legacy of a history that goes back centuries further than that of all but a handful of European cities – and there are now finally signs of a revival in the Baixa (downtown) and surrounding residential *bairros*.

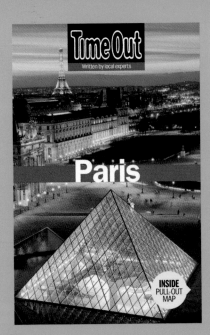
Time Out
Written by local experts

Paris

INSIDE
PULL-OUT
MAP

Written by
local experts,
rated 'Top
Guidebook
Brand'
by Which?

Travel
beyond
the
Rewritten, redesigned
and better than ever.
clichés

Keep up, join in **Time Out**

TOURISM AND REGENERATION

The flurry of urban rehabilitation work is thanks in part to an influx of foreign investment, but also to a change in attitude from young Portuguese professionals, who are coming around to the charms of city living.

An unprecedented tourism boom has also helped: a record 18 million passengers passed through Lisbon airport in 2014, up two million on 2013, and the number of overnight stays by foreign visitors (an increasing number in newly renovated rental apartments) was up by around 15 per cent. The quantity and quality of local hotels continues to rise, with several popping up even in the long-neglected Baixa.

No wonder visitors find Lisbon attractive. With some 2,800 hours of sunshine a year, it is Europe's sunniest capital, as well as having the mildest winters. Summers are hot, but rarely unbearably so thanks to the freshening Atlantic breezes.

The Portuguese are invariably friendly and helpful, and increasingly speak good English – certainly by comparison with their linguistically and phonetically challenged neighbours in Spain. They are also touchingly keen to know what you think of their country, especially if it is positive – although they yield to none in their own eagerness to pinpoint its failings.

Then there is the tasty, affordable food and wine, and the buzzing nightlife – with old haunts such as the Bairro Alto complemented by emerging hubs such as Cais do Sodré and Intendente, and Lux regularly featuring on lists of Europe's best nightclubs.

Lisbon's compact size means that you could cover the main sights on foot in a couple of days – if it weren't for its hilly topography, that is. On the upside (so to speak), all those hills guarantee a range of stunning views.

The tourism boom of the past few years is the result of growing numbers of Europeans – and increasingly North Americans and others – taking advantage of cheap flights to discover what was once a rather marginal destination but is now consistently rated as one of the best places for a city break.

INFRASTRUCTURE AND AUSTERITY

Not that Lisbon lacks for problems. With more ageing buildings than either the public or private sector can conceivably maintain or renovate, and chronic problems with its downtown drainage systems – not to

'Lisbon, once a rather marginal destination, is now consistently rated as one of the top places for a city break.'

mention unrepaired potholes, cars parked up on pavements and ubiquitous dog mess in residential areas – the challenges are many.

When the global financial crisis hit, Lisbon's city council found itself mired in debt to an even greater extent than most of the country's local authorities. One of the main tasks of the Socialist mayor who took office in 2007, António Costa, was to ensure that the city paid what it owed to small suppliers of goods and services, who had long been squeezed as a direct result of the council's poor money management.

Despite the shortage of cash – which only worsened with the recession and the austerity policies that followed Portugal's move to seek a euro-zone bailout in 2008 – the council has continued a tradition of organising or fostering free cultural events aimed at both locals and tourists. And long-awaited initiatives such as the redevelopment of the historic Ribeira das Naus area – part of a broader movement for the city to restore its relationship with the River Tagus – have gone ahead, if more slowly.

Costa also showed talent in bringing on board (and so neutralising) independent leftists in the city council. Since, at the time of writing, the mayor looked set to step aside soon, having become national leader of the opposition Socialist Party in the run-up to the 2015 general election, his deft handling of rivals as potential allies seemed to point to the kind of coalitions he might build if he were to win that election.

CULTURE SHAKE-UPS

In the field of culture, the austerity of recent years has left scars. Lisbon's theatre and dance troupes are among those that have felt the cuts most keenly, some losing all their state funding. In other cases, more efficient management, organisational reforms and inventive initiatives have saved the day.

The Museu Nacional de Arte Antiga (*see p95*), a treasure-house of Portuguese art

Lux. See p19.

(see p157), a lynchpin of Lisbon's Belém district, and lost no time in tabling similar proposals for what is Portugal's largest concentration of museums and historical monuments.

With 2015 marking the 500th anniversary of the construction of the Torre de Belém, the timing for such an initiative certainly looks right. As Lamas explained to journalists soon after his appointment, the idea is to get the managers of a score of local sights actively working together, to make the most of the five million or so tourists who visit the area each year.

STATE OF THE STREET ART

Away from the big state-subsidised institutions, Lisbon has emerged as a major centre for urban art (see p26) – with many initiatives again fostered by the council. Economic upheaval has bequeathed the city many derelict buildings ripe for use as giant canvases. Given the continuing problems of the financial sector – with the collapse in 2014 of one of the country's biggest banks – the supply of empty properties seems unlikely to run out any time soon.

LISBON AND PORTUGAL

Still, in many respects the capital is untypical of Portugal. It's the country's wealthiest region – with a GDP that even exceeds the European Union average – as well as being home to most of the foreign multinationals. It also has a much higher concentration of immigrants.

Ethnic minorities aren't the only incomers, either. Unlike Portugal's second city, Porto, where a larger proportion of the population has deep local roots, the capital has always sucked in people from Portugal's rural interior.

But while migration can dislocate social networks and generate alienation, in Lisbon that does not seem to have happened. In Mouraria, Intendente and other poor inner city neighbourhoods, ethnic diversity has in recent years been celebrated in an annual festival with the inclusive name of 'Todos', as well as ongoing community initiatives that seek to involve all locals, native and non-native.

Across the city, while pickpockets can plague touristy areas (particularly the no.28 tram), violent crime remains rare in comparison with most other European cities. For all these reasons and more, Lisbon is one of the most welcoming places a visitor could choose to explore, alone or in company.

that had always been rather conservatively managed, has shaken things up through a partnership with a leading entertainment promoter best known for organising rock festivals. The resulting slick promotion of temporary exhibitions at the museum – which have included an unprecedented exchange of artworks with Madrid's Museu del Prado – helped drive a 60 per cent surge in visitor numbers in 2014 (in a country that has one of the lowest museum attendances in Europe).

Elsewhere, the success in Sintra of a state-municipal joint venture in creating a virtuous circle of rising visitor numbers and investment in that town's natural and built heritage could soon be replicated in the capital if the former chief executive in charge of Sintra parks and heritage, António Lamas, has his way. In late 2014, he took over at the Centro Cultural de Belém

WISH YOU WERE HERE, WISH I WERE THERE
The meaning of saudade.

Central to the Portuguese sensibility is an evocative word whose meaning is tricky to capture in English. To feel *saudade* is to suffer an intense yearning or nostalgia for a place, person or just about anything that you know is out of reach, perhaps forever.

Fado, the melancholy musical form that emerged from Lisbon's mean streets, is filled with references to the *saudades* endured by this nation of hardy seafarers and emigrants. It shines a light into the soul of a nation where the sentimental fatalism of an Atlantic temperament seems to be in constant conflict with a sunnier Mediterranean side.

Saudade is what women feel when their menfolk have been long at sea. Or perhaps it better describes the yearning of those men for their hearths, the comforting arms of their wives and a stiff fish stew. *Saudade* is what the emigrant feels for his home town as decades of separation slip by.

Since the time voyagers first rounded the Cape of Good Hope, millions of Portuguese have gone forth, seeking riches or just escaping poverty. Throughout the 19th and 20th centuries, hardship at home meant that a move to northern Europe or across the Atlantic was the clearest path to a better life. Emigrants' remittances came to make a major contribution to Portugal's balance of payments. Again, the women did not always accompany their men abroad,

and some spent most of their lives barely every seeing their loved ones, if at all.

But sometimes the men did come back – because they were in the grip of *saudade*. Like the Spanish, many Portuguese believe their village, town or city is the most blessed patch of earth on the planet, and none of the finery of Paris or London would deter them from saving their cash for the day when they can build a fancy pile back home.

You're unlikely these days to come across black-clad fishwives sending a heart-rending fado out across the waves. After the 1974 Revolution, Lisbon's traditional music fell out of fashion and, in the first few years of the 21st century, the country even became a net recipient of immigrants for the first time. But during the past few years, recession and austerity have seen the situation revert to the historical norm, now with a fresh wave of emigration made up of tens of thousands of youngsters – members of the best-educated generation in Portugal's history – who had expected to thrive in their homeland.

So it is perhaps not surprising that fado is once more back in fashion, including among youngsters: releases by rising young *fadistas* regularly top the charts and *casas de fado* (see p149) are multiplying. Meanwhile, there are still several million Portuguese living abroad, and *saudade* and the sea remain defining features of the national character.

Café Luso. *See p150.*

Itineraries

*Plot out your perfect
break with our step-
by-step Lisbon planner.*

Clockwise from below:
**Castelo de São Jorge;
Feira da Ladra; Igreja de
São Roque; Solar do
Vinho do Porto**.

Day 1

9AM Head up to the **Castelo de São Jorge** (p64) to get your bearings, taking the antique no.28 tram (or a bus if you want to ride all the way up). The castle battlements afford breathtaking views of the river and the city draped over a series of hills.

10AM Wander down towards the atmospheric **Alfama** neighbourhood (p64), stopping off at the **Museu-Escola de Artes Decorativas** (p65) if you have a taste for applied arts, or detouring to the remains of the **Teatro Romano** (p62).

NOON If it's a Tuesday or Saturday, take in the **Feira da Ladra** (p66), a sprawling flea market. The cloisters of the nearby **Mosteiro de São Vicente** (p67) feature magnificent *azulejo* panels – and more stunning views. Lunch on a plate of grilled sardines or *bacalhau* at a local *tasca*, or go for a more exotic alternative.

2PM

2PM After lunch, catch the tram across to **Chiado** (p72) for some shopping or people-watching. Of the many local churches, the highlight is the **Igreja de São Roque** (p82) just uphill, with its lavish Baroque decoration.

4PM Art lovers may want to fit in a visit to the predominantly Portuguese **Museu Nacional de Arte Antiga** (p95) or the wider-ranging **Museu Calouste Gulbenkian** (p116), across town. The latter has a lovely garden, but keen botanists will find more to marvel at closer to hand at the **Jardim Botânico** (p86) in Príncipe Real.

6PM Time for an aperitif, with the **Solar do Vinho do Porto** (p84) an excellent place for it. It's on the edge of the **Bairro Alto** area, which is home to myriad restaurants (pp82-84) and late-opening bars (p144). When these finally close, you can head home to sleep – or downhill to **Lux** (p148) or another all-night club.

10AM

Clockwise from above: **Mosteiro dos Jerónimos**; **Parque das Nações**; **Maria da Mouraria** fado house; **Crêperie da Ribeira**.

1PM

Day 2

10AM You should set aside half a day to explore **Belém** (p98), a district that will be forever linked with the Discoveries, the golden age of Portuguese maritime exploration. As well as being home to key examples of the late Gothic Manueline style of architecture, Such as the **Mosteiro dos Jerónimos** (p100), the area features museums galore and a fine modern art collection. Take a break from the culture to indulge in some of the famous custard tarts at the **Antiga Confeitaria de Belém** (p103): it's almost considered a sin by Lisboetas to walk past here without stepping inside.

1PM At lunchtime, head for the **Docas** or one of our recommended restaurants in **Alcântara**, **Santos** or **Cais do Sodré** (pp90-103), such as Crêperie da Ribeira. Many of them offer views of the mighty Tagus.

3PM Cross town to the **Parque das Nações** (p126), the former site of Expo 98, whose theme was the oceans and the Discoveries. It has treats for visitors of all ages, with the **Oceanário** (p126) the prime attraction. To cover more ground, you can let the cable car take the strain.

Alternatively, hire a bike or a pair of skates (p225).

6PM Head back into town for a late-afternoon drink at one of the numerous **miradouros**, Lisbon's wonderful look-out points (p57, p67 & p89).

8PM Dine at a **casa de fado** (p149), where singers will pour their hearts out to you, accompanied by a lute-shaped Portuguese guitar. The origins of the *saudade* they're expressing lie in part in seafarers' homesickness and the longing of the women they left behind.

Urban Art

Whether it's thanks to a centuries-old tradition of open-air art in the form of *azulejos*, the legacy of the revolutionary murals of the 1970s and '80s, or the creative ferment generated by an unprecedented economic crisis, Lisbon has become a great place for urban art.

The city council has done much to foster the trend, its Gabinete de Arte Urbana (GAU) providing a sanctioned outlet for the talents of local youngsters – and often the paint too. GAU started modestly, with seven panels on Calçada da Glória (the route of the funicular that links the Baixa with Bairro Alto) and neighbouring Largo da Oliveirinha. They're still there, but the initiative has now spread out into the suburbs.

Lisbon garnered international media coverage after GAU called in leading foreign artists for the 12-month Crono project, starting on a group of abandoned buildings on Avenida Fontes Pereira de Melo. At no.24, a giant masked vandal painted by Brazilian duo Os Gémeos emerges from the façade, taking aim with a slingshot in the form of a besuited, bespectacled figure. Round the side of the same building, Italian artist Blu has a monstrous Big Oil figure literally sucking the earth's resources. Next door, a dark giant by Spanish artist Sam3 sprawls across bricked-up windows on which a starry sky is painted; and further down is a Godzilla-like crocodile by Erica II Cane. Round the block are the fruits of a separate project also backed by GAU, featuring local artists Vanessa Teodoro and Paulo Arraiano.

Subsequent phases of Crono also involved locals, including one of the project's driving forces, Alexandre Farto, aka Vhils. Widely acknowledged as Portugal's leading urban artist, influenced by both graffiti and advertising, he explores the dialogue – or cacophony – between these and other occupiers of public space. Vhils is best known for his unique method of creating relief compositions through 'reverse stencilling', cutting through layers of posters or brick with drills, chisels or even explosives.

In 2014, an extensive exhibition of his work was staged, indoors and out, at the Museu de Electricidade, one of Lisbon's prime art spaces. It was temporary, but you can still see Vhils pieces in, among other places, Alcântara (on Avenida da Índia), at the riverside Jardim do Tabaco (with Pixel Pancho) and even in Alfama (in Travessa das Merceeiras, just up from the cathedral).

Other big names whose work has popped up include Dutch artist Niels Shoe, French stencil wizard C215 and Italy's Cripsta and Dilen. Downtown, there's a towering skeletal horse by globe-trotting Spanish artist Aryz on Rua Manuel Jesus Coelho.

Jardim do Tabaco.

But GAU-sponsored projects can be found in all sorts of places. The once depressing underpass in the Alcântara-Mar railway station has now been livened up by lesser-known local writers; even the city's bottle banks are fair game, with a programme specifically aimed at covering them with art.

The biggest single project so far is *Rostos do Muro Azul* (Faces of the Blue Wall), on Rua das Murtas in Alvalade, a street that skirts three sides of a large hospital complex. Dozens of local and foreign writers took part, with the eastern wall worked only by female artists because 'blue is not just for boys'.

For the latest, check GAU's Facebook page, where photographs are posted of the latest local art. There's also an online magazine with fabulous illustrations (www.issuu.com/galeriadearteurbana) and a 200-page book, *Street Art Lisbon*, on sale at local bookshops.

Celebrated youngsters aside, you can still come across fading remnants of old revolutionary graffiti on walls around town. In the Bairro Alto, there's a brand-new mural of the same kind, with the vanguard of the proletariat yelling its way down Travessa dos Fiéis de Deus. It was painted not by a teenager, but by António Alves, a veteran of the ideological battles of the 1970s and '80s. This time round he didn't have to work under cover of night, but produced the scene on the side wall of Galeria Zé dos Bois (*see p85*).

LISBON FOR FREE
Save your pennies in the Portuguese capital.

FREE MUSEUMS
National museums and monuments are free on the first Sunday of the month. The privately owned Gulbenkian is free every Sunday. The Museu Berardo and MUDE – Museu de Design e da Moda are always free.

MUSIC TO YOUR EARS
Free music abounds in Lisbon, from regular classical concerts in the Palácio Foz to jam sessions on Tuesdays and Wednesdays at legendary jazz venue Hot Clube de Portugal. From June to September, myriad open-air concerts are laid on by the council.

TRANSPORTS OF DELIGHT
There are ways to negotiate some of the city's hills without being out of pocket. If you're downtown and heading for the Bairro Alto, enter Baixa-Chiado metro station and cross the ticket hall to ride a series of free escalators up to Largo do Chiado.

BEACH LIFE
On sunny weekends, locals pour out of the city for the region's top free attraction: its beaches. Join them or – better still – go during the week, when they're emptier. For a more energetic day out, take the train to Cascais and pick up a free bike from BiCas – the stand is right by the station.

MUDE.

Diary

*Plan your perfect break
with our year-round guide
to the Portuguese capital.*

In Portugal, there are *festas* dotted throughout the year – often marking saints' days – and many Lisboetas are close enough to their rural roots to keep track of goings-on in their ancestral village. Though religious in origin, *festas* tend to involve drinking, listening and dancing to bad music, setting off firecrackers and eating sugar-covered doughnuts. In the capital, more sophisticated seasonal pleasures are on offer – from jazz festivals to major sporting events. Tickets for most are available via www.ticketline.sapo.pt or at the ABEP booth in Praça dos Restauradores. Note that in addition to the public holidays listed (see p29), government employees are given certain days off, such as Shrove Tuesday. Four public holidays were revoked in 2012 as part of an austerity drive – Corpus Christi (60 days after Easter), Republic Day (5 Oct), All Saints' Day (1 Nov) and Restoration of Independence (1 Dec) – but one or more may be reinstated by a future government.

Meia Maratona de Lisboa.

Spring

Moda Lisboa

Various venues (21 321 3000, www.modalisboa.pt).
Date early Mar, mid Oct.
Portuguese designers display their wares at this twice-yearly clothes show. *Photo p30.*

Meia Maratona de Lisboa

Various courses (21 441 3182, www.meiamaratona delisboa.com). **Admission** *Half-marathon* €25-€50; *mini-marathon* €20-€35. **Date** late Mar.
Tens of thousands take part in the 21km Lisbon half-marathon, many for the unique opportunity to run across the city's Ponte 25 de Abril. There's a parallel elite event and a 7km mini-marathon, which also takes in the bridge.

Senhor dos Passos

Igreja da Graça (21 887 3943). **Date** 2nd Sun in Lent.
This 500-year-old procession sees a figure of a bleeding Christ carried on a litter of violets around one of Lisbon's hills, starting and ending at the Igreja da Graça. It's attended by leading socialites.

PUBLIC HOLIDAYS

Good Friday (Sexta-feira Santa)
Friday before Easter Sunday (date varies)

Freedom Day (Dia da Liberdade)
25 April

Worker's Day (Dia do Trabalhador)
1 May

**Portugal Day (Dia de Portugal,
de Camões e das Comunidades)**
10 June

**St Anthony's Day
(Dia de Santo António)**
13 June

**Assumption
(Assunção de Nossa Senhora)**
15 August

**Immaculate Conception
(Imaculada Conceição)**
8 December

Christmas Day (Natal)
25 December

New Year's Day (Ano Novo)
1 January

Moda Lisboa. *See p29.*

Festa do Jazz do São Luiz

Teatro de São Luiz (21 325 7640, www.teatro saoluiz.pt). **Admission** €15/day; €25/2 days. **Date** early Apr.

Both amateurs and professionals perform in this friendly festival of Portuguese jazz, which takes place over a weekend. There's the odd free concert too.

★ Peixe em Lisboa

Pátio Galé, Praça do Comércio (21 031 2700, www.peixemlisboa.com). **Admission** €15/day; free under-13s. **Date** mid Apr.

Also dubbed Lisbon Fish & Flavours for the benefit of foreign visitors, the city's biggest gastronomic event focuses on seafood. As well as the chance to sample a range of delicious dishes, it features cooking demonstrations by top local and foreign chefs, fine Portuguese wines to match with your food, and stalls selling all kinds of gourmet ingredients.

Dias da Música

Centro Cultural de Belém, Praça do Império, Belém (21 361 2400, www.ccb.pt). **Tickets** €4-€10.50. **Date** late Apr/early May.

Three 'Days of Music' packed with cut-price classical concerts from morning to night, on a different musical theme each year. The CCB (*see p157*) also organises a one-day Festa da Primavera (Spring Party) in March, with some free concerts.

Dia da Liberdade

Information: Associação 25 de Abril (21 324 1420). **Date** 25 Apr.

A national holiday for the anniversary of the 1974 coup that ended decades of dictatorship and ushered in democracy. Official speeches are made (these days usually outside Lisbon, to avoid anti-government protests) while nostalgic lefties parade down the capital's Avenida da Liberdade.

Feira do Livro

Parque Eduardo VII (21 843 5180, www. feiradolivrodelisboa.pt). **Date** late Apr. Bookstalls take over Lisbon's central park, with side events such as author talks and concerts.

IndieLisboa

Various venues (21 315 8399, www.indielisboa. com). **Tickets** €1-€4. **Date** late Apr/early May. The Lisbon International Festival of Independent Cinema has expanded hugely since its debut in 2004 and now comprises various competitive sections, as well as showcases of feature films and shorts from around the world. There's also a parallel Indie Júnior festival for kids. Films are screened at a variety of venues, including Cinema São Jorge. *See also p136.*

Portugal Open

Estádio Nacional, Complexo Desportivo do Jamor, Cruz Quebrada (information 21 303 4900, www. portugalopen.pt). **Tickets** *Ground admission* €5; free under-6s. *Centre court* €20-€45; €18-€40 reductions. *Tournament pass* €130. *Qualifying stages* free. **Date** late Apr-early May. Portugal's most important tennis tournament usually attracts a big international name or two.

FIMFA Festival Internacional de Marionetas e Formas Animadas

Various venues (information 21 242 7621, www. fimfalx.blogspot.pt). **Tickets** €5-€16. **Date** May. Puppeteers from around the world put on inventive shows, with the language barrier rarely presenting a problem.

Estoril Jazz

Casino Estoril (www.projazz.pt, tickets: 21 003 6300, www.ticketline.sapo.pt). **Tickets** €30/day; €90/7-day pass. **Date** mid May. One of Portugal's oldest music festivals, this invariably boasts a top-quality programme with familiar faces from the jazz world.

Rock in Rio Lisboa

Parque de Boavista (http://rockinriolisboa.sapo.pt). **Tickets** €61/day. **Date** mid-late May. A biennial event (next in 2016) spread over two long weekends and two stages, this slick Brazilian import boasts big Portuguese, Brazilian and international names (Justin Timberlake and The Rolling Stones were on the bill in 2014). DJs keep pumping out the music until the early hours. *Photo p32.*

Alkantara Festival

Various venues (information 21 315 2267, www. alkantara.pt). **Tickets** €12; €5-€6 reductions. **Date** late May-early June. Cross-cultural fertilisation is the theme of Lisbon's largest performing arts festival, a biennial affair (next in 2016) with local and visiting dance and theatre troupes performing around town.

FESTAS DOS SANTOS POPULARES
Partying with the people's saints.

The **Festas dos Santos Populares** (see p32) is not one party but a whole month of them, during which 'the people's saints' – António, João and Pedro – have their days. These are the excuse for some pretty unusual celebrations. Local favourite Santo António, a native of Lisbon who even has his own museum (see p60), is patron of lovers. In the run-up to his day on 13 June, secret admirers hand over pots of *manjerico* (sweet basil) with corny poems attached to a paper carnation. Things are somewhat less romantic during Oporto's big rave-up on 23 June, in honour of São João – complete strangers will hit you over the head with giant plastic hammers or shove bunches of giant garlic under your nose.

In Lisbon, the afternoon of 12 June sees the wedding of the Noivos de Santo António, during which 13 lucky pairs of *noivos* (bride and groom) get married with all expenses paid by the city council. That evening a colourful parade, the Marchas Populares, inches down Avenida de Liberdade; each bairro organises a group dressed in themed costumes who perform a song written for the competition. There's only limited tiered seating, and the pavements are crowded; to get a proper look at the groups, you could instead attend one of the pre-competition showcases held some ten days earlier at the Pavilhão Atlântico (see p152). That gives you a sense not only of how much work goes into the enterprise, but also of the fierce rivalries involved: the mood in the arena when Alfama, Castelo and Mouraria are in action recalls a football derby – and fists have been known to fly. After the Marchas on the night of 12 June, many residents of the older *bairros populares* set up an *arraial* (street party), with grilled sardines and sangria served to allcomers; in Alfama you may have to queue to sit down and the area is packed until sunrise. In the early hours, the atmosphere here and in Mouraria can get a little fraught as the proportion of tipsy teenagers rises. Other traditional *bairros* such as Madragoa or Bica can be just as fun, with more elbow room.

The following afternoon – St Anthony's Day itself, a municipal holiday – there's a procession from Igreja de Santo António to Sé Catedral. The two are only a stone's throw apart, yet it takes a couple of hours for the procession to snake its way around Alfama. Afterwards, the saint's devotees linger, placing a mountain of candles around his statue.

That's not the end of it, though. Throughout June, *arraiais* are held around town, and the council puts on lots of free shows as part of the official Festas de Lisboa.

Summer

★ Out Jazz
Various venues (21 342 1546, www.ncs.pt/outjazz).
Admission free. **Date** May-Sept.
This free outdoor festival of music stretches either side of summer. Concerts take place on weekend afternoons (sometimes on Fridays as well) in a different park or garden each month.

★ Festas dos Santos Populares
Around town (www.egeac.pt). **Date** June.
See p31 **Festas dos Santos Populares**.

Festival de Sintra
Various venues in and around Sintra (information 21 910 7110, box office 21 910 7118, www.festival desintra.pt). **Tickets** €5-€20. **Date** June-July.
Classical music dominates this highlight of the year for cultured locals, which has been going for almost half a century. Concerts take place at the Centro Cultural Olga de Cadaval in Sintra, and in palaces and country estates around the region.

Cool Jazz
Various venues in Mafra, Oeiras and Cascais (70 723 4234, www.cooljazzfest.com). **Tickets** €25-€50. **Date** June-July.
More cool than jazz, this festival tends to feature mainstream performers such as Diana Krall and her ilk, performing in leafy settings.

Nós Alive
Passeio Marítimo de Algés (21 393 3770, www. nosalive.com). **Tickets** €50/day; €90/3 days.
Date mid July.
One of Lisbon's top music festivals: a long weekend by the river with big mainstream, indie and dance names on three stages, and a plethora of sideshows and attractions. It's heavily marketed in the UK.

Super Bock Super Rock
Herdade do Cabeço da Flauta, Meco (www. superbock.pt). **Tickets** €48/day; €90/3 days (incl camping). **Date** mid July.
Lisbon's longest-running music festival, sponsored by a brewery, has changed format several times but always keeps its edge. Nowadays it takes place over three days amid pine trees and sand on the Caparica coast, south of the River Tagus. That means clouds of dust (though not usually mud). Big names in 2014 included Disclosure, Foals and Kasabian.

Festival Internacional de Teatro
Various venues (21 273 9360, 21 275 2175, www. ctalmada.pt). **Tickets** €5-€17. *Festival pass* €70; €40 under-26s. **Date** July.
Many of the shows by Portuguese and foreign groups in this, Portugal's leading theatre festival, are staged at venues in Almada (*see p127*), as well as places such as the CCB (*see p157*).

Rock in Rio Lisboa. *See p30.*

Festival Músicas do Mundo Sines
Venues in and around Sines (269 630 665, www. fmm.com.pt). **Admission** free-€10. **Date** late July.
This festival of fine music from around the world draws spectators from far and wide to the port town of Sines, 90 minutes south of Lisbon. Concerts are staged in the medieval castle, on the seafront, and now also in the pretty beach village of Porto Covo.

Jazz em Agosto
Centro de Arte Moderna, Rua Dr Nicolau de Bettencourt (21 782 3483/74, 21 782 3700, www.musica.gulbenkian.pt/jazz). **Tickets** €12-€20; €6-€14 reductions. **Date** early Aug.
International and local artists – including big names in experimental jazz – perform at the outdoor amphitheatre in the gardens of the Fundação Calouste Gulbenkian (*see p159*).

Autumn

★ Festa do Avante
Quinta da Amora, Seixal (21 222 4000, www. festadoavante.pcp.pt). **Tickets** *In advance* €21/3 days. *On the gate* €23/Fri; €27.50/Sat; €17/Sun; €32/3 days. **Date** 1st wknd in Sept.
They don't get so many votes these days, but Portugal's communists know how to hold a party. Cross the Tagus for this three-day extravaganza featuring rock, roots and even classical music, plus well-priced food and drink from around the country.

Festa do Chiado
Information: Centro Nacional de Cultura (21 346 6722, www.cnc.pt). **Date** mid Oct.
A week of concerts, exhibitions, open-air bookstalls, free guided tours and talks in one of Lisbon's most fashionable neighbourhoods.

Queer Lisboa
Various venues (91 376 5343, www.queerlisboa.pt). **Tickets** free-€4. **Date** late Sept.

chrysanthemums at the gates of cemeteries as families leave flowers and candles on graves. Lisbon's largest necropolis is the Cemitério do Alto do São João, in the north-east of the city.

Lisbon & Estoril Film Fest

Various venues in Lisbon & Estoril. **Admission** *Films* €3-€5. *Workshops* €2. **Date** mid Nov.
One of the country's highest-profile film festivals, this is the brainchild of Portugal's leading producer, Paulo Branco. It features screenings, lively debates and workshops with top international names.

São Martinho

Date 11 Nov.
Roast chestnut parties are held to celebrate the opening of the first barrels of *água pé* (new wine). Some restaurants and fado houses discreetly observe the tradition, but strict hygiene rules mean that these days the equally traditional *jeropiga* (sugary fortified wine) is often served instead.

Experimenta Design

Various venues (21 099 3045, www.experimenta design.pt). **Admission** free. **Date** Nov-Dec.
Exhibitions, debates and 'urban interventions' from this cultural biennale (next in 2015) dedicated to design, architecture and creativity. Expect multi-disciplinary events with a very international flavour.

Portugal's only showcase for gay, lesbian, bisexual, transgender and transsexual cinema is also Lisbon's longest-established film festival.

Dia da República

Paços do Concelho, Praça do Município. **Date** 5 Oct.
Though no longer a public holiday, Republic Day is a key date for Portugal's leftists – and for Lisbon. The first republic was declared back in 1910 from the balcony of city hall, and it is from this same spot that the mayor and Portugal's president continue to make speeches to mark the date.

Rock 'n' Roll Maratona de Lisboa

(21 441 6830, www.pt.competitor.com).
Admission *Marathon* €35-€50; *half-marathon* €16-€22; *mini-marathon* €13-€19. **Date** early Oct.
The city's marathon is less scenic than the Meia Maratona *(see p29)*, as it avoids hills to attract record-chasing athletes. In recent years it has started in Cascais, running along the Atlantic coast and the north bank of the Tagus into the heart of Lisbon.

DocLisboa

Various venues (information 21 888 3093, www.dodisboa.org). **Tickets** €3.20-€4; €2.15-€3.50 reductions. **Date** late Oct.
Worth a special trip if you love documentaries, this long-running festival screens a feast of films from around the world in competitive and themed sections.

Seixal Jazz

Various venues, Seixal (21 097 6103, 91 563 5090, www.cm-seixal.pt/seixaljazz). **Tickets** €10; €7.50 reductions; €40/5 days. **Date** late Oct.
This south-bank festival is a highlight of the year for jazz fans, attracting international musicians as well as local favourites.

Dia de Todos os Santos

Date 1 Nov.
Florists do a roaring trade on All Saints' Day – also known as Dia dos Mortos (Day of the Dead) – selling

Winter

Música em São Roque

Largo Trindade Coelho, Bairro Alto (information 21 323 5444, www.scml.pt). **Tickets** €3-€3.50.
Date mid Nov-early Dec.
Two or three cut-price concerts – mainly *música antiga* (early music) – are staged each week, some in the lavish 16th-century Saint Roch church and some in the adjoining museum.

Natal

Date 24, 25 Dec.
Christmas announces its arrival early these days, with the Baixa, Chiado and Avenida da Liberdade decked out in fairy lights from late November. Christmas dinner, of *bacalhau*, takes place on the evening of 24 December; the next day people are out and about, and many cafés are open.

Ano Novo

Date 31 Dec, 1 Jan.
New Year is seen in with fireworks downtown (and at several points on the south bank visible from Lisbon) and usually a concert by a leading Portuguese artist.

Carnaval

Date Feb (start of Lent).
Children dress up for parties, but otherwise this religious festival is pretty low-key in the capital.

Lisbon's Best

*There's something
for everyone with our
hand-picked highlights.*

Castelo de São Jorge.

Sightseeing

VIEWS

Castelo de São Jorge p64
Castle with strategic overview
of the city.
Miradouro de Santa Luzia p64
A view of Alfama, framed
by flowers.
Nossa Senhora do Monte p66
Lisbon's highest hill, with an
ancient chapel.
**Miradouro de São Pedro
de Alcântara** p81
Locals and visitors alike
gather here to gaze across
to the castle.
Cristo Rei p127
This huge south-bank
monument provides a
different perspective.

ART & DESIGN

**Museu Colecção
Berardo** p102
Top-notch modern painting,
sculpture and installations.
**Museu Calouste
Gulbenkian** p116
A treasure-house of
Western and Oriental art.
**MUDE – Museu de Design
e da Moda** p46
Design and fashion combined
under one roof.
**Museu Nacional de Arte
Antiga** p95
Portuguese fine art through
the centuries.
**Museu Nacional do
Azulejo** p124
All about Portugal's
wonderful ceramic tiles.

Praia do Guincho.

ARCHITECTURE
Mosteiro de Jerónimos p100
Torre de Belém p103
Aqueduto das Águas Livres p112
The Baixa pp42-57
Oceanário p126, p132
Pavilhaõ de Portugal p126
Champalimaud Centre for the Unknown p100

HISTORY
Sé Catedral p62
Planted triumphantly on the site of a mosque.
Teatro Romano p60
Most visible reminder of Lisbon's Roman heritage.
Museu de Lisboa p121
Tells the story of the city before and after the 1755 earthquake.
Museu do Oriente p97
Reflecting on 500 years of Portuguese encounters in Asia.

OUTDOORS
Boat trip on the Tagus p225
For the wind in your hair and a fresh view of the city.
Praia do Guincho p168
This beach is one of the region's most spectacular.
Sintra pp176-179
Forested hills that offer escape from the city heat.
Reserva Natural do Estuário do Tejo p127
A birdwatcher's paradise.

CHILDREN
Parque das Nações p126
Lots of open space, plus educational attractions.
Tram ride p131
Fun for all ages.
Jardim Zoológico de Lisboa p132
Well-run zoo with a variety of shows.
Watersports p171
Combine a beach trip with surf lessons.
KidZania p132
Slick 'world of work' where kids pretend to be grown-ups.

Eating & drinking

BLOWOUTS
Belcanto p72
Reinventing Portuguese cuisine, with two Michelin stars.
Pap'açorda p83
Still fashionable after all these years.
Gambrinus p51
Here the customer is king.
Bica do Sapato p124
Fab food in a trendy riverside setting.
Peixe em Lisboa p30
Also known as Fish & Flavours, this festival is Lisbon's biggest gastronomic event.

Belcanto. See p35.

Parque das Nações. See p35.

Museu Colecção Berardo. See p34.

Solar do Vinho do Porto p84
A unique venue to sample a
unique drink.
Terraço BA p84
Laidback bar with a great view.

Shopping

GIFTS & DESIGN
A Arte da Terra p63
A panoply of handicrafts in
an old stables.
A Vida Portuguesa p69, p80
Classy crafts and vintage
brands in charming packaging.
Vista Alegre Atlantis p80
Portugal's best porcelain
and glassware.
Loja do Burel p79
Clothing and accessories
made from rustic burel fabric.
Pelcor p63
Designs in cork.
Ratton p110
Traditional tiles, but in
contemporary designs.

LOCAL FASHION
Embaixada p87
A range of Portuguese
clothing and footwear.
Storytailors p80
Fabled designer duo with
celebrity fans.
Lidja Kolovrat p88
Daring pieces from the
eponymous designer.
Fly London p55
Funky footwear that's
actually Portuguese.

SEAFOOD
Ramiro p69
Only classy crustaceans
are admitted here.
Sea Me p75
Great fish served in a
funky atmosphere.
Senhor Peixe p127
The freshest of fish,
mainly served grilled.
Fortaleza do Guincho p222
For cordon bleu seafood.

TRADITIONAL
1º de Maio p82
Simple dishes, served
with a smile.
De Castro p107
Trendy but informal eatery
with great traditional food.
Casa do Bacalhau p125
For cod obsessives.
Stop do Bairro p113
The quintessential local
tasca, with a huge wine list.

Taberna Ideal p96
One of the most successful
of Lisbon's new *tabernas*.

GLOBAL
Malaca Too p97
A culinary tour of Asia.
Maharaja p54
The best of a growing bunch
of Indian eateries.
Zambeze p64
Fancy versions of favourite
African dishes.

CAFÉS & BARS
Café A Brasileira p76
A Lisbon classic that's worth
visiting, if only to gawp.
**Café Martinho da
Arcada** p46
Lisbon's oldest café, favoured
by leading cultural figures.
Pois, Café p66
Cosy Austrian-run venue
in Alfama.

Luvaria Ulísses p79
Famous glove specialist.

FOOD & DRINK

GN Cellar p47
Best for Portuguese wine.
Manteigaria Silva p52
Stop by this *bacalhau*
specialist even if you're
not buying the stuff.
**Antiga Confeitaria
de Belém** p103
The best cream tarts
– or at least the best
pastéis de Belém.
Mercado da Ribeira p94, p95
Old market hall, revamped
by our local partner, *Time
Out Lisboa*.

BOOKS & MUSIC

Fnac p78
The city's best-stocked
bookshop; world music too.
Discoteca Amalia p47
Fado specialist.
Flur p126
Where local DJs browse, this
is also a good place for tips
on parties.

Nightlife

BARS

Maria Caxuxa p144
Where Lisbon's arty types
meet up.
Pensão Amor p146
The beating heart of the
Cais do Sodré scene.
Lounge p146
This hipster hangout
predates its neighbours.
Pavilhão Chinês p145
Probably Lisbon's best decor
– and one of Europe's most
attractive bars too.
Cinco Lounge p145
The place to head for well-
mixed cocktails.

CLUBS

Lux p148
Lisbon's essential
nightlife stop.
Europa p147
They take their dance music
seriously here.
Op Art Café p148
To dance until dawn.

LIVE MUSIC

Hot Clube de Portugal p153
The famous old jazz venue
is as lively as ever.
MusicBox p154
Offers the city's most
interesting programming.
Mesa dos Frades p151
A safe bet among Lisbon's
many fado venues.
B.Leza p153
We defy you not to dance at
this classic African club.

Performing arts

FESTIVALS

**Festas dos Santos
Populares** p32
Lisbon's big party, in June,
with lots of free music laid on.
Nós Alive p32
Top international bands and
some Portuguese ones.
Jazz em Agosto p32
Experimental jazz outdoors
at the Gulbenkian.
Festa do Avante p32
There's always a good range
of Portuguese music at the
Communists' September bash.

CLASSICAL MUSIC
& OPERA

Fundação Gulbenkian p159
Private foundation supporting
an orchestra and choir.
**Teatro Nacional São
Carlos** p159
Affordable opera in a fine
neoclassical building.
**Orquestra Metropolitana
de Lisboa** p157
Many concerts organised by
the city's orchestra are free.
**Centro Cultural de
Belém** p157
Its modern auditoriums often
host classical performances.

DANCE & THEATRE

Chapitô p162
Fun physical theatre at a circus
school with a great terrace.
Teatro Dona Maria II p161
Lisbon's national theatre
often plays host to visiting
foreign troupes.
Teatro Camões p160
Home of Portugal's national
ballet company.
**Festival Internacional
de Teatro** p32
Portugal's largest theatre
festival, with events north
and south of the river.

Teatro Nacional São Carlos.

Explore

Central Lisbon

EXPLORE

The devastating 1755 earthquake paved the way for a despotic but enlightened first minister to stamp his rationalist mark on the heart of the city. The Baixa – literally 'low' – is a grid of streets leading down to the river at the majestic Praça do Comércio. Long the city's welcome mat, this grand square remains the entry point for thousands of commuters who cross over the Tagus from the south bank every day. At the northern end of the Baixa is the less formal square known as Rossio, from where it's just a short walk to Avenida da Liberdade, the city's main axis, forging uphill to the green expanse of Lisbon's central park, Parque Eduardo VII.

Elevador de Santa Justa.

Don't Miss

1 Praça do Comércio The vast riverside square that locals still call Terreiro do Paço (p42).

2 Baixa shopping Haberdashers, jewellers and modern crafts inhabit this 18th-century grid (p46).

3 Elevador de Santa Justa This century-old iron tower boasts some lofty views (p43).

4 Rossio The city's crossroads for two millennia (p47).

5 Avenida da Liberdade Lisbon's central axis, lined with trees and luxury stores (p53).

Praça do Comércio.

THE BAIXA

A walk around the Baixa, Lisbon's traditional downtown, gives a flavour of how things were done in the days before shopping malls. Old-fashioned emporia, long driven out of business in other cities, here survive thanks to rent controls. Thus you can wander down streets where trades have clustered for centuries: jewellers linger on **Rua do Ouro** (also marked on some maps by its old name, Rua Aurea), **Rua dos Sapateiros** is still a 'street of shoemakers' and **Rua dos Fanqueiros** is home to textile merchants and fabric shops, as it has always been.

Or, at least, as it's been since the mid 18th century. Before then, the heart of medieval Lisbon was a labyrinthine tangle of narrow streets. Then, as now, the poles were two squares: the **Terreiro do Paço** on the waterfront, later remade as the Praça do Comércio but more often known locally by its old name; and the **Rossio** (now officially Praça Dom Pedro IV) at its upper end, where the low ground splits into two valleys. The centre of commerce was **Rua Nova**, which cuts east–west across the lower end of the modern grid. The largest of Lisbon's Jewish quarters, the **Judiaria Grande**, occupied a big chunk of the Baixa, centred around the synagogue that stood between Rua da Conceição and Rua de São Nicolau, at their eastern end.

The 1755 Earthquake put paid to all that. Charged with the job of reconstruction, the Marquês de Pombal based his plan on a military encampment, with each street having a specific function. The orderly rows still stand as he planned them, though some took until the next century to finish – the Arco Triunfal (Triumphal Arch) capping the street of the same name was completed in 1873. That's Glory on top of the arch, holding wreaths above the heads of Genius and Bravery. Below are Viriatus, Nun'Álvares Pereira, Vasco da Gama and the Marquês de Pombal. The Tagus is the River God

on the left, the Douro is on the right. Since mid 2013 the **Arco da Rua Augusta**, as it now tends to be known, has been open to the public.

The Baixa's grid retains nothing of medieval Lisbon, yet has accumulated a patina of history in the past 250 years. In the waterfront **Praça do Comércio**, Pombal wanted a majestic square to rival anything found in Europe, and architects Carlos Mardel and Eugênio dos Santos more or less gave him what he wanted. It was designed with one side open to the river and the other three for government ministries, with its centrepiece Joaquim Machado de Castro's 14-metre-high equestrian statue of Dom José I, monarch at the time of the Quake. Long condemned to life as a car park, the centre of the square is now once again in use as a public space, and esplanades line its western and eastern flanks. Nearby is the **Lisbon Story Centre**.

Along the bottom edge of the square, traffic still surges, partly severing it from the river. Yet the **Cais das Colunas** – a monumental stone jetty – draws canoodling couples and tourists in search of a scenic selfie. A few steps east, rush-hour crowds pour on and off ferries linking the capital with the south-bank towns of Montijo and Barreiro. In the other direction is the revamped Ribeira dos Naus riverfront, where ocean-going *naus* were built for centuries.

Under the arcades along the top of the square handicrafts stalls set up on weekends. On the

EXPLORE

Many businesses hereabouts still have appealing old fronts, such as the dilapidated art nouveau button shops and haberdashers on **Rua da Conceição**. Between the tram tracks near the junction with Rua da Prata, a rectangular manhole cover marks the way down to some Roman tanks, often referred to as 'baths' or fish-salting tanks, but probably the foundations of a temple or other large building. They are normally flooded and open to the public only once a year, in the autumn. Interested in Roman Lisbon? Step into the **Núcleo Arqueológico da Rua dos Correeiros** or head over to the **Casa dos Bicos** (*see p60*) or up to the **Teatro Romano** and related museum (*see p62*). Baixa's tallest landmark is the **Elevador de Santa Justa**, the 19th-century solution to the problem of getting up to the Chiado without breaking into a sweat. Today the series of escalators in Baixa-Chiado Metro station do part of the job, but are underground. On the eastern side of the Baixa, the misleadingly named **Ascensor do Castelo** (Rua dos Fanqueiros 170, open 9am-9pm daily), a modern lift inside a building, is just the first step up to the castle hill; for the next bit, take the lift inside the Chão do Loureiro car park, which whisks you up to Costa do Castelo.

square's north-east corner, the **Café Martinho da Arcada** has been open since 1782. Lisbon's iconic poet Fernando Pessoa was a regular during the 1920s and '30s. On the north-west corner you'll find the **Lisbon Welcome Centre** (www.visitlisboa.com) with a walk-in tourist office and a range of souvenirs.

A stone plaque on the wall nearby recalls the assassination, on 1 February 1908, of the then king, Dom Carlos I, and the crown prince, Luís Filipe. The gunmen represented the violent fringe of a republican movement that was to triumph two years later, with the proclamation of the Portuguese Republic just around the corner.

The **Paços do Concelho**, housing Lisbon's Câmara Municipal (city council), sits on the west side of the Baixa on Praça do Município. Built in 1867, it was renovated after a 1996 fire that mysteriously broke out in the department of financial records. Check at the desk about guided visits (usually two Sunday mornings a month). The Câmara's grand balcony was where the Republic was proclaimed on 5 October 1910, and the square is the setting for annual Republic Day celebrations – even if the public holiday was revoked a couple of years ago.

Rua do Arsenal, running west from here to Cais do Sodré, is principally famous for the smell of *bacalhau* emanating from its store-fronts. By contrast, **Rua dos Bacalhoeiros** running east from the Baixa no longer boasts the *bacalhau* sellers its name advertises, but does have one of Lisbon's most delightful old shops: the **Conserveira de Lisboa** (*see p63*).

Many of the Baixa's streets are now pedestrianised, notably the main drag, **Rua Augusta**, which has café esplanades, shops, buskers and fast-food joints along its length, and the **Museu de Design e da Moda** at its southern end. The workaday lunch crowd head for the cluster of cheap restaurants on Rua dos Correeiros or to more obscure eateries through doorways devoid of signs.

Sights & Museums

Arco da Rua Augusta
Rua Augusta (21 194 1099). Metro Terreiro do Paço. **Open** 9am-7pm daily. **Admission** €2.50; free under-6s. *Joint ticket with Lisbon Story Centre* €8; €4.50-€6.50 reductions; free under-6s. **Map** p45 H5 **❶**
There's nothing much to see in this grand structure, but its roof affords a unique view of the Baixa – and of the statues atop the arch – despite it being a comparatively low vantage point.

★ Elevador de Santa Justa
Rua do Ouro (21 342 7944). Metro Baixa-Chiado. **Open** *Lift* Oct-May 7am-10pm daily. June-Sept 7am-11pm daily. *Miradouro* 8.30am-8.30pm daily. **Admission** *Lift* €5 return. *Miradouro* €1.50. **No credit cards. Map** p45 G4 **❷**
The industrial-age iron tracery of the Santa Justa lift – sometimes called the Elevador do Carmo – is one of Lisbon's most beloved landmarks but became a national monument only in 2002. It was built by Portuguese-born Eiffel disciple Raul Mesnier de Ponsard, and officially opened in August 1901. It links downtown Rua do Ouro with the square next to the Carmo church up above, via a 15m viaduct. On the top floor, up a spiral staircase, a viewing platform offers 360° views. The Elevador is part of the public transport system, so if you have a payment card a one-way trip is equivalent to a bus journey; on board only pricey return tickets are on sale. For a budget alternative view, head for department store Pollux (*see p47*), whose top-floor café also has cheap coffee.

EXPLORE

EXPLORE

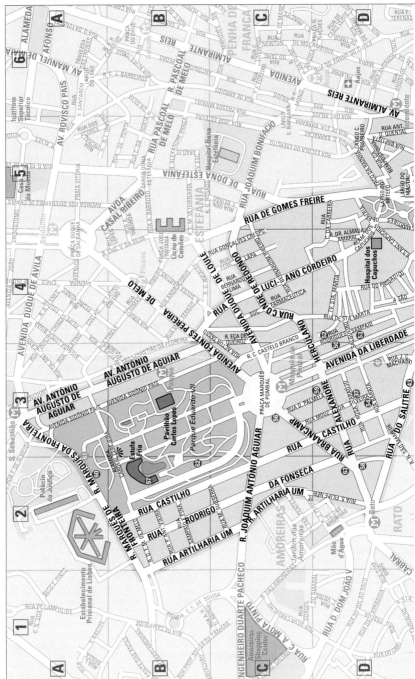

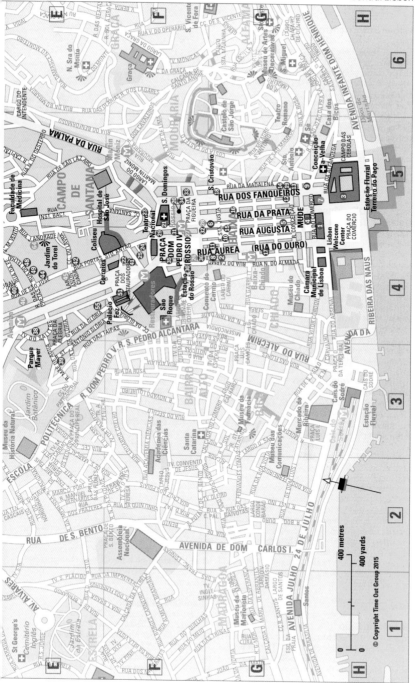

Lisbon Story Centre

Praça do Comércio 78-81 (21 194 1099, www. lisboastorycentre.pt). Metro Terreiro do Paço. **Open** 10am-8pm daily (last entry 7pm). **Admission** €7; €3-€6 reductions; free under-6s. *Joint ticket with Arco da Rua Augusta* €8; €4.50-€6.50 reductions; free under-6s. **Map** p45 H5 ❸

This privately run space aims to take visitors on a journey through time, using sets with costumed figures, maquettes, and multimedia and sensory experiences to recreate key events in Lisbon's history. These include the city's mythical and documented beginnings, its growth and status at the centre of a global empire, and the 1755 earthquake and its aftermath. There are audioguides in various languages included with your ticket.

★ [FREE] MUDE – Museu de Design e da Moda

Rua Augusta 24 (21 888 6117, www.mude.pt). Metro Baixa-Chiado or tram 12, 28. **Open** 10am-6pm Tue-Sun. **Admission** free. **Map** p45 G5 ❹

Lisbon's Museum of Design and Fashion highlights the links between the two disciplines: the permanent displays were donated to the city by a private collector with an interest in both fields. It's housed in a cavernous former bank headquarters. The underground vault and second-floor gallery host temporary exhibitions, while the ground floor showcases the main collection: iconic and experimental clothing, footwear and accessories, household design and furniture – even the odd scooter.

[FREE] Núcleo Arqueológico da Rua dos Correeiros

Rua dos Correeiros 9 (21 113 4496). Metro Baixa-Chiado or tram 12, 28. **Guided tours** (English or Portuguese) hourly 10am-noon, 2-5pm Mon-Sat. **Admission** free. **Map** p45 G5 ❺

Under the Millennium BCP bank headquarters in Rua Augusta (enter round the back), the Archaeological Centre offers a glimpse of what's lurking below the Baixa. In Roman times, this was a river beach, where locals made sauces by mixing fish and shellfish bits with salt, spices and herbs. The ingredients were then put in tanks and left to rot over time into a suitably tasty decomposed mush. When the bank wanted to redo its head office in 1991, the construction teams unearthed the ancient complex. Experts were called in and the centre opened to the public in 1995. On display are artefacts found during the dig, as well as ancient walls, a holding tank and an intact section of mosaic floor.

Restaurants

★ João do Grão

Rua dos Correeiros 220-226 (21 342 4757). Metro Rossio or Baixa-Chiado, or tram 12, 15. **Open** noon-3pm, 6-10pm daily. **Main courses** €7.50-€13.90. **Map** p45 G5 ❻ **Portuguese**

Lisbon Story Centre.

In a street packed with touristy eateries, this renowned restaurant has remained popular with locals and visitors in the know by keeping standards up and prices down (relatively speaking). The *grão* (chickpeas) of the name turn up in one of the *bacalhau* staples and in *mão de vaca* (cow's hoof) *com grão*. There are various other grilled fish and meat dishes, plus traditional fare such as game.

Cafés & Bars

Café Martinho da Arcada

Praça do Comércio 3 (21 887 9259, www. martinhodaarcada.com). Metro Terreiro do Paço or tram 15, 18, 25, 28. **Open** *Café* 7am-11pm Mon-Sat. *Restaurant* noon-4pm, 7-11pm Mon-Sat. **Map** p45 H5 ❼

This establishment began life in 1782 as a shop selling drinks and ice. The café and adjacent restaurant it was to become were two of poet Fernando Pessoa's favourite haunts. A few tables in the restaurant (main courses €15-€24) are now also reserved for living greats, such as painter Júlio Pomar. The café is worth a stop for the renowned *pastéis de nata*. The terrace is beset by exhaust fumes.

Shops & Services

Araújos

Rua Áurea (Rua do Ouro) 261 (21 346 7810). Metro Rossio. **Open** 10am-7pm Mon-Fri; 10am-1pm Sat. **Map** p45 G4 ❽ **Jewellery**

Established in 1878 and now run by the fourth generation of the same family – pretty much with the same decor as when it first opened – this jeweller has unusual gold and silver pieces, some of them copies of old designs. This is one of the best places to hunt for fine traditional Portuguese filigree.

Chapelaria d'Aquino

Rua do Comércio 16A (91 227 7783). Metro Terreiro do Paço or Baixa-Chiado, or tram 12, 28. **Open** 10am-7pm Mon-Sat. **Map** p45 G5 ❾ **Accessories**

A scion of one of Lisbon's long-established hatters has teamed up with another local retailer in this clean, modern space. It stocks a vast range of headgear,

EXPLORE

from top hats and Panamas to flat caps and turbans. Most are products of Portugal's still thriving felt-hat industry, although some are imported.

Dama de Copas

Rua de Santa Justa 87 (21 195 5997, www.dama decopas.pt). Metro Rossio or Baixa-Chiado. **Open** 10am-8pm Mon-Sat; 11am-7pm Sun. **Map** p45 G4 ⑩ **Lingerie**
According to the two friends who opened this lingerie consultancy in 2009, more than 90% of women wear bras that don't quite fit; their mission is to help you find just the right size, in styles for any occasion. Bra (or bikini) fittings and advice are free. The formula works: they have shops in Oporto and Madrid too.

Discoteca Amália

Rua Áurea (Rua do Ouro) 272 (21 342 0939). Metro Baixa-Chiado. **Open** 9.30am-1pm, 3-7pm Mon-Fri; 9.30am-1pm, 3-5pm Sat. **Map** p45 G4 ⑪ **Music**
A specialist in fado and other traditional music, with plenty of classics from Amália and her ilk, as well as contemporary artists.
Other location Van on Rua do Carmo, Chiado (21 347 0276, closed Sun).

★ GN Cellar

Rua da Conceição 20-26 (21 885 2395, www. garrafeiranacional.com). Metro Baixa-Chiado or Terreiro do Paço, or tram 12, 28. **Open** 10am-9pm daily. **Map** p45 G5 ⑫ **Food & drink**
A spin-off of leading wine and spirit merchant Garrafeira Nacional (Rua de Santa Justa 18-24, 21 887 9080, www.garrafeiranacional.com), this bright store with inventive window displays is aimed squarely at foreign wine-lovers. The stock is clearly displayed and staff are knowledgeable and speak good English. There are weekly wine tastings.

Napoleão

Rua dos Fanqueiros 70 (21 887 2042, www. napoleao.co.pt). Metro Baixa-Chiado or Terreiro do Paço, or tram 12, 28. Open 9.30am-8pm Mon-Sat; 3-7pm Sun. **Map** p45 G5 ⑬ **Food & drink**
Just across the street from GN Cellar (*see above*), staff at this or the Napoleão on the other street corner at Rua da Conceição 15 will help you choose from a wide range of Portuguese wines and ports. There's a Roman ruin visible through a glass floor.
Other locations throughout the city.

Numismática Diamantino

Rua da Madalena 89 (21 887 5113, www.nnd. com.pt). Metro Baixa-Chiado or tram 28. **Open** 9.30am-1pm, 2-7pm Mon-Fri; 9.30am-1pm Sat. **Map** p45 G5 ⑭ **Coins**
A numismatist's delight, Diamantino sells notes and coins, mainly from Portugal and the former colonies, including currency dating well back into monarchical times. On Saturday, visitors are advised to call ahead.

Nunes Corrêa

Rua Augusta 250 (21 324 0930, www.nunescorrea. com). Metro Baixa-Chiado or tram 28. **Open** 10am-7pm daily. **Map** p45 G4 ⑮ **Fashion**
Jacinto Nunes Corrêa, the founder of this lovely wood-panelled store, made clothes for the royal family in the late 19th century. They no longer make suits to measure, but stock excellent off-the-peg combos, plus good-quality shirts, shoes and silk ties.

A Outra Face da Lua

Rua da Assunção 22 (21 886 3430, www.aoutra facedalua.com). Metro Baixa-Chiado or Rossio, or tram 12, 28. **Open** 10am-8pm Mon-Sat; noon-7pm Sun. **Map** p45 G5 ⑯ **Fashion**
Recycled and second-hand clothes, plus retro gear such as flower-power minis. The shop also stocks vintage wallpaper and other decorative objects, smoking paraphernalia, kitsch tin toys and gadgets, and lots of different teas.
Other location Avenida Almirante Reis 94A (21 826 9578).

Papelaria Fernandes

Rua Áurea (Rua do Ouro) 145 (21 322 4830, www.papelariafernandes.pt). Metro Baixa-Chiado. **Open** 9am-7pm Mon-Fri; 10am-7pm Sat. **Map** p45 G4 ⑰ **Stationery**
This century-old retailer is where locals head to when they want a particular kind of envelope, staple-gun or log book. On the top floor (entrance also at Rua Vitória 41) are cards and wrapping paper and packaging, as well as a decent range of art supplies.
Other location Largo do Rato 13 (21 382 6230)

Pollux

Rua dos Fanqueiros 276 (21 881 1200, www.pollux.pt). Metro Rossio or tram 12, 15. **Open** 10am-7pm Mon-Sat. **Map** p45 G5 ⑱ **Department store**
This nine-storey department store is jammed with everything from fine glassware and ceramics to suitcases and stationery. The rooftop terrace, with a fantastic view, is a bonus.

Santos Ofícios Artesanatos

Rua da Madalena 87 (21 887 2031, www.santos oficios-artesanato.pt). Metro Baixa-Chiado or Terreiro do Paço, or tram 12, 28. **Open** 10am-8pm Mon-Sat. **Map** p45 G5 ⑲ **Handicrafts**
A cut above the usual souvenir shops, stocking a fine selection of handmade blankets, rugs, toys, pottery, clothes and baskets. There are also more modern offerings such as tiles with unusual designs and bags made of coffee packets sewn together.

ROSSIO

Most people moving around the city will pass through Rossio at least once a day. It's also a central meeting point, and was once a market

EXPLORE

CHERRY AID

A local drink for local people.

Could this be the world's most localised drinking phenomenon? Clustered around Rossio – with a handful of outliers elsewhere – are tiny bars that survive almost entirely by selling a drink you won't spot in Lisbon's fancier venues: a sticky cherry liqueur called *ginjinha*. Opening early and closing at midnight, these bars never lack custom – partly because they're in one of the most touristy parts of Lisbon, and partly because *ginjinha*, which some older folks still make at home, reminds sentimental locals of their grandmothers.

The biggest-selling brand is Ginja Sem Rival, which comes with or without whole cherries. But Ginja Espinheira, showcased in **A Ginjinha** at Largo de São Domingos 8 (open 7am-midnight daily), makes for stiff competition. A fixture since 1840, this bar also serves home-made lemonade and Eduardino, a herbal liqueur. A few yards away, at Rua das Portas de Santo Antão 7, another minuscule place with an ancient frontage serves Ginja Sem Rival (open 8am-midnight daily) and Eduardino. Further up, at No.61, is **Ginginha Popular** (open 7am-midnight Mon-Fri, 9am-midnight Sat & Sun).

Round the corner at Rua Barros Queirós 27, **Ginjinha Rubi** (open 7am-10.30pm daily) is the only establishment with its own production in the city itself (up the road in Anjos). On the southern side of Rossio, **Tendinha** (open 7am-9pm Mon-Fri, 8am-7.30pm Sat) claims to be Lisbon's oldest *tasca*.

Elsewhere, there are also *ginjinha* bars at Travessa da Ribeira 24 and Largo de Trindade Coelho 17. In Alfama, **Ginja d'Alfama** (Rua de São Pedro 12, open 10am-midnight Mon, Wed-Sun) and **Ginja da Sé** (Rua São João da Praça 3, open 4pm-2am Mon, Wed-Sun) sell the sticky stuff to a modish young crowd.

Local shops sell some attractive bottles of *ginjinha*. The best presented is Ginja Sem Rival with cherries, but the finest is Ginginha de Alcobaça, a lighter-coloured, less alcoholic tipple sold in a conical bottle. After a few *ginjinhas* you might start thinking one of these would make a lovely souvenir. But face facts: back home it'll only gather dust at the back of the drinks cabinet. Try it in Lisbon, where it belongs.

– florists still operate at the southern end. It was here that a flower seller is supposed to have given a carnation to a soldier on 25 April 1974, thus earning the Revolution the nickname Revolução dos Cravos (Carnation Revolution). But most of the cafés that the nervous dictator Salazar had 15 years earlier ordered to ban *tertúlias* – informal discussion groups – have disappeared. Of those that remain, **Café Nicola**, here since the late 18th century, has the most historical resonance. Around the square, crowds of commuters queue for buses and tourists browse at kiosks selling foreign-language newspapers.

Meanwhile, Africans cluster around the steps of the **Teatro Nacional Dona Maria II** (*see p161*), catching up with news from Guinea-Bissau or other distant homelands: the area first became a magnet for them because the nearby Igreja de São Domingos traditionally had a black priest. In the square in front of the church, businessmen peruse the newspaper as they get a shoeshine and shopworkers fortify themselves with a nip of *ginjinha*, the cough syrup-like brandy made from morello cherries that is served from stand-up bars in the area (*see left* **Cherry Aid**).

Now believed to mark the site of the Roman hippodrome, by medieval times Rossio was the open marketplace at the top of town. Pombal intended his more rectangular version to be secondary to the Praça do Comércio. Instead, Rossio increased in importance as the city expanded north. Its official name, Praça Dom Pedro IV, is something you'll only see on maps or the odd business card. King Pedro is remembered with a statue on top of the square's 23-metre-tall central column, while figures around the base represent Justice, Wisdom, Courage and Restraint. *See also p49* **In the Know.**

Restraint was not always Rossio's hallmark. The Teatro Nacional stands on the site of a royal palace that was taken over by the Inquisition, and many an auto-da-fé (public judging of heretics) ended with the condemned being burned at the stake in the square. Some 40,000 people were judged guilty during the history of the Portuguese Inquisition, of whom 1,800 were consigned to the flames.

Next to Rossio lies the less gracious **Praça da Figueira**. Here the statue, erected in 1971, is of Dom João I. If you've visited before and could have sworn the plinth has moved, you're right: when replaced after the construction of an underground car park, it was aligned with the vista down Rua da Prata, instead of returning to the square's centre. Praça da Figueira is ringed with nondescript shops, the exception being the **Hospital das Bonecas**, a sweet doll's hospital and shop. At night the square's population runs from skateboarders to ageing prostitutes; in winter the homeless warm themselves over the Metro vents. Round the corner, in the lobby of the

EXPLORE

Lisboa Tejo Hotel (see p211), the Poço de Borratém is an ancient well whose water was long used to cure itching and liver ailments.

On the north side of Largo de São Domingos stands blood-red **Palácio de Independência** (21 324 1470), one of the few large structures in the area that survived the 1755 Earthquake virtually intact. Its name comes from the fact that it was here, in 1640, that 40 aristocratic conspirators – known as the Conjurados – planned to end decades of Spanish rule. Guided visits to the palace and its *azulejo*-lined garden patio may be arranged during the week or you can just stop at the café-restaurant, which also has a peaceful inner patio.

The pedestrian-only **Rua das Portas de Santo Antão** leads north from here. It's lined with restaurants, almost all tourist traps where no self-respecting local foodie would be seen dead. If you must stop and eat in this area, try the grilled fowl at **Bonjardim**, or push the boat out at **Gambrinus** or **Solar dos Presuntos**. One discreet doorway at no.58 marks the **Casa do Alentejo**, a home from home for *alentejanos* with amazing neo-Moorish decor and a restaurant (21 340 5140, open 10am-11pm daily) open to all that serves so-so regional dishes. A few paces north, up Beco de São Luís da Pena, is the **Igreja de São Luís dos Franceses** (91 919 4614, www.saint-louis-des-francais.org) – the church of the city's French community since 1572. Normally open only for Sunday mass (11am), it's worth a look for the stucco work by Manuel Franciso dos Santos (who also decorated the Palácio dos Marqueses da Fronteira, see p117) and a painting attributed to Amaro do Vale that is said to be one of only three that depict Lisbon before the 1755 earthquake. It's high up on the north side of the nave.

Portas de Santo Antão is also the address of the cavernous **Coliseu dos Recreios** (see p152), the Lisbon Coliseum, opened in 1890 and nowadays a concert venue that hosts both classical and rock, as well as touring ballet and circus companies.

**IN THE KNOW
CAST-OFF BRONZE?**

Dom Pedro IV is the monarch whom the bronze figure atop the column in Rossio nominally represents. But a stubbornly persistent local rumour insists that it is actually a likeness of Emperor Maximilian of Mexico. In 1870, a ship bearing his statue is said to have docked at Lisbon, en route from Marseille, when word came of his assassination. By chance, Portugal had ordered a statue of Pedro IV from the same sculptor, Elias David, and a deal to take over the now unwanted Maximilian was supposedly struck.

A smaller entrance in the same building, at no.100, leads into the Sociedade de Geografia and its Museu Etnográfico. Further up is the **Ateneu Comercial de Lisboa**, founded in a former aristocratic residence in 1880 as a sort of social club for Lisbon shop assistants. The decaying building still provides a roof for everything from chess to dance classes and basketball, and now also two bars: **Primeiro Andar** (see p143) and a top-floor garden terrace.

A little further along is the **Ascensor da Lavra** (open 7.45am-8pm Mon-Fri; 9am-8pm Sat & Sun), a funicular that bears weary Lisboetas and wearier tourists up to Campo de Santana. For a non-touristy lunch, keep walking north on Portas de Santo Antão until it turns into **Rua de São José**, which is lined with more eateries – this time serving mainly local workers.

Sights & Museums

Hospital de Bonecas
Praça da Figueira 7 (21 342 8574, www.hospital debonecas.com). Metro Rossio. **Open** *Museum* 10.30am-12.30pm, 3.30-5pm Mon-Sat. *Shop* 10am-7pm Mon-Fri; 10am-6pm Sat. **Admission** *Museum* €2. **No credit cards. Map** p45 F5 ⑳
Generations of Lisbon children have brought battered toys to this 'dolls' hospital' for surgery, which takes place upstairs. The little museum built up over the years here is a treasure-trove of antique dolls and other toys and knick-knacks. In the ground-floor shop you can update your doll's wardrobe, pick up a Portuguese rag doll or porcelain doll, or choose from a selection of Barbies. On the third floor of the same building is Plum (see p52), a space shared by several young jewellery makers.

FREE ★ Igreja de São Domingos
Largo de São Domingos (21 342 8275). Metro Rossio or tram 12, 15. **Open** 7.30am-7pm daily. **Map** p45 F5 ㉑

Praça da Figueira.

EXPLORE

A succession of natural catastrophes has laid waste to this Dominican church since it was founded by Dom Sancho II in 1242 – most notably the earthquakes in 1531 and 1755 but, most recently, a fire in 1959. After nearly 40 years of renovation it reopened in 1997, but the still flame-ravaged interior gives the church a striking cave-like look. The high altar was completed in 1748 to the designs of Ludovice, architect of the monastery of Mafra. The Dominicans were central to the Inquisition, which was based across the square, and autos-da-fé often included a procession that began from here. The best time to visit is between 12.30pm and 5pm, when there's no mass going on.

Restaurants

Bonjardim
Travessa de Santo Antão 7 & 10 (21 342 7424). *Metro Rossio or Restauradores.* **Open** noon-11pm daily. **Main courses** €8.50-€19.60. **Map** p45 F4 ❷ **Portuguese**

WALK FLOWER POWER

How the fall of the dictatorship became the Carnation Revolution.

A visit to Rossio helps to explain how the 1974 military coup that ended 48 years of dictatorship in Portugal came to be known as the Revolução dos Cravos, or Carnation Revolution. Amid jubilant celebrations, flower sellers in the square pressed red carnations on the young soldiers who had toppled the old regime. The motif of the flower in a rifle barrel, evoking the relatively bloodless nature of the coup, remains a powerful symbol of Portugal's transition to democracy. The florists are still here, though fewer in number and now in unsightly metal kiosks at the southern end of the square, rather than at its centre. Every 25 April, the date of the coup, there's a carnation-strewn march down Avenida da Liberdade, but numbers fluctuate and never match those in the first few heady years.

Looking up and south-west from Rossio you'll see, high above the rooftops, the ruined arches of the **Convento do Carmo** (see p72), toppled by the 1755 Earthquake. It was in the square beside this church that the main confrontation of the Revolution took place.

Following the map, take Calçada do Carmo, which leads from the west side of Rossio to a steep flight of steps opposite the side entrance to Rossio railway station. From the top of the steps turn left and follow the same street up into a tree-lined square, Largo do Carmo. On the left are the arched entrances, designed for cavalry, of the headquarters of the Guarda Nacional Republicana, Portugal's paramilitary national guard. A new **Museu da GNR** (21 321 7000) here should shortly be open to the public, its circuit including rooms that witnessed key events on 25 April 1974.

It was to this barracks that the leaders of the old regime fled after the uprising. These included Marcello Caetano, who had taken over from Salazar as prime minister in 1968, President Américo Tomás, and several government ministers. In support of the rebel troops, crowds packed into the square, cheering from the tops of tanks for their surrender. Caetano told Captain Salgueiro Maia, the young rebel officer demanding his capitulation, that he feared 'power would fall to the mob' and as a matter of dignity he should surrender only to a general.

General António de Spínola, a charismatic, monocle-wearing figure, was telephoned and agreed to intervene, although he had played no part in the coup. He spoke with the rebel officers and entered the barracks. As word

EXPLORE

The self-styled 'King of Chicken', comprising two restaurants on either side of the street, is a favourite for a cheap downtown feed. Chicken grilled over charcoal comes with chips, salad and the ubiquitous (and thankfully optional) hot piri-piri sauce. There are other dishes on the menu but the place aims for quick turnover, so service can be on the brusque side. Note that prices for eating on the terrace are 20% higher. Of the two buildings, heading upstairs in the southern one is the 'local' option. There are takeaways available too.

came that he'd accepted the unconditional surrender of Caetano and his colleagues, the crowd rejoiced. The next day the deposed leaders flew to exile in Brazil.

Just a few streets away another confrontation was unfolding. Leave Largo do Carmo by Travessa do Carmo and turn left into Rua Serpa Pinto, where on the first floor of no.12B the restaurant Aviz was once a glittering gathering place for the rich and famous. After most of its patrons fled following the Revolution, left-wing visitors such as Jean Paul Sartre, Simone de Beauvoir and some of the young 'Captains of April' who had led the coup helped to keep it in business.

Turn right into Rua Garrett, then second left into Rua Antónia Maria Cardoso. No.26, at the end of the street on the left, was the headquarters of the PIDE, the despised and feared secret police of the Salazar-Caetano regime. A plaque on the wall commemorates the four people who were killed when PIDE agents fired into the crowd that surrounded the building on 25 April 1974. Their deaths represented the last violent throes of the regime.

After standing empty for decades, the building was converted into luxury flats. The move outraged many, with calls for it instead to be turned into a museum honouring the regime's opponents, some of whom were detained, interrogated and tortured in cells here. The campaign came to nothing, and Lisbon still has no museum dedicated to the dictatorship and its overthrow. So for now the keeper of the flame remains the Associação 25 de Abril, which hosts small-scale exhibitions on the Revolution. To visit it, double back to Largo do Chiado, turn left, then right up Rua da Misericórdia to No.95.

Everest Montanha
Calçada do Garcia 15 (21 887 6428). Metro Rossio. **Open** noon-3.30pm, 7pm-midnight daily. **Main courses** €7.75-€12.75. **No credit cards.** **Map** p45 F5 **㉒** **Indian**
Up an alley off Largo de São Domingos, this friendly Nepali-owned place offers tasty food at what are reasonable prices, given its central location. The menu has a wide range of Indian standards, among them several vegetarian and vegan dishes.

Gambrinus
Rua das Portas de Santo Antão 23 (21 342 1466, www.gambrinuslisboa.com). Metro Rossio or Restauradores. **Open** noon-1.30am daily. **Main courses** €22-€42. **Map** p45 F4 **㉔** **Portuguese**
In this discreet gourmet haven, amid stained glass and wood panelling, liveried waiters glide to and fro, bearing plates of seafood. Eating here can cost a packet if you order any of those, or the fancier traditional dishes on offer, but the place also built its reputation with *pregos* (steak sandwiches) and delicious meat croquettes. So you can do as many locals do and just snack at the long bar. Here or in the two dining rooms (smoking and non-smoking, the latter with a huge fireplace), it's worth asking what is available other than what's printed on the menu.

O Marquês
Travesso do Ferro 11 (21 346 8070). Metro Restauradores or Rossio. **Open** 9am-10pm Mon-Sat. **Main courses** €4.80-€6.75. **Map** p45 F4 **㉕** **Portuguese**
The last in a row of cheap *tascas*, O Marquês offers the best value of any. Locals crowd in here for a reason, in the shape of tasty grilled fish and meats, and filling traditional fare such as *feijoada* (bean, meat and vegetable stew) or *alheira de caça* (game sausage). Order a *meia dose* (half serving) or split a full dose between two.

Cafés & Bars

★ Café Nicola
Praça Dom Pedro IV (Rossio) 24 (21 346 0579). Metro Rossio or tram 12, 15. **Open** 8am-midnight daily. **Map** p45 F4 **㉖**
Nicola and its grand façade have been here since 1929, but occupy the site of a famous 18th-century café where poet Manuel Maria Barbosa du Bocage held court (his statue is still toasted nightly). In the 20th century, Nicola was a centre for political intrigue, with the dictatorship's secret police assigned to keep tabs on would-be agitators. Its marble, steel and glass interior is the result of a 1990s renovation, but the paintings are 1935 originals by Fernando Santos.

Casa Suíça
Praça Dom Pedro IV (Rossio) 96 (21 321 4090, www.casasuica.pt). Metro Rossio or tram 12, 15. **Open** 7am-9pm daily. **Map** p45 F4 **㉗**

Suiça's extensive selection of sticky pastries is as good as ever (including prize-winning *pastéis de nata*) but there are also sandwiches, salads, yoghurts and shakes. It has terraces both front and back.

★ Confeitaria Nacional

Praça da Figueira 18B (21 342 4470, www. confeitarianacional.pt). Metro Rossio or tram 12, 15. **Open** 8am-8pm Mon-Sat; 9am-9pm Sun. **Map** p45 F5 ㉓

The plaque outside boasting 'over 100 years of existence' is itself an antique; Nacional was founded in 1829 and retains its glass cases and painted panels. With fast, pleasant service, it's a good place to buy biscuits or cakes to take away, but there is also a sit-down café. They even have their own brand of coffee.

Shops & Services

★ Azevedo Rua

Praça Dom Pedro IV (Rossio) 69 & 72-73 (21 342 7511, 93 343 5294, www.azevedorua.com). Metro Rossio. **Open** 9.30am-7pm Mon-Fri; 10am-2.30pm Sat (Nov, Dec to 7pm). **Map** p45 F4 ㉙ **Accessories**

Rossio used to be home to a whole community of hatters; only this one, founded in 1886, remains. Black, rabbit-skin felt hats, worn by Portuguese horsemen, and the style favoured by Fernando Pessoa are stacked up to the ceiling. There's also a large range of berets, Panama hats and bowlers.

Celeiro

Rua 1º de Dezembro 65 (21 030 6030, www.celeiro. pt). Metro Rossio. **Open** 8.30am-8pm Mon-Fri; 8.30am-7pm Sat. **Map** p45 F4 ㉚ **Food & drink**

Health-food chain selling vegan products, cereals, beans, pulses and vitamins, as well as traditional Portuguese and imported herbal cures. It also has a decent selection of breads and snacks, plus some organic fruit and veg. There are self-service restaurants in the basement and next door.

Other locations throughout the city.

★ Manteigaria Silva

Rua Dom Antão de Almada 1C-D (21 342 4905). Metro Rossio. **Open** 9am-7.30pm Mon-Sat. **Map** p45 F4 ㉛ **Food & drink**

The Portuguese have been eating *bacalhau* (salt cod) for centuries. It's sold dried and salted. In traditional places such as this one, the smelly, kite-shaped cod carcasses are stacked up whole, ready to be chopped up to order. Alternatively, you can buy *caras* (cod faces) and *línguas* (cod tongues). The shop also stocks canned fish and has a cheese and *presunto* (cured ham) counter. It now has a spin-off stall in the Mercado da Ribeira (*see p95*), open daily until 2am.

Manuel Tavares

Rua da Betesga 1A-B (21 342 4209, www.manuel tavares.com). Metro Rossio. **Open** 9.30am-7.30pm Mon-Sat. **Map** p45 F4 ㉜ **Food & drink**

Founded in 1860, this traditional delicatessen stocks a vast range of *presunto* (cured ham) and sausages including *morçela* (black pudding) and *chouriço doce* (with honey and almonds). There are also smoked pig's tongues, Portuguese cheeses, dried fruit, *bacalhau* and a good range of ports.

Mercado Praça da Figueira

Praça da Figueira 10B (21 886 7464, www. casapereira.pt). Metro Rossio. **Open** 8.30am-8pm Mon-Sat. **Map** p45 F5 ㉝ **Food & drink**

A narrow entrance lined with fruit displays opens out into a small supermarket that stocks gourmet and foreign foods, plus an excellent selection of Portuguese wines. There's also a proper butcher's section. It makes for an atmospheric place to shop, under the original Pombaline arches and beams, and (a later addition) lots of *azulejos*.

Plum

Praça da Figueira 7, 3D (21 343 2322). Metro Rossio. **Open** 10am-6pm Mon-Fri. **Map** p45 F5 ㉞ **Jewellery/Accessories**

Upstairs from the Hospital de Bonecas (*see p49*) is another box of delights: the shared atelier-cum-showroom of several young artisans. (There's no sign: just knock on the door on the right off the third flight of stairs.) Here Vera Manzoni (91 611 4546, www.veramanzoni.com) continues a family tradition of making costume jewellery: her exclusive designs (necklaces from €25) often use quite simple materials in striking combinations, though she's also a trained goldsmith and works with precious and semi-precious stones, especially river pearls. Paula Paour (93 651 3619) makes more austere contemporary pieces, above all using silver and semi-precious stones. Like Manzoni, she can recondition jewellery. Sónia Estêvão (91 815 9790, www.soniaestevao.com) also uses mainly silver (plain and gilded).

Seaside

Largo Dom Pedro IV (Rossio) 57 (96 152 4010, www.seaside.pt). Metro Rossio or Restauradores. **Open** 10am-9pm Mon-Sat; 10am-8pm Sun. **No credit cards. Map** p45 F4 ㉟ **Fashion**

One of Portugal's best-value footwear retailers, whose three-storey flagship store sells functional men's and women's styles. Most are made in Portugal and some in Spain, despite English- and Italian-sounding brand names. There are several branches in the vicinity, including two on Praça da Figueira. **Other locations** throughout the city.

Tabacaria Monaco

Praça Dom Pedro IV (Rossio) 21 (21 346 8191). Metro Rossio. **Open** 9am-7pm Mon-Fri; 9am-2pm Sat. **No credit cards. Map** p45 F4 ㊱ **Press & periodicals**

This splendid vintage tobacconist's, inaugurated in 1894, sells a wide range of European and US newspapers and a fair number of foreign glossies.

EXPLORE

Praça dos Restauradores.

RESTAURADORES & AVENIDA DA LIBERDADE

Avenida da Liberdade began as an extension of the Passeio Público, a late 18th-century garden promenade. This busy boulevard, built on the Champs-Elysées model, was completed in 1886, forming an axis that connects the 18th-century downtown with new areas built in the 19th century. Where Lisbon had previously clustered along the river, now it expanded inland to the north. Carrying several lanes of traffic between the Praça dos Restauradores and the Praça Marquês de Pombal roundabout, Avenida da Liberdade has been spruced up in recent years and is now an elegant home to office blocks, big hotels and upmarket fashion shops.

At the southern end, just north-west of Rossio, is the neo-Manueline façade of Rossio station, completed in 1892. It's built against the hillside, its main hall and platforms on the top floor. This is normally the terminus of the Sintra line, but delays in repairs to the tunnel through which trains exit Lisbon mean it is closed for now.

The obelisk in Praça dos Restauradores commemorates the 1 December 1640 restoration of independence from Spain, inscribed with dates of decisive battles in the 28 years of war. The Eden cinema here was once an outstanding art deco landmark by Cassiano Branco, but as an aparthotel, the VIP Executive Suites Éden, it now retains only the façade and a monumental staircase.

Next door, the **Palácio Foz** (*see p159*) housed a notorious nightclub in the 1920s, and later the Ministry of Propaganda. Its ground floor is now home to Lisbon's main tourist office, the tourist police and the Loja dos Museus, a shop with replicas from Portugal's museums that make good souvenirs. There are also concerts most Wednesdays and Fridays, and some Saturdays,

upstairs in the gilded Sala de Espelhos – access is via the door on the far right of the façade. The same door is the entrance to the **Cinemateca Júnior** (21 463 2157, 21 347 6129; open 10am-5pm Mon-Fri, 11am-6pm Sat), an offshoot of **Cinemateca Portuguesa** (*see p135*). It has a display of magic lanterns and other pieces relating to early cinema and its precursors, and screens films for kids at 3pm on Saturday.

Round the corner is the **Ascensor da Glória** (open 7am-11.55pm Mon-Thur, 7am-12.25am Fri, 8.30am-12.25am Sat, 9am-12.25am Sun), a funicular that takes the strain if you're heading up to the Bairro Alto. Across the square is the central post office and also the **ABEP kiosk** (*see p156*), which sells tickets for films, plays, bullfights and other sports and cultural events.

The tree-lined Avenida was long a tolerated prostitution zone, spilling out from the red-light district around the green **Praça da Alegria**, home for decades to venerable jazz venue **Hot Club** (*see p153*). Nowadays it's known more for high-end clothes shopping: long a showcase for posher Portuguese brands such as the venerable Rosa & Teixeira and Lanidor, in recent years it has become a magnet for luxury fashion names such as Prada and Hugo Boss. **Fashion Clinic** (21 354 9040, www.fashionclinic.pt), in the Tivoli Forum shopping centre halfway up on the avenue's eastern side, stocks lots of well-known brands. Meanwhile, the rash of new kiosks dotted either side of the avenue each boasts its own speciality – everything from gourmet hot dogs to fruit cocktails. At night, groups of youngsters chat over DJ-driven soundtracks.

A few blocks north of Praça Restauradores on the west side, two art deco pillars mark the entrance to **Parque Mayer**, a decaying 1920s complex that was home to Portuguese *revista* – revue theatre – but where all stages but one have now gone dark. Longstanding plans to redevelop this prime real estate have been shelved for lack of funds. One of the disused theatres, the **Capitólio** (*see p204*), has been listed, which any future project must respect.

Across the street, the curved lines of the modernist building at **no.170** stand out from the derivative architecture that predominates around it. Another work by Cassiano Branco, from 1936, as the Hotel Vitória it was frequented by German spies during World War II, but is now owned by the local Communist Party. A little further up is the **Teatro Tivoli**, a neoclassical former cinema built in 1924 by Raul Lino. It was renovated in the 1990s and has established itself as a venue for slick comedies. The striking red kiosk in front was installed in 1925 by the owners of **Diário de Notícias**, whose modernist editorial offices (1936) stand further north.

Back on the west side of the avenue, the **Cinema São Jorge** (*see p136*), completed in

1950 to a design by Fernando Silva, is the last of Lisbon's old picture palaces, now owned by the council and used mainly for festivals. By contrast, the **Cinemateca Portuguesa** (see p135) round the corner in Rua Barata Salgueiro has a packed programme of Portuguese and international classics and art movies. Opposite, the Sociedade Nacional de Belas Artes is one of several art spaces in the area; on the next road north, the **Casa-Museu Medeiros e Almeida** boasts one of Portugal's finest collections of decorative arts.

If you want to get up, up and away from the city streets, take the lift to the Hotel Tivoli Lisboa's **Sky Bar** or head up Rua do Salitre, past the excellent vegetarian retaurant **Os Tibetanos**, to the **CS Vintage Hotel Lisboa** (Rua Barata Salgueiro 55). Its rooftop bar, the Varanda do Castelo (open 5pm-midnight daily) boasts a great view across the city to the castle – as its name suggests.

Sights & Museums

FREE Casa-Museu Medeiros e Almeida

Rua Rosa Araújo 41 (21 354 7892, www.casamuseumedeirosealmeida.pt). Metro Marquês de Pombal. **Open** free guided tours noon 1st & 3rd Sat of mth or paid pre-booked tours (min 6) 1-5.30pm Mon-Sat. **Admission** free-€6. **Map** p44 D3 ③
The foundation that late businessman António Medeiros e Almeida created in 1973 has 26 rooms across two floors showing 2,000 pieces (out of total holdings of 9,000 pieces), the legacy of years of hoarding. They include Chinese porcelain, clocks, paintings, furniture, gold and jewellery, sacred art, sculpture and textiles. The 19th-century building was previously the Vatican's embassy. For the free one-hour tours on alternate Saturdays, turn up ten minutes early.

Restaurants

Avenue

Avenida da Liberdade 129 (21 601 7127, www.avenue.pt). Metro Avenida. **Open** 12.30-3pm, 7.30-11pm Mon-Thur; 12.30-3pm, 7.30-11.30pm Fri; 7.30-11.30pm Sat. **Main courses** €14-€29. **Map** p45 E4 ③ **Portuguese**
As a woman, Marlene Vieira is a rarity among Lisbon's star chefs, but it is her talent in creatively applying new techniques and flavours to traditional dishes that has won her fame. Starters might include *ovos verdes* (egg cooked at low temperature, served with watercress cream) or *pipis de pato* (duck liver terrine and gizzard confit, served with Madeira wine). As well as hearty meat dishes such as roast pork belly, tuck into the likes of red mullet served with crunchy fried breadcrumbs and seaweed, or *polvinhos à lagareiro* (roast octopus). Ask for a table by the window for views of the Avenida.

Jardim dos Sentidos

Rua Mãe d'Água 3 (21 342 3670, www.jardim dosentidos.com). Metro Avenida. **Open** noon-3pm, 7-11pm Mon-Thur; 7-11pm Fri, Sat. **Main courses** €8-€9.90. **No credit cards**. **Map** p45 E3 ③ **Vegetarian**
The delightful garden with palm trees is perhaps the main attraction here, as the menu is fairly limited: vegetarian lasagne, stuffed aubergine and so on. The lunch buffet is great value (€8.90 with tea, €10.60 with fresh juice); there's also a kids' menu. The interior is stylishly simple, with original stone window frames dividing the space. Out back is an alternative therapy centre.

★ Maharaja

Rua do Cardal de São José 21-23 (21 346 9300, 96 256 1787). Metro Avenida. **Open** noon-3pm, 6.30-11pm Tue-Sun. **Main courses** €7.50-€16. **Map** p45 E4 ⑩ **Indian**
This plush den specialising in Mughlai food is hidden away in a back street – make the effort, though, as it's great value. The kitchen turns out delicious tandoori kebabs, coconut shrimp curry and the like, and there are more than a dozen vegetarian mains.

Pinóquio

Praça dos Restauradores 79 (21 346 5106). Metro Restauradores. **Open** noon-midnight daily. **Main courses** €11-€22. **Map** p45 F4 ⑪ **Portuguese**
Pinóquio stands out from its neighbours for its juicy clams and succulent prawns, plus delicious nibbles such as *pica pau* (marinated meat) and steak served with the famous house sauce.

★ Solar dos Presuntos

Rua das Portas de Santo Antão 150 (21 342 4253, www.solardospresuntos.com). Metro Restauradores. **Open** noon-3.30pm, 7-11pm Mon-Sat. **Main courses** €14.50-€27.50. **Map** p45 E4 ⑫ **Portuguese**

Maharaja.

Fans of Portuguese country cooking – particularly from the northern Minho region – make a beeline for this upscale restaurant, with a wood-panelled interior lined with photos of celeb regulars. It's pricey but worth it. If you like *bacalhau* you should try it *assado* (roasted). The octopus is excellent too. In season, they also offer unusual dishes such as fried *sável* (shad).

★ Os Tibetanos

Rua do Salitre 117 (21 314 2038, www.tibetanos. com). Metro Avenida. **Open** 12.15-2.45pm, 7.30-10.30pm Mon-Fri; 12.45-3.45pm, 8-11pm Sat. **Main courses** €9-€13. **No credit cards.** **Map** p44 D3 ⑬ Vegetarian

Lisbon's longest-running vegetarian dining option is as good as ever. It offers dishes including Tibetan *momo*, *seitan* steak and tofu sausages. The lunchtime set menus are excellent value, and there's French cider if you don't fancy one of the many herbal teas. Seating in the dining room is rather cramped, so this isn't a place to relax over a long meal. A small shop at the entrance sells Tibetan items, and there's a Buddhist centre upstairs (open 10am-3pm, 4.30-7pm Mon-Fri).

Zé Varunca

Rua de São José 54 (21 346 8018, www.zevarunca. com). Metro Avenida. **Open** 12.30-3pm, 7.30-10.30pm Mon-Sat. **Main courses** €9.50-€12.50. **Map** p45 E4 ⑭ Portuguese

This rustic little place is a haven for lovers of Alentejo food (and wine). It's the third restaurant the eponymous owner has opened in the Lisbon region, after his successes in Parede and Oeiras. The menu changes daily, but everything is good, from *sopa de cação* (dogfish soup) to *arroz de pato* (duck rice) or *carne de porco à alentejana* (pork with clams).

Cafés & Bars

Champanheria do Largo

Largo da Anunciada 20 (21 347 0392). Metro Restauradores. **Open** noon-midnight Mon-Sat. **Map** p45 E4 ⑮

Enjoy a champagne cocktail or two in this airy wine bar opposite the Lavra funicular accompanied by tasty snacks such as veal carpaccio or *queijo da ilha* (tangy cheese from the Azores). You can also dine here until 11.30pm, on dishes such as suckling pig.

Delta Q

Avenida da Liberdade 144 (no phone). Metro Avenida. **Open** 9am-7pm Mon-Thur; 9am-midnight Fri, Sat. **Map** p45 E4 ⑯

This flagship store for Portugal's leading coffee distributor, Delta, is a pleasant place for a break from shopping or sightseeing. As well as the café and lounge, there's a gourmet store and boutique, with information and advice about types of coffee, machines and accessories.

Sky Bar

Hotel Tivoli Lisboa, Avenida da Liberdade 185 (21 319 8832). Metro Avenida. **Open** May-Oct 5pm-1am daily. **Map** p44 D3 ⑰

In a relaxed, comfortable setting (cushions and pouffes aplenty), staff serve tasty cocktails and finger food. In high summer, there are DJs here every Thursday, Friday and Saturday.

Shops & Services

Carbono

Rua do Telhal 6B (21 342 3757, www.carbono. com.pt). Metro Avenida. **Open** 11am-7pm Mon-Sat. **Map** p45 E4 ⑭ Music

Carbono is an alternative music store that sells (and buys) local and international releases on CD, including new and second-hand, as well as lots of vinyl. It's a good source of information about new Portuguese artists and musical projects.

Castanheira Só Música

Rua do Telhal 8A/B (21 342 1870, www.castanheirasomusica.com). Metro Avenida. **Open** 10am-1pm, 2.30-5pm Mon-Fri; 10.30am-1pm Sat. **Map** p45 E4 ⑭ Musical instruments

One door up from Carbono (*see above*), this spacious store is a good place to pick up local instruments such as a *guitarra* (lute-shaped, 12-stringed Portuguese guitar) and *cavaqu inho* (probable ancestor of the Hawaiian ukelele). The shop is also a good place for tips about local workshops and jam sessions.

★ Fly London

Avenida da Liberdade 230 (91 059 4564, www.flylondon.com). Metro Avenida. **Open** 10am-7pm Mon-Sat. **Map** p44 D3 ⑩ Fashion

This Portuguese brand's distinctive footwear selection was a hit in the UK and elsewhere even before this outlet opened in 2010. This flagship store stocks the latest women's lines – plus the odd men's range – along with some clothes and accessories.

★ Loja dos Museus

Palácio Foz, Praça dos Restauradores (21 343 3008, www.patrimoniocultural.pt). Metro Restauradores. **Open** 9.30am-6.30pm Mon-Sat. **Map** p45 F4 ⑪ Gifts & souvenirs

Porcelain, textiles, tiles, glassware and silverware are among the top-quality items stocked at this downtown outlet of the institution that runs Portugal's national monuments.

Other locations throughout the city.

Oficina Mustra

Rua Rodrigues Sampaio 112 C/V (21 314 7009). Metro Avenida. **Open** 10am-7.30pm Mon-Sat. **Map** p44 D4 ⑫ Fashion

Off-the-peg and made-to-measure suits designed by a former creative director for an Italian clothing company. After your visit to the showroom, the

EXPLORE

resulting designs are sent to Naples where a team of tailors stitch them together. Shirts, shoes and ties can also be made to order.

Rosa & Teixeira
Avenida da Liberdade 204 (21 311 0350, www.rosaeteixeira.pt). Metro Avenida. **Open** 10am-7.30pm Mon-Sat. **Map** p44 D4 ⑤ **Fashion**
Portugal's business elite have long had suits made to measure at this, the avenue's longest-established menswear specialist. Techniques perfected over generations are applied by tailors upstairs, at prices that run to thousands of euros. Downstairs, off-the-peg suits from leading foreign brands line the racks.

Sociedade Nacional de Belas Artes
Rua Barata Salgueiro 36 (21 313 8510, www.snba. pt). Metro Marquês de Pombal. **Open** noon-7pm Mon-Fri (Aug 2-6pm). **Map** p44 D3 ⑤ **Gallery**
Three airy exhibition spaces run by artists for artists, where many leading figures of the Portuguese scene began their careers. It also runs competitions.

Sunrise Press
Avenida da Liberdade 9 (21 347 0204). Metro Restauradores. **Open** 9am-9pm daily. **Map** p45 E4 ⑤ **Press & periodicals**
A tunnel of a shop that sells one of the best selections of foreign newspapers and specialist magazines anywhere in Lisbon.

MARQUÊS DE POMBAL & PARQUE EDUARDO VII

At the top of the Avenida stands an enormous column from which the statue of the Marquês de Pombal lords it over the eponymous Praça – really a roundabout that's a seething mass of cars. Atop his column, he serenely overlooks the distant urban plan he imposed on the old city.

Behind him is the **Parque Eduardo VII**, laid out in the late 19th century as the natural extension of the Avenida da Liberdade axis, and later named after the British king Edward VII during his 1903 visit to Portugal. The layout of much of the park is rather formal, but the **Estufa Fria** gardens and greenhouse on its west side provide welcome shade.

Two fascist pillars at the park's upper end now enclose a pile of stones – purportedly, a sculpture by João Cutileiro – supposed to commemorate the 1974 Revolution. A pond garden in the upper eastern corner has a café with a pleasant terrace. Note, though, that at night parts of the park serve as a gay cruising area. Beyond Alameda Cardeal Cerejeira is a garden named after fado singer Amália Rodrigues (*see p149*). Nearby is a hulking gourmet restaurant, **Eleven**, and one of Lisbon's most serene esplanades, the **Linha d'Água**. But for a truly relaxed vibe (and live music while you eat), head to the **Associação Caboverdeana**.

Sights & Museums

FREE Arte e Finança
Praça Marquês de Pombal 3 (21 350 8975). Metro Marquês de Pombal. **Open** 9am-7pm Mon-Sat. **Admission** free. **Map** p44 C3 ⑤⑥
In a state-of-the-art building in the heart of the business district, this privately funded endeavour provides a downtown showcase for contemporary art. The permanent collection comprises some 1,000 photography-based works by 280 artists, including the likes of Cindy Sherman and Wolfgang Tillmans.

Estufa Fria
Parque Eduardo VII (21 388 2278). Metro Marquês de Pombal or Parque. **Open** *Summer* (from last Sun in Mar) 10am-7pm daily. *Winter* (from last Sun in Oct) 9am-5pm daily. **Admission** €3.10; reductions from €1.55; free under-6s & all Sun to 2pm. **No credit cards. Map** p44 B2 ⑤
This greenhouse garden on the north-west side of Parque Eduardo VII was completed in 1930. The promenade around the pond leads into three areas containing a total of some 300 species: the Estufa Quente, or hothouse; the Estufa Fria itself, a cool greenhouse covered by a porous wooden roof; and the Estufa Doce, the 'sweet' greenhouse with drier conditions. The foliage, statues and cascades are ideal for a romantic stroll.

Restaurants

Assinatura
Rua do Vale de Pereiro 19 (21 386 7696, www. assinatura.com.pt). Metro Rato or Marquês de Pombal. **Open** 7.45-10.30pm Mon; 12.30-3pm, 7.45-10.30pm Tue-Thur; 12.30-3pm, 7.45-11.30 Fri, Sat. **Main courses** €23-€32. **Map** p44 D2 ⑤ **Portuguese/International**
A fixture on the Lisbon gourmet scene for some years, Assinatura has seen chefs come and go, but now looks in safe hands with Vitor Areias. Drawing on experience at top European restaurants such as Mugaritz and Noma, he brings a touch of molecular magic to Assinatura. His four- and six-course tasting menus (€47 and €56; matching wines €24 or €34) start with inventive amuse-bouches before moving on to a starter – perhaps smoked goat's cheese with white beans, fresh cherries and herbs – then a main such as shoulder of lamb with bell pepper sauce and crunchy salsify glacée. Desserts show real visual flair.

★ Associação Caboverdeana
Rua Duque de Palmela 2, 8th floor (21 353 1932, www.acaboverdeana.org). Metro Marquês de Pombal. **Open** *Lunch* 12.30pm-3pm Mon-Fri. **Main courses** (for 2 people) €9.50-€11.50. **No credit cards. Map** p44 D3 ⑤ **African**
For a cheap lunchtime treat, take the lift to the eighth-floor canteen of this Cape Verdean social club. Here inexpensive, tasty African dishes such

as *cachupa*, fish *mukeca* or chicken with peanut sauce are served to an appreciative clientele made up in part of local office workers. On Tuesdays and Thursdays there's live music (1-2.30pm) and the same crowd spend their lunch break dancing cheek-to-cheek to *mornas*.

Eleven

Rua Marquês de Fronteira, Parque Eduardo VII (21 386 2211, www.restauranteleven.com). Metro Parque. **Open** 12.30-3pm, 7.30-11pm Mon-Sat. **Main courses** €29-€49. **Map** p44 A2 ⑥ Mediterranean

The first restaurant to bring a Michelin star to the city centre back in 2006, with the elegant Mediterranean cuisine of Joachim Koerper, Eleven briefly lost, then won back, that honour but now seems to have a firm grip. In what is essentially a large concrete box, whose floor-to-ceiling windows afford panoramic views, Lisbon's elite coo over elaborate dishes produced using the freshest seafood, vegetable and herbs, and prime meats. Desserts, such as coconut crème brûlée or passionfruit soufflé, are divine. The minimalist decor – wood, iron and stone – makes it feel like a place that's geared towards a business crowd, and the lunchtime 'express menu' (€31.50 for three courses) fits with that. But there are various tasting menus (from €90) to be enjoyed at leisure.

Cafés & Bars

Linha d'Água

Rua Marquês de Fronteira, Jardim Amália Rodrigues (21 381 4327). Metro São Sebastião. Open *Summer* 10am-10pm daily. *Winter* 10am-8pm daily. **No credit cards. Map** p44 A3 ①
At the very top of Parque Eduardo VII, this modern café by a circular pool is a haven of tranquillity. Fine salads, cakes and light meals are served inside to a cool musical soundtrack, while outside water laps beneath a boardwalk. On the eastern side of the park, Cafeteria Botequim do Rei (21 315 4611, closed Mon) also has a pleasant terrace.

Shops & Services

Clube VII

Parque Eduardo VII (21 384 8300, www.clubevii. com). Metro Marquês de Pombal. **Admission** €35/day. **Map** p44 B2 ② Sports club/spa
Buy a day pass at this posh sports club in a leafy park and you get access to the chlorine-free indoor pool and gym, plus two hours on covered tennis courts (rackets are available for hire). Treatments in the well-appointed spa are extra.

★ Lanidor

Rua Braancamp 48 (93 203 2428, www.lanidor. com). Metro Marquês de Pombal. **Open** 10am-7.30pm Mon-Fri; 10am-1pm Sat. **Map** p44 D2 ⑥ Fashion

Lanidor offers stylish and restrained women's fashion plus clothes for children and young teens, and is now making inroads into foreign markets. This is one of the more upmarket Portuguese chains and a safe bet in terms of both price and quality. It has branches in all the main shopping centres, or you can order online.
Other locations throughout the city.

CAMPO DE SANTANA

Rising in the fork between the two Avenidas, Almirante Reis and da Liberdade, is a mixed bag of a neighbourhood with an uncommon number of hospitals. This makes it the perfect location for the statue of Sousa Martins, which stands on the well-greened square of **Campo dos Mártires de Pátria** (invariably still known by its original name of Campo de Santana) outside the Faculdade de Medicina.

José Thomaz de Sousa Martins died in 1897 having gained great favour among the poor for his even-handed approach to curing the sick. Though the man himself was entirely secular in outlook, grateful locals have since made him a religious cult hero and many keep candles burning in his memory. The stone plaques around the base have been left in thanks for miracle cures attributed to the divine medic.

The **Jardim do Torel**, a small park off Rua de Júlio de Andrade, has fine views, exercise equipment and benches designed for lounging. Just below it is the spacious **Esplanada do Torel**. The park may be reached from downtown by catching the Lavra funicular on Largo da Anunciada (at the top, turn left and then left again into the park) or, from Avenida Metro station, head up Rua das Pretas and 50 metres up its continuation, Rua do Telhal, and then climb the stairs on your right.

Cafés & Bars

Esplanada do Torel

Jardim do Torel (93 040 4702). Metro Avenida then 10min walk, or Ascensor do Lavra. **Open** *Winter* 11am-7pm daily. *Summer* 11am-midnight daily. **Map** p45 E4 ⑥
This esplanade on the hill that noses its way into the centre of Lisbon is one of the city's best-kept secrets. A few steps below the leafy Jardim do Torel, drinks and burgers are served from a kiosk and consumed on a large terrace. The view makes it a great place for a sundowner, especially in summer when it often hosts live music or DJs. A safe kids' playground is within eyeshot. In August, the area has been known to be transformed into an urban beach, complete with sand and a large fountain serving as a pool. The kiosk was undergoing renovation at the time of writing, but should be functioning again from summer 2015.

EXPLORE

East of Baixa

From the orderly streets of Baixa, Lisbon loses all decorum as it scrambles on to its alleged seven hills, all of them with white churches dotted about. On its eastern side, above the clutter of terracotta rooftops, the skyline is topped by the brooding Castelo de São Jorge, with the higgledy-piggledy Alfama below it. Densely populated, Alfama is still a community. The poor linger in tiny rent-controlled apartments, though rooftop flats are much sought after by wealthier newcomers. It looks cheerful and postcard-perfect in summer, and the city, aware of the area's attractiveness to visitors, subsidises the maintenance of façades. But many houses are in dire need of renovation. In this area, you'll also find the 12th-century Sé Catedral and many of the city's finest *miradouros*, lookout points that reward the efforts of footsore visitors.

EXPLORE

Feira da Ladra.

Don't Miss

1 Castelo de São Jorge The castle is essential viewing (p64).

2 Museu-Escola de Artes Decorativas A treasure house of applied arts (p65).

3 Igreja e Mosteiro de São Vicente de Fora Fabulous *azulejo* panels and panoramic views (p67).

4 Feira da Ladra Treasure and tat abound at this flea market (p66).

5 Intendente Supremely trendy area, but still with enough edge (p68).

SÉ

Lisbon's most picturesque tram ride – the no.28 east from Baixa up to Graça – heads past **Igreja de Santo António**, built at the birthplace of the city's favourite saint, the neighbouring **Museu de Santo António**, and the 12th-century **Sé Catedral**. As it skirts the hill below the Castelo, the street changes name so many times that locals often refer to it as Rua do Eléctrico da Sé – 'Street of the Tram of the Cathedral'.

Unlike nearby Alfama, this area was greatly modified after the 1755 earthquake, with the building of wider streets and elegant houses. It's also home to the Aljube, once Salazar's secret police prison and now destined to become a museum if all goes well.

The Teatro Romano, Portugal's only known Roman amphitheatre, was begun during the reign of Augustus and rebuilt under Nero in AD 57. A section can be seen fenced off under a shed on Rua de São Mamede, but it isn't very revealing; a video reconstruction can be seen at the nearby **Museu do Teatro Romano**, which has entrances both on Rua de São Mamede and from the tram route.

Follow any of the narrow alleys that run downhill to the right of the Sé and you'll pop out on to the Campo das Cebolas (Field of the Onions). A big, open square lined with souvenir shops and cheap restaurants, its main attraction is the spiky façade of the **Casa dos Bicos**, a 16th-century merchant's house. It now houses the foundation that promotes the work of the late Nobel Prize-winning writer José Saramago, but is open to the public. Turning west on Rua da Alfândega brings into view the medieval stone façade of the **Igreja da Conceição-a-Velha**.

Sights & Museums

FREE Casa dos Bicos

Rua dos Bacalhoeiros 10 (21 880 2040, www. josesaramago.org). Metro Terreiro do Paço. **Open** 10am-6pm Mon-Sat (last entry 5.30pm). **Admission** free. **Map** p61 A5 ❶

This striking building was erected between 1521 and 1523, on the orders of Brás de Albuquerque, the son of the first Viceroy of India. Its unusual façade, covered by a grid of point-cut diamonds commonly known as 'bicos', was inspired by Italian Renaissance models, namely the Palazzo dei Diamanti in Ferrara. Inside, a ground-floor exhibit run by the Museu de Lisboa lays bare (literally) the plot's history from Roman through medieval times, including sections of the ancient city wall, traces of a production centre for fish preserves, and ceramics and glassware from later centuries. The upper floors house the Fundação José Saramago (21 751 3215, www.josesaramago.org). It has a bookshop and a good stock of the writer's work and hosts regular debates on literary and social topics.

FREE Igreja da Conceição-a-Velha

Rua da Alfândega (21 887 0202). Tram 18, 25. **Open** 9am-5pm Mon-Fri (mass 1pm Tue-Fri); 10am-12.30pm Sun. **Map** p61 A5 ❷

This site originally housed a church built in 1534 dedicated to Nossa Senhora da Misericórdia (Our Lady of Mercy), who can be seen above the portal sheltering various notables under her mantle. The 1755 earthquake demolished the main structure, leaving only the wonderful Manueline-style façade. In 1770, the church reopened to house the congregation of Nossa Senhora da Conceição-a-Velha, whose original home, a converted synagogue in the Baixa, had been flattened. The simple post-quake interior has one nave and contains an image of Our Lady of Restelo, donated to the earlier Conceição church by Prince Henry the Navigator. Major restoration work is underway but the church remains open.

FREE Igreja de Santo António

Largo de Santo António da Sé (21 886 9145). Tram 12, 28 or bus 737. **Open** 8am-7pm daily. Breaks for mass (30-45mins) at 11am & 5pm Mon-Fri; 11am, 5pm & 7pm Sat, Sun. **Map** p61 A5 ❸

This small Baroque church opened in 1787, 20 years after construction began. It replaced a structure destroyed in the 1755 earthquake, on the spot where Fernando Bulhões, later known as St Anthony of Padua, was born around 1190. St Anthony became famous as a travelling preacher and miracle worker, the latter charisma still being frequently invoked, particularly in his capacity as patron saint of things lost. Mass marriages for those too poor to afford individual ceremonies, known as 'St Anthony's weddings', are held here in June (*see p31*).

Museu de Santo António

Largo de Santo António da Sé 22 (21 886 0447). Tram 12, 28 or bus 737. **Open** 10am-1pm, 2-6pm Tue-Sun. **Admission** €1.50; €0.75 reductions; free under-15s & all 10am-1pm Sun. **No credit cards**. **Map** p61 A5 ❹

This recently renovated museum on St Anthony, next to the church dedicated to him (*see above*), contains iconographic sculptures, paintings and

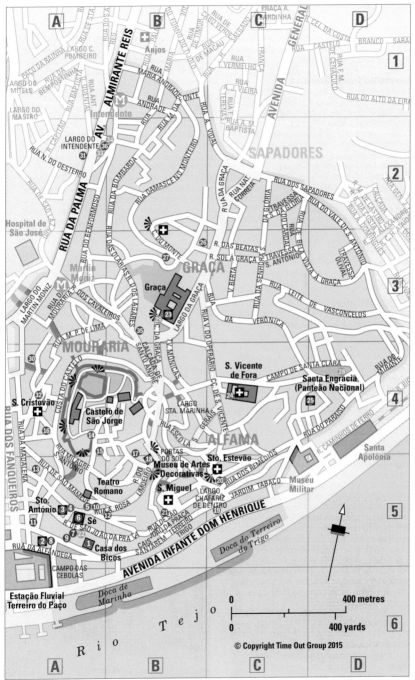

EXPLORE

biographical documents, plus some rather more offbeat representations of the saint in the form of soft furnishings and collages. It's an offshoot of the Museu de Lisboa (*see p121*).

Museu do Teatro Romano

Pátio do Aljube 5, Rua Augusto Rosa (21 882 0320, www.museuteatroromano.pt). Tram 12, 28 or bus 737. **Open** 10am-6pm Tue-Sun. **Admission** €3; €1.50 reductions. **Map** p61 A5 ⑤

Due to reopen in mid 2015 after an archaeological dig and refurbishment, this little museum just up from the Sé provides some context for the Roman Theatre that's visible to passers-by on Rua de São Mamede. This is probably Portugal's only Roman amphitheatre, seating perhaps 5,000, and is proof that Olisipo, as Lisbon was then known, was a major outpost. A first-century wall that was designed to prevent the whole pile from sliding down the slope is visible on the museum's upper floor, next to a pretty covered patio. It also houses columns and other decorative elements from the site, including an inscription dedicating the theatre to Nero and a copy of a sculpture of Silenus. The museum occupies a renovated 19th-century factory.

★ FREE Sé Catedral

Largo da Sé (21 887 6752). Tram 12, 28 or bus 737. **Open** *Church* 9am-5pm Mon, Sun; 9am-7pm Tue-Sat. *Cloisters* Summer 10am-5pm Mon; 10am-6.30pm Tue-Sat. Winter 10am-5pm Mon-Sat. *Treasury* 10am-5pm Mon-Sat. **Admission** *Church* free. *Cloisters* €2.50; €1.25 reductions; free under-11s. *Treasury* €2.50; €1.25 reductions; free under-11s. *Cloisters & treasury* €4, €2 reductions. **No credit cards. Map** p61 A5 ⑥

Lisbon's cathedral is a symbol of the Christian Reconquest, having been built in the 12th century on the site of the main mosque. It was enlarged in subsequent centuries and facelifts were made necessary by earthquake damage, particularly after the 1755 quake: the south tower collapsed and the interior chancel, chapels and high altar were damaged. The Sé's current appearance is the result of restoration work completed in 1930 that removed many Baroque trappings and reconstructed the rose window from fragments of the original. In the original Romanesque scheme, the Sé was laid out in the form of a Latin cross with three naves. Gothic cloisters were added under Dom Dinis (early 14th century). The treasury has artefacts and vestments, but visitors may be more interested in the cloisters, where parts of the mosque wall have been uncovered, as well as a section of Roman road and remains of the Visigothic occupation.

Restaurants

Esperança da Sé

Rua São João da Praça 103 (21 887 0189). **Open** 7.30pm-12.30am Mon-Fri; 1-4pm,

7.30pm-12.30am Sat, Sun. **Main courses** €9-€16.75. **Map** p61 A5 ⑦ **Pizza**

A good range of thin-crust pizzas, risottos and burgers are served at this little place just below the cathedral – an offshoot of a popular restaurant in the Bairro Alto with a similar name. In summer, they set up a pleasant little terrace across the street next to the cathedral wall.

Hua Ta Li

Rua dos Bacalhoeiros 109 (21 887 9170, www. restaurantechines.pt). Tram 15, 18, 28. **Open** noon-3.30pm, 6.30-11pm daily. **Main courses** €5.40-€12.80. **Map** p61 A5 ⑧ **Chinese**

Other Chinese eateries come and go, but this busy restaurant by Praça do Comércio has been going strong for nearly three decades. It's now run by the son of the founder. Food is top-notch and portions are generous. The decor is a cut above many of its peers and service is fast.

Taberna Moderna

Rua dos Bacalhoeiros 18 (21 886 5039). Metro Terreiro do Paço or tram 12, 28. **Open** 6pm-midnight Mon-Sat. **Snacks** €5-€9. **Map** p61 A5 ⑨ **Portuguese**

With bright, modern decoration, a convivial terrace and a long list of cocktails, Taberna Moderna draws fashionable locals happy to mix and match the delicious tapas on offer. These include *peixinhos da horta* (deep-fried green beans), *pica da vazia* (beef in the house special sauce), Galician-style octopus, braised tuna, and top-seller *arroz de choco* (cuttlefish rice). The brownies are great too. While the kitchen closes at midnight, the bar stays open later.

Sé Catedral.

EXPLORE

Shops & Services

★ A Arte da Terra

Rua Augusto Rosa 40 (21 274 5975, www.aarte daterra.pt). Tram 12, 28 or bus 737. **Open** 11am-8pm daily. **Map** p61 A5 ⓾ **Souvenirs**
Displayed in stone mangers in the 12th-century former stables of the Sé cathedral is an immense variety of handicrafts and other *típico* products. Linen, embroidery, rustic clothing, fado and folk CDs, toys and pottery can all be found at this wonderful showcase of Portuguese culture, as well as dozens of figurines of the city's favourite son, Santo António.

★ Conserveira de Lisboa

Rua dos Bacalhoeiros 34 (21 886 4009, www. conserveiradelisboa.pt). Metro Terreiro do Paço or tram 12, 28. **Open** 9am-7pm Mon-Sat. **Map** p61 A5 ⓫ **Food & drink**
This small, wood-panelled space opened in 1930 and is lined with a dazzling array of colourfully packaged tins – sardines, tuna, anchovies, fish paste and the like. The store now also stocks a range of gourmet jams and liqueurs for tourists.

★ Fabula Urbis

Rua de Augusto Rosa 27 (21 888 5032, www.fabulaurbis.pt). Tram 12, 28 or bus 737. **Open** 10am-1.30pm, 3-8pm daily. **Map** p61 B5 ⓬ **Books**
Most Lisbon bookshops have English-language sections, but stock few books about the city itself. This little place fills that gap. As well as a fine selection of Portuguese non-fiction and fiction, translated into English, French, German and several other languages, there are plenty of glossy coffee-table tomes about Portuguese country gardens and the like.

Pelcor

Rua das Pedras Negras 28 (21 886 4205, www. pelcor.pt). Tram 12, 28. **Open** 10am-1pm, 2-7pm Mon-Fri; 11am-1pm, 3-6pm Sat. **Map** p61 A5 ⓭ **Accessories**
The cork bags and accessories on display at this showcase for an award-winning brand come in a variety of colours, offset by the clean white decor. You'll be amazed at the fine items – from wallets, belts and hats to iPad cases – that can be made from this truly environmentally friendly material (its use contributes to protect a unique ecosystem).

CASTELO

Lisbon began on the hill of Castelo, with an Iron Age settlement that was later occupied successively by Romans, Visigoths and Moors, all of whom added their own fortifications. Some of the oldest segments, thought to be of Roman origin, are near the No.737 bus stop. These are the outer walls, enclosing both the **Castelo de São Jorge** itself and the small *intramuros* ('within the walls') neighbourhood.

From here, the way in is through the Arco de São Jorge; on the left a niche houses an image of St George, dragon-killing patron of the castle – and of Portugal. The ticket office for the castle proper is beyond it; at the top of the rise is the Casa do Governador, now a shop selling classy souvenirs. Off to the right, narrow streets lead into a neighbourhood where the number of older residents living in rent-controlled flats is dwindling, while incomers pay fortunes for renovated pads. At the end of Rua da Santa Cruz do Castelo, the Igreja da Santa Cruz do Castelo is on the shady Largo of the same name and contains a statue of St George. The original church was built on top of a mosque right after the 1147 reconquest; the present post-earthquake one dates from 1776.

In Castelo de São Jorge itself, the open square just past the entrance has unrivalled views over the city. Cannons projecting over the parapet recall the fortification's original purpose, but today overlook orange and lemon trees in the gardens below. Further in are a moat and keep, whose courtyards and ramparted walkways make up the heart of the medieval castle.

Just outside the walls of the Castelo area, at the far end of Chão da Feira from the Arco de São Jorge, is a curious urinal, much photographed by tourists despite its odour. The **Palácio Belmonte** (*see p216*), through the nearby archway, was renovated with city council funds and is now a top-notch hotel.

The tunnel here through to the Pátio de Dom Fradique is a public right of way; take it to pass through a square surrounded by tumbledown houses with a view east towards the dome of the Panteão Nacional de Santa Engrácia. Through the arch at the bottom is Rua dos Cegos – Street of the Blind – where the 16th-century house at no.20 is one of the city's oldest. The octagonal shape of the large church to your left, the Baroque **Igreja do Menino de Deus** (mass 8.30am on Sat & Sun) is unique in Portugal. If the door is locked, ask next door at no.27 (7am-7pm Mon-Fri). From here, streets lead into the Alfama and Mouraria.

EXPLORE

The street circling below and around the castle in the other direction from the Arco de São Jorge is called Costa do Castelo. It rewards walkers with views out over the city, including those from the terraces of the **Chapitô** (*see p162*) restaurant-bar and theatre, and the café of the restored 19th-century **Teatro Taborda** (*see p163*). A staircase, the Escadinhas de São Crispim, follows the course of the old Moorish walls down towards the Sé from near Chapitô.

Sights & Museums

★ Castelo de São Jorge
Rua de Santa Cruz do Castelo (21 880 0620, www. castelosaojorge.pt). Tram 12, 28 or bus 737. **Open** *Nov-Feb* 9am-6pm daily. *Mar-Oct* 9am-9pm daily. **Admission** €8.50; €5 reductions; free under-11s. **Map** p61 A4 ㉔

The hilltop was fortified even before the arrival of the Roman legions; in later centuries the castle walls were strengthened by Visigoths and Moors, before falling to Portugal's first king, Afonso Henriques, in 1147. His statue stands in the square just past the main gate. From the 14th to the 16th centuries, Portugal's kings resided in the Palácio de Alcaçovas, the remains of which now house a snack bar and a display of finds from the ongoing archaeological digs. The castle itself has undergone numerous transformations. Back in the 1930s, several government offices and a firehouse were removed from the grounds, exposing the walls, which were duly topped with supposedly authentic-looking battlements. There have been several makeovers since then. The battlements of the Castelejo (keep) have ten towers, which may be climbed; in one is a Câmara Obscura (10am-5pm) from which you can see key city monuments and spy on people downtown, as well as learning how the contraption works. Beyond the keep is an area where labelled displays trace out dwellings from prehistoric times and the late Islamic period, as well as the ruins of the last palatial residence on this hill, destroyed by the 1755 earthquake.

Restaurants

Arco do Castelo
Rua Chão da Feira 25 (21 887 6598). Tram 12, 28 or bus 737. **Open** noon-11pm Mon-Thur; noon-midnight Fri, Sat. **Main courses** €8.75-€13.50. **Map** p61 A4 ⑮ **Indian**

Judging from the basic furniture, plain tablecloths and bottle-lined walls you might think this tiny place was a cheap Italian, but in fact it's one of Lisbon's few genuinely Goan restaurants. The menu only runs to two pages, but includes *xacuti* (chicken with coconut and aromatic spices), *balchão de porco* and *sarapatel* (pork dishes, the former in a rich sauce containing dried shrimp, the latter in a rich ginger gravy). Booking is essential for dinner; note that the kitchen closes an hour before the restaurant does.

★ Zambeze
Calçada Marquês dos Tancos, Edifício EMEL, Mercado Chão do Loureiro (21 887 7056, http://zambezerestaurante.pt). Tram 28. **Open** 10am-11pm daily. **Main courses** €13-€22. **Map** p61 A4 ⑯ **African/Portuguese**

Dishes from Mozambique, beautifully prepared and presented in an airy space, plus a huge terrace with stunning views of Lisbon: what's not to like? The place also has dishes from the Beiras region of central Portugal. There's a Portuguese touch to the decoration, too, in the form of Bordallo Pinheiro ceramics. Zambeze is on the roof of a multi-storey car park, so if you're on foot take the Elevador do Castelo (Rua dos Fanqueiros 170; open 9am-9pm daily) then cross the road to the car park, where another lift (by the Pingo Doce supermarket) whisks you up to the roof.

Shops & Services

Arte Bruta
Largo do Contador Mor 17 (21 887 0489). **Open** *Apr-Dec* 11am-7pm daily. *Jan-Mar* noon-6pm daily. **Map** p61 B4 ⑰ **Arts & crafts**

No tourist tat in this little shop, which stocks only genuine – and often unusual – Portuguese arts and crafts, plus gourmet foods. Manager Lila has scoured the nation for the best products, from traditional Viana gold filigree to contemporary design pieces, including wonderfully colourful ceramics.

ALFAMA

A *miradouro* with a beautiful view introduces visitors to Alfama. On the 12 and 28 tram lines, the Miradouro de Santa Luzia, just below Largo das Portas do Sol, has a rose garden, wading pool and grapevine trellises that combine to provide one of Lisbon's most serene views. On the outside wall of the nearby **Igreja de Santa Luzia** (the Order of Malta's headquarters in Portugal), are two tile panels: one maps downtown Lisbon before the 1755 quake, the other shows Christians storming the castle in 1147. Another twist of the road up the hill leads to Largo das Portas do Sol (Sun Gate Square), graced by a statue of Lisbon's official patron, São Vicente (St Vincent), bearing the city's symbol (a boat with two ravens).

On the southern side of the square, the former city palace of the Visconde de Azurara is now occupied by the **Museu-Escola de Artes Decorativas**, while the adjacent Cerca Moura bar-café is in an old stone tower that was once part of the Moorish siege walls. Its terrace overlooks an expanse of red Alfama roofs where TV antennae sprout like weeds. Over the next hill, the white marble churches of São Vicente and Santa Engrácia mark the eastern boundary of Alfama. The ugly slab in the foreground is the roof of the neighbourhood car park, where vehicles are stored and fetched completely automatically.

Running down the south-eastern slope of the hill topped by the Castelo, Alfama is Lisbon's oldest *bairro* (quarter) after the castle. It's an appealing warren of narrow streets and blind alleys, stooping archways and twisting staircases. Some buildings stand on foundations dating back to the Visigoths, but the street pattern is Moorish. Washing flutters everywhere. Children chase through alleys as grown-ups chatter outside shops and cafés.

The name Alfama probably comes from the Arabic word *al-hama*, which means springs or fountains. Most of this well-watered area stood outside the Moorish siege walls, which stretched from Portas do Sol along Rua Norberto Araújo and Rua da Adiça down to the river. The fountain in Largo do Chafariz de Dentro, after which the square is named, has been in use since medieval times, while the Chafariz d'el Rei on Rua Cais de Santarém has also been dishing out water for more than seven centuries. In the 17th and 18th centuries, the taps were segregated: blacks used the tap on one side, whites the other.

At the eastern end of narrow Rua de São Pedro, Largo de São Rafael opens on to a remaining portion of the Moorish siege walls, complete with a private lemon-tree garden on top. Below this, Rua da Judiaria is a small side street, home to Alfama's Jewish community in medieval times. A museum dedicated to its history is planned here. Nearby Largo de São Miguel is a sloping square centred around a palm tree and fronted by the white façade of the Igreja de São Miguel – like so many, a post-earthquake reconstruction of an earlier church. Narrow Rua de São Miguel leads off it; this is a main street of sorts, with grocery stands, butchers, and tiny *tascas*. The tiny alleys off Rua de São Miguel lead into wondrous networks of staircases, terraces and gardens.

What's missing in Alfama is the sound of motor vehicles. They can't get in here – a factor that acts as a brake on gentrification. Morning rush hour in Alfama is accompanied by the sound of birds singing and footsteps scurrying to work. The traffic gathers down on Largo do Chafariz de Dentro, where tourist buses decant their camera-toting passengers. On summer evenings, crowds head into Alfama looking for an outside table, a dinner of grilled sardines and plenty of red wine. A number of fado houses crowd the bottom end of the neighbourhood: the **Parreirinha de Alfama** (*see p151*) is one of the city's most renowned. Just across the main road at the bottom of Alfama is the **Museu do Fado**.

A good way to get a more intimate look at Alfama is to step up (via Rua dos Remédios) to the Igreja de Santo Estêvão, whose veranda-cum-*miradouro* provides yet another fine view. From here you can see grapevines growing in the back lots of some houses. Leading off here are streets up to the Igreja de São Vicente de Fora and the neighbourhood named after it, and to the more bustling Graça district. But the ideal way to get to know Alfama is to wander and get a little lost – something visitors will find almost impossible to avoid. Be aware, though: pickpockets do operate, so don't flash fancy cameras around.

Sights & Museums

★ Museu-Escola de Artes Decorativas

Largo das Portas do Sol 2 (21 888 1991, www.fress.pt). Tram 12, 28, or bus 737. **Open** 10am-5pm Mon, Wed-Sun. **Admission** €4; €2 reductions; free under-15s. **Map** p61 B5 ⑬

Banker Ricardo do Espírito Santo Silva – admirer of Salazar, intimate with *fadista* Amália, builder of the Ritz Hotel – was also a leading collector of Portuguese applied arts. In 1947, he bought a 17th-century palace and created the Museum of Applied Arts and attached school. The collection of 16th- to 19th-century Portuguese, French and English furniture is the most important in the country, and is displayed in reconstructions of the original rooms. Tapestries, silverware, porcelain, antique books and tiles make up the rest of the exhibits. The shop sells items produced by the school and workshops' staff, who are skilled in 21 different crafts.

Museu do Fado

Largo do Chafariz de Dentro 1 (21 882 3470, www.museudofado.pt). Metro Santa Apolónia. **Open** 10am-6pm Tue-Sun. **Admission** €5; €3 reductions; free under-16s. **Map** p61 C5 ⑲

Permanent displays at this city museum tell the history of this ever-popular musical form; you can book a guided visit that includes a live fado performance. On summer weekends there are also excellent free fado tours of Alfama during which local singers

Museu do Fado.

perform – check the website for details. There is a museum café, and the attached restaurant, Travessa do Fado (91 026 3613, open 7pm-2am) serves up delicious snacks and has a good selection of wines. Fado singers often perform here too.

Restaurants

★ Páteo 13
Calçadinha de Santo Estêvão 13 (21 888 2325). *Metro Terreiro do Paço or Santa Apolónia.* **Open** (summer only) 11am-11pm Tue-Sun. **Main courses** €8-€13. **Map** p61 C5 ⑳ **Portuguese**
Shaded by vines, Páteo 13 is one of the most atmospheric places to eat fish or cuts of meat straight off the charcoal grill. The big seller is sardines, traditionally served with boiled potatoes, salad and grilled peppers, all washed down with sangria. What you see on arrival – the terrace – is what you get: there's no indoor dining room. Pateo 13 only functions in the warmer/drier months, with no set dates.

Santo António de Alfama
Beco de São Miguel 7 (21 888 1328, www.site antonio.com). Metro Terreiro do Paço or Santa Apolónia, or tram 12, 28. **Open** 12.30-5pm, 7.30pm-2am daily. **Main courses** €13.50-€19. **Map** p61 B5 ㉑ **Portuguese**
This restaurant became an Alfama fixture by being a tad more sophisticated than its local rivals (slogan: 'no fado or sardines') and is sticking to the formula after almost two decades. It has a wide variety of starters and desserts, and some decent main courses, though grilled fish and steak dominate.

Cafés & Bars

★ Pois, Café
Rua São João da Praça 93 (21 886 2497, www.pois cafe.com). Tram 12, 28 or bus 737. **Open** 1-11pm Mon; 11am-11pm Tue-Sun. **Map** p61 A5 ㉒
This Austrian-run café is a great place in which to lounge, reading the foreign newspapers and magazines provided. The rustic decoration, mismatched furniture, and games and toys scattered about add to the informal atmosphere. Sandwiches, salads, fine cakes and fragrant Austrian lemonade are all on offer.

SÃO VICENTE & GRAÇA

Between the **Igreja e Mosteiro de São Vicente de Fora** and the white dome of the **Panteão Nacional de Santa Engrácia** – both of whose roofs offer fabulous views of Lisbon – lies the hillside space known as the Campo de Santa Clara. Here, from dawn until early afternoon (Tue, Sat), the **Feira da Ladra** flea market is held.

Whereas Alfama feels like a busy village, Graça, on the hill above São Vicente, is more like a small town. Indeed, it has several *vilas operárias*, built by the more enlightened late 19th-century

Igreja e Mosteiro de São Vicente de Fora.

industrialists to house their workers in decent conditions, with patios and verandas. The no.28 tram stops at Largo da Graça, site of one of the largest, Vila Sousa. (You can find others off nearby Rua da Senhora da Glória and Rua do Sol à Graça, and a whole *bairro operário*, the Bairro Estrela de Ouro, off Rua Virginia at the northern end of Graça.) To the west is the **Esplanada da Graça**, an open-air café with great sunset views. The **Igreja da Graça** is one of Lisbon's oldest churches, built in 1271 but enlarged in the mid 16th century. The attached monastery became a military barracks after religious orders were dissolved in 1834.

The small promontory above Graça (turn left on Rua Damasceno Monteiro, then bear right up the Calçada do Monte) is the highest of Lisbon's hills, topped by the chapel of **Nossa Senhora do Monte** (open 3-6pm daily). In front of the chapel is a glass-encased image of the Virgin, while a sit-down inside on the stone chair of St Gens – a bishop martyred during Roman times, after whom the chapel was originally named – is supposed to ease the pangs of childbirth; the chair was popular with Portuguese queens over the centuries. The *miradouro* is a favourite with lovers and a fine place to catch the sunset.

Sights & Museums

FREE Igreja da Graça
Largo da Graça (21 887 3943). Tram 28 or bus 734. **Open** 9.30am-12.30pm, 3-6pm Tue-Sat; 9.30am-12.30pm, 5-8pm Sun. **Admission** free. **Map** p61 B3 ㉓

The original monastery of Graça was built in 1271 and completed with an image of Nossa Senhora da Graça (Our Lady of Grace), salvaged from the sea off Cascais that same year. Renovated in the mid 16th century, most of the church fell in the 1755 earthquake. The later renovation reduced three naves to one, and removed much austere marble in favour of rococo decoration. During Lent, the church organises the Senhor dos Passos procession.

★ Igreja e Mosteiro de São Vicente de Fora

Largo de São Vicente (21 882 4400 church, 21 888 5652 cloisters). Tram 28 or bus 734. **Open** *Church* 8am-1pm, 2.30-5pm Tue-Sat; 8am-noon Sun. *Cloisters* 10am-6pm Tue-Sun. **Admission** *Church* free. *Cloisters* €4; €2 reductions; free under-13s. **No credit cards. Map** p61 C4 ❷

Portugal's first king, Afonso Henriques, laid the foundation stone for the first church of St Vincent 'Outside' – that is, beyond the then city walls – hardly a month after taking Lisbon from the Moors in 1147. He was fulfilling a vow to construct Christian houses of worship on the sites where Portuguese soldiers and northern European crusaders lay buried. In 1580, Portugal's then ruler King Philip II of Spain decided to start from scratch and brought in his own architect, Juan Herrera (builder of the Escorial). With Italian architect Filippo Terzi, Herrera designed a new church in Italian mannerist style. It was inaugurated in 1629, but was severely damaged in the 1755 earthquake, when the main dome and roof collapsed on a crowd of worshippers. The big draw are the cloisters, richly decorated with early 18th-century tile panels, some illustrating La Fontaine fables. Inside there's the royal pantheon of the Braganza family, the last dynasty to rule Portugal. The figure of a weeping woman kneels before the twin tombs of Dom Carlos I and Crown Prince Luís Filipe, shot by assassins in 1908.

Panteão Nacional de Santa Engrácia

Campo de Santa Clara (21 885 4820). Tram 28 or bus 734. **Open** 10am-5pm Tue-Sun. **Admission** €5; €2 reductions; free under-13s & all 1st Sun of mth. **No credit cards. Map** p61 D4 ❷

The dome of this church was completed in 1966, a mere 285 years after the building was begun; hence the Lisbon expression 'a job like Santa Engrácia' – one that takes forever. The church is on the site of an earlier one, which was torn down after being desecrated by a robbery in 1630. A Jew was blamed and executed, but later exonerated. Before dying he is said to have prophesied that the new church would never be completed because an innocent man had been convicted. The first attempt at a new Santa Engrácia duly collapsed in 1681 (construction error, compounded by a storm, may have been to blame) and work restarted the following year. The new plan, by master stonemason João Antunes, bears many similarities to Peruzzi's plans for St Peter's in Rome,

and marble in various colours dominates the interior. In 1916, the Republican government decided the then still roofless Santa Engrácia would become the national Pantheon, a temple to honour dead Portuguese heroes. Among those since laid to rest here is General Humberto Delgado, an opposition leader assassinated by the secret police in 1962, and fado diva Amália Rodrigues.

Restaurants

Haweli Tandoori

Travessa do Monte 14 (21 886 7713). Tram 28. **Open** noon-3pm, 7-10.30pm Mon, Wed-Sun. **Main courses** €6.75-€9.50. **No credit cards. Map** p61 B3 ❷ **Indian**

This place serves some of the most dependable Indian food in Lisbon. The brothers who have been running it for more than two decades hail from Portuguese India and their menu is influenced by the culinary mingling that went on there. Vegetarians are well catered for. Arrive early for dinner to avoid the queues. The same extended family runs Calcuta and Calcuta 2 in the Bairro Alto (www.restaurant calcuta.com), and the unmarked Caxemira (Rua Condes de Monsanto 4, 1st floor, 21 886 5486).

Via Graça

Rua Damasceno Monteiro 9B (21 887 0830, www. restauranteviagraca.com). Tram 28. **Open** 12.30-3pm, 7.30-11pm Mon-Fri; 7.30-11pm Sat, Sun. **Main courses** €16-€35. **Map** p61 B3 ❷ **Portuguese**

Via Graça serves up one of Lisbon's best views, attentive service and excellent traditional dishes from around Portugal. Choose from one of the *bacalhau* dishes on offer, or perhaps the likes of octopus rice or game pie, and wash it down with a full-bodied Alentejo red, as you gaze at the illuminated ramparts of the castle. You may want to take a taxi to get here, but the tram stop is only a short walk away.

Cafés & Bars

Clara Clara

Jardim do Bôtto Machado, Campo de Santa Clara (21 885 0172). Tram 12 or bus 734. **Open** *Winter* 10am-8pm daily. *Summer* 10am-midnight daily. **Map** p61 D4 ❷

On days when there's no Feira da Ladra (*see p68*), the little park in Campo de Santa Clara is a peaceful oasis with a surprising view over the river. It has well-shaded lawns, a children's playground, tables where old locals play cards, and now also this little kiosk and terrace, with coffee, herbal tea, home-made snacks and lemonade, and free Wi-Fi. Note that on chilly or rainy days, it may close slightly early.

★ Esplanada da Graça

Largo da Graça (no phone). Tram 28 or bus 35. **Open** 10am-2am daily. **No credit cards. Map** p61 B3 ❷

With one of Lisbon's best views, this large esplanade next to the church in Graça fills with tourists and locals alike on sunny afternoons. The toasted sandwiches and fresh lemonade are excellent.

MOURARIA & INTENDENTE

Mouraria is the district wedged on the hillside between the Castelo and Graça. The defeated Moors were allowed to settle here, and in the 12th and 13th centuries two mosques were still functioning. A 1471 Muslim petition to the king mentions that Mouraria was enclosed by walls and that residents locked the gates at night. Twenty-five years later, non-Christians were either converted or expelled from the country.

In the 19th century, Mouraria was known for its prostitutes, seedy *tascas* and fado houses – the area is still scruffy, but no less authentically *lisboeta* than Alfama. The most famous fado house of the 19th century, run by singer A Severa, was in Rua do Capelão. The building traditionally identified as the Casa da Severa was renovated by the city in 2013 and is now fado house **Maria da Mouraria** (*see p151*), run by *fadista* Hélder Moutinho, brother of the more famous Camané.

Mouraria's main street is Rua dos Cavaleiros/Calçada do Santo André, which the no.12 tram climbs up. The lower part of it has been taken over by Indian-run discount stores, and the Centro Comercial Mouraria, down on Largo Martim Moniz, bustles with Asian and African shops.

This multi-ethnic area is, appropriately, where the Society of Jesus began training missionaries, including St Francis Xavier, to send out across the world. On Rua Marquês de Ponte de Lima is the former Convento de Santo Antão-o-Velho; a plaque indicates that the world's first Jesuit foundation was founded here in 1542. It now serves as the church of the Socorro parish.

Mouraria meets the Baixa in Largo do Martim Moniz. This was once the heart of Mouraria, but in the 1950s and '60s old byways, patios and churches were bulldozed in the name of urban renewal. For three decades what is now a large square was a maze of rubble and temporary sheds put up to house displaced shopkeepers. Successive city administrations inflicted architectural atrocities on the area – tacking the Centro Comercial Mouraria on to the back of the tiny chapel of Nossa Senhora da Saúde and dotting the square with strange metal kiosks. These seem finally to have found their vocation, as food stalls serving everything from ceviche to vegetarian burgers; on summer evenings live music and DJ sets liven up the square.

At other times, Martim Moniz serves as a meeting place for the immigrants who have adopted it; on Sundays, you might even catch a cricket game at the southern end of the square. The **Hotel Mundial** (*see p209*) has a rooftop bar with one of Lisbon's best views.

Running north from Martim Moniz towards the airport, the Rua da Palma/Avenida Almirante Reis axis is a workaday contrast to the glitzier Avenida da Liberdade. At this end it's a down-at-heel shopping district devoid of landmarks, save for the municipal **Arquivo Fotográfico** at Rua da Palma 246, which has regular exhibitions and a pleasant bar-café. The narrow street behind this block, Rua do Benformoso, is believed to date back to Roman times. The medieval house at no.101 may be Lisbon's oldest.

Lined with Chinese shops, Pakistani butchers and Portuguese *tascas*, and with residents hailing from dozens of other nations, this street finally opens up after half a kilometre into a large open space, Largo do Intendente. Long a round-the-clock precinct of sleaze featuring dodgy bars and occasional stabbings, Intendente has undergone a miraculous makeover in the past couple of years. Now, believe it or not (and locals themselves hardly can), it's one of the city's trendiest areas – though certainly still with a bit of an edge. There are even rumours that Catalan super-chef Albert Adrià, brother of Ferran, is considering opening a restaurant here. For now, as well as the flagship **A Vida Portuguesa** store and bustling **Largo Café Estúdio**, the square is also home to the popular Casa Independente bar, among others.

Restaurants

Cantinho do Aziz

Rua São Lourenço 3 (21 887 6472). Metro Martim Moniz or Rossio, or tram 12, 28. **Open** noon-4pm, 7-10pm Mon-Sat. **Main courses** €5-€9.50. **Map** p61 A4 ⓾ **African/Indian**
For a real taste of Africa in Europe, you could do far worse than this canteen. The cuisine is Mozambican, with Goan recipes thrown in for good measure, and

EXPLORE

A Vida Portuguesa.

all of it is halal. As well as the *chamussas* (samosas), we recommend the *frango à Zambeziana* (grilled chicken marinated in coconut milk), but there are many different fish and meat curries plus a couple of vegetarian mains.

Ramiro

Avenida Almirante Reis 1H (21 885 1024, www. cervejariaramiro.pt). Metro Intendente or tram 28. **Open** noon-1am Tue-Sun. **Shellfish** €11-€89/kilo. **Map** p61 A2 ⓩ **Seafood**

Senhor Ramiro, a native of Galicia in Spain, is what Lisboetas call a *cromo*, 'a card'. After helping his father run a snack bar in what was then a dodgy part of town, he transformed it into this celebrated *marisqueira*. As the fame of his sublime Spanish-style *gambas a ajillo* and other fresh shellfish spread, Ramiro bought the shop next door, then the next and the next. Service and turnover are rapid.

Restaurante São Cristovão

Rua de São Cristovão 28-30 (91 475 2102). Metro Rossio or tram 28. **Open** 11am-midnight daily. **Main courses** €8.50-€13.90. **No credit cards**. **Map** p61 A4 ⓩ **African**

The food at this little canteen is simple Cape Verdean fare, but the place has a great vibe, especially when the night ends in an impromptu late jam session – and perhaps a glass of home-made *ponche* (honey spirit).

Cafés & Bars

Largo Café Estúdio

Largo do Intendente 16 (21 888 5420, http:// largoresidencias.com). Metro Intendente. **Open** 9am-midnight Tue-Thur, Sun; 9am-2am Fri, Sat. **Map** p61 A2 ⓩ

This café on the ground floor of a building that houses a number of artists' *ateliers* describes itself as 'a space for meetings, conversations and concerts', and also serves as an art gallery. There's an excellent range of teas and home-made cakes and quiches, and the terrace is a great place to absorb the atmosphere of this happening neighbourhood.

O das Joanas

Largo do Intendente 28 (21 887 9401). Metro Intendente. **Open** *Mid Oct-June* 9am-11pm Mon, Wed, Thur; 9am-2am Fri; 10am-2am Sat; 10am-11pm Sun. *July-mid Oct* 9am-11pm Mon-Thur; 9am-2am Fri; 10am-2am Sat; 10am-11pm Sun. **No credit cards**. **Map** p61 B2 ⓩ

This capacious café sells breakfast, brunch and a great variety of soups, salads, quiches and cakes. Drinks made in-house include lemonade, herbal tea and mulled wine. There's plenty of space inside the *azulejo*-fronted building, but on warm days the large terrace is the big attraction.

Shops & Services

Cortiço & Netos

Calçada de Santo André 66 (21 136 2376, www.corticoenetos.com). Metro Martim Moniz or tram 12. **Open** 10am-7pm Mon-Sat. **Map** p61 B3 ⓩ **Tiles**

Unlike other *azulejo* shops listed in this guide, this place stocks mostly mass-produced tiles. But with hundreds of discontinued lines, it's a veritable museum of style through the decades and a great place to pick up one-off decorative bargains. For years, the owner snapped up stock from factories as they closed; now his grandchildren (the *netos* of the name) are busy selling it. Buy now while you can.

★ A Vida Portuguesa

Largo do Intendente 23 (21 197 4512, www. avidaportuguesa.com). Metro Intendente. **Open** 10.30am-7.30pm daily. **Map** p61 A2 ⓩ **Vintage**

This wasn't the first of Catarina Portas's wildly successful vintage shops to open, but it's the largest and most painstakingly restored. Everything from the shelving and cabinets to the packaging of the products is calculated to delight. Stock includes many of the best and most unusual Portuguese gourmet products, as well as traditional soaps and creams. There are also large items for the home.
Other location Rua Anchieta 11, Chiado (21 346 5073).

West of Baixa

During the 19th and early 20th centuries the Chiado, with Rua Garrett as its main axis, was the very centre of Lisbon's intellectual life. The dictatorship, not keen on the life of the mind, pressurised this inheritance. Then, in August 1988, much of what remained went up in smoke when fire destroyed Lisbon's only two department stores. Reconstruction work was overseen by renowned Oporto architect Alvaro Siza Vieira, who ensured that some of the former grandeur endured in this neighbourhood of cafés and booksellers, theatres and boutiques. The neighbouring areas of Bica and Bairro Alto are a contradiction in terms: they're old-fashioned residential areas that are dotted with bars and restaurants and, increasingly, funky shops. Further uphill, Príncipe Real is known as the city's thriving gay hub, but it also has bookshops and antiques traders aplenty, and a central garden favoured by card-playing oldies.

EXPLORE

Igreja de São Roque.

Don't Miss

1 Chiado shops & cafés Lisbon's most elegant place to dawdle (p76).

2 Museu Nacional de Arte Contemporânea For a crash course in modern Portuguese art (p72).

3 Igreja de São Roque Home to the city's most lavish chapel (p82).

4 Belcanto Lisbon's only restaurant with two Michelin stars (p72).

5 Bairro Alto nightlife Bar bonanza (p144).

CHIADO

The ascent from Rossio up Rua do Carmo and then along Rua Garrett is reasonably gentle and leads into the heart of the Chiado. On the way, as the road passes under the viaduct of the Ascensor da Santa Justa, modern boutiques rub shoulders with ancient establishments selling first editions or fine gloves. At the bottom of Rua Garrett is the **Armazéns do Chiado**, a compact mall anchored by Fnac that has a top-floor food court with some good Portuguese eateries, plus loos with a view. To enjoy a similar panoramic view, but comfortably seated and with a well-mixed drink in your hand, head next door to the **Hotel do Chiado** (*see p217*) on Rua Nova de Almada and take the lift to its Entretanto bar and terrace.

As you climb up Rua Garrett, you pass Portugal's oldest bookshop, **Livraria Bertrand**, inaugurated here in 1773. On Largo do Chiado, **Café A Brasileira** is a traditional meeting point, though too expensive for most locals actually to eat anything. It was once a haunt of writer Fernando Pessoa, whose bronze likeness has a seat on the terrace.

Down towards the river, the **Museu Nacional de Arte Contemporânea** houses a collection of Portuguese art from the 19th and 20th centuries. The nearby **Teatro Nacional de São Carlos** (*see p159*), inaugurated in 1793, was built on the model of the great Italian opera houses of the time. On the street above, the **Teatro Municipal de São Luíz** is notable for the ironwork fire escapes that lace its rear façade.

Up from the other side of Rua Garrett, Largo do Carmo is one of Lisbon's prettiest squares, fronted by the ruined **Igreja do Carmo**, next to the former convent of the same name that is the headquarters of the GNR – the paramilitary National Republican Guard. This was the scene of one of the most memorable moments of the 1974 Revolution, serving as a refuge for the prime minister, Marcello Caetano (*see p50* **Walk**), and should soon be open for visits. The walkway from the top of the towering **Elevador da Santa Justa** (*see p43*) is just beside the convent; there's no ticket office, but if you have a Carris bus and tram ticket or pass already charged up, you may use this elevator.

Sights & Museums

Igreja do Carmo/Museu Arqueológico

Largo do Carmo (21 347 8629, www.museu arqueologicodocarmo.pt). Metro Baixa-Chiado or tram 28. **Open** 10am-6pm Mon-Sat (to 7pm June-Sept). **Admission** €3.50; €2 reductions; free under-16s. **No credit cards. Map** p73 D4 **①**
The Gothic lines of the Church of Our Lady of Mount Carmel went up on the orders of Nun'Álvares Pereira, who helped Dom João I consolidate the rule

of Portugal's second dynasty, the House of Avis. Pereira, known as the Condestável, or Constable, founded the church and attached convent to fulfil a pledge made before a battle, and was adamant in his choice of location – despite the nearby precipice and various false starts after foundations caved in. During the 1755 earthquake the roof fell in on a crowd of All Saints' Day worshippers, leaving the structure near collapse with only the walls and some vault ribbing still standing. Said by many to be the most beautiful church in Lisbon, it has been left roofless ever since. The Archaeological Museum, a ragbag of European finds, is at the far end of the church.

★ Museu Nacional de Arte Contemporânea – Museu do Chiado

Rua Serpa Pinto 4 (21 343 2148, www.museuarte contemporanea.pt). Metro Baixa-Chiado or tram 28. **Open** 10am-6pm Tue-Sun. **Admission** €4.50; €2.25 reductions; free under-13s & all 1st Sun of mth. **No credit cards. Map** p73 C5 **②**
Founded in 1911, this state-run museum reopened in 1994 after a hiatus following the Chiado fire. Notwithstanding the cool, modernist redesign by French architect Jean-Michel Wilmotte, the name – National Museum of Contemporary Art – is a little ambitious given the place's size and budget. Still, the rehang of a couple of years ago, involving 100 works from the permanent collection, offers an instructive overview of 150 years of Portuguese art – from romanticism through naturalism to neo-realism, surrealism and abstractionism – up to 1975. There are also changing exhibitions of contemporary art, and a pleasant café and patio that hosts jazz concerts on some summer afternoons.

Restaurants

★ Aqui Há Peixe

Rua da Trindade 18A (21 343 2154, www.aquiha peixe.pt). Metro Baixa-Chiado. **Open** noon-4pm, 7-11pm Tue-Fri; 7-11pm Sat, Sun. **Main courses** €14-€32. **Map** p73 D4 **③** Seafood
This prettily decorated restaurant brings a breath of sea air to the city: while its regulars include local artists and politicians it has retained its informal ambience. The seafood is wonderful – from the more affordable grilled fish of the day, or squid in beurre blanc sauce, to the blowout *cataplana* stew or shellfish sold by the kilo. The home-made desserts are a big draw too. For unreconstructed meat-eaters there's Brazilian *picanha* beef, served with black beans.

★ Belcanto

Largo de São Carlos 10 (21 342 0607, www. belcanto.pt). Metro Baixa-Chiado. **Open** 12.30-3pm, 7.30-11pm Tue-Sat. **Main courses** €31-€42. **Map** p73 C5 **④** Portuguese
José Avillez had already made his name with his adventurous approach to Portuguese cuisine when he took over this space opposite the opera house in

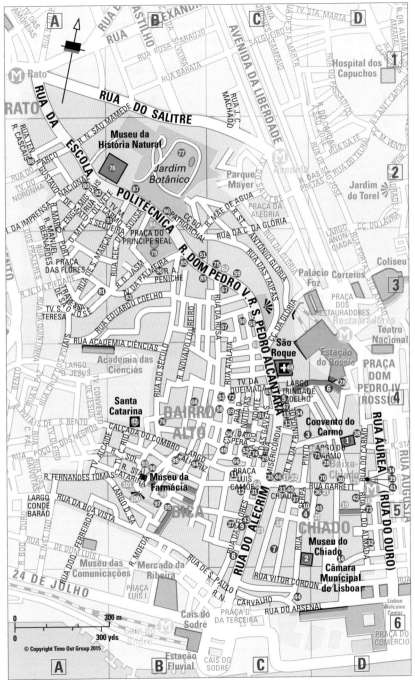

EXPLORE

EXPLORE

NO ORDINARY JOSÉ

Stars aplenty for Lisbon's culinary wizard.

José Avillez already had five restaurants – including one of Portugal's most celebrated – in Lisbon's elegant Chiado area, plus a new venture in Oporto and a thriving catering business. What else could he possibly want?

Well, a second Michelin star, for one – which he finally secured in late 2014 for his flagship, **Belcanto** (*see p72*). It was just the latest recognition for the most renowned of a new generation (he was born in 1979) of Portuguese chefs who value local traditions while applying up-to-the-minute techniques – in his case learned while working with the likes of Ferran Adrià and Alain Ducasse.

In late 2009, Avillez became the first Portuguese chef to bring a Michelin star to Lisbon. (At the time, the region's few starred venues were all run by foreigners.) That was at Tavares (Rua do Misericordia 35), a restaurant in Chiado that dates back to 1784 and is worth a look for its gilt interior alone.

Avillez flew the coop two years later, bent on a project of his own, and Tavares lost its star soon afterwards. It took him less than a year to persuade the Michelin judges to star his new place, Belcanto. This was another long-established gastronomic haven, by now somewhat fusty and serving a dwindling band of regulars. To spare their sensibilities and some history, bits of the old menu were salvaged, above all *ovos à professor* – an egg dish invented by a customer in the 1960s. This dish now appears in a '21st-century' version at **Cantinho do Avillez** (*see p75*), the chef's more informal eatery nearby (now replicated up north in Oporto too).

There are further riffs on local tradition at his **Café Lisboa** (21 191 4498, www.cafelisboa.pt), which operates out of the Teatro Nacional de São Carlos on the square of the same name: the coffee sauce on the house steak is a Chiado classic, while the fried meat pasty (dubbed '*pastel Lisboa*') is said to have its origins in the 12th century. Round the corner in Rua António Maria Cardoso, there are gourmet snacks, modish drinks and a DJ-driven ambience at **Mini Bar** (21 130 5393, www.minibar.pt), Avillez's 'gastronomic bar' in the Teatro São Luiz. Finally, he now has a pizzeria down the street from the Cantinho as well, **Pizzaria Lisboa** (21 155 4945, www.pizzarialisboa.pt).

All of Avillez's ventures offer great food and good value, but for a real sense of his culinary

Top: **José Avillez (left)**.
Bottom: **Belcanto**.

wizardry you must book a table at Belcanto. Its menu features signature dishes from his spell at Tavares such as *mergulho no mar* (sea bass with seaweed and bivalves), plus classics-in-the-making such as *salmonete braseado com molho de fígados e xerém de amêijoas à Bulhão Pato* (braised red mullet, served with a liver sauce and cornmeal with clams, garlic and coriander) or *leitão revisitado* ('suckling pig revisited' – a remake of this ultra-traditional repast). Service and presentation are impeccable, and everything from the amuse-bouches to the pretty petits fours goes towards making a meal at Belcanto an experience involving all the senses.

As for Avillez, after launching red, white and rosé wines under his JA label, penning several books and presenting numerous TV shows, his latest challenge is helping the national tourist board to promote new Portuguese cuisine abroad. In his absence, the kitchen at Belcanto has been run by his associate, David Jesus. In 2014, Jesus was named a Chef de l'Avenir (Chef of the Future) by the International Academy of Gastronomy (AIG). The question now is where and when this promising youngster will want to launch a project of his own.

2010. Within a year, it had won a Michelin star and, for many, established itself as Lisbon's top restaurant. In 2014, it won a second star, thanks to the continuity provided by David Jesus as head chef. Avillez has four more informal eateries in the area (see p74 **No Ordinary José**) but you must book a table at Belcanto to try his 'revisited' Portuguese cuisine, exemplified in dishes such as *cozido à portuguesa* – a traditional stew, but with each flavour clearly distinguishable. Full tasting menus start from €75; there are also lunch menus (€40-€60).

Bistro 100 Maneiras

Largo da Trindade 9 (91 030 7575, http://www. restaurante100maneiras.com). Metro Baixa-Chiado or tram 28. **Open** 7.30pm-2am Mon-Sat (kitchen closes at midnight). **Main courses** €14-€30. **Map** p73 C4 ❺ **Portuguese/International**
At this more informal spin-off of Ljubomir Stanisic's original 100 Maneiras (see p82), the menu ranges further afield, taking in his native Yugoslavia. Perennials include Balkan-style *burek* pastry stuffed with chard and cheese, sole with *açorda* (traditional Portuguese bread soup), steak tartare, and a salmon burger served in bread made with cuttlefish ink.

Café Buenos Aires

Calçada do Duque 31 (21 342 0739). Metro Rossio or Baixa-Chiado. **Open** 6pm-1am daily. **Main courses** €15.50-€24.80. **No credit cards**. **Map** p73 D4 ❻ **Argentinian/International**
It's all about the cross-cultural vibe at this evocatively decorated bistro run by an Argentinian and a Portuguese who met in Paris. The steak is good, as are the margaritas, although there isn't much else beyond *tartines* and salads, and it isn't exactly cheap. But the wine list is decent and the terrace buzzes in summer. Space in the original Buenos Aires is at a premium, but there's now a larger and equally charmingly decorated offshoot round the corer, Café Buenos Aires na Fábrica (Rua do Duque 22).

Cantinho do Avillez

Rua dos Duques de Bragança 7 (21 199 2369, http://cantinhodoavillez.pt). Metro Baixa-Chiado or tram 28. **Open** 12.30-3pm, 7.30pm-midnight Mon-Fri; 12.30-3pm Sat. **Main courses** €8.75-€39.50. **Map** p73 C5 ❼ **Portuguese**
This, the second restaurant from star chef José Avillez (see p74 **No Ordinary José**) is round the corner from Belcanto (see p72). It's an informal affair, with casually dressed staff, quirky decoration and less elaborate dishes than at his flagship. Though it's not exactly cheap, you're pretty much guaranteed an enjoyable meal. There are tasty starters such as *peixinhos da horta* (deep-fried green beans, here with lemon salt and tartare sauce), *farinheira* (floury garlic sausage with a coriander cornbread crust), and foie gras terrine with figs and balsamic vinegar. If you're short of time or on a budget, there are also three versions of the classic *prego* (steak sandwich).

And there are mains ranging from seared scallops with tomato, asparagus and sweet potato, to lamb tagine and other hearty dishes. The desserts are inventive and delicious.

Charcutaria Lisboa

Rua do Alecrim 47 (21 346 0672). Metro Baixa-Chiado or Cais do Sodré. **Open** noon-3.30pm, 7-11pm daily. **Main courses** €8-€27. **Map** p73 C5 ❽ **Portuguese**
The elegant offshoot of a long-established restaurant in the Campo de Ourique neighbourhood, Charcutaria is a veritable culinary embassy for the Alentejo region. After nibbling some cured ham, regional cheese or one of the famed chicken pies, you might order a hearty soup such as *sopa de cação* (dogfish, complete with poached egg) or dig into a main dish such as stewed partridge, hare with beans, or pork with *migas de espargos* (fried breadcrumbs with asparagus). Leave room for dessert.

★ Das Flores

Rua das Flores 76 (21 342 8828). Metro Baixa-Chiado or tram 28. **Open** noon-3.30pm daily. **Main courses** €10-€19. **Map** p73 C5 ❾ **Portuguese**
Beware: there are several places to eat in and around Rua das Flores with similar names, but this undoubtedly offers the best value. The meat croquettes are famous, but there's plenty of other delicious simple fare such as *alheira* (garlic sausage) and *arroz de pato* (duck rice), as well as plenty of salads and vegetable dishes to choose from. Das Flores is only open for lunch – book ahead or arrive early.

Largo

Rua Serpa Pinto 10A (21 347 7225, www.largo.pt). Metro Baixa-Chiado or tram 28. **Open** noon-3pm, 7.30pm-1am Mon-Sat. **Main courses** €17.50-€24.50. **Map** p73 C5 ❿ **Portuguese/International**
Largo's interior, by designer Miguel Câncio Martins, features a gantry and lightbox above the entrance and three giant aquariums with jellyfish. More importantly, the kitchen is overseen by Miguel Castro e Silva, one of Portugal's top chefs. Dishes are prepared just so: Portuguese cod cooked at precisely 80°C (176°F) and served with fried breadcrumbs seasoned with wild mint and pennyroyal, say, or roast pork from the Iberian black pig with grilled polenta. The lunchtime executive menu is fantastic value at €18, and there's a good range of gin cocktails (from €7.50). There are smoking and non-smoking areas, plus free Wi-Fi and valet parking. Castro e Silva's talents are also now on display at his De Castro restaurants.

Sea Me

Rua do Loreto 2 (21 346 1564, www.peixaria moderna.com). Metro Baixa-Chiado or tram 28. **Open** 12.30-3.30pm, 7.30pm-midnight Mon-Sat; 1pm-midnight Sun. **Main courses** €10-€28. **Map** p73 C5 ⓫ **Seafood/Japanese**

EXPLORE

'Peixaria Moderna' – a modern fishmonger – is how Sea Me styles itself: it seeks to combine the excellence of the fresh seafood found in gourmet restaurants with the informality of traditional Lisbon *marisqueiras*. This is not the place for a leisurely or intimate meal – the tables are packed in tight and noise levels can be alarming – but it is good for a fast, delicious feast of molluscs, grilled fish or sushi, and there's an excellent selection of wines to boot. Like any *marisqueira*, they also do *prego* (a garlic-steak sandwich), served here in a sweet *bolo do caco* bun from Madeira – it's so popular that there's now a spin-off in Príncipe Real, O Prego da Peixaria (see *p87*), dedicated to serving this dish.

Taberna da Rua das Flores

Rua das Flores 103 (21 347 9418). Metro Baixa-Chiado or tram 28. **Open** 11.30am-10.30pm Mon-Sat. **Snacks** €5.50-€8.50. **Main courses** €8-€12. **No credit cards. Map** p73 C5 ㉒ **Portuguese**
Founded by three veterans of the Lisbon scene, this tiny place (come early or queue) specialises in traditional Lisbon lunch fare such as *iscas com elas* (liver in a sauce made from pig's spleen), *meia-desfeita de bacalhau* (codfish fins) and *miomba* (a sandwich made with finely sliced pork shoulder). For dinner, there might be *mexilhões à Bulhão Pato* (mussels in a garlic and coriander sauce), *lingueirão na chapa* (seared razor clams) or *pâté de ovas de pescada* (haddock roe pâté served with toast). Only Lisbon wines are served, including Bucelas, Fonte das Moças, Cadaval and Casal Figueira, drunk from a tiny traditional *copo de três*. You can buy gourmet products to take away too.

Tacho à Mesa by Faz Gostos

Rua Nova da Trindade 11 (92 528 6086, www.fazgostoslx.com). Metro Baixa-Chiado. **Open** 6.30pm-1.30am Mon-Sat. **Main courses** €12.50-€19.50. **Map** p73 C4 ㉓ **Portuguese**
A transplant from the Algarve that thankfully brought with it some of the best of what that region has to offer. That means rice dishes with *ameijoas* (clams) or *lingueirão* (razor clams), as well as a range of meats and sausages. The decor blends modernity with tradition (in the form of a lovely sweep of *azulejos*) and dining here is informal: your food arrives still in the cooking pot – ideal for splitting between diners to keep prices down. The all-in menus are good value too.

★ Tágide

Largo da Academia Nacional de Belas Artes 18 (21 340 4010, www.restaurantetagide.com). Tram 28 or metro Baixa-Chiado. **Open** 12.30-3pm, 8pm-midnight Mon-Sat. **Main courses** €20-€26.50. **Map** p73 D5 ㉔ **Portuguese**
Away from the hustle of Chiado's main drag, this refined yet friendly restaurant has one of the most amazing views you'll find in any Lisbon dining room. The food is fairly conservative Portuguese

fare, expertly prepared and served, in the form of seasonal lunch and dinner à la carte menus that include tasty vegetarian options, or a more elaborate *degustação* (tasting menu, €43.50). Reservations are essential but Tágide Wine & Tapas is a walk-in bar downstairs with a similarly stunning view and a range of excellent Portuguese wines and snacks.

Umai

Rua da Misericórdia 78 (96 727 1281, http:// restauranteumai.blogspot.pt). Metro Baixa-Chiado or tram 28. **Open** noon-3pm, 7.30pm-midnight. **Main courses** €10-€20. **Map** p73 C4 ㉕ **Asian**
Sushi isn't cheap anywhere in Europe, and Lisbon is no exception. But here you're in safe hands as the kitchen is overseen by Paulo Morais, one of Portugal's leading exponents of Japanese and fusion cuisine. The fish is as fresh as it can be (note that Umai doesn't use endangered bluefin tuna, instead sourcing related fish from the Azores) and the rice is perfect. You can eat well here for a reasonable price: *menus de degustação* (tasting menus) start at €29, and at lunchtime there are Vietnamese, Thai, Korean and sushi set menus from €9.

Cafés & Bars

Bar Entretanto

Hotel do Chiado, Rua Nova de Almada 114 (21 325 6100, www.hotelchiado.pt). Metro Baixa-Chiado. **Open** 11am-midnight daily. **Map** p73 D5 ⑯
The jaw-dropping view from this seventh-floor terrace is worth paying a little extra for, whether you stick to coffee or a cocktail, or order something to snack on (the toasted salmon sandwich is a good option). The kitchen is overseen by talented young chef Igor Martinho, and light meals are served until 10.30pm. Afternoon tea is also available, complete with scones.

★ Café A Brasileira

Rua Garrett 120 (21 346 9541). Metro Baixa-Chiado or tram 28. **Open** 8am-2am daily. **Map** p73 C5 ⑰
When this café opened in 1905, customers not only got a free *bica* when they bought a bag of beans, but the waiters were courteous too. These days prices are steep and the service is off-hand. Inside is a little cheaper and you can gawp at the carved wood interior and modern art. At its 1920s peak, A Brasileira contributed greatly to the idea that while Coimbra studied and Oporto worked, Lisbon talked and made revolution. Now it's all about tourists taking snaps by the Pessoa statue or listening to buskers playing in the square. It only really has any atmosphere after midnight, when flotsam from the Bairro Alto – including the odd tipsy local intellectual – washes in.

Café no Chiado

Largo do Picadeiro 10 (21 346 0501, www.cafe nochiado.com). Metro Baixa-Chiado or tram 28. **Open** 10am-2am daily. **Map** p73 C5 ⑱

Civilised yet informal, this café is great for settling down to an afternoon with the papers. The terrace has better and cheaper coffee than Café A Brasileira and is more peaceful; even the trams rattling past provide a photo opportunity. The place is a lunch favourite with media types, who tuck into caesar salad and English roast beef, as well as Portuguese fare. It's owned by the Centro Nacional de Cultura, a non-state body that was a cultural catalyst during the dictatorship; its library and internet space are upstairs (open 10am-6pm Mon-Fri).

Fábulas

Calçada Nova de São Francisco 14 (21 601 8472, www.fabulas.pt). Metro Baixa-Chiado. **Open** *Nov-Feb* noon-11pm Mon-Thur; noon-1am Fri, Sat. *Mar-Oct* 11am-midnight Mon-Thur; 11am-1am Fri, Sat. **Map** p73 D5 ⑲
The jumble of old furniture dotted about this cave-like former storage space makes for a pleasantly informal drinking experience. Fábulas has swiftly become a magnet for Lisbon's bright young things. As well as couscous, crêpes and unusual toasted sandwiches, which go down nicely with the well-priced house red, there are yummy cakes and tarts and a range of herbal teas. A roomy annexe has more seating and art exhibitions.

★ Kaffeehaus

Rua Anchieta 3 (21 095 6828, www.kaffeehaus-lisboa.com). Metro Baixa-Chiado or tram 28. **Open** noon-midnight Tue-Fri; 11am-midnight Sat; 11am-8pm Sun. **Map** p73 D5 ⑳
This Austrian-owned café brings a touch of Viennese class to Lisbon. The hearty fare on offer includes wiener schnitzel, *spätzle*, *apfelstrudel* and *sachertorte*, and there's delicious hot chocolate too. There are also vegetarian options and a brunch menu at weekends. A range of foreign newspapers hang by the door.

Maria em Lisboa

Rua Garrett 47, 1D (93 614 5044). Metro Baixa-Chiado. **Open** 11.30am-1pm Mon-Thur; 11.30am-midnight Fri; 10.30am-midnight Sat; 10.30am-7pm Sun. **No credit cards. Map** p73 D5 ㉑
For a quiet break from Chiado shopping, head up a flight of stairs to this first-floor café above the Amorino ice-cream parlour (open 11am-11pm daily). Furnished with vintage pieces snapped up by its owners around Portugal, it retains traces of its previous long life as a hairdressing salon. As well as a range of teas and home-made cakes, there are well-priced Portuguese snacks and wines.

Pastelaria Bénard

Rua Garrett 104 (21 347 3133). Metro Baixa-Chiado or tram 28. **Open** 8am-11pm Mon-Sat. **Map** p73 D5 ㉒
Top-notch coffee and cakes are served here, in a tearoom that's one of Lisbon's oldest (and whose waiting staff certainly act as though they've seen it all before). You can also lunch at Bénard, but as at neighbouring Café A Brasileira (*see p76*) prices all but triple if you sit outside.

Quinoa

Rua do Alecrim 54 (21 347 9326). Metro Baixa-Chiado or tram 28. **Open** 9am-7pm Tue-Sat; 9am-4pm Sun. **Map** p73 C5 ㉓
All the bread in the bakery here is made from organic grains – with up to a dozen different types every day (none of them cheap), not to mention Lisbon's bagels, biscuits and cakes. The café serves breakfast and a renowned Sunday brunch buffet, plus sandwiches and burgers.

★ Royale Café

Largo Rafael Bordalo Pinheiro 29 R/C E (21 346 9125, 93 861 1370, www.royalecafe.com). Metro Baixa-Chiado. **Open** 11am-midnight Mon-Sat; 11am-8pm Sun. **Map** p73 D4 ㉔
A Scandinavian café serving Mediterranean food – that more or less sums up this stylish place where everything except the rye bread is made on site. Ingredients feature organic or regional specialities such as *chouriço de cebola* (onion sausage) and *queijo da serra* cheese, the herbal teas are made from loose leaves, and there are old-fashioned tipples such as *quinado* (a fortified wine flavoured with quinine) and *licor de pinho* (pine liqueur) served with orange, mint and cinnamon. The café's patio is delightful.

★ Santini

Rua do Carmo 9 (21 346 8431, deliveries 91 500 1103, www.santini.pt). Metro Baixa-Chiado. **Open** 11am-midnight. **Map** p73 D5 ㉕
The original ice-cream parlour in Cascais, opened in 1949 by Italian expat Attilio Santini, was patronised by local high society, including the Spanish royal family in exile. At this Lisbon outlet the firm's wonderful all-natural ice-creams and sorbets are just as popular. They deliver too.
Other location Time Out Mercado da Ribeira, Avenida 24 de Julho.

Vertigo Café

Travessa do Carmo 4 (21 343 3112). Metro Baixa-Chiado. Open 10.30am-7pm Mon-Sat. **Map** p73 D5 ㉖
The stained glass and wood panelling give Vertigo a central European feel, and it draws local bohos as well as tourists. It's a great place to linger over a pot of exotic tea, snack on a toasted sandwich (try the salmon), cake or bagel, or browse the papers.

Shops & Services

BdMania

Rua das Flores 67 (21 346 1208, 93 446 1207, www.bdmania.pt). Metro Baixa-Chiado or tram 28. **Open** 10.30am-7.30pm Mon-Sat. **Map** p73 C5 ㉗ **Comics**

EXPLORE

As well as importing comics from the US, France, Spain and Belgium, BDMania issues some of its own publications. Avid collectors will also find all the related merchandise (posters, models and T-shirts) they could possibly want.

Brio
Travessa do Carmo 1 (21 342 7324, www.brio.pt). Metro Baixa-Chiado. **Open** 9am-8pm Mon-Fri; 10am-8pm Sat; noon-7pm Sun. **Map** p73 D4 ㉘ **Food & drink**
Hidden away amid sleek buildings designed by Álvaro Siza Vieira (after the 1998 Chiado fire) is this well-stocked health-food store and café with terrace. It carries a good range of organic fruit and veg, some meat, nuts and grains, and a good range of fresh breads and cakes.

A Carioca
Rua da Misericórdia 9 (21 346 9567). Metro Baixa-Chiado or tram 28. **Open** 9am-7pm Mon-Fri; 9am-1pm Sat. **No credit cards.** **Map** p73 C5 ㉙ **Food & drink**
Established in 1936, and still with the original interior, this shop sells everything from cheap coffee-chicory mixtures at €2 per kilo to specialist beans costing up to €20. Staff make up blends on request and grind them to suit your coffee-maker; they're also happy to let you taste other products.

Casa Pereira
Rua Garrett 38 (21 342 6694). Metro Baixa-Chiado or tram 28. **Open** 9am-7pm Mon-Sat. **No credit cards.** **Map** p73 D5 ㉚ **Food & drink**
Another shop redolent of a bygone age that sells coffee from Timor, Brazil and other former Portuguese colonies. It also imports a handsome range of tea, biscuits and chocolates.

★ Cutipol
Rua do Alecrim 113-115 (21 322 5075, www.cutipol.pt). Metro Baixa-Chiado or tram 28. **Open** 10am-2pm, 3-7pm Mon-Sat. **Map** p73 C5 ㉛ **Homewares**
Portugal's leading Portuguese cutlery maker, selling both machine-produced and gold-trimmed, hand-made pieces with striking designs in stainless steel or silver. The main store also sells a selection of other high-quality homewares. Across the road at no.84 is another Cutipol showroom.

Eureka
Rua Nova do Almada 26 (21 346 8173, www.eurekashoes.com). Metro Baixa-Chiado. **Open** 10am-7.30pm Mon-Sat. **Map** p73 D5 ㉜ **Fashion**
Striking modern footwear by local designers including Lidja Kolovrat and Nuno Gama are on sale at this store owned by Alberto Sousa, one of Portugal's largest shoe manufacturers. There's a wide range of men's and women's styles, from restrained to bold, for people not too obsessed with following trends.

Other location Dolce Vita Monumental, Avenida Praia da Vitória 71, Saldanha (21 315 0466).

Fábrica Features
Rua Garrett 83, 4th floor (21 325 6765). Metro Baixa-Chiado. **Open** 10am-8pm Mon-Sat; 11am-7pm Sun. **Map** p73 C5 ㉝ **Design**
Located on the top floor of a large Benetton, this is one of only three such spin-offs set up by the Italian company worldwide. It stocks imported design goods alongside funky locally produced artefacts, many made using recycled materials. There's also a space for art exhibits. The place has wonderful views over the Chiado.

★ Fnac
Armazéns do Chiado, Rua do Carmo 2 (707 313 435, www.fnac.pt). Metro Baixa-Chiado or tram 28. **Open** 10am-10pm daily. **Map** p73 D5 ㉞ **Books & music**
The anchor store for the Armazéns do Chiado mini-mall, Fnac is a pleasant place to while away an hour or two browsing the shelves. It has a good range of Portuguese literature in translation, as well as lots of originals in English, French and Spanish. The CD department also has a great selection: Portuguese, Brazilian and African music, jazz, classical, world, pop and rock. There are decent computer, camera and audiovisual departments, a counter where you can buy tickets for most major shows, and a café with a programme of films and concerts.
Other locations Centro Colombo (see p120); Centro Vasco da Gama (see p127).

★ Leitão & Irmão
Largo do Chiado 16 (21 325 7870, www.leitao-irmao.com). Metro Baixa-Chiado or tram 28. **Open** 10am-8pm Mon-Fri; 10am-7pm Sat, Sun. **Map** p73 C5 ㉟ **Jewellery/tableware**
After a complete makeover in 2005, the flagship store of Portugal's most famous gold- and silversmith showcases its tableware and jewellery to stunning effect. Leitão & Irmão first opened a store here in 1877 – and was patronised by the court as it spearheaded a revival of Portuguese gold-working traditions – but from its original home in Oporto the company was already goldsmith to Brazilian royalty, with branches in Paris and London. (Its workshop is now in the Bairro Alto.) Some pieces, such as the 1942 crown of Our Lady of Fátima, are one-offs, but other historic lines – such as a 1917 silver cutlery set by René Lalique – are still in production.
Other locations Travessa da Espera 8-14, Bairro Alto (21 342 4107, closed Sat & Sun); Hotel Ritz Four Seasons (see p214, 21 192 3454).

Livraria Bertrand
Rua Garrett 73-75 (21 347 6122, www.bertrand.pt). Metro Baixa-Chiado or tram 28. **Open** 9am-10pm Mon-Sat; 11am-8pm Sun. **Map** p73 D5 ㊱ **Books**

Bertrand was founded in 1732 (it moved to its current location some 50 years later), making it Portugal's oldest bookshop. Apart from local literature, it stocks a reasonable selection of English novels, as well as guidebooks and foreign magazines. **Other locations** throughout the city.

★ Loja do Burel
Rua Serpa Pinto 15B (21 245 6910, www. burelfactory.com). Metro Baixa-Chiado. **Open** 10am-8pm Mon-Sat. **Map** p73 C5 ❸ **Fashion & handicrafts**
Burel is a material made from compacted wool, long used by shepherds in the Serra da Estrela, Portugal's highest mountain range, to protect them from cold, wet winters. The capes, jackets and bags sold here are made in one of the last remaining factories in the hill town of Manteigas, in both traditional and colourful new designs. The shop also stocks herbs and other food items from the Serra da Estrela, helping to preserve the culture of a unique region.

★ Luvaria Ulisses
Rua do Carmo 87A (21 342 0295, www.luvaria ulisses.com). Metro Baixa-Chiado or Rossio. **Open** 10am-7pm Mon-Sat. **Map** p73 D4 ❸ **Accessories**
In this tiny shop – in business since 1925 and now the only one of its kind in the country – rows of drawers contain exquisite gloves indexed by size, colour and material, available in quarter sizes. There are leather, lace, crocheted and sporting varieties, lined with fur, cashmere or silk. All come with a simple guarantee: a free, unlimited repair service.

Loja do Burel.

Parfois
Armazéns do Chiado, Rua do Carmo 2 (93 226 4370, www.parfois.com). Metro Baixa-Chiado. **Open** 10am-10pm daily. **Map** p73 D5 ❸ **Accessories**
With scores of outlets in Portugal, this nimble chain has now spread to dozens of foreign markets where it's battling it out with the UK's Accessorize. Its products come from a similar mould: cheap and cheerful styles, in everything from earrings and keychains to travel bags and umbrellas.
Other locations throughout the city.

Paris em Lisboa
Rua Garrett 77 (21 342 4329, www.parisem lisboa.pt). Metro Baixa-Chiado or tram 28. **Open** 10am-7pm Mon-Sat. **Map** p73 C5 ❹ **Home furnishings**
The name and façade reflect a Portuguese fixation with French style that dates back to well before 1888, when the shop first opened. Local *senhoras bem* (posh ladies) still flock here to stock up on towels, bedlinen and tablecloths, even if some of the best are now made in Portugal.

Pedra Dura
Armazéns do Chiado, Rua do Carmo 2 (21 134 6452, www.pedradura.net). **Open** 10am-10pm daily. **Map** p73 D5 ❹ **Accessories**
A deservedly successful purveyor of costume jewellery, whose unusual designs – some imported and many exclusive – stress fantasy rather than ostentation. Items are stashed in drawers, adding a sense of discovery.
Other locations Amoreiras (see p113, 91 653 8288); Centro Colombo (see p120, 91 256 9129); Dolce Vita Monumental, Avenida Praia da Vitória 71, Saldanha (91 222 8748).

Rulys
Rua Nova do Almada 89-101, Chiado (21 342 4036, www.rulys.pt). Metro Baixa-Chiado. **Open** 11am-7.45pm Mon-Fri; 10am-8pm Sat. **Map** p73 D5 ❷ **Fashion**
This sprawling store is the flagship for a Portuguese brand with an established presence up north, offering mid-priced casual clothing and accessories for men and women, designed with an eye to international trends. It offers a bit more quality and variety than Spanish invader Zara.

Sant'Anna
Rua do Alecrim 95 (21 342 2537, www.santanna. com.pt). Metro Baixa-Chiado or tram 28. **Open** 9.30am-7pm Mon-Sat. **Map** p73 C5 ❸ **Tiles**
Sant'Anna has been producing handmade tiles since 1741 and sells copies of designs dating from the 17th and 18th centuries. The shop is happy to manufacture to order and ship abroad.
Other locations Factory showroom, Calçada da Boa-Hora 94B, Ajuda (21 363 8292).

EXPLORE

★ Storytailors

Calçada do Ferragial 8 (21 343 2306, www.story tailors.pt). Metro Baixa-Chiado or tram 28. **Open** noon-8pm Mon-Sat. **Map** p73 C6 ❹ **Fashion**
Plunge into a world of fantasy tales with Portuguese designer duo Luís Sanchez and João Branco, who are renowned for their funky yet sophisticated ready-to-wear and made-to-measure clothes. Everything from corsets to capes feature exquisite detail and opulent fabrics. The atelier-cum-store is an atmospheric place to indulge.

★ A Vida Portuguesa

Rua Anchieta 11 (21 346 5073, www.avida portuguesa.com). Metro Baixa-Chiado or tram 28. **Open** 10am-8pm Mon-Sat; 11am-8pm Sun. **Map** p73 D5 ❹ **Gifts & souvenirs**
Though this shop stocks handicrafts, it's best known for giving a new lease of life to venerable Portuguese brands of soap and other toiletries, processed foods, stationery and toys. All are beautifully presented, many in old-style packaging that triggers bouts of nostalgia among older customers. A Vida Portuguesa is a good place to look for well-priced, unusual gifts; the newer Intendente shop is the larger of the two.
Other location Largo do Intendente Pina Manique 23 (21 197 4512).

★ Vista Alegre Atlantis

Largo do Chiado 20-21 (21 346 1401, www.vista alegre.pt). Metro Baixa-Chiado or tram 28. **Open** 10am-8pm Mon-Sat. **Map** p73 C5 ❹ **Tableware**
Vista Alegre is the best-known Portuguese porcelain brand, with a wide range of plates, crockery, vases and bowls in traditional designs, Oriental styles and modern classics. Atlantis Crystal is part of the same group: handmade Portuguese lead crystal, ranging from copies of 18th-century goblets to modern glassware. There are Vista Alegre Atlantis stores in all the city's largest shopping centres.
Other locations throughout the city.

We3

Rua da Misericórdia 102 (21 347 2293). Metro Baixa-Chiado or tram 28. **Open** 10.30am-7.30pm Mon-Sat. **Map** p73 C4 ❹ **Fashion & Accessories**
This is a showcase for three independent Portuguese brands: hence the name. Here you'll find elegant shoes by Catarina Martins, delicately embroidered Asian-inspired designs by TMCollection, and gorgeously coloured handbags and other leather goods by Muu. Note that the shop occasionally closes for lunch (1.30-2.30pm).

BAIRRO ALTO

When Dom Manuel I moved his residence down from the castle to the waterfront in the early 1500s, the axis of Lisbon's development shifted west: harbour activity expanded along Cais do

Jardim de São Pedro de Alcântara.

Sodré, while up the hill the level ground outside the 14th-century Muralha Fernandina city wall was divided into lots and sold to aristocrats and the emerging merchant class. The Jesuits set up in the **Igreja de São Roque** and the quarter became known as the Bairro Alto de São Roque (upper neighbourhood of St Roch). Wealthy merchants later gave way to small shopkeepers and, for a while, there were print shops and newspaper offices. Both Rua de O Século and Rua do Diário de Notícias are named after newspapers once based here.

Though maps differ, the Bairro Alto is essentially bounded by Rua do Século (as it's usually written) to the west, Rua Dom Pedro V to the north, Rua de São Pedro de Alcântara and Rua da Misericórdia to the east, and Rua do Loreto to the south. This layout predates the Baixa; this was the first district in Lisbon to have straight, regular streets. Straight and regular by the standards of the time, that is. In many ways it's as maze-like as other old quarters, with enough kinks and dead ends to get even locals confused as to what's where – especially after a crawl through the many bars.

During the day the Bairro Alto is relatively quiet, especially since almost all cars were banished a few years ago. Children play ball in the streets while old ladies chat and hang out the laundry. Interesting shops are dotted about, many of which are at the cutting edge of Lisbon's fashion scene. There are also plenty of second-hand bookstores, specialist music shops and art supplies places. But it's mainly a residential area and by day the streets rarely bustle.

At night it's another story. Every weekend thousands of revellers cram into these narrow streets, hopping from bar to bar or jamming nexus points such as the junction of Rua da Atalaia and Travessa da Queimada outside the **Portas Largas** bar (*see p145*). The area is also full of restaurants, ranging from *tascas* to places serving smart cosmopolitan cuisine. Funky shops are multiplying, too, with most open from mid to late afternoon until midnight or so. (This is the best part of town to hunt for club- and streetwear, but beware poor quality imports sold with a hefty mark-up.) Another late starter is arts collective **Galeria Zé dos Bois**, which promotes new artists working in less conventional fields such as radical multimedia and body arts, and hosts concerts of experimental music.

The Bairro Alto also has Lisbon's largest collection of fado houses – 20 or so – which have been in this quarter since long before the more fashionable bars and clubs began opening up in the 1980s. **Café Luso** on Travessa da Queimada is Lisbon's oldest, with **Adega Machado** (for both, *see p150*) on Rua do Norte almost as venerable, whereas **Tasca do Chico** (*see p149* **In the Know**) is cheaper and less formal. All these places love tourists, but Portuguese frequent them too. Sometimes, as the Bairro Alto begins to close down around 3am, rising above the clatter you'll hear someone singing fado on the street – a lament for the end of the night.

At the southern edge of the Bairro Alto is Praça Luís de Camões, a square ringed with umbrella pines and adjoining Largo do Chiado to the east. A monumental statue designed by Vítor Bastos was unveiled in 1867 at its centre; it represents the 16th-century epic poet Luís de Camões, standing on a pedestal ringed by smaller statues of Portuguese authors – all now atop an underground car park. The square's antique-style kiosk serving coffee, *capilé* and other traditional Portuguese *refrescos* is a relatively recent addition.

For fine views down to the river, pop into the **Bairro Alto Hotel** (*see p217*) on the south side of the square, whose top-floor **Terraço BA** bar is popular with well-heeled locals for an early-evening snifter. A short way down Rua do Alecrim is another literary statue, of 19th-century novelist and scourge of hypocrisy Eça de Queirós unveiling Truth.

In the opposite direction, up Rua da Misericórdia, duck into the **Espaço Chiado** (at no.14) for a sight of the 14th-century Fernandine city walls. Further uphill at no.95, the **Associação 25 de Abril** (21 324 1420, open 10am-12.30pm, 1.30-5.30pm Mon-Sat) strives to keep memories of the 1974 Revolution alive, with changing exhibitions on the ground floor. Further uphill, in front of the Igreja de São Roque, is Largo de Trindade Coelho, although Lisboetas tend to call it Largo da Misericórdia, after the social

welfare institution whose head offices are there. The presence of the Santa Casa da Misericórdia also explains the bronze statue of a lottery ticket seller: the 'Holy House' has a not-so-holy monopoly on the lottery business. Several antiquarian and second-hand bookshops cluster in this area, for example on Rua Nova da Trindade, which is also the address of the **Teatro da Trindade** (*see p161*) and the wonderfully tiled **Cervejaria Trindade**. A scenic staircase, the Calçada do Duque, leads from the square down to Rossio, passing Café Buenos Aires and several other restaurants, and more bookshops.

The third open space bounding the Bairro Alto is the **Jardim de São Pedro de Alcântara**, a garden *miradouro* laid out in the early 19th century that offers splendid views over the Avenida da Liberdade business district, the Baixa, Castelo and the river. The area around the kiosk here is lively on weekend evenings, with live music some nights. A flight of steps leads down to another esplanade.

The **Ascensor da Glória** funicular has been whisking passengers down and up the steep Calçada da Glória between Jardim de São Pedro de Alcântara and Restauradores since 1885. The fit climb on leg power alone; those who tire can hitch a handhold on the back of the car and get pulled up. The **Solar do Vinho do Porto**, a swish bar dedicated to port wine, is across from the funicular's upper terminal point. The building was once known as the Palácio Ludovice, after the architect of Mafra, who built it as his city residence in 1747 at a time when Bairro Alto was the 'in' neighbourhood. The palace is organised around an inner courtyard and takes up an entire block.

The street running north past the *miradouro* is named after the Convento de São Pedro de Alcântara, at its upper end. Until recently an active nunnery, it could soon be open to visitors. In the meantime it's worth a look at the blue-tiled depiction of St Peter of Alcântara's stigmata, by the entrance.

The north of the Bairro Alto was barely affected by the 1755 Earthquake. Today it is relatively quiet. An alley halfway down Rua da Rosa leads to the Colégio dos Inglesinhos, founded in 1628, a time when English Catholics were forced to flee their country or be thrown in prison. The religious foundation was closed in 1973, and the building was turned into a luxury residential complex.

On the Bairro Alto's western edge, the quiet Rua do Século is home to Portugal's constitutional court, a dance conservatory and galleries. At no.79 is the 16th-century palace built by Sebastião de Carvalho e Melo, grandfather of the future Marquês de Pombal (who was born here). It was the family's main residence until the 1755 Quake. Now municipally owned, it houses a lively arts space, **Carpe Diem** (21 197 7102, open 1-7pm Wed-Sat). At no.123, the **Convento de Cardaes** (21 342 7525, open 2.30-5.30pm Mon-Sat) is still an active religious institution but runs guided tours and has a shop with lovely handicrafts. Round the corner in Rua da Academia das Ciências is a venerable scientific academy whose **Museu Geológico** (no.19, 21 346 3915, closed Sun) is one of Portugal's oldest museums with historically important collections, including a vast range of fossils.

Sights & Museums

★ FREE Igreja de São Roque/ Museu de São Roque

Largo de Trindade Coelho (21 323 5444, www. museudesaoroque.com). Metro Baixo-Chiado or Restauradores then Ascensor da Glória. **Open** *Church* (with break for mass 12.15pm Tue-Sat, 12.30pm Sun) Oct-Mar 2-6pm Mon; 9am-6pm Tue-Sun. Apr-Sept 2-7pm Mon; 9am-7pm Tue, Wed, Fri-Sun; 9am-8pm Thur. *Museum* Oct-Mar 2-6pm Mon; 10am-6pm Tue-Sun. Apr-Sept 2-7pm Mon; 10am-7pm Tue, Wed, Fri-Sun; 10am-8pm Thur. **Admission** *Church* free. *Museum* €2.50; €1.25 reductions; free under-15s & all Sun to 2pm. **No credit cards. Map** p73 C4 ⓸⓷

The Igreja de São Roque was built for the Jesuits with the assistance of Filippo Terzi on the site of an earlier chapel dedicated to São Roque (St Roch). Most of the single-nave structure was built between 1565 and 1573, although it was roofless for another decade. The ceiling is a wonder of sorts. The original architect had planned a vaulted roof, but in 1582 a decision was made to flatroof the space in wood, and sturdy timber from Prussia was richly painted. The paintings in the inner sacristy are worth seeing, but the main attraction is the side chapel dedicated to St John the Baptist: its lavish ivory, gold and lapis lazuli attests to Portugal's colonial wealth and extravagance. Built in Rome and shipped to Lisbon in 1749 after being blessed by the Pope, it took four years to reassemble, not least because of the detailed mosaic above the altar. The neighbouring museum contains items from the chapel, including Italian goldsmiths' work, paintings and richly embroidered vestments.

Restaurants

★ 1° de Maio

Rua da Atalaia 8 (21 342 6840). Metro Baixa-Chiado or tram 28. **Open** noon-3pm, 7-11pm Mon-Fri; 7-11pm Sat. **Main courses** €10.50-€18.50. **Map** p73 C4 ⓸⓽ **Portuguese**

The queue outside the saloon-style swing doors from around 8pm every weeknight testifies to the popularity of this budget classic. At lunchtime, too, canny regulars cram round snugly fitted tables, tucking into grilled fish or meat dishes, served fast and with a smile, at reasonable prices. For something a bit

fancier, go for stewed osso buco (oxtail) or partridge. The restaurant is a rock-solid option for Portuguese standards, including desserts such as *bolo de bolacha* (a cake made from layers of biscuits and cream) or traditional *sericaia*, made with eggs, milk and flour, and flavoured with cinnamon and lemon.

100 Maneiras

Rua do Teixeira 35 (91 030 7575, www.restaurante 100maneiras.com). Metro Baixa-Chiado or Restauradores then Ascensor da Glória. **Open** 7.30pm-2am daily (kitchen closes 11pm). **Set menu** €55. **Map** p73 C3 ⓹⓪ **Portuguese/International**

This tiny restaurant, a gourmet showcase for talented Serbian-born chef Ljubomir Stanisic, aims to be recession-proof. Its *menu de degustação*, comprising ten elegantly (and often humorously) presented dishes, costs quite a bit less than some rivals. Pairing wines with your food adds €35, or €60 for premium wines – all overseen by a very knowledgeable sommelier and served in crystal glasses.

Antiga Casa Faz-Frio

Rua Dom Pedro V 96 (21 346 1860). Metro Rato. **Open** noon-3pm, 7-11pm Mon-Sat. **Main courses** €8-€15. **No credit cards. Map** p73 B3 ⓹⓵ **Portuguese**

This old-fashioned local restaurant comes complete with antique wooden dining compartments for conspiring or canoodling. There's a different cod dish every day, as well as the house specialities – breaded prawns and shellfish paella. Faz-Frio may not be for sophisticated foodies, but it can be relied upon for solid home cooking.

Calcuta

Rua do Norte 17 (21 342 8295, www.restaurant calcuta.com). Metro Baixa-Chiado or tram 28. **Open** noon-midnight Mon-Sat; 6pm-midnight Sun. **Main courses** €9-€12. **Map** p73 C4 ⓹⓶ **Indian**

One of Lisbon's longest-established Indian eateries, largely playing safe with the Mughlai standards that go down so well with foreign tourists and, increasingly, locals. But it does offer one main dish from former Portuguese India, *sarapatel* (marinated pork), and one dessert, *bebinka*, a sort of cross between tiramisu and Portugal's own eggy *pudim*. **Other location** Calcuta 2, Rua da Atalaia 28 (21 346 8165).

Casanostra

Travessa Poço da Cidade 60 (21 342 5931, www. restaurantecasanostra.com). Metro Baixa-Chiado or tram 28. **Open** 12.30-2.30pm, 8-11pm Mon-Fri, Sun; 8-11pm Sat. **Main courses** €8.50-€18. **Map** p73 C4 ⓹⓷ **Italian**

Portugal's first decent Italian restaurant when it opened almost three decades ago, Casanostra is still a staple of the Bairro Alto dining scene. Rivals have sprung up since, but it keeps ahead of the pack with authentic ingredients flown over from Italy and designer pasta from owner Maria Paola. For pizza, look to sister restaurant Casanova (*see p125*) or a takeaway spin-off at Príncipe Real, Pizza à Pezzi (Rua Dom Pedro V 84, 93 456 3170, open noon-2am daily).

Cervejaria Trindade
Rua Nova da Trindade 20C (21 342 3506, www. cervejariatrindade.pt). Metro Baixa-Chiado or tram 28. **Open** 10am-midnight Mon-Thur; 10am-1am Sat, Sun. **Main courses** €10.50-€27.50. **Map** p73 C4 ⑤④ **Beer hall**
This beer hall within the walls of a former monastery is above all renowned for the fabulous *azulejo* panels that line its walls. The food is unremarkable, though adequate if you're after nothing more sophisticated than prawns or steak (there are some pricier shellfish options too). Meals are served at all hours.

Decadente
Rua de São Pedro de Alcântara 81 (21 346 1381, www.thedecadente.pt). Metro Baixa-Chiado. **Open** *Restaurant* noon-3pm, 8-11pm Mon-Fri; 12.30-4pm, 8-10pm Sat; noon-4pm, 8-11pm Sun. *Bar* 6pm-midnight Mon-Wed, Sun; 6pm-1am Thur; 6pm-2am Fri, Sat. **Main courses** €9-€14. **Map** p73 C3 ⑤⑤ **Portuguese**
This restaurant on the ground floor of one of Lisbon's new breed of hostels offers interesting dishes made from excellent Portuguese ingredients, whipped up by a capable young chef. The funky decor and vibe help to make it popular with both locals and tourists, so it's worth booking ahead. The back patio is sheltered from sun and wind, and has a retractable roof for when it rains. Of the snacks, the tomato soup and *pica pau* (marinated strips of beef) are good. This is a nice spot for Sunday brunch, a mid-afternoon snack or a cocktail. On the hostel's roof, the pricier Insólito (closed Mon & Sun) has a breathtaking view across to the castle and a menu that ranges from oysters and carpaccio to sophisticated vegetarian fare. The bar is open from 6pm, the restaurant from 7pm.

★ Fidalgo
Rua da Barroca 27 (21 342 2900). Metro Baixa-Chiado or tram 28. **Open** noon-3pm, 7-11pm Mon-Sat. **Main courses** €9.50-€17.50. **Map** p73 C4 ⑤⑥ **Portuguese**
Fidalgo is a *tasca* at heart, despite the contemporary decor and occasional flight of culinary fancy. You'll find well-prepared dishes such as *arroz de garoupa*, *medalhões de javalí* and *bacalhau à brás*. The desserts are delicious: try the profiteroles or wild berry tart. All in all, a meal here is unlikely to disappoint.

Flor da Laranja
Rua da Rosa 206 (21 342 2996). Metro Baixa-Chiado or bus 758, 790. **Open** *Lunch* by reservation only. *Dinner* 7pm-midnight Mon-Sat (last entry 10.30pm). **Main courses** €10-€16. **Map** p73 C3 ⑤⑦ **Moroccan**
The most authentic of Lisbon's few Moroccan eateries, with traditional starters such as spinach with preserved lemon and marinated carrots, and then decent helpings of couscous royale or lamb tagine with prunes (or vegetarian alternatives). To finish, the passionfruit and orange egg pudding is a house standard. For lunch, call ahead to book as they sometimes host cookery workshops.

★ Pap'açorda
Rua da Atalaia 57 (21 346 4811). Metro Baixa-Chiado or tram 28. **Open** 8-11.30pm Tue-Sat. **Main courses** €15-€28. **Map** p73 C4 ⑤⑧ **Portuguese**
It is quite a challenge to stay on top for more than three decades in a neighbourhood packed with restaurants, but Pap'açorda has kept its edge. The dishes are unique – try the gourmet *açorda* (Portuguese bread soup, here served with prawns or lobster) that gives the place its name, or the justly famed chocolate mousse – while the decoration and atmosphere are also exceptional. Though pricier than other places nearby, this remains one of the city's hippest spots.

EXPLORE

Decadente.

EXPLORE

La Paparrucha

Rua Dom Pedro V 18 (21 342 5333, www. lapaparrucha.com). Metro Baixa-Chiado or Restauradores then Elevador da Glória. **Open** noon-3pm, 7-11.30pm Mon-Fri; 12.30-3.30pm, 7-11.30pm Sat, Sun. **Main courses** €17-€39. **Map** p73 C3 ➏ **Argentinian**

Argentinian flavours and excellent meat are the order of the day at this cosy restaurant with a terrace overlooking the city. Inside, try booking a table near the windows and come early to enjoy an appetiser outside. Worth a visit just for the special: smoked sausage steak.

Primavera do Jerónimo

Travessa da Espera 34 (21 342 0477). Metro Baixa-Chiado or tram 28. **Open** 7.30-11.30pm Mon-Sat. **Main courses** €9-€12.50. **No credit cards. Map** p73 C4 ➏ **Portuguese**

If you want simple Portuguese grub, look no further than this long-established haven, known to locals simply as Primavera, where you can get a full meal with wine for no more than €20. The menu features hearty soups, clams in white wine, braised liver and other meaty concoctions from the north, as well as grilled fresh fish and *bacalhau*. The kitchen is on full view from the tiny dining room, where tiles bearing Portuguese proverbs, framed articles and a photograph of Josephine Baker above the table where she ate all make good talking points.

Sinal Vermelho

Rua das Gáveas 89 (21 346 1252). Metro Baixa-Chiado or tram 28. **Open** 7.30-11.30pm Mon; 12.30-2.30pm, 7.30-11.30pm Tue-Thur; 12.30-2.30pm, 7.30pm-midnight Fri; 7.30pm-midnight Sat. **Main courses** €9.90-€14.90. **Map** p73 C4 ➏ **Portuguese**

The name means ' red light' and anyone looking for reliably good food would do well to make a stop at this bustling Bairro Alto standard. *Peixinhos da horta* (tempura green beans) and baked cod are among the house staples. They pack the tables in tight but staff are pretty competent.

Cafés & Bars

Lost In

Rua Dom Pedro V 56D (91 775 9282, www.lostin. com.pt) Metro Baixa-Chiado or metro Avenida then Ascensor da Glória. **Open** 4pm-midnight Mon; 12.30pm-midnight Tue-Sat. **No credit cards. Map** p73 C3 ➏

Duck through a tunnel past a store selling Indian clothing and trinkets to this terrace with a breathtaking view over central Lisbon. Here you can nestle in a brightly painted wicker chair and sip a drink or snack on a salad or wrap (full meals are available 7.30-10.30pm). You can order tea and scones at any time too.

★ Solar do Vinho do Porto

Rua de São Pedro de Alcântara 45 (21 347 5707, www.ivdp.pt). Metro Baixa-Chiado or Restauradores then Ascensor da Glória. **Open** 11am-midnight Mon-Fri; 3pm-midnight Sat. **Map** p73 C4 ➏

A cool haven on the ground floor of the 18th-century Palácio de Ludovice, its interior given a tasteful makeover by leading Portuguese designer Paulo Lobo. Waiters serve port by the glass from a menu of more than 300, from some 60 producers; you can also buy bottles to take away.

★ Terraço BA

Bairro Alto Hotel, Praça Luís de Camões 2 (21 340 8288, www.bairroaltohotel.com). Metro Baixa-Chiado or tram 28. **Open** *Summer* 10.30am-1am daily. *Winter* 10.30am-10pm Mon-Thur, Sun; 10.30am-1am Fri, Sat. **Map** p73 C5 ➏

Padded wicker chairs and sofas await on this shaded terrace with a magnificent view over Cais do Sodré and the river: relax over a late breakfast or sip a sundowner to a chillout soundtrack. There's also a good lunch and snack menu, and drinks such as home-made iced tea and mojitos.

Shops & Services

★ Arcádia

Largo Trindade Coelho 11 (21 347 1280, www. arcadia.pt). Metro Baixa-Chiado. **Open** 10am-8pm Mon-Fri; 10am-6pm Sat, Sun. **Map** p73 C4 ➏ **Food & drink**

Founded in 1933, this Oporto-based *chocolatier* has been turning out traditional treats ever since. But it only started opening shops in Lisbon a couple of years ago. Among its most famous products are simple *línguas de gato* (literally 'cat's tongues') – slabs of delicious dark and milk chocolate – and sugared almonds in various shapes and colours.

Other locations Avenida da República 37A (21 793 2562); Avenida de Roma 14D (21 840 8670); Rua de Belém 53 (21 362 1897); Rua Almeida e Sousa 29A, Campo de Ourique (21 395 1602); Avenia João Crisóstomo 48 (21 316 2001).

★ Cork & Co

Rua das Salgadeiras 10 (21 609 0231, www.
corkandcompany.pt). Metro Baixa-Chiado or tram
28. **Open** 11am-10pm Mon-Wed; 11am-midnight
Thur-Sat. **Map** p73 C5 ⑥⑤ **Accessories**
One of several companies that are doing sterling
work finding amazing uses for one of Portugal's
most important products. Here you'll find
everything from handbags to lampshades and even
umbrellas made out of cork. If you don't know how
the raw material is harvested and processed, do ask
– it's fascinating. Note that, like many stores in this
area, Cork & Co keeps late opening hours, staying
open until midnight at the weekends.

Galeria da Arcada

Rua Dom Pedro V 49, Porta A (21 346 8518).
Bus 758, 790. **Open** 10.30am-1pm, 3-7pm Mon-
Sat. **Map** p73 C3 ⑤⑦ **Antiques**
An impressive collection of religious carvings
from the 15th to the 19th centuries, primarily from
Portugal, ranging from tiny crucifixes right up to
life-size depictions of Biblical scenes.

Galeria Graça Brandão

Rua dos Caetanos 26A (21 346 9183, 91 986
4469, www.galeriagracabrandao.com). Metro
Baixa-Chiado. **Open** 11am-7pm Tue-Sat. Closed
Aug. **No credit cards. Map** p73 B4 ⑥⑧ **Gallery**
The spotlight at this commercial gallery is on
high-quality art from Portuguese-speaking countries, especially Brazil. Albano Afonso and Lygia
Pape are among artists represented in a modern
space that retains traces of its industrial past.

Galeria Zé dos Bois

Rua da Barroca 59 (21 343 0205, www.zedosbois.
org). Metro Baixa-Chiado or tram 28. **Open**
6pm-2am Mon-Thur, Sun; 6pm-3am Fri, Sat.
Map p73 C4 ⑥⑨ **Gallery**
For two decades, this not-for-profit centre based in
an 18th-century former palace has showcased and
promoted contemporary creativity of various kinds:
from visual and performing arts to film and music.
It hosts frequently changing exhibitions, plus other
events, such as artist residencies, workshops, theatre and dance performances, and concerts of experimental music (*see p154*). Its rooftop terrace is a great
place to lounge on summer evenings.

Gardénia

Rua Garrett 54 (93 451 3158, www.gardenia.com.
pt). Metro Baixa-Chiado or tram 28. **Open** 10am-
10pm Mon-Thur; 10am-11pm Fri, Sat; 11am-8pm
Sun. **Map** p73 D5 ⑦⓪ **Fashion & acessories**
Tiny Gardénia is a compulsory stop for local footwear fetishists, thanks to an always interesting
selection of funky foreign and Portuguese brands. It
sells some clothes too. There are branches in several
major shopping centres, as well as round the corner
in Rua Ivens (with accessories), up on Largo Rafael

Bordalo Pinheiro (men's shoes only), and down the
road in Armazéns do Chiado.
Other locations throughout the city.

José António Tenente

Travessa do Carmo 8 (21 482 7220, www.
joseantoniotenente.com). Metro Baixa-Chiado
or tram 28. **Open** by appointment only. **Map**
p73 D4 ⑦① **Fashion**
The established Cascais-born designer produces
men's and women's suits, cotton shirts, shoes, bags
and other accessories along more conservative lines
than you'll find in many Bairro Alto boutiques.

Lena Aires

Rua da Atalaia 96 (21 346 1815, www.lena-aires.
com). Metro Baixa-Chiado or tram 28. **Open**
2-8pm Mon-Sat. **Map** p73 C4 ⑦② **Fashion**
Distinctive, colourful womenswear is on show here,
designed by a native of the remote Trás-os-Montes
region who has also worked in London.

Louie Louie

Escadinhas do Santo Espírito da Pedreira (21 347
2232). Metro Baixa-Chiado. **Open** 11am-7.30pm
Mon-Sat; 3-7.30pm Sun. **Map** p73 D5 ⑦③ **Music**
Thousands of new and second-hand CDs (from €5)
and vinyl records are on display in this airy store
accessed via a quiet stairway that connects Rua
Nova de Almada to Rua do Crucifixo. Genres range
widely, from hip hop to dark and industrial, and
there's plenty of Portuguese and Brazilian music to
delve into.

Sneakers Delight

Rua do Norte 32 (21 347 9976). Metro Baixa-
Chiado or tram 28. **Open** 1pm-midnight Mon-Fri;
2pm-midnight Sat. **Map** p73 C4 ⑦④ **Fashion**
A minimalist store specialising in… well, you can
guess. The footwear is drop-dead trendy and a DJ is
often on hand to get you in the mood.

Solar

Rua Dom Pedro V 70 (21 045 8993, http://solar.
com.pt/pt). Metro Rato or bus 58, 790. **Open**
10am-7pm Mon-Fri; 10am-1pm Sat (closed Sat
in July & Aug). **Map** p73 C3 ⑦⑤ **Tiles**
An incredible collection of over half a million
antique *azulejos* from the 15th to the 19th centuries,
displayed chronologically. They come mainly from
old palaces, churches and houses.

Tom-Tom Shop

Rua do Século 4A-E & 19 (21 347 9733).
Metro Baixa-Chiado or tram 28. **Open** 11am-
8pm Mon-Fri; 11am-7pm Sat. **Map** p73 B4
⑦⑥ **Homewares**
Stylish homeware, designer kitchenware and a good
selection of lights, teapots, picture frames and door
knobs. This is the ideal spot if you're looking for
cheap gift possibilities.

EXPLORE

PRÍNCIPE REAL

Rua Dom Pedro V leads north to Praça do Príncipe Real. There are antiques and book shops here, as well as the **Pavilhão Chinês** (*see p145*), the bar with the best interior decor in Lisbon. Príncipe Real is really a continuation of the Bairro Alto, especially for the gay and lesbian community, who have plenty of bars and clubs to choose from in this area.

The Praça do Príncipe Real is one of the city's most romantic garden settings, with two café-esplanades on which to linger. The park was laid out in 1860, with lots of exotic imported greenery. On sunny afternoons old men play cards at one end, while lovers curl up on benches under the century-old cedar tree, grown out horizontally to provide more shade. At its centre, steps lead down into the **Reservatório da Patriarcal**, a cavernous water tank that occasionally hosts concerts. The garden itself also hosts the weekly **Mercado Biológico do Príncipe Real** (open 8am-2pm Sat), Lisbon's longest-running organic market, where you can pick up herbs, olive oil and bread as well as fresh fruit and vegetables.

The square is ringed by pastel-painted buildings, the most notable of which is the Arabesque palace at no.26, built in the late 19th century as the Palácio Ribeiro da Cunha and now housing a trendy shopping gallery, **Embaixada**. It and another a few doors down, **Entre Tanto**, were developed by a foreign company that is said to have bought no fewer than 20 properties in the area for various commercial and residential projects – confirmation that the area is on the up. The streets between Príncipe Real and São Bento are a gridiron of townhouses that are home to, among others, the British Council on Rua de São Marçal. Eça de Queiroz's novel *Cousin Bazilio* portrays the life of an upper-class housewife, living in boredom in this neighbourhood.

Rua da Escola Politécnica is home to the **Museu de Ciência**; the path lined with palm trees leads to the faculty's **Jardim Botânico**. Next door is the **Teatro da Politécnica** (*see p163*), the current home of one of Lisbon's most active theatre companies, Artistas Unidos.

Sights & Museums

Jardim Botânico da Faculdade de Ciências

Rua da Escola Politécnica (21 392 1800, www. mnhnc.ulisboa.pt). Metro Rato. **Open** *Nov-Mar* 9am-5pm Mon-Fri; 9am-6pm Sat, Sun. *Apr-Oct* 9am-8pm daily. Last entry 30mins before closing. **Admission** €2; free under-6s. **No credit cards. Map** p73 B2 ⑦

The shaded walkways of the university's Botanical Garden, laid out between 1858 and 1878, are surrounded by some 10,000 plants. It's a lovely place to wander on hot days – though do remember that what goes down must come up, and the garden is on the slope of a hill. The Borboletário (butterfly house), home to an unrivalled range of Iberian species, is open from mid March to November (10am-5pm Tue-Fri, 11am-6pm Sat & Sun).

Museu de Ciência/ Museu de História Natural

Rua da Escola Politécnica 56 (21 392 1808, www. mnhnc.ulisboa.pt). Metro Rato. **Open** 10am-5pm Tue-Fri; 11am-6pm Sat, Sun. **Admission** €5; €3 reductions; free under-6s & all Sun to 2pm. **No credit cards. Map** p73 B2 ⑦

The Science Museum, part of a university-run collective of small museums, was founded in 1985. It's interactive, child-friendly and accessible to all. Phenomena such as momentum, centripetal force, the properties of a vacuum and the speed of sound are demonstrated in entertaining and practical ways. The museum has a collection of antique instruments and organises temporary exhibitions, lectures and courses for non-specialists, some housed next door in the 19th-century planetarium. Also in the main building, the Natural History Museum (21 392 1817) houses historically important anthropological and zoological collections, from seashells to stuffed animals. A mineralogical department (closed Sat morn, Sun) displays astonishing glittery rocks.

Reservatório da Patriarcal

Jardim do Príncipe Real (21 810 0215). Metro Rato. **Open** 10am-6pm Mon-Sat. **Admission** €1; €0.50 reductions; free under-13s. **No credit cards. Map** p73 B3 ⑦

Inaugurated in 1856, this underground reservoir was once crucial to Lisbon's downtown water distribution system, but it has been disused since the 1940s. After a prize-winning renovation, it's now used as an atmospheric venue for concerts and exhibitions.

Restaurants

Comida de Santo

Calçada Engenheiro Miguel Pais 39 (21 396 3339, www.comidadesanto.pt). Metro Rato. **Open** 12.30-3.30pm, 7.30pm-1am Mon, Wed-Sun. **Main courses** €16.50-€21. **Map** p73 A2 ⑳ **Brazilian**

This deservedly enduring restaurant serves hearty Brazilian food in hearty Brazilian surroundings: greenery, papier-mâché toucans and other tropical tat. Its *feijoada* and other classic dishes are as good as any in town, but the real secret is the cosy atmosphere. There's a surprisingly good selection of vegetarian dishes on offer, plus lots of sticky Brazilian desserts.

Honorato

Rua da Palmeira 33A (93 265 0001, 21 346 0248). Metro Rato. **Open** noon-midnight Mon-Thur; noon-2am Fri, Sat; noon-midnight Sun. **Main courses** €5-€9. **Map** p73 A3 ㉛ **Burgers**

It was Márcio Honorato who, back in 2011, started what was to become something of a local craze for gourmet burgers; he now has three other branches in Lisbon (and one across the pond in his native Brazil). The burgers here, from the austere Troika to the over-the-top Honorato, come in standard and mini sizes, with a generous helping of perfectly crispy chips. There are caipirinhas and other cocktails, and DJ sets on Thursday, Friday and Saturday nights. **Other locations** Rua da Santa Marta 35 (21 351 0425, 93 879 5298); Rua de Belém 116 (93 527 3971); Time Out Mercado da Ribeira, Avenida 24 de Julho.

★ O Prego da Peixaria
Rua da Escola Politécnica 40 (21 347 1356, www. opregodapeixaria.com). Metro Rato. **Open** 12.30pm-midnight Mon-Thur, Sun; 12.30pm-1am Fri, Sat. **Main courses** €8.50-€13. **Map** p73 A2 ❷ **Burgers**
When *prego* (steak sandwich) in a sweet *bolo do caco* bun became the biggest seller at modish seafood restaurant Sea Me, its owners were quick to open this spin-off. Besides five meat versions, there are tuna and vegetarian ones (the latter a portobello mushroom in a tandoori bun); burgers made from cod, cuttlefish and shrimp; and salads. Chips are made from spuds brought in daily or, if you prefer, sweet potatoes. Desserts include old-style *arroz doce* (rice pudding). Cocktails are good too.

★ Terra
Rua da Palmeira 15 (21 342 1407, www.restaurante terra.pt). Metro Rato. **Open** *Restaurant* 12.30-3.30pm, 7.30pm-midnight Mon-Sat (kitchen closes 10.30pm). **Buffet** €15.90 (Mon-Fri lunch €12.50). **Map** p73 B3 ❸ **Vegetarian**
Buffet dining only, with a plethora of organic vegetarian delights: sushi, kebabs, an adaptation of *cozido* (Portuguese stew), plus home-made vegan ice-cream and crumble. Only drinks – including juices made on the premises (try the ginger), beer and wines – are extra. In an 18th-century building, two dining areas are filled with Portuguese furniture and decorative items from around the world. Out back are more tables in a garden with a fountain.

Cafés & Bars

Esplanada do Príncipe Real
Praça do Príncipe Real (21 096 5699). Metro Rato or bus 758, 773. **Open** 9am-11pm Mon-Wed, Sun; 9am-2am Thur-Sat. **No credit cards.** **Map** p73 B2 ❹
Arty types, scruffy teachers (the British Council is nearby) and geeky students mingle at this popular meeting spot, where the sangria and cocktails flow freely. There's seating inside but, if you can, sit outside to take advantage of the great people-watching opportunities: this small park is both a social centre for the local oldies and the heart of Lisbon's gay district. The place stays open later than advertised on busy nights.

Shops & Services

Charcutaria Moy
Rua Dom Pedro V 111 (21 346 7011). Metro Rato or bus 758, 790. **Open** 10am-8pm Mon-Sat. **Map** p73 B3 ❺ **Food & drink**
This rather pricey delicatessen carries a decent range of French and Italian luxury foods, as well as good-quality local products, including fine wines.

Embaixada
Praça do Príncipe Real 26 (21 340 4150, 96 530 9154, www.embaixadalx.pt). Metro Rato. **Open** *Shops* noon-8pm daily. *Café-bar* noon-midnight Mon-Wed, Sun; noon-2am Thur-Sat. **Map** p73 B2 ❻
This self-appointed 'conceptual shopping gallery' in an iconic 19th-century neo-Moorish building (revamped by Pritzker Prize-winner Eduardo Souto Moura) hosts the grooviest of Portuguese retailers. Among fashion stores here, don't miss Shoes Closet (21 099 8983, www.shoesclosetstore.com), a family-run company with gorgeous exclusive designs assembled by hand in a workshop up north. Elsewhere, there's jewellery, organic cosmetics and babywear, and design goods. Café-bar Le Jardin makes good use of the spectacular interior patio.

Entre Tanto
Rua da Escola Politécnica 42 (96 120 4571, www.entretanto.pt). Metro Rato. **Open** *Shops* noon-8pm daily. *Restaurant* 10am-2am daily. **Map** p73 B2 ❼ **Mall**
Another new-generation mall, where the stress is less on promoting trendy Portuguese products than serving trendy locals. So far, that has meant a juice bar and a nail bar, plus boutiques selling fashion, homewares, childrenswear and accessories.

Embaixada.

EXPLORE

Galeria Luís Serpa

Rua Tenente Raúl Cascais 1B (21 396 0548, http://galerialuisserpaprojectos.blogspot.pt). Metro Rato. **Open** 3-7pm Mon-Fri. Closed Aug. **No credit cards**. **Map** p73 A2 ⑱ **Gallery**

During the past three decades, Luís Serpa has exhibited many high-profile artists, mainly of Portuguese and Brazilian extraction. Although not the most cutting-edge of local galleries, it regularly shows exceptional pieces.

Lidija Kolovrat

Rua Dom Pedro V 79 (21 387 4536, www.lidijakolovrat.org). Metro Rato. **Open** 11am-8pm Mon-Sat. **Map** p73 B3 ⑲ **Fashion & accessories**

Art meets fashion in this magnificently revamped former bakery run by Bosnian-born but longtime Lisbon resident Kolovrat. The price tags on her creations are reasonable; whether you'd walk down the street in them is another matter. The space also showcases other designers' work, accessories and perfumes, as well as staging art shows and events.

Lisbon Lovers

Praça do Príncipe Real 28 (213 928 799, http://shop.lisbonlovers.com). Metro Rato. **Open** 10am-8pm Mon-Sat. **Map** p73 B2 ⑳ **Souvenirs**

The vast variety of postcards, T-shirts and trinkets in funky and original Lisbon-themed designs stocked here delights tourists and locals alike. **Other location** In front of Mosteiro dos Jerónimos, Belém.

Livraria Britânica

Rua de São Marçal 83 (21 342 8472, http://livrariabritanica.pt). Metro Rato. **Open** 9.30am-7pm Mon-Fri; 9.30am-1pm Sat. **Map** p73 B2 ㉑ **Books & music**

Although a specialist in study books, this English-language bookshop round the corner from the British Council also has an excellent range of novels, classics, children's books, bestsellers and recent releases. They will also order.

BICA & SANTA CATARINA

The **Ascensor da Bica** funicular (7am-8.55pm Mon-Sat, 9am-8.55pm Sun) snails its way up a steep street from Cais do Sodré to the lower end of the Bairro Alto, beginning its journey in a building down on Rua de São Paulo. It climbs through one of Lisbon's quirkiest old *bairros*, an area where fashionable restaurants and bars coexist with tatty grocers and taverns.

A landslide swept away much of an earlier Bica during an earthquake in 1598. Topping out the neighbourhood now is the **Esplanada do Adamastor** (aka Santa Catarina *miradouro*), where the kiosk often serves drinks deep into a summer night. Crowds admire the wonderful view over the Tagus, or lie on the lawn under

Pharmácia.

the statue of the Adamastor – the mythical monster who guarded the Cape of Good Hope in Camões's *Lusiads*. The pink mansion beyond the square above the *miradouro* is the HQ of the pharmacists' association, housing the surprisingly good **Museu da Farmácia** and café-restaurant **Pharmácia**.

If you like to wash away your sins in gilt, head down Calçada do Combro to the **Igreja de Santa Catarina**, which boasts one of the city's most sumptuous interiors. Behind the church (under the arch and down the alley beside it) is a quiet esplanade mainly patronised by locals. For somewhere more fashionable – and great views – walk back up to the multi-storey car park and take the lift to fashionable rooftop bar **Park** (*see p145*).

Sights & Museums

Igreja de Santa Catarina

Calçada do Combro (21 346 4443). Tram 28. **Open** 9am-noon, 2-5pm daily. **Admission** free. **Map** p73 B4 ㉒

The original religious foundation here dates from 1647, but it was remodelled after the 1755 Earthquake. The adjoining monastery is now a National Guard barracks, but the church is still in use and contains giltwork dating to the late 17th century, as well as a ceiling that's a masterpiece of 18th-century stucco in rococo style. Paintings on the side walls include works by Vieira Lusitano and André Gonçalves, two of Portugal's leading 18th-century artists.

Museu da Farmácia

Rua Marechal Saldanha 1 (21 340 0680). Metro Baixa-Chiado or tram 28. **Open** 10am-6pm Mon-Fri; 2-6pm Sat. **Admission** €5; €3.50 reductions. **No credit cards**. **Map** p73 B5 ㉓

The Pharmaceutical Museum is a treasure trove of fascinating items: European medical implements and model infirmaries from medieval times onwards, ancient Roman and Greek artefacts,

Tibetan medical charts and Arab medicine chests. The full-scale mock-ups of pharmacies through the centuries are painstakingly done.

Restaurants

★ Casa Liège
Rua da Bica de Duarte Belo 72 (21 342 2794, 91 898 3036). Metro Baixa-Chiado or tram 28. **Open** noon-3pm, 6.30-10.30pm Mon-Sat. **Main courses** €5-€7.50. **No credit cards. Map** p73 B5 **⑨⑭ Portuguese**
A friendly *tasca* at the top of the Elevador da Bica, Casa Liège makes a great pit stop if you're on a budget. For three decades the cook has turned out local favourites such as *pernil de porco* (leg of pork), *pataniscas de bacalhau* (cod fritters), *bitoque* (cheap steak, served with egg and chips) and, in summer, grilled meats. Casa Liège is popular with groups of local and foreign students, and noise levels tend to be high.

Estrela da Bica
Travessa do Cabral 33 (21 347 3310). Metro Baixa-Chiado or Cais do Sodré, or tram 28. **Open** 5pm-1am (dinner from 8pm). **Main courses** €8.70-€13. **Map** p73 B5 **⑨⑤ Portuguese/International**
The lower end of Bica has become rather trendy of late and this café-bar-restaurant draws an arty crowd. Its battered wooden tables and chairs look as if they were salvaged from an old school, as do the maps on the wall and the slates on which the day's offerings are chalked up. The food is a bit different from your average Lisbon tavern: beetroot burgers, say, or salmon with a chia crust.

Pharmácia
Rua Marechal Saldanha 1 (21 346 2146). Metro Baixa-Chiado or tram 28. **Open** 1pm-1am Tue-Sun. **Main courses** €11-€15. **Map** p73 B5 **⑨⑥ Portuguese**
The garden terrace of the Museu da Farmácia (*see p88*) is its big draw, but the kitchen that serves it is overseen by Susana Felicidade, culinary brains behind Taberna Ideal (*see p96*) and a leading light of Lisbon's *taberna* revival. So tasty snacks abound, from salads and *tibornas* (open sandwiches) to duck croquettes, aubergine rolls with goat's cheese, dates and fresh mint, and fried cuttlefish and sardines. More substantial dishes include rice with *lingueirão* (razor clams) and coriander. As well as excellent Portuguese wines, there are cocktails with alarming pharmaceutical names.

Santa Bica
Travessa do Cabral 37 (21 823 4089, www.santa bica.com). Metro Baixa-Chiado or Cais do Sodré, or tram 28. **Open** 6pm-2am Tue-Sun. **Main courses** €12-€14. **Map** p73 B5 **⑨⑦ Portuguese**
In what was once a bakery, the old chequered marble floor and marble counter remain – but advance down the shiny grey corridor to your table and you're

definitely in the 21st century. The restaurant's trump card is its back patio, which is shaded in summer and covered in winter, but there are several dining rooms if you want something cosier. The crowd here is well-heeled and the menu not particularly adventurous; snacks predominate, from deep-fried potato skins to octopus salad and the house steak sandwich.

Toma Lá Dá Cá
Travessa do Sequeiro 38 (21 347 9243). Metro Baixa-Chiado or tram 28. **Open** noon-3pm, 7-11.30pm Mon-Sat. **Main courses** €7.50-€14. **Map** p73 B5 **⑨⑧ Portuguese/International**
This unpretentious little restaurant with a *calçada à portuguesa* mosaic floor serves food that's pretty fancy for the price you pay. Dishes range from grilled or fried fish, *nacos de vitela Maronesa* (succulent veal chunks) or pork steak gratiné, to fondue and emincé with rösti, as well as a dozen types of fish, including grilled tuna and salmon. You can't book, so turn up early or be prepared to wait on the street.

Cafés & Bars

Bica à Esquina
Rua da Bica de Duarte Belo 1 (96 494 2506, 91 942 6815). Metro Baixa-Chiado or Cais do Sodré, or tram 28. **Open** 4pm-midnight Tue-Thur; 4pm-2am Fri, Sat. **Map** p73 B5 **⑨⑨**
At the happening bottom end of Bica, this cosy café-cum-bar with its carpet and armchairs is a bit like your auntie's sitting room, except with sangria, caipirinhas, mojitos and, in winter, mulled wine. Smoking is allowed. There's a loudspeaker directing music on to the street, so most people end up outside.

Esplanada do Adamastor
Miradouro de Santa Catarina (21 343 0582). Metro Baixa-Chiado or tram 28. **Open** *Nov-Apr* 10am-10pm daily. *May-Oct* 10am-2am daily. **Map** p73 B5 **⑩⓪**
Head along Rua Marechal Saldanha for this laidback little terrace with fine views of the river. On warm nights, the little square below fills up with young-sters – and the smell of dope – surveyed disapprovingly by the statue of the monstrous Adamastor.

Noobai
Miradouro do Adamastor (21 346 5014, www. noobaicafe.com). Metro Baixa-Chiado or tram 28. **Open** noon-midnight daily. **No credit cards. Map** p73 B5 **⑩①**
Right next to the Esplanada do Adamastor (*see above*) and boasting the same river views, Noobai is set apart from the noisy scene that takes over the area as the night wears on. On sunny days there are tables on the rooftop terrace, but there's more space downstairs. A modish menu offers Med snacks such as stuffed vegetables, risottos and couscous. There's also a range of tarts, cakes and scones, plus some great caipirinhas. It's a fine choice for those with young kids as there's a well-stocked play area.

EXPLORE

Western Waterfront

The banks of the River Tagus once provided the berths for fishing boats and the shipyards that fitted out the caravels and *naus* of the Discoveries. With the reclamation of land and laying of a rail line and roads, Lisbon turned its back on the river. It finally woke up to the wonders of the waterfront in the 1980s, and the area has drawn restaurants, bars and joggers ever since. Tourists troop daily through Belém, a museum of museums ranging from the Mosteiro dos Jerónimos to the city's leading cultural centre, the Centro Cultural de Belém. Once you've gorged yourself on culture, take time to indulge in another of the area's unmissable treats – the famous custard tarts of the Antiga Confeitaria de Belém. It's almost considered a sin by Lisboetas to walk past here without stepping inside to munch a few of its specialist *pastéis de Belém*.

LX Factory.

Don't Miss

1 **Belém** Historic coaches, modern art and pastries galore (p98).

2 **Museu Nacional de Arte Antiga** Portuguese art in full (p95).

3 **Time Out Mercado da Ribeira** Gourmet food hall pioneered by *Time Out Lisboa* (p94).

4 **LX Factory** A 'creative city' in an old industrial area (p96).

5 **Cais do Sodré** The city's buzziest nightlife (p92).

EXPLORE

CAIS DO SODRÉ

Immediately west of Praça do Comércio is a walkway along the river to the Cais do Sodré train, Metro and boat stations. This area – the **Ribeira das Naus** – has been transformed in the past couple of years, with a new promenade, steps down to the river and lawns laid out next to the remains (now open to view) of the docks where ships were built that explored the world's oceans during the 15th and 16th centuries. Moored at its far end, near two EU agencies, is *Trafaria Praia* – a floating work by Portugal's most successful contemporary artist, Joana Vasconcelos (*see p101* **A Woman's Touch**).

At rush hour at Cais do Sodré, commuters head every which way (beachgoers too in summer) as this is the end of the line for many buses, trains on the Cascais line and the Metro's green line, as well as the terminal for ferries to Cacilhas. From here, a new cycle path runs along the river to **Belém** (*see p98*), with Pessoa's *Ode to the Tagus* spooling out on the tarmac.

There has long been a port-like red-light area just in from the river, and a few prostitutes do still loll around Praça de São Paulo. Nowadays, though, the area has been all but taken over by a stream of trendy bars and offers some of the city's buzziest nightlife (*see p146*).

The **Mercado da Ribeira**, built in 1882, is a grand old market hall on Avenida 24 de Julho; with cafés that open early, it's a spot for late-night revellers to sip hot chocolate in winter while waiting for the first train home. A little later, stallholders start unpacking fruit and veg, and in the afternoon the place is a blaze of colour as the flower sellers take over. The first floor is often used for book and music fairs, or to host live music. But the biggest recent development has been the transformation of the western nave by our sister magazine *Time Out Lisboa* into foodie heaven (*see p94* **In the Market for Gourmet Food**).

Sights & Museums

Trafaria Praia
Praça Europa (22 340 2500, www.dou., www.douazul.com).
Metro Cais do Sodré. **Open** 10am-7pm Tue-Sun.
River trips 11am, 3pm, 6pm. **Admission** €6;
€3 reductions; free under 4s. *River trip* €18;
€9 reductions; free under 4s. **Map** p93 G6 ❶
This old ferry was transformed by Joana Vasconcelos into Portugal's pavilion for the 2013 Venice Biennale. The artist covered part of the exterior with a tile panel that depicts Lisbon today; inside, some of her most tactile artworks are on show. Three times a day, the vessel takes a one-hour turn on the Tagus. *See also p101* **A Woman's Touch**.

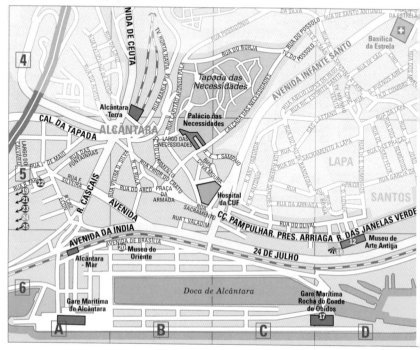

Restaurants

Confraria Lx

Rua do Alecrim, 12A (21 342 6292, www.confraria sushi.com). Metro Cais do Sodré or tram 15, 18. **Open** 12.30pm-midnight Mon-Thur, Sun; 12.30pm-1am Fri, Sat. **Main courses** €9-€29. **Map** p93 G6 ❷ **Japanese**

It can be hard to get a table at this prettily decorated offshoot of Cascais favourite Confraria (Rua Luis Xavier Palmeirim 14, 21 483 4614), housed in a boutique hotel, so book ahead. All the sushi is good, but the *gyoza* and *niguiri* are really special. There's occasional live music too.

La Crêperie da Ribeira

Rua da Moeda 1A (21 243 1565, www.lacreperie. pt). Metro Cais do Sodré. **Open** 9am-midnight Mon-Fri; 10am-midnight Sat; 10am-8pm Sun. **Main courses** €5-€11. **Map** p93 G5 ❸ **Pancakes**

Giant galettes made from (gluten-free) buckwheat are stuffed with tasty savoury fillings and served with a colourful side salad, making them great value. There are sweet crêpes, too – choose from spreads such as creamed chestnut, salted caramel or sugar and lemon – plus soups, toasted sandwiches, breakfast menus and set lunches. This is a civilised place to eat if the nearby Mercado da Ribeira (*see p95*) is too crowded.

Ibo

Cais do Sodré (21 342 3611, www.ibo-restaurante.pt). Metro Cais do Sodré. **Open** 12.30-3pm, 7.30-11pm Tue-Sat; 12.30-3.30pm Sun. **Main courses** €18-€22. **Map** p93 G6 ❹ **African/Portuguese**

Best known for serving food with a Mozambican influence, Ibo is also notable for its pleasing design and fantastic riverside location. The menu is fairly simple: chicken and goat curries (with a strong Goan influence) dominate, alongside tenderloin steak served with various sauces. For dessert, try the stuffed papaya.

Taberna Tosca

Praça de São Paulo 21 (21 803 4563, www. tabernatosca.com). Metro Cais do Sodré. **Open** noon-midnight Mon-Thur, Sun; noon-2am Fri, Sat. **Petiscos** (snacks) €6.50-€12.50. **Map** p93 G6 ❺ **Portuguese**

Tosca is one of the new breed of gourmet *tabernas* situated in Lisbon's hottest nightlife zone. It serves traditional snacks, such as fried cuttlefish, *pataniscas de bacalhau* (cod fritters) or eggs with *farinheira* sausage, in decent portions – three or four make a light supper for two. There's a wide range of wines served by the glass. You can eat in the tastefully renovated interior, complete with stone arches, or out on the square.

EXPLORE

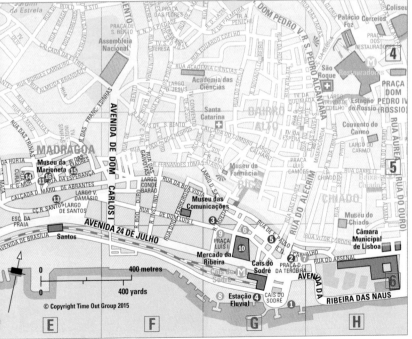

Cafés & Bars

Café Tati
Rua da Ribeira Nova 36 (21 346 1279, www. cafetati.blogspot.com). Metro Cais do Sodré. **Open** 11am-1am Tue-Sun. **No credit cards.** **Map** p93 G6 ⑥
The old port quarter retains a slightly decadent air, and this relatively new arrival with a French/Latin flavour fits right in. Tasty snacks and drinks are served all day and well into the night. There's live jazz or African music on Wednesdays from 10pm.

Leitaria Caneças
Rua Bernardino da Costa 36 (21 342 3748). Metro Cais do Sodré or tram 15, 18. **Open** 7am-7.15pm Mon-Fri. **No credit cards. Map** p93 G6 ⑦
Leitaria Caneças has delicious pastries, but it really stands out for its unusually wide range of breads. The place is hugely popular with commuters from Cais do Sodré station looking for a caffeine-and-sugar fix on their way to work; service is swift and usually with a smile. You can also grab lunch at the counter.

Meninos do Rio
Rua da Cintura, Armazém 225 (21 322 0070, http://meninosdorio.com). Metro Cais do Sodré or tram 15, 18. **Open** *Winter* (sunny days only) 12.30pm-midnight daily. *Summer* 12.30pm-4am daily. **No credit cards. Map** p93 G6 ⑧
This dockside terrace is often thick with *betos* (Portuguese posh kids), but the palm trees and balmy riverside location are a saving grace. Indoors, the restaurant serves soups, salads, hamburgers and a few Portuguese standards (it also has a children's menu). Upstairs, the more interesting Sushi Rio (21 322 0070; closed Mon, Sun dinner) serves regular and fusion sushi daily until around midnight, and has enviable river views and a balcony – open all year, thanks to heaters.

IN THE MARKET FOR GOURMET FOOD

For well-priced delicacies from top local chefs, head for this old market hall.

Opened with great fanfare in early 2014, the gourmet food court in the western nave of Lisbon's main market hall has been a roaring success. Every afternoon and evening the new **Time Out Mercado da Ribeira** (Avenida 24 de Julho 50, open 10am-midnight Mon-Wed & Sun, 10am-2am Fri & Sat) pulls in hundreds of trendy locals and foreign visitors eager to sample snacks and drinks dreamed up by top local chefs.

It was in 2010 that the city council started seeking bids for the concession to manage this part of the dilapidated Mercado da Ribeira (see p95) and inject new life into it. The challenge was taken up by the company that publishes our local sister magazine, *Time Out Lisboa* – and it ended up winning with an ambitious proposal to bring in top culinary talent and gourmet products.

Leading chefs whose creations can be tasted here include Miguel Castro e Silva of Largo (see p75), Alexandre Silva of Bica do Sapato (see p124), Marlene Vieira of Avenue (see p54), and Dieter Koschina of the Michelin-starred Vila Joya in the Algarve. You can order wine by the glass – and even blend your own – or choose from a great range of fruit juices. For dessert there are the prize-winning *pastéis de nata* of Aloma (see p113), cakes and Santini ice-creams. If you just want a sandwich, head out to the Soundwich kiosk (see p95) in the garden outside – their sarnies are also devised by top local chefs.

Soundwich

Praça Dom Luís I (93 790 0311). Metro Cais do Sodré. **Open** 10am-midnight Mon-Wed, Sun; 10am-2am Thur-Sat. **Map** p93 G6 ⑨
This kiosk in the garden next to the Mercado da Ribeira adapts a concept from a wildly popular venture of the same name in Oporto. It offers seven gourmet sandwiches, each designed by a leading chef who is either from Lisbon or works here.

Shops & Services

Mercado da Ribeira

Avenida 24 de Julho 50 (21 346 2966). Metro Cais do Sodré. **Open** *Fresh produce* 6am-2pm daily. *Flowers* 6am-8pm daily. *Collectors' market* 9am-1pm Sun. **Map** p93 G6 ⑩ **Market** *See p94* **In the Market for Gourmet Food**.

SANTOS & MADRAGOA

Avenida 24 de Julho is pretty empty during the day, but at night bar-hopping youngsters are often out until dawn. Fast-food stops in Santos stay open late, serving *caldo verde* (cabbage soup with a slice of sausage) and *pão com chouriço* (sausage bread), warm from brick ovens.

The area was named after three saintly Christian siblings – Verissimus, Julia and Maxima – who according to tradition were martyred by the Romans on the beach here in the early fourth century. It remains home to crumbling monasteries and nunneries, and there are tales of secret tunnels used by enterprising monks in search of lonely nuns. One old royal palace on Rua de Santos-o-Velho is now the French Embassy; legend has it that Christopher Columbus was introduced to his (Portuguese) wife here.

The road running west from the Igreja de Santos-o-Velho – the church believed to stand on the site of the fourth-century shrine – is Rua das Janelas Verdes or 'Street of the Green Windows', after the nickname of the old Alvor Palace that now houses the **Museu Nacional de Arte Antiga**. Its shaded rear garden, with a view out over the river, serves as a terrace for the museum café. The area has long been a favourite of visiting artists and writers. Graham Greene and John le Carré are among past guests of nearby posh *pensão* York House (*see p220*), while charming hotel **As Janelas Verdes** (*see p219*) was once the home of Portuguese novelist Eça de Queiroz and is said to have inspired two of his novels.

Just above the eastern end of Santos is one of Lisbon's most traditional neighbourhoods, Madragoa. A feast of fado and fishwives, it once housed a colony of African fishermen, their waterfront irreverence contrasting with the holy orders dwelling in the many nearby houses of religion. Since those days, the railway line and Avenida 24 de Julho have cut the neighbourhood

off from the river, and the religious orders were abolished in Portugal back in 1834. The former Convento das Berardas on Rua da Esperança now hosts the **Museu da Marioneta** and a fine restaurant, Luso-Belgian **Travessa**.

Sights & Museums

Museu da Marioneta

Convento das Bernardas, Rua da Esperança (21 394 2810, www.museudamarioneta.pt). Tram 15, 18, 25. **Open** 10am-1pm, 2-6pm Tue-Sun. **Admission** *Museum* €5; €3 reductions; free under-3s & all Sun 10am-noon. *Shows* €7.50; €5 reductions. **No credit cards. Map** p93 E5 ⑪
Housed in a grand 18th-century former convent, the Puppet Museum contains more than 800 marionettes from Portugal and around the world, some created for operas staged by its founders, puppet-maker Helena Vaz and the late composer João Alberto Gil. The convent's former chapel serves as a theatre for puppet shows.

★ Museu Nacional de Arte Antiga

Rua das Janelas Verdes (21 391 2800, www. museudearteantiga.pt). Tram 15, 18, 25. **Open** 2-6pm Tue; 10am-6pm Wed-Sun. **Admission** €6; €3 reductions; free under-12s & all 1st Sun of mth. **Map** p92 D6 ⑫
Housed in a 17th-century former palace, the National Museum of Ancient Art is the only truly comprehensive view of Portuguese art from the 12th to the early 19th centuries. Its most prized possession is Nuno Gonçalves's enigmatic late 15th-century masterpiece, usually known as the *Panels of St Vincent*, although its subject is hotly disputed: some say the central figure is Dom Fernando, the Infante Santo (holy prince) who died in captivity in Fez in 1443. The collection also includes Flemish Renaissance paintings (including a triptych by Hieronymous Bosch), Chinese porcelain, Indian furniture and African carvings. There are some fascinating products of the stylistic mix fostered by the 15th- and 16th-century Discoveries and empire, such as Indo-Portuguese cabinets with legs in the form of buxom women or snarling tigers. The shop is excellent.

Restaurants

Estado Líquido

Largo de Santos 5A (21 397 2022, www.estado liquido.com). Tram 25, 28. **Open** 12.30-3pm, 8pm-1am Mon-Wed; 12.30-3pm, 8pm-3am Thur; 12.30-3pm, 8pm-4am Fri; 1-3pm, 8pm-4am Sat; 1-3.30pm, 8pm-2am Sun. **Main courses** €10-€20. **Map** p93 E5 ⑬ **Japanese**
With lighting as low as the tables, an insistent soundtrack and late, late opening hours, the upstairs Sushi Lounge at Estado Liquido helps get your night off to a funky start. The food is good too: Japanese with a smidgeon of São Paulo fusion. Tuck into the

likes of scallop carpaccio with caviar and a spicy sauce. Wash it all down with saké or a Sakerinha – a twist on the caipirinha.

★ Guarda-Mor

Rua do Guarda-Mor 8 (21 397 8663, 96 275 2752, 91 839 3817, www.guarda-mor.com). **Tram 25. Open** 12.30-3pm, 8pm-midnight Tue-Fri; 8pm-midnight Sat, Sun. **Main courses** €11-€20. **Map** p93 E5 ⓩ **Portuguese**
This smart, friendly place serves affordable traditional dishes. As well as some great fried snacks, there's a legendary fish soup. There are fado sessions on Wednesday nights.

★ Taberna Ideal

Rua da Esperança 112-114 (21 396 2744). **Tram 25, 28. Open** 7pm-2am Wed-Sat; 1.30pm-12.30am Sun. **Snacks** €6-€10. **Map** p93 E5 ⓯ **Portuguese**
The twin secrets of this wildly popular place – one of the first of Lisbon's new generation of *tabernas* to open, back in 2008 – are its laidback atmosphere and delicious grub. The menu varies daily, but you'll find starters such as mushrooms sautéed with chestnuts or scrambled eggs with game sausage, and mains such as *arroz de polvo* (octopus rice).

Travessa

Travessa do Convento das Bernardas 12 (21 390 2034, 21 394 0800, www.atravessa.com). **Tram 25, 28. Open** 8pm-midnight Mon, Sat; 12.30-3.30pm, 8pm-midnight Tue-Fri. **Main courses** €24.50-€35. **Map** p93 E5 ⓰ **Portuguese/International**
This Luso-Belgian restaurant is in the Convento das Bernardas – a former nunnery that also houses the Museu da Marioneta (*see p95*). Owners Viviane Durieu and António Moita are usually on hand to guide you through a seasonal menu with five dishes each of fish and meat, plus steak cooked several ways. Look out for *tamboril flamejado* (seared monkfish), *raia a vapor* (steamed ray), and *pernil da pata negra assado* (roast shank of black pig). The wine list is exhaustive and there's Belgian beer.

Último Porto

Estação Marítima da Rocha do Conde de Óbidos (21 397 9498). **Tram 15, 18. Open** 12.30-3.30pm Mon-Sat. **Main courses** €8.50-€13.50. **Map** p92 D6 ⓱ **Seafood**
This dockside restaurant (lunch only) in an old boat station is known as one of the best places in Lisbon to tuck into fresh fish, grilled over charcoal, at affordable prices. There are grilled meats too. If the weather's fine, come early to snag an outside table.

Cafés & Bars

Le Chat

Jardim 9 de Abril, Rua das Janelas Verdes (21 396 3668, www.lechat-lisboa.com). **Tram 25 or bus 713, 727, 760. Open** *Summer* 12.30pm-2am Mon-Thur;

12.30pm-3am Fri, Sat; 12.30pm-midnight Sun. *Winter* 12.30pm-midnight Tue-Thur; 12.30pm-3am Fri, Sat; 12.30-8pm Sun. **Map** p92 D6 ⓲
Perched on a cliff next to the Museu Nacional de Arte Antiga (*see p95*), the glass-walled Le Chat is a great place for a coffee or early-evening cocktail. There are DJ sets most evenings from 5pm and 11pm. At weekends, brunch is served until 5.30pm.

ALCÂNTARA & DOCAS

The westernmost end of Avenida 24 de Julho meets the Alcântara district in the shadow of the Ponte 25 de Abril. It was the longest suspension bridge in Europe when it was built in 1966 as the Ponte Salazar. Its four lanes were then more than enough to handle all foreseeable traffic, but within a few decades it had become Lisbon's biggest traffic bugbear, with rush-hour jams that lasted hours. The opening in 1998 of the Ponte Vasco da Gama in eastern Lisbon to relieve the pressure hasn't solved beach-related jams. In 1999, a railway track that was part of the original design was suspended underneath.

High on the eastern side of the Alcântara valley are the pink walls of the 18th-century Palácio das Necessidades, now the Foreign Ministry. Its leafy park, the **Tapada das Necessidades**, contains a notable collection of exotic plants, including one of Europe's oldest cactus gardens, as well as the abandoned cages and animal houses of a royal zoo. Concerts and DJ sets are staged on the lawn on summer weekends; at other times women are advised not to wander here alone.

Up on the western slopes is the **Tapada de Ajuda**, a former royal hunting ground where weekend guided walks (21 365 3553 or ceabn@isa. utl.pt) are organised by the agricultural institute there. A little further west is the hilltop **Capela de Santo Amaro**, a pretty, round hermitage built in 1549. It opens only for mass (10am, 1st Sun of mth) but early 17th-century polychrome tile panels recounting the life of St Amaro can be seen in the porch; others from the 18th century tell the story of how the chapel was founded by grateful Galician sailors saved from a shipwreck.

The lower part of Alcântara around the busy public transport hub of Largo do Calvário was transformed in the 1990s, with nightclubs and restaurants carved out of old warehouses. Along Rua Rodrigues Faria are African venues such as **Casa da Morna**. At its far end, a new 'creative city' has taken shape in the form of **LX Factory**. Across thousands of square metres, former workshops and storerooms house design studios and art spaces, but also shops, cafés, restaurants and clubs. The neighbouring tram terminal houses the **Museu do Carris**.

Across the railway tracks and under a flyover is the **Doca de Santo Amaro**, a yachting marina with outdoor terraces and indoor bars.

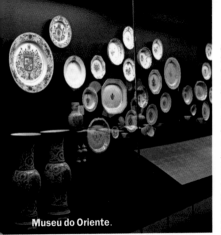

Museu do Oriente.

Most of the restaurants offer conveyor-belt cuisine – if you hate noise and crowds, don't venture here on weekend nights. If you live on a boat, the Doca de Alcântara, to the east, is a better place to tie up. It's home to one of the city's best museums, the **Museu do Oriente**.

Sights & Museums

Museu do Carris
Rua 1° de Maio 101 (21 361 3087, http://museu. carris.pt). Tram 15, 18. **Open** *10am-6pm Mon-Fri; 10am-1pm, 2-6pm Sat. Multimedia show hourly 10am-4pm Mon-Fri; 3pm Sat.* **Admission** *Museum €4; €2 reductions; free under 6s. Multimedia show €5. Combined ticket €7.50.* **Map** *p92 A5* ⑲
At the city transport company's Alcântara hub, kids will delight in decommissioned horse-drawn and electric trams and double-decker buses, while adult buffs can pore over plans and scale models – such as an 1892 model of the city. Don't miss the show 'Lisboa, Who Are You?', in which digital technology is applied to paintings, engravings and tile panels to give a sense of the city's history, to a soundtrack featuring top Portuguese musicians.

★ Museu do Oriente
Avenida de Brasília (21 358 5200, www.museu dooriente.pt). Train to Alcântara Mar from Cais do Sodré, tram 15, 18, or bus 712. **Open** *10am-6pm Tue-Thur, Sat, Sun; 10am-10pm Fri.* **Admission** *€6; €2-€3.50 reductions; free under-6s & all 6-10pm Fri.* **Map** *p92 B6* ⑳
The Portuguese were the first Europeans to have an enduring presence in Asia and the Museum of the Orient, opened in 2008, tells the story. The core exhibition includes unique maps and charts, priceless 17th- and 18th-century Chinese and Japanese painted screens and other Namban (Western-influenced) art, and an important collection of artefacts from Timor. The separate 'Shadows of Asia' display has shadow puppets from a swathe

of countries from Turkey to south-east Asia, drawn from the vast Kwok On collection. The museum runs courses on everything from languages to cuisine and ikebana, as well as hosting concerts of Asian, fusion and world music and dance. The top-floor restaurant (21 358 5258) has fine views.

Restaurants

Cantina LX
LX Factory (Edifício C), Rua Rodrigues Faria 21 (21 362 8239). Train to Alcântara Mar from Cais do Sodré or tram 15, 18. **Open** *noon-3pm, 7.30pm-12.15am Mon; noon-3pm, 7.30-11pm Tue-Sat; noon-4pm Sun.* **Main courses** *€11.80-€18.70.* **Map** *p92 A5* ㉑ Portuguese
In this former industrial space – the restaurant makes use of the wood-fired oven and battered tables and chairs from its previous long life as a workers' canteen – you can eat well and cheaply. There are several fresh fish and *bacalhau* dishes, while meat options might include pork cheek with asparagus *migas* or duck leg.

Casa da Morna & Semba
Rua Rodrigues Faria 21 (21 362 1169, 96 180 0700). Train to Alcântara Mar from Cais do Sodré or tram 15, 18. **Open** *7.30pm-12.30am Mon-Thur, Sun; 7.30pm-2am Fri, Sat.* **Main courses** *€12.50-€16.* **Map** *p92 A5* ㉒ African
Good Cape Verdean and Angolan food is served in a formal setting that warms up when the live music starts, often performed by veteran Cape Verdean musician Tito Paris. The *mornas* and *sembas* played during dinner complement the tasty *moamba*, *cachupa*, *cafriela*, *moqueca* and other classic dishes. All this plus the art for sale on the walls adds up to a sophisticated version of Africa, in mood and price.

★ Malaca Too
LX Factory (Edifício G), Rua Rodrigues Faria 103 (213 477 082, 96 710 4142). Train to Alcântara Mar from Cais do Sodré or tram 15, 18. **Open** *12.30-3pm, 8-11pm daily.* **Main courses** *€12.50-€17.50.* **Map** *p92 A5* ㉓ Asian
This restaurant takes its inspiration from the voyages through Asia of 15th- and 16th-century Portuguese mariners. You might find tempura and yakitori, satay, Thai salad, red and green curries, Korean beef (stir-fried with peppers and mushrooms) or spicy steamed fish, plus at least one vegetarian option. Desserts invariably include black sticky rice pudding and green tea ice cream. The lunch menus are good value.

Cafés & Bars

Landeau
LX Factory, Rua Rodrigues Faria 103 (91 727 8939, www.landeau.pt). Train to Alcântara Mar from Cais do Sodré or tram 15, 18. **Open** *noon-7pm daily.* **Map** *p92 A5* ㉔

EXPLORE

When a place makes a good living by selling only one thing, you know there has to be something special about it. In this case, it's a rich chocolate cake deemed by many to be the city's best.
Other location Rua das Flores 70, Chiado (91 181 0801).

Shops & Services

★ Ler Devagar

LX Factory (Edifício G), Rua Rodrigues Faria 103 (21 325 9992, www.lerdevagar.com). Train to Alcântara Mar from Cais do Sodré or tram 15, 18. **Open** *noon-9pm Mon; noon-midnight Tue-Thur; noon-2am Fri, Sat; 11am-9pm Sun.* **Map** p92 A5 ㉕ **Books**
Housed in an old printing works, this ambitious venture – dubbed 'Read Slowly' – is an important cultural centre with a busy programme of concerts, debates and exhibitions. As for the books, the English section has political and social science tomes, as well as literature and the arts, but the shop is stronger on French- and Portuguese-language titles.

BELÉM, AJUDA & ALGÉS

Belém was originally separate from the city of Lisbon, and bore the name Restelo (now limited to the residential region uphill). The lower part was dubbed Belém (Bethlehem) in the 16th century by Dom Manuel I. Once a prime anchorage spot, its history is intertwined with the Discoveries. In 1415, the first overseas expedition left Restelo beach on the way to conquer Ceuta in Morocco. In March 1493, Christopher Colombus stopped in on his way back from the Americas; and in 1497, Vasco da Gama departed with his fleet for India – a scene recorded in Luís de Camões's 16th-century epic poem *The Lusiads*. In 1588, during Spanish rule, Belém was the assembly point for the Spanish Armada sent forth against England.

For a trip through history, start at the **Torre de Belém**, one of Lisbon's most recognisable symbols. Nearby is a V-shaped monument to Portugal's dead in the African colonial wars that raged through the 1960s, ending only with the 1974 Revolution.

In 1940, to divert attention as World War II raged around neutral Portugal, the Salazar regime put on a show called the Exhibition of the Portuguese World, celebrating various anniversaries, including 300 years since the restoration of Portugal's independence from Spain. The waterfront at Belém was dolled up and the Praça do Império levelled out in front of the Mosteiro dos Jerónimos. Remnants of the show are a museum of folk art (now closed), the reflecting pools, and a building that houses a branch of the Portugália chain of beer halls. Another leftover is the monolithic **Padrão dos Descobrimentos**, beside the marina.

Inland, the **Mosteiro dos Jerónimos** is one of Portugal's most famous landmarks, containing the tombs of Vasco da Gama and Luís de Camões, both laid to rest here in the 19th century. The longer wing, facing the Praça do Império, was built in the 19th century and houses the **Museu Nacional de Arqueológia, Museu da Marinha** and **Planetário Calouste Gulbenkian** (*see p132*). Uphill from Jerónimos are **Belenenses** (*see p121* **Football Crazy**), the Lisbon club with the best view, and the **Museu Nacional de Etnologia**.

The modern complex facing Praça do Império is the **Centro Cultural de Belém**, or CCB (*see p157*), erected as a showpiece for Portugal's 1992 presidency of the European Union. Originally controversial for its cost, this striking building soon settled into its role as host of cultural events and, since 2007, the priceless collection of modern art of the **Museu Colecção Berardo**.

One block of the old residential district of Belém survives amid the monumentality. The houses along Rua de Belém used to be on the river, which has since retreated to the other side of the train tracks. Opposite, the **Antiga Confeitaria de Belém** has been serving its lovely speciality *pastéis de Belém*, a creamy custard tart topped with cinnamon and sugar, since 1837; the place is invariably packed.

An alley leading off the main street, next to no.118, leads into a tiny square with a column. The five bands on this *pelourinho* (pillory) stand for the five members of the aristocratic Távora family who were executed here in 1759 for their alleged complicity in an assassination attempt against Dom José I. (In fact, it's believed that the Marquês de Pombal used the incident as an excuse to clear some powerful rivals out of the way.) The Marchioness of Távora was decapitated; her husband and sons were tortured and their bones crushed. Salt was spread on their property so nothing would grow there; today weeds peek up among the cobbles around the *pelourinho*. Round the corner and up the Calçada do Galvão, the elegant neoclassical **Igreja da Memória** marks the spot of the assassination attempt.

On the way up there you'll pass the entrance to one of two botanical gardens in the area. Created in 1906 as the Jardim do Ultramar, the **Jardim Botânico Tropical** (Largo dos Jerónimos, 21 360 9660, www.iict.pt) features ponds and exotic lush foliage. One building houses the Xiloteca, a scholarly collection of woods from some 15,000 species of tree (visits by appointment only).

Between the eastern end of Rua de Belém and the river is shady Praça Afonso de Albuquerque, named after the fiery Indian Ocean governor who established Portugal's pepper empire in the early 16th century. The salmon-coloured building opposite is the official residence of the president of Portugal. The **Museu da Presidência** (21 361 4660, www.museu.presidencia.pt, closed

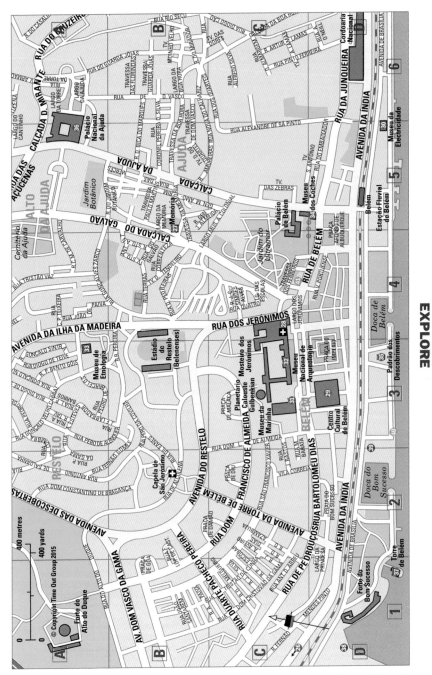

EXPLORE

EXPLORE

IN THE KNOW REGAL REGO

The **Museu da Presidência** (see p98) isn't a big draw for foreign visitors, but art lovers joining the Saturday guided tours will get to see Paula Rego's specially commissioned series on the life of the Virgin Mary. The theme is unusual for the artist, but recalls the area's name, which means Bethlehem. For more works by Rego, visit the Casa das Histórias (see p175) in Cascais, a museum dedicated to her work.

Mon) has curiosity value, with glass cases of official decorations and gifts from foreign heads of state, but the palace itself (guided tours 11am-5pm Sat) is more interesting (*see above* **In the Know**). Each summer there are guided tours of the lovely gardens (June-mid Aug 2-6pm Sun). Next door to the palace is tourist favourite the **Museu Nacional dos Coches**. The hulking concrete structure on the eastern side of the square – together with the larger raised exhibition hall behind it, was designed by Paulo Mendes da Rocha, a Pritzker Prize-winning Brazilian architect – as the museum's future home, but a lack of funds to put the finishing touches to it and pay to move the museum's priceless coaches means that no date has yet been set.

On the river side of the railway tracks is the Belém boat station for ferries to Trafaria (beyond which stretches the Costa da Caparica, weekend beach destination of many locals). Beside it stands the **Museu da Electricidade**, housed in what was Portugal's first power station. It has hosted many interesting art exhibitions, but the curvy **Centro de Artes e Tecnologia** – designed by British architect Amanda Levete – now taking shape next door is expected to play a still bigger role on the city's arts scene. The project is overseen by Fundação EDP, an offshoot of the privatised energy utility of the same name.

Back inland, the Calçada de Ajuda runs along the side of the Coach Museum and past the 18th-century **Jardim Botânico da Ajuda** (21 362 2503, www.jardimbotanicodajuda.com). Portugal's first botanical garden, it was created by order of Dom José I to grow plants from around the world. Further uphill is the **Palácio da Ajuda**, begun in 1802 but left unfinished. Beyond Ajuda is Monsanto Forest Park, created in the 1930s at the behest of Salazar's energetic minister of public works, Duarte Pacheco. Comprising almost an eighth of the city's territory, it serves as its green 'lung', freshening the west wind as it breezes in. Long a haunt of prostitutes and drug dealers, Monsanto is now much better used by locals, who walk, cycle, attend open-air concerts and bring their kids here for council-sponsored activities.

West of Belém lies Algés, a transport hub. Its **Centro de Arte Manuel de Brito** is home to one of the most important collections of Portuguese 20th-century art in the country. On the riverbank between Belém and Algés looms the **Champalimaud Centre for the Unknown**, a privately funded scientific research and clinical centre designed by Indian architect Charles Correa that is one of Portugal's most impressive recent buildings. It houses a lovely restaurant, Darwin's Café, and a cheaper cafeteria (open 8am-8pm Mon-Fri) with a terrace offering views right across the mouth of the Tagus.

Sights & Museums

Centro de Arte Manuel de Brito

Palácio Anjos, Alameda Hermano Patrone (21 411 1400, http://camb.cm-oeiras.pt). Train to Algés or tram 15. **Open** 10am-6pm Tue-Fri; noon-6pm Sat, Sun (last entry 30mins before closing). **Admission** €2; €1 reductions; free under-18s, over-64s & all Sun. **Map** p99 C1 ㉖

In a leafy garden west of Belém, this municipal arts centre shows off works by Paula Rego, Amadeo de Souza Cardoso and other leading Portuguese artists from the past century in a beautifully restored mansion. The collection was amassed by the late Manuel de Brito, founder of Lisbon's Galeria 111, and the centre has exhibition space for contemporary work too.

FREE Igreja da Memória

Largo da Memória, Calçada do Galvão (21 363 5295). Tram 18 or bus 729, 732. **Open** 2-7pm Mon-Sat (mass 6pm); 8am-noon Sun (mass 9.30am). **Admission** free. **Map** p99 B5 ㉗

Ironically for a building that today houses the mortal remains of the Marquês de Pombal, most of its construction took place during the reign of his sworn enemy, Dona Maria I. The Church of Memory is so named because it marks the spot of the 1759 assassination attempt on Dom José I, having been projected the following year as an expression of gratitude for his survival. After the death of its Italian architect, Giovanni de Bibbiena, a few months after the foundation stone was laid, work continued for a couple of years then halted. In 1779, it resumed under Mateus Vicente, architect of the larger Basílica de Estrela; elements here are reminiscent of that church, such as the dome and drum.

★ Mosteiro dos Jerónimos

Praça do Império (21 362 0034, www.mosteiro jeronimos.pt). Train to Belém from Cais do Sodré, tram 15, or bus 28, 714, 727, 751. **Open** Oct-Apr 10am-5.30pm Tue-Sun. May-Sept 10am-6.30pm Tue-Sun (last entry 30mins before closing). **Admission** Church free. Cloisters €10; €5 reductions; free under-13s & all 1st Sun of mth. *Combined ticket with Torre de Belém €12.* **Map** p99 C4 ㉘

Jerónimos is the masterpiece of the Manueline style, the Portuguese twist to late Gothic. Construction of the church and cloisters for the Hieronymite religious order began in 1502 on the orders of Dom Manuel I, in thanks for the divine favour bestowed through the Discoveries and to commemorate Portugal's maritime prowess. The site had previously housed a chapel dedicated 50 years earlier by Prince Henry the Navigator. The west-facing entrance to the church is obscured by a 19th-century extension that now houses the Museu Nacional de Arqueologia (*see p102*), but the sculptural relief of

the south lateral entrance still captivates. The hierarchic pile of stonework saints is topped by the image of St Mary of Bethlehem (Belém), patron saint of the church and monastery. Immediately inside the church are the tombs of Vasco da Gama and Luís de Camões. Jerónimos is famed for the quality of light that sweeps into the nave during the day: a visit during a choir performance is enough to make the wicked long for redemption. The exquisite cloisters, designed by master architect Diogo de Boytac and completed by João de Castilho, are often the setting for concerts and other events. Boytac is also thought

---

A WOMAN'S TOUCH

Lisbon is awash with works by leading artist Joana Vasconcelos.

The reconditioned Trafaria Praia ferry (*see p92*) is the most visible piece by Portugal's most prominent contemporary artist, Joana Vasconcelos (www.joanavasconcelos.com), but there are plenty of other works in the city, indoors and out. Often colourful, even tactile, they invariably provoke reactions of delight and amusement.

In 2010, Vasconcelos was the first Portuguese artist to be given a large-scale retrospective at the Museu Colecção Berardo (*see p102*) – the museum owns several of her works, including *Coração Independente* ('Independent Heart', 2005), a giant filigree heart ingeniously woven from plastic cutlery rather than gold. That same year, *Marilyn* (2009), an over-sized pair of shoes made from steel cooking pans, was auctioned at Christie's for £505,000. And in 2013, a display at the Palácio de Ajuda (*see p103*) of 38 of her works (a scaled-down version of an earlier show at Versailles) was seen by 235,000 people – a record in Portugal. (During its first month, it drew more visitors than the palace usually does in a year.)

Vasconcelos' open-air installations – turning a building or bridge into an artwork by decking it out with textiles or colourful stuffed shapes – display an ambition unmatched by her peers, as well as a markedly Portuguese sensibility. Born in Paris in 1971 to Portuguese parents, she has her atelier in Lisbon's Alcântara docks. Her frequent use of domestic crafts (she stresses the fact that only the aid of dozens of skilled female hands enables her to realise many of her conceptions) gives the works a feminist – or at least feminine – twist.

One of her most frequent approaches is to wrap in crochet ceramic beasts designed by the 19th-century artist Rafael Bordalo

Portugal a Banhos.

Pinheiro and produced at the factory that he founded in the spa town of Caldas da Rainha. So Vasconcelos was the obvious choice to create an outdoor showcase for his work in the gardens of the Museu de Lisboa (*see p121*) in northern Lisbon – where snakes, wasps, wolves, cats and lobsters now lurk in fountains and bushes.

Her piece *Portugal a Banhos* ('Portugal Goes Swimming', 2010) – a full-size pool in the shape of the country – was first installed at Praça do Comércio and now towers over the Docas de Santo Amaro marina. Her stated aim with the piece was to symbolise Portugal's maritime links; in the current economic crisis, though, the joke is that 'Portugal has sprung a leak'.

EXPLORE

to have overseen the construction in 1514 of a pretty hermitage uphill, the Capela de São Jerónimo (guided visits, Wed only, can be booked at the monastery).

★ FREE Museu Colecção Berardo

Centro Cultural de Belém, Praça do Império (21 361 2878, www.museuberardo.pt). Train to Belém from Cais do Sodré, tram 15, or bus 28, 714, 727, 751. **Open** 10am-7pm Tue-Sun. **Admission** free. **Map** p99 D3 ❷

The culturally vital Centro Cultural de Belém opened in 1993. Its Centro de Exposições is the best art space in town, dominated since 2007 by the Museu Colecção Berardo. This showcase for the collection of Madeiran-born mining-to-media magnate José 'Joe' Berardo runs to hundreds of pieces, from Picasso and Duchamp to Warhol, Bacon and local girl Paula Rego. In fact, there's only room for some 900 of Berardo's more than 4,000 works (by some 550 different artists), representing dozens of modern movements.

FREE Museu da Electricidade

Avenida de Brasília (21 002 8190, www.fundacao edp.pt/museu-da-electricidade). Train to Belém from Cais do Sodré, tram 15, or bus 28, 714, 727, 729, 751. **Open** 10am-6pm Tue-Sun. **Admission** free. **Map** p99 D5 ❸

Although highly visible, this cathedral-like former power station by the river is not that easy to get to. The best way is probably on foot, via the footbridge at Belém rail station. The Central Tejo, as it originally was, powered Lisbon for three decades from 1918, before being relegated to the status of a back-up powerplant. Its boilers and generators, many dating from the 1930s, were last used in 1972. The museum opened in 1990 and was given a revamp in 2005 to turn it into a real technology museum (a leaflet in English is available). Fans of industrial architecture will enjoy wandering among giant machines in this tall, red-brick building with arched windows, pilasters, pediments and cornices – a dramatic backdrop for the art and fashion shows often held here.

Museu da Marinha

Praça do Império (21 362 0019, http://museu. marinha.pt). Train to Belém from Cais do Sodré, tram 15, or bus 28, 714, 727, 729, 751. **Open** *Oct-Apr* 10am-5pm Tue-Sun. *May-Sept* 10am-6pm Tue-Sun. **Admission** €6; €3 reductions; free under-13s & all 1st Sun of mth. **No credit cards. Map** p99 C3 ❸

The Naval Museum has an enormous collection, all owned by the Defence Ministry. The display starts with scale models of every type of Portuguese boat, and ends with a hangar full of gilded royal barges. Along the way are maps, navigational instruments, and crypto-fascist statues from the Salazar years.

Museu Nacional de Arqueologia

Praça do Império (21 362 0000, www.museu arqueologia.pt). Train to Belém from Cais do Sodré, tram 15, or bus 28, 714, 727, 729, 751.

Open 10am-6pm Tue-Sun. **Admission** €5; €2.50 reductions; free under-13s & all 1st Sun of mth. **No credit cards. Map** p99 C3 ❸

Although the Archaeological Museum has been housed in a wing of the Mosteiro dos Jerónimos for more than a century, it has only existed in its current form since 1990. There's too little space to display more than a small proportion of the permanent collection at any one time, but on show are usually an impressive collection of Egyptian artefacts and (often excellent) temporary exhibitions.

Museu Nacional de Etnologia

Avenida da Ilha da Madeira (21 304 1160). Bus 28, 714, 732. **Open** *Museum* 2-6pm Tue; 10am-6pm Wed-Sun. *Library* 9.30am-5.15pm Mon-Fri. **Admission** €3; €1.50 reductions; free under-13s & all 1st Sun of mth. **No credit cards. Map** p99 A3 ❸

The National Museum of Ethnology has a vast collection of items from rural Portugal and the former colonies that are regularly rotated and displayed in well-researched temporary exhibitions. A permanent show on rural life comprising some 3,000 pieces may be visited (with a guided tour, 2.30pm Tue, 10.30am & 2.30pm Wed-Fri). Staff are very helpful and the shop has books in English.

★ Museu Nacional dos Coches

Praça Afonso de Albuquerque (21 361 0850, www. museudoscoches.pt). Train to Belém from Cais do Sodré, tram 15, or bus 28, 714, 727, 729, 751. **Open** 10am-6pm Tue-Sun (last entry 5.30pm). **Admission** €6; €3 reductions; free under-13s & all 1st Sun of mth. **Map** p99 D5 ❸

Housed in an 18th-century royal riding hall (commissioned by Dom João V in 1726), the Coach Museum claims to have the world's largest and most valuable collection of horse-drawn coaches – 45 of them in all. The oldest, used by Spanish incomer Philip II (Philip

Museu Nacional dos Coches.

III of Spain) in the early 17th century, was outwardly austere so as not to stoke resentment among his new subjects, but plush inside. The art of coach-making reached its height in three Italian Baroque confections sent to Pope Clement XI by Dom João V; even their wheels are elaborately carved.

Padrão dos Descobrimentos

Avenida de Brasília (21 303 1950, www.padrao dosdescobrimentos.pt). Train to Belém from Cais do Sodré, tram 15, or bus 28, 714, 727, 729, 751. **Open** *Oct-Feb* 10am-6pm Tue-Sun. *Mar* 10am-7pm Tue-Sun. *Apr-Sept* 10am-7pm daily. Last entry 30mins before closing. **Admission** €3; €2 reductions; free under-13s. **Map** p99 D3 ㉟

The original temporary Monument to the Discoveries was put up for the 1940 Exhibition, and the permanent stone Salazarist glorification of the Discoveries opened to the public only in 1960. From the side, it takes the form of a tall oblong; at the base, sculpted figures of discoverers line a stylised prow jutting over the Tagus. They're led by Prince Henry the Navigator. Viewed head on, the monument appears as a giant sword-cum-cross, its point embedded in the riverbank, marking the entrance to the little exhibition space. Inside there's a lift to the top for fine views. As the sun follows its course, the shadow of the monument traces the progress of Portuguese explorers around a marble map of the world on the square below. Key dates, such as Vasco da Gama's rounding of the Cape of Good Hope in 1498 and Pedro Álvares Cabral's landing in Brazil in 1500, are marked.

Palácio da Ajuda

Largo da Ajuda (21 363 7095, www.palacioajuda. pt). Tram 18 or bus 729, 732. **Open** 10am-6pm Mon, Tue, Thur-Sun. **Admission** €5; €2.50 reductions; free under-13s & all 1st Sun of mth. **No credit cards.** **Map** p99 A5 ㊱

Construction began in 1802, but was interrupted in 1807 when the royal family high-tailed it to Brazil to escape Napoleon's armies. The palace was never finished and still looks sawn in half. Nevertheless, it served as a royal residence in the late 19th century. Some wings are open as a museum, while others house the Ministry of Culture.

★ Torre de Belém

Praça da Torre de São Vicente (21 362 0034, www. torrebelem.pt). Train to Belém from Cais do Sodré, tram 15, or bus 723, 729. **Open** *Oct-Apr* 10am-5.30pm Tue-Sun. *May-Sept* 10am-6.30pm Tue-Sun. **Admission** €6; €3 reductions; free under-13s & all 1st Sun of mth. *Combined ticket with Mosteiro de Jerónimos* €12. **Map** p99 D1 ㊲

The Tower of Belém was put up to guard the river entrance into Lisbon harbour. Built on the orders of Dom Manuel the Fortunate, it has stonework motifs recalling the Discoveries, among them twisted rope and the Catholic Crosses of Christ, as well as Lisbon's patron saint St Vincent and a rhinoceros.

Restaurants

Darwin's Café

Champalimaud Centre for the Unknown, Avenida Brasília (21 048 0222, www.darwincafe.com). Tram 15. **Open** 12.30-4pm Mon; 12.30-3.30pm, 4.30-6.30pm, 7.30-11pm Tue-Sun. **Main courses** €12.50-€25. **Map** p99 D1 ㊳ **International**

The location of this restaurant in a private scientific foundation on a curve of the river just before it meets the ocean is enough to take your breath away. Add to that the landmark building and the restaurant's dramatic interior, and dining here is a real occasion. The food is inevitably hard pressed to match the setting, but is good and pretty well priced, with a range of pasta and risotto dishes as well as more elaborate *bacalhau* and meat dishes, plus an excellent wine list. You can also enjoy tea or a drink on the café terrace.

Feitoria

Altis Belém Hotel, Doca do Bom Sucesso (21 040 0200, www.restaurantefeitoria.com). Tram 15. **Open** 7.30-11pm Mon-Sat. **Main courses** €29-€39. **Map** p99 D3 ㊳ **Portuguese/Asian**

This Michelin-starred restaurant and wine bar in the riverside Altis Belém (*see p219*) offers something unique in Lisbon: Portuguese auteur cuisine, but with oriental touches. For your main dish, choose from five fish and five meat dishes or go for one of the full *menus de degustação*: three courses for €70, five for €120, six for €155 (prices without wine).

Cafés & Bars

À Margem

Doca do Bom Sucesso (91 822 5548, 91 862 0032, www.amargem.com). Train to Belém from Cais do Sodré or tram 15. **Open** *Summer* 10am-1am daily. *Winter* 10am-10pm Mon-Thur, Sun; 10am-1am Fri, Sat. **Map** p99 D3 ㊵

On sunny days, this riverside terrace is one of Lisbon's busiest. At weekends book ahead or be prepared to wait for a table. The secret of À Margem's success is its simplicity: it's a white steel-and-glass box, as pleasant inside as out, with ambient music to suit the hour. The food isn't outstanding, but the spot is ideal for a lunchtime salad, afternoon tea and scones, or a glass of wine at sunset.

★ Antiga Confeitaria de Belém

Rua de Belém 84-92 (21 363 7423, www. pasteisdebelem.pt). Train to Belém from Cais do Sodré or tram 15. **Open** *July-Sept* 8am-midnight daily. *Oct-June* 8am-11pm daily. **Map** p99 C4 ㊶

The world-famous *pastéis de Belém* – warm, creamy tarts with puff pastry made according to a secret recipe – fairly fly out of the door here. Customers with time to spare scoff them two at a time in a warren of rooms lined with tiles depicting Belém in the early 17th century. Others take them away by the half-dozen in specially designed cardboard tubes.

EXPLORE

São Bento & Beyond

Parliamentarians gather at the Assembly of the Republic in São Bento, an area that in historical terms could be labelled the African inner city – it still retains something of an African feel. Up the hill towards Príncipe Real and Rato is the domain of antiques shops and twee cafés, as well as the former home of famed fado diva Amália Rodrigues. Further west are Estrela, with its white-domed basilica built on the orders of Dona Maria I to fulfil a promise over the birth of a male heir; middle-class Campo de Ourique; and the well-heeled Lapa district – home to many foreign diplomats. With several interesting museums and pleasant gardens, yet off the main tourist track, these are good places for relaxed sightseeing, with or without the aid of the antique trams that cut through the area.

EXPLORE

Aqueduto das Águas Livres.

Don't Miss

1 Aqueduto das Águas Livres This aqueduct withstood the quake (p112).

2 Basílica da Estrela Serene church with stunning views (p110).

3 Fundação Arpad Szenes – Vieira da Silva Striking modern art on show (p112).

4 Rua de São Bento Browse antiques and glassware aplenty (p106).

5 Pastelaria Aloma Tuck into some prize-winning *pastéis de nata* (p113).

SÃO BENTO

The neighbourhood in front of the Palácio de São Bento, the massive old Benedictine monastery that now houses the Portuguese parliament, takes its name from the building. Perhaps the best approach to the *palácio* is from the narrow Travessa da Arrochela, a typical old street with laundry draped from the windows. Capping the view at the bottom of the street are the huge pediment and columns of the palace, now known as the **Palácio da Assembléia da República**. Up Rua de São Bento, a street dotted with antiques shops, is the former home of Amália, the greatest 20th-century *fadista*. It's now the **Casa-Museu Amália Rodrigues**. In the other direction, the broad Avenida Carlos I leads down to Santos.

In the 16th century, the area around busy Rua do Poço dos Negros (Well of Negroes) to the east of Avenida Dom Carlos I reeked of rotting bodies – African slaves dumped in a depository at the bottom of the hill after serving their use. It's now a lively residential area served by cheap *tascas*, some with an African feel. Round the corner in Travessa do Convento de Jesus, the **Centro InterculturaCidade** (No.16A, 21 820 7657, http://interculturacidade.wordpress.com, open 3-7pm Mon-Fri, 3-6pm Sat) hosts exhibitions relating to immigrant communities or former Portuguese colonies; many evenings it holds percussion workshops, dance classes, concerts and African dinners (donations from €10) too.

Turn into Rua do Vale for a view up to the imposing former Convento de Jesus (now the parish church of Mercês) and the city's newest museum, the **Atelier-Museu Júlio Pomar** modern art space. Further uphill, Praça das Flores is a delightfully leafy square with a cluster of fashionable cafés and restaurants.

De Castro.

Atelier-Museu Júlio Pomar.

Sights & Museums

FREE Atelier-Museu Júlio Pomar
Rua do Vale 7 (21 817 2111, www.ateliermuseu juliopomar.pt). Tram 28. **Open** 10am-6pm Tue-Sun. **Admission** free. **Map** p109 G6 ❶
The city council acquired this derelict 17th-century warehouse in 2000 to house a workshop-cum-museum for Lisbon native Júlio Pomar, one of Portugal's leading artists. But it was only in 2013 that the building – transformed by renowned Oporto architect Álvaro Siza Vieira – was finally unveiled. The new art space comprises an airy central exhibition area and mezzanine, plus an auditorium. As well as showcasing several hundred paintings, sculptures, drawings, engravings, collages, ceramics and installations donated by Pomar (who continues to work here), it also hosts exhibitions of fellow artists' works.

Casa-Museu Amália Rodrigues
Rua de São Bento 193 (21 397 1896, www.amalia rodrigues.pt). Metro Rato or bus 706, 727, 773. **Open** 10am-1pm, 2-6pm Tue-Sun. **Admission** *Guided tours* €5. **No credit cards**. **Map** p109 E5 ❷
The house of fado diva Amália Rodrigues is a shrine to the memory of the greatest exponent of Lisbon's soulful music (for more on fado, *see p149*). Lined with 18th-century *azulejos*, it has been restored and adapted, displaying portraits of the star by leading Portuguese artists, her favourite glittery outfits, jewellery, and decorations awarded by adoring politicians. Guided tours are conducted in Portuguese or English. Amália, as she is invariably known, died in October 1999 after a career that spanned decades, having won the hearts of her compatriots and fame in Italy, France and Brazil. Since 2002, her remains have been in the National Pantheon (*see p67*).

EXPLORE

FREE Palácio da Assembléia da República

Largo das Cortes, Rua de São Bento (21 391 9625, 21 391 9773, www.parlamento.pt). Tram 25, 28 or bus 6, 713, 727, 773. **Open** Sessions from 3pm Wed, Thur; from 10am Fri. *Guided visits* 3pm, 4pm last Sat of mth. **Admission** free. **Map** p109 F5 ❸

The imposing façade of the Palácio de São Bento seems as if it ought to face more than just a huddle of red-roofed neighbourhoods kept at bay by the stone lions at its entrance. Portugal's Assembly of the Republic is housed in this former monastery, the Mosteiro de São Bento (Saint Benedict), which was turned over to parliament in 1834 when religious orders were abolished. Major renovation work has left little evidence of the original late 16th-century structure, but the building contains notable artworks, especially the upstairs murals (1920-26) by Rafael Bordalo Pinheiro. Guided tours (1hr 30mins) take place once a month; book by noon the previous day by phone or email (cic.rp@ar.parlamento.pt). When parliament is in session, you can also enter the viewing galleries (entrance on Praça de São Bento, to the right of the palace). Up the hill behind parliament is the prime minister's official residence.

Restaurants

Café de São Bento

Rua de São Bento 212 (21 395 2911, www.cafe saobento.com). **Open** 12.30-2.30pm, 7pm-2am Mon-Fri; 7pm-2am Sat, Sun. **Main courses** €9.90-€23.40. **Map** p109 F5 ❹ **Steakhouse**
The Café de São Bento is small and rather formal, but the quality of the steak and accompanying sauces and chips, not to mention the well-pulled beer, are the main thing here. There are uncomplicated salads and starters involving smoked salmon or fine cheeses and hams, plus a range of desserts that include a delicious tarte tatin.

★ De Castro

Rua Marcos Portugal 1 (21 590 3077, www.decastro. pt). Tram 28 or bus 706, 727, 773. **Open** 12.30-3pm, 7.30-11pm Tue-Sat; 12.30-3pm Sun. **Main courses** €10.80-€17.50. **Map** p109 E6 ❺ **Portuguese**
'Portuguese cuisine with a modern twist' is how chef Miguel Castro e Silva defines what he's about at this, his latest culinary project. This white-painted space is cosy and casual, making it a fun place to dip into snacks such as octopus fillets, duck liver and *morcela* sausage. Alternatively, go for the menu for two at €40; there's also a range of delicious desserts.

Cafés & Bars

Casa de Chá de Santa Isabel

Rua de São Bento 700 (21 388 7040). Metro Rato. **Open** 11.30am-7pm Tue-Fri; 11.30am-7pm Sat, Sun. Closed Aug. **No credit cards. Map** p108 D5 ❻

COFFEE SPEAK

How to order the right brew.

The usually simple task of ordering a coffee can be fraught with perils in Lisbon. You could just say '*um café, por favor*', but then brace yourself for a tiny dose of a potent, bitter brew that, drunk neat, can disable tastebuds for hours.

For a milky coffee, served in a glass, ask for *um galão*, but add the words *da máquina* (from the machine) or the coffee may come from a tankful that's been standing around for an hour. The nearest thing to a cappuccino is *uma meia da leite* (half of milk). To make sure it's strong and hot, end the phrase with *da máquina com leite quente* (with hot milk).

Most locals don't bother with wimpy additions such as milk. They opt for a straight *bica* (Lisbon waiters' slang – as the customer, you order *um café* unless you're tacking on an adjective) or *um duplo* (double) when in need of extra caffeine, and offset the bitterness with sugar. Alternatively, they might cut it with a drop (*um pingo*) of milk, ordering *um café pingado*. The other way round – a few drops of coffee in milk – is *um garoto* (literally 'a young boy'); even this can be qualified with the words *claro* or *escuro* (light or dark).

If a simple *bica* doesn't do it for you any more, try *uma italiana* – effectively, a thimbleful of hot coffee essence. Or get finicky and order *um café cheio/curto* (that is, weaker/stronger). The faint-hearted order *um carioca*, a diluted *bica* and not to be confused with *um carioca de limão*, which is lemon rind in hot water. *Um abatanado* is still more diluted, and thus served in a larger cup. For a different kind of boost, try *um café com cheirinho* – 'with a whiff' of *aguardente* (grape mash distillate). A decaf is *um descafeinado*.

The pickiest customers refuse to accept a cup from on top of the coffee machine, where crockery is left to dry. If they want piping hot coffee yet without burning their lips (don't you just hate it when that happens?) they order *uma bica escaldada numa chávena fria* ('scalded' in a cold cup).

To test the staff's reactions, you could even order *uma bica descafeinada escaldada pingada numa chávena fria*. But perhaps that would be taking things just a little too far.

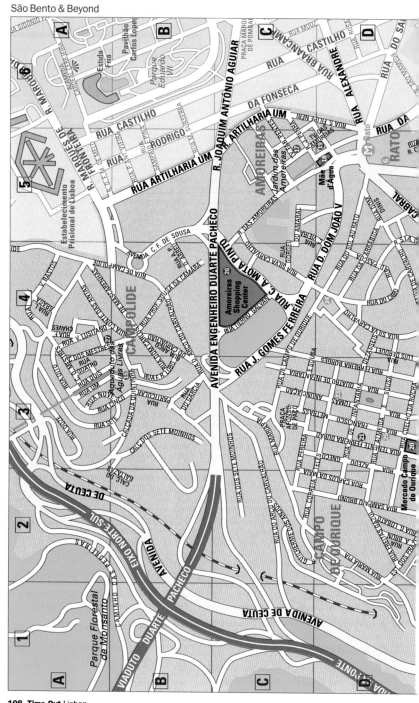

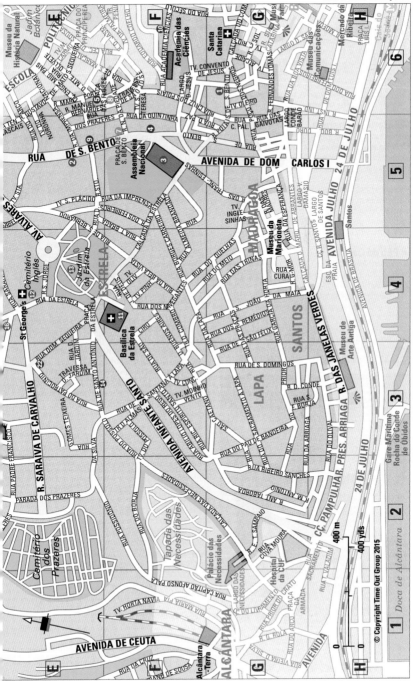

EXPLORE

Still known to locals as 'As Vicentinhas', after the religious order that ran it for decades, this recently revamped tearoom hands all its profits to local charitable works. As well as sweet and savoury snacks, full meals are available between 12.45pm and 3pm. After that, home-made scones and cakes are displayed in all their sticky glory for what is arguably Lisbon's best afternoon tea.

Gelateria Nannarella

Rua Nova da Piedade 68 (91 630 2201). Tram 28. **Open** noon-7.30pm Mon-Sat. **Map** p109 F5 ⑦
Rome natives Constanza and Filippo lived in Lisbon for a couple of years before they thought to open this little ice-cream parlour. But it quickly found success, with queues forming outside at peak hours. Ingredients in the sorbets and ices include locally sourced fresh fruit (including the very Portuguese rocha pear), pistachios and almonds imported from Italy, port wine and Óbidos *ginja* (cherry liqueur).

★ Pão de Canela

Praça das Flores 27 (21 397 2220, www.canela.pt). Metro Rato or bus 773. **Open** 7.30am-11pm daily. **Map** p109 F6 ⑧
This discreetly fashionable café serves tasty quiches and cakes. Its terrace is blissfully free of traffic fumes, and there's even a mini-café for kids with craft activities to complement the playground in the square. The attached restaurant (mains €7.50-€14) stays open until 11pm, and at weekends lays on a great brunch (€18). The latest offshoot is Canela Grill (at no.40).

Pão de Canela.

Shops & Services

★ Depósito da Marinha Grande

Rua de São Bento 418 (21 396 3096, www. dmg.com.pt). Tram 28 or bus 706, 727, 773. **Open** 9am-7pm Mon-Fri; 9am-1pm Sat. **Map** p109 E5 ⑨ **Glassware**
Thousands of pieces of hand-blown glasswork in copies of old, unusual designs from the town of Marinha Grande, where the industry dates back to 1769. Prices are reasonable, with large goblets selling for around €15. There's another, smaller shop at no.234 (21 396 3234).

★ Ratton

Rua Academia das Ciências 2C (21 346 0948, http://galeriaratton.blogspot.com). Tram 28. **Open** 3-7pm Mon-Fri. **No credit cards.** **Map** p109 F6 ⑩ **Tiles**
Contemporary designs, in collaboration with Portuguese and foreign artists, including Júlio Pomar and Paula Rego. The gallery has some temporary exhibits but most designs are in catalogues; a reproduction will set you back €50-€150 per tile.

LAPA & ESTRELA

West of São Bento, the neighbourhoods are more well-to-do. **Lapa**, on a hillside facing south over the river, is home to Lisbon's diplomats. A walk along Rua do Sacramento, Rua do Caetano or Rua de São Domingos shows what Lisbon has to offer in the way of discreet luxury. **Estrela** is based around the late 18th-century **Basílica da Estrela**. Tram 28 passes by here, on the west end of its run up and down old Lisbon. The **Jardim da Estrela** opposite the church is a popular stop for parents with children in tow.

Beyond the roundabout at its eastern end is an art nouveau building housing the free **Museu João de Deus** (Avenida Álvares Cabral 69, 21 396 0854, www.joaodeus.com, closed Sat & Sun), dedicated to the poet-pedagogue but most interesting for its 19th-century art. There are paintings by José Malhoa in the office to the right of the lobby, and by Rodrigo Soares in one on the left; in the conference room are cartoons and a vase by the multi-talented Bordalo Pinheiro. On the other side of Rua de São Jorge is the **Cemitério Inglês** and, round the corner, St George's Church; they're among several local features with Anglo connections (*see p111* **In the Know**).

Sights & Museums

★ FREE Basílica da Estrela

Praça da Estrela (21 396 0915). Tram 25, 28. **Open** *Church* 7.30am-7.45pm daily. *Roof terrace* 10am-6.30pm Mon-Sat; 3-6.30pm Sun. **Admission** *Church* free. *Roof terrace* €4; €2 reductions. **Map** p109 F4 ⑪

Basílica da Estrela.

The ornate white dome of the Basílica da Estrela is one of Lisbon's best-loved landmarks. Construction took ten years (1779-89), with statues sculpted by artists from the Mafra School. The church is richly decorated inside with Portuguese marble, although many of the paintings are by Italian masters. Climb the 114 steps for fine views of the city.

FREE Cemitério Inglês
Rua de São Jorge à Estrela (no phone). Tram 25, 28 or bus 709, 720, 738. **Open** *9am-1pm daily.* **Map** p109 E4 **⑫**
Across the street from the top end of the Jardim da Estrela, a tall wall encloses the English cemetery, which dates back to a 1654 agreement between Dom João IV and Oliver Cromwell over the need for a Protestant burial ground given the many British merchants in Lisbon. Intentions were made good

---

IN THE KNOW
OUR FRIENDS FROM THE NORTH

The establishment of the **Cemitério Inglês** (*see above*) in Estrela encouraged several anglophone institutions to move to the neighbourhood. St George's Church, in Rua São Jorge, was built in 1889 on the site of an earlier Anglican church (after which the street was named). The British Hospital, Portugal's first private hospital, closed in 2009, ripe for redevelopment into luxury flats. But the Lisbon Players, its thespian neighbours in Estrela Hall (*see p162*), are resisting the British Embassy's efforts to winkle them out.

---

seven decades later, and the first body was officially laid to rest in 1729. Among them is 18th-century novelist Henry Fielding, who came to Lisbon to improve his health and promptly died. A small Jewish area – in use in the first half of the 19th century – is hidden behind a wall on the west side. If the gate isn't open, ring the bell (repeatedly) and somebody should come and let you in.

FREE Jardim da Estrela
Praça da Estrela (no phone). Tram 25, 28 or bus 9, 720, 738, 773. **Open** *7am-midnight daily.* **Map** p109 E4 **⑬**
Also known as the Jardim Guerra Junqueiro, the Estrela Garden was laid out in 1842 across the street from the Basílica. The bandstand near the top end of the park once graced the public promenade that became Avenida da Liberdade; it has been here since the 1930s. There's a swan lake overlooked by a café, several other kiosks, and a large playground.

Shops & Services

Cristina Guerra Contemporary Art
Rua Santo António à Estrela 33 (21 395 9559, www. cristinaguerra.com). Tram 25, 28. **Open** *noon-8pm Tue-Fri; 3-8pm Sat.* **Map** p109 E3 **⑭ Gallery**
This gallery showcases works in a range of media by heavyweights such as Matt Mullican, Michael Biberstein, Julião Sarmento and João Onofre, who has been with Guerra almost from the start of his career. New shows appear every couple of months.

CAMPO DE OURIQUE & AMOREIRAS

Campo de Ourique is a middle-class district above Estrela that was laid out in the 19th century on a grid pattern. The house on Rua Coelho da Rocha where poet Fernando Pessoa spent the last 15 years of his life is now the **Casa Fernando Pessoa**, one of Lisbon's more active small cultural institutions. The **Mercado de Campo de Ourique**, one of the city's best markets, is now home to a host of gourmet food stalls too. To the west, at the end of the No.28 tram route, is a vast city of the dead spread beneath lonely cypresses, the municipal Cemitério dos Prazeres (literally 'Pleasures'), named after the local church dedicated to Our Lady of that ilk). The cemetery has a small museum (closed Mon).

The northern end of Campo de Ourique is marked by a pile of pastel postmodernism. Architect Tomás Taveira boasted in the mid 1980s that his goal with the **Amoreiras** towers – which look a bit like giant Liquorice Allsorts studded with smoked glass – was to provide a skyline counterbalance to the Castelo de São Jorge. Most feel he missed the mark, but the towers are still there and Amoreiras is one of the capital's most popular malls. Down Rua das Amoreiras, above

EXPLORE

busy Largo do Rato, is the pretty Jardim das Amoreiras, located under the arches at the end of the **Aqueduto das Águas Livres** before it terminates at the **Mãe d'Água**. A café here serves light lunches.

The **Fundação Arpad Szenes – Vieira da Silva** has a permanent collection of the work of Portuguese modernist painter Maria Helena Vieira da Silva and her Hungarian husband, along with works by associated artists. The museum is housed in a former textile workshop. The whole area was set up as an industrial park in the late 18th century, which is why so many of the streets are named after factories, such as Travessa da Fábrica dos Pentes (Comb Factory Way).

Lisbon's central synagogue, the **Sinagoga Shaaré Tikvá** (Alexandre Herculano 59, 21 393 1130, www.cilisboa.org), is just off Largo do Rato, set well back from the street: when it was built, in 1904, non-Catholic places of worship weren't permitted to front on to a public thoroughfare. To book a weekday guided visit, call 96 735 0685.

Sights & Museums

Aqueduto das Águas Livres

Access from Calçada da Quintinha (EPAL gate) (21 325 1652). Bus 2. **Open** *Mar-Nov* 10am-5.30pm Tue-Sat. **Admission** €3; €1.50 reductions; free under-13s. **Map** p108 B3 ⑮

Lisbon's aqueduct spans the Alcântara valley. Construction began in 1731, and by 1748 the first water was flowing from a source 58 kilometres to the north-west. It bridges the valley on a series of 35 arches, the largest of which rises 64 metres from the ground; giddy heights indeed when you walk along the parapet. When built, these were the tallest stone arches in the world. They were sturdy too – they survived the 1755 Earthquake unscathed. The aqueduct was taken out of service in 1967. Guided walks, taking in some of the surrounding area, can be booked through the Museu da Água (*see p124*).

Casa Fernando Pessoa

Rua Coelho da Rocha 16 (21 391 3270, http://casa fernandopessoa.cm-lisboa.pt). Tram 25, 28. **Open** 10am-6pm Mon-Sat (library Mon-Fri). **Admission** €3; €2 reductions; free under-6s. **Map** p109 E4 ⑯

Dedicated to poetry in general, and Portugal's most celebrated modernist poet in particular, the Casa Fernando Pessoa is where he lived during the last 15 years of his life. The Casa organises poetry readings and publishes monographs on Pessoa, as well as hosting art exhibitions and the odd jazz concert. There's a restaurant (21 395 0704) round the back.

Fundação Arpad Szenes – Vieira da Silva

Praça das Amoreiras 56 (21 388 0044, 21 388 0053, www.fasvs.pt). Metro Rato. **Open** 10am-6pm Tue-Sun. **Admission** €4; €2 reductions; free to all 10am-2pm Sun. **Map** p108 C5 ⑰

A plain building that was once the Royal Silk and Textile Workshop now houses this foundation, dedicated to exhibiting and promoting research into the work of Portuguese modernist Maria Helena Vieira da Silva and her Hungarian husband and fellow painter Arpad Szenes. Although the couple lived in France for many years and played a central role in the School of Paris, they're also iconic figures in Portugal. As well as housing and displaying its large permanent collection of their works, the foundation puts on regular exhibitions of artists with links to the couple, such as Fernand Léger and Marc Chagall.

Mãe d'Água

Praça das Amoreiras (21 325 1644). Metro Rato. **Open** 10am-12.30pm, 1.30-5.30pm Tue-Sat. **Admission** €5; €2.50 reductions; free under-13s. **Map** p108 D5 ⑱

The Aqueduto das Águas Livres ends at the Mãe d'Água (Mother of Water), a large stone building that looms behind the Socialist Party headquarters on Largo do Rato. Construction began in 1745 and work carried on until 1834. Inside, the central tank has a capacity of 5,500 cubic metres, and the cool stone interior has the feel of an eerie grotto. Arriving water tumbles into the central pool over an ever-growing mound of scale. The walkways around the tank and a floating platform are used for art exhibitions. Visitors can climb the stairs to peer down the aqueduct passage.

Restaurants

★ Estórias na Casa da Comida

Travessa das Amoreiras 1 (21 388 5376, www.casadacomida.pt). Metro Rato. **Open** 7pm-midnight Mon-Sat. **Main courses** €18.50-€26. **Prix fixe** €40, €60. **Map** p108 D5 ⑲ Portuguese

A famous gourmet spot, the Casa da Comida has been given a gastronomic makeover by new chef Miguel Carvalho. His seasonal menus include elaborate dishes based on traditional Portuguese cuisine, but with an international twist. The sommelier, Ricardo Morais, is one of Lisbon's best. You can just drink and snack in the wine bar, or head for the restaurant and its romantic *azulejo*-lined patio.

Mercado do Campo de Ourique

Rua Coelho da Rocha (21 132 3701, www. mercadodocampodeourique.pt). Tram 25, 28 or bus 709, 774. **Open** 10am-11pm Mon, Tue; 10am-midnight Wed, Sun; 10am-1am Thur-Sat; 10am-midnight Sun. **Main courses** €4-€10. **Map** p108 D3 ⑳ Portuguese/International

Not one restaurant but a whole gourmet food court in one of Lisbon's liveliest surviving market halls. Stalls include a gin bar and an oyster bar, as well as Portuguese favourites such as suckling pig and gourmet burgers. On weekend nights there's live music or DJs. Meanwhile the old business of selling fruit, vegetables, fish and meat goes on next door.

Amoreiras.

★ Stop do Bairro
Rua Tenente Ferreira Durão 55A (21 388 8856). Tram 28 or bus 774. **Open** noon-4pm, 7-11pm Tue-Sun. **Main courses** €8.50-€20. **Map** p108 D3 ㉔ **Portuguese**
This neighbourhood favourite remains as resolutely unglamorous as ever, its walls decked with football scarves and slogans in Portuguese of the 'You don't have to be mad…' variety. Among well-priced dishes on its extensive menu are *caras de bacalhau* (codfish cheeks), Azorean *polvo guisado* (stewed octopus) and, on Fridays, *cabidela de galinha* (chicken cooked in blood). Helpings are generous – in some cases even a *meia dose* (half serving) is enough for two – but it's worth saving space for dessert. The wine list is outstanding for this price bracket. You can't reserve, so come early. Note that smoking is allowed and there are just three tables outside.

Tasca da Esquina
Rua Domingues Sequeira 41C (21 099 3939, www.tascadaesquina.com). Tram 25, 28 or bus 709. **Open** 7.30-11.30pm Mon; 12.30-3.30pm, 7.30-11.30pm Tue-Fri; 1-3.30pm, 7.30-11.30pm Sat. **Main courses** €9-€20. **Map** p109 E3 ㉒ **Portuguese**
A *tasca* in name only, this recession-busting gourmet restaurant is overseen by leading Portuguese chef Vítor Sobral. There are two ways to approach a meal here, both involving delicious starters: order à la carte from a menu that includes dishes of the day, or go for a combo with four to seven starters. Offal looms large here but there are other options, such as squid sautéed with mushrooms or flaked *bacalhau* with potato and egg.

Cafés & Bars

Lomar
Rua Tomás de Anunciação 72 (21 385 8417). Tram 25, 28. **Open** 7.30am-7.30pm Mon-Fri; 7.30am-4pm Sat. **No credit cards**. **Map** p108 D3 ㉓
This stylish neighbourhood *pastelaria* attracts a mixture of local *tias* (literally 'aunts', but meaning ladies who lunch) and students, who come in to natter over coffee and sample the sweets and savouries that are made on the premises. There's a good coffee and 'cake of the week' deal for €1.40.

Panificação Mecânica
Rua Silva Carvalho 209 (21 381 2260). Metro Rato or bus 758. **Open** 7am-8pm Mon-Fri; 7am-3pm Sat. **No credit cards**. **Map** p108 D4 ㉔
Chandeliers, tiles depicting ears of wheat, coloured enamel pillars, painted moulded ceilings and wall mirrors make this one of Lisbon's most over-the-top *pastelarias*. It has been supplying the middle classes and local businesses with top-notch bread and cakes for more than a century. There's no seating area, but you can stand at the high table or counter for a drink and a snack.

★ Pastelaria Aloma
Rua Francisco Metrass 67 (21 396 3797). Tram 25, 28. **Open** 8am-7pm daily. **No credit cards**. **Map** p108 D3 ㉕
Inaugurated in 1943 and named after a sarong-clad character played by film star Dorothy Lamour, this place won national fame in 2012 and 2013 when its *pastéis de nata* (custard tartlets) were declared Portugal's best in a blind tasting.

Shops & Services

Amoreiras
Avenida Engenheiro Duarte Pacheco (21 381 0240, www.amoreiras.com). Metro Rato or bus 711, 718, 723, 748, 753, 758. **Open** 10am-11pm daily. **Map** p108 C4 ㉖ **Mall**
Architect Tomás Taveira based the postmodernist design for Portugal's first shopping centre on the Brazilian concept of many small entrances making it easy to get in. A maze-like layout and poor signage means it can be rather more tricky to find your way back out, though. Expect the usual selection of local and international chains, a supermarket, a multiplex and a chapel.

Módulo – Centro Difusor de Arte
Calçada dos Mestres 34A-B (21 388 5570). Bus 701, 702, 712, 742. **Open** 3-8pm Mon-Sat. **No credit cards**. **Map** p108 A4 ㉗ **Gallery**
This 'art diffusion centre' is home to one of Lisbon's most interesting exhibition spaces. Work by exciting new artists predominates, with photography a particular focus.

Further Afield

The wooded walkways that became the Avenida da Liberdade once marked the northern edge of the city. Now, the roundabout at its far end is just the starting point for avenues that spin off towards today's office districts. Still, many points of interest for visitors are dotted across northern Lisbon.

In the 1800s, writer Almeida Garrett described the low hills to the east of Lisbon as full of gardens and orchards. By the 1860s, the area was changed as trains chugged alongside the river, heralding the arrival of factories and warehouses. A highway parallel to the river links Praça do Comércio with the Expo 98 site – now the Parque das Nações.

The settlements south of the river are definitely in the city's orbit, with commuters streaming over the two giant bridges and on to ferries each morning. This is also where the iconic statue of Cristo Rei guards the southern end of the Ponte 25 de Abril.

Cristo Rei.

Don't Miss

1 Museu Nacional do Azulejo An overview of that archetypal Portuguese decoration – the tile (p124).

2 Museu Calouste Gulbenkian Fine arts at their finest (p116).

3 Parque das Nações Open spaces, plus mall and multiplex (p126).

4 Bica do Sapato One of Lisbon's top eateries, run by chef with flair (p124).

5 Cristo Rei Views of river, bridge and city (p127).

Museu Calouste Gulbenkian.

Northern Lisbon

SETE RIOS & BENFICA

Praça de Espanha is infamous at rush hour; the grassy space in the middle now sports an aqueduct arch that used to constrict traffic further downtown until it was uprooted to here. On one side is Palácio de Palhavã, the official residence of the Spanish ambassador. Uphill, towering department store **El Corte Inglés**, with its well-stocked supermarket and gourmet groceries, also does sterling work for Spanish-Portuguese relations.

Opposite the embassy is the Fundação Calouste Gulbenkian, one of Lisbon's most important cultural institutions. Its **Museu Calouste Gulbenkian** has a rich collection of artefacts, while its **Centro de Arte Moderna** showcases modern art and, in summer, open-air jazz. There are more shows on offer on the south-western corner of Praça de Espanha, at the **Teatro Aberto** (see p162) and **Teatro da Comuna** (see p163). On the northern side of Praça de Espanha is a ramshackle market with stalls selling everything from buckets to imitation designer T-shirts. Continue past it to reach the **Jardim Zoológico de Lisboa** (see p132).

Now a sprawl of bank headquarters and airport-style hotels, Sete Rios still has some old jewels, such as the **Palácio dos Marqueses da Fronteira**, famed for its gardens and tiles depicting exotic hunting scenes. A little further north is the **Biblioteca-Museu República e Resistência** (Estrada de Benfica 419, 21 771 2310, closed Sat & Sun), a leftist archive housed in a *vila operária*. The **Museu da Música** is nearby, inside the Alto dos Moinhos Metro station. From here it's a short walk to the giant stadium of **Sport Lisboa e Benfica** (see p121 **Football Crazy**), a powerhouse of European football in the 1960s and a perennial candidate, with FC Porto and Sporting, for the league title.

Across the ring road is the huge **Centro Colombo**. Beyond this giant shopping centre is Benfica itself, once a quiet town, now a concrete suburb.

Sights & Museums

★ Centro de Arte Moderna José de Azeredo Perdigão

Fundação Calouste Gulbenkian, Rua Dr Nicolau Bettencourt (21 782 3474, guided visits & activities 21 782 3800, www.cam.gulbenkian.pt). Metro São Sebastião. **Open** 10am-5.45pm Tue-Sun. **Admission** €5 (€15 with Museu Calouste Gulbenkian and all exhibitions); €2.50 reductions; free under-13s, over-64s & all Sun. **Map** p118 C6 ❶

Part of the terrific Gulbenkian complex (see p158 **Prospecting for Culture**), the CAMJAP is a fine modernist building on the edge of a lovely park, with a canteen and bookshop. Its collection is a fine foil to the Old Masters of the main Museu Calouste Gulbenkian (see below), displaying Portuguese works from the last century. Modernism is represented by key artists, such as surrealists António Pedro and António Dacosta. There's also a collection of modern British art, amassed over decades.

★ Museu Calouste Gulbenkian

Avenida de Berna 45 (21 782 3461, guided visits & activities 21 782 3455, www.museu. gulbenkian.pt). Metro Praça de Espanha. **Open** *Museum* 10am-6pm Tue-Sun (last entry 5.30pm). *Library* 9.30am-7pm Mon-Fri. **Admission** €5 (€15 with Centro de Arte Moderna and all exhibitions); €2.50 reductions; free under-13s & all Sun. **No credit cards. Map** p118 C5 ❷

It's difficult to know where to start in this, one of Europe's leading fine arts museums, with exhibits dating from 2000 BC to the early 20th century. From the ancient world come Egyptian scarabs, Greco-Roman jewellery and a giant ninth century BC Assyrian bas-relief in alabaster of a warrior. Perhaps the two outstanding rooms are those containing Islamic and Oriental art: carpets, robes, tapestries, tiles and glassware, mainly from 16th- and 17th-century Persia, Turkey, Syria and India; and porcelain, jade, paintings and lacquered boxes from China and Japan. The section on European art displays medieval manuscripts, and ivory and wood diptychs. Further on are Italian Renaissance majolica ware and tapestries, and a selection of 18th-century French furniture and silverware. Among the painters represented are Domenico Ghirlandaio, Rubens, Hals and Rembrandt, Gainsborough, Manet and Corot. Save time for the final room and its breathtaking glass and metal art nouveau jewellery by René Lalique. Audio-guides are available in English, French, Spanish and Portuguese to help you get the most from the experience. There are also excellent temporary exhibitions, with pieces lent by institutions around the world. Downstairs is an art library (which often hosts midday classical recitals on Sundays), an excellent café and a small gift shop. There's a larger bookshop in the lobby of the main building. Don't miss the Centro de Arte Moderna (*see p116*) at the southern end of the park.

Museu da Música

Alto dos Moinhos Metro station, Rua de Freitas Branco (21 771 0990, www.museudamusica.pt). **Open** 10am-6pm Mon-Sat. **Admission** €3; €1.50 reductions; free under-13s. **No credit cards**. **Map** p118 A2 ❸

Although it's off the beaten track, the Museum of Music is definitely worth a trip if you're an enthusiast. Some real treasures are on display from the 16th century to the 20th century – everything from pocket fiddles and a plethora of *guitarras* (12-stringed Portuguese guitars) to Baroque harpsichords – plus related documents. There's also a specially-strengthened piano that Franz Liszt brought to Lisbon for a much-feted series of concerts, and which he left behind as a gift to the queen, Dona Maria II. The shop (closed Mon) has a good range of books and classical CDs, as well as miniature instruments.

★ Palácio dos Marqueses da Fronteira

Largo de São Domingos de Benfica 1 (21 778 2023, www.fronteira-alorna.pt). Metro Parque Zoológico or bus 770. **Open** *Guided tours* (palace and garden) June-Sept 10.30am, 11am, 11.30am, noon Mon-Sat. Oct-May 11am, noon Mon-Sat. *Garden* 11am-1pm, 2.30-5pm Mon-Fri; 11am-1pm Sat. **Admission** *Tours* €7.50; free under-14s. *Gardens* €3; free under-14s. **No credit cards**. **Map** p118 A4 ❹

IN THE KNOW SEE SHANTIES

Even before leaving the airport, you may catch sight of remnants of the *bairros de lata* (literally, 'tin neighbourhoods'). Some were founded by white *retornados* who arrived, destitute, after the African colonies won independence. Most have long since moved on, their ingeniously built homes often taken over by African immigrants. In Cova da Moura, north-west of Lisbon, the local youth club (21 497 1070, sabura. visitas@gmail.com) has made a once notorious neighbourhood accessible with tours that include Cape Verdean food.

The idyllic setting of this palace, at the foot of Monsanto Forest Park, is in sharp contrast to the concrete jungle of Sete Rios, across the railway tracks. The palace was built for the Mascarenhas family, who still own it. Jesuit super-missionary St Francis Xavier is supposed to have said mass in the chapel before leaving for India in 1541. Most of the palace was put up in the 1670s, then rebuilt after the 1755 Earthquake. Its Sala das Batalhas is decorated with 17th-century *azulejos* depicting battles against Spain during the War of Restoration (1640-68), while the rest of the halls, courtyards and gardens are full of statuary. You may visit the garden independently but the palace is only accessible with a guided tour. Tours last about an hour; arrive a few minutes early.

Restaurants

★ De Castro Elias

Avenida Elias Garcia 180 (21 797 9214, www. decastroelias.com). Metro São Sebastião or Campo Pequeno. **Open** 12.30-3pm, 7.30-11pm daily. **Main courses** €11.80-€16.30. **Map** p118 D5 ❺ **Portuguese**

Tucked away in the lee of the Gulbenkian, this sleek but informal stablemate of a similarly named restaurant in São Bento (*see p107*) delights in reinventing traditional snacks such as *moelas* (chicken gizzards, sautéed and served in a spicy sauce), *feijão branco* (white beans) cooked with shrimp, or *morcela da Beira* (blood sausage), here seasoned with apple and cinnamon. There's a good range of wines.

Grand'Elias

Avenida Elias Garcia 109 (21 797 5359, www. grandeliasrestaurantebar.com.pt). Metro Campo Pequeno. **Open** noon-4pm, 6pm-midnight daily. **Main courses** €7.80-€13.80. **Map** p118 D5 ❻ **Portuguese**

A specialist in rustic fare from the northern Minho region, Grande Elias has built up its reputation over decades with dishes such as roast *bacalhau* and octopus, grilled *javali* (wild boar), *rojões com castanhas* (pork loin with chestnuts) and tender *rabo de boi* (oxtail). The decor is quaint, to say the least, staff are friendly and the wine cellar is vast.

Oh! Lacerda

Avenida da Berna 36A (21 797 4057, 96 323 1029). Metro Praça de Espanha. **Open** noon-4pm, 7-11pm Mon-Sat. **Main courses** €8.50-€15.50. **Map** p118 C5 ❼ **Portuguese**

The quirky name heralds a quirkier interior, with clay jugs and bunches of garlic hanging from the rafters, and bank-notes plastered on the walls. The space was once a butcher's (before 1946, that is). Steak is one of the house specialities, but try one of the more elaborate fish or meat dishes instead, such as *arroz de cherne* (grouper and rice), *folhado de pato* (duck pasty) or *cabrito assado* (roast kid). It's unreconstructed traditional cuisine, so come hungry.

EXPLORE

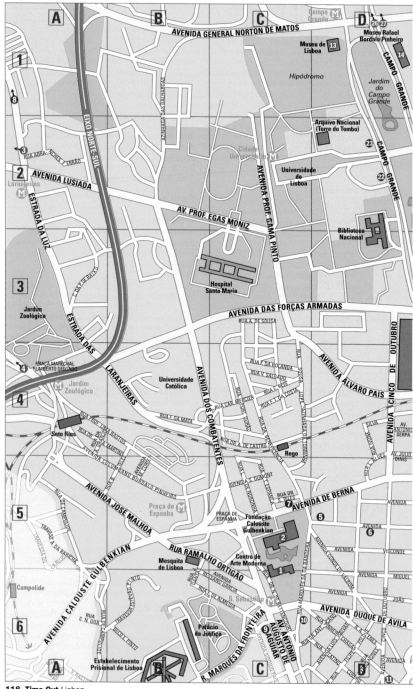

EXPLORE

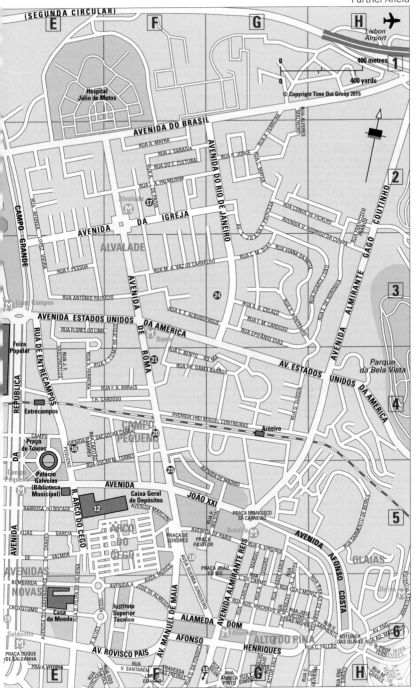

Shops & Services

Centro Colombo
*Avenida Lusíada, Benfica (21 711 3600, www.
colombo.pt). Metro Colégio Militar-Luz.* **Open**
10am-midnight daily. **Map** p118 A1 ❽ **Mall**
This giant mall boasts a wealth of international and
Portuguese chains, lots of fast food (including some
local stalls of reasonable quality), a cinema and a
bowling alley.

★ El Corte Inglés
*Avenida António Augusto de Aguiar 31, Praça
de Espanha (21 371 1700, www.elcorteingles.pt).
Metro São Sebastião.* **Open** 10am-10pm Mon-
Thur; 10am-11.30pm Fri, Sat; 10am-8pm Sun.
Map p118 C6 ❾ **Department store**
This flagship branch of the Spanish chain opened in
2001. In the basement is one of Lisbon's best supermarkets and a separate gourmet deli, plus cinemas
and a varied food court. Across the other 12 floors
are departments from stationery and electronics
through surfwear to home textiles.

★ Miosótis
*Rua Marquês Sá da Bandeira 16A (21 795 9357).
Metro São Sebastião.* **Open** 9am-8pm Mon-Sat.
No credit cards. Map p118 C6 ❿ **Food & drink**
This organic grocery has a wide range of local and
imported fresh produce and prepared dishes, herbal
teas and vitamins, plus hard-to-find ingredients
such as pecans. They also sell seeds for planting.

SALDANHA & AVENIDAS NOVAS

There are bustling office blocks along the new
avenues off Avenida da República and busy
shopping centres with cinema multiplexes around
Praça Duque de Saldanha. Yet bits of an older,
gentler city remain: the **Casa-Museu José
Anastácio Gonçalves** is a monument to
tasteful acquisitiveness; at the beginning of
Avenida da República, **Pastelaria Versailles**
retains its bourgeois appeal; and across the
avenue at no.38 stands an art nouveau gem.

Further up Avenida da República, ringed by
brick-red cupolas, is a neo-Moorish bullring,
the Praça de Touros do Campo Pequeno, built
in 1892. On the south side of the square is the
Palácio Galveias, an elegant former palace that
houses the city's central library, where the then
unknown José Saramago spent countless hours
feeding his passion for literature, many years
before he won fame as a writer and eventually a
Nobel Prize. Its main reading room is now named
after him. The palace's lovely walled garden has
a terrace. Round the corner is Portugal's biggest
building, the headquarters of state savings
bank Caixa Geral de Depósitos, which is home
to **Culturgest** (*see right*), one of the city's
leading arts venues.

Avenida da República continues north to
Entrecampos. At the time of writing, the old
Feira Popular fairground (96 402 5890) here
was operating only from the last weekend in
November to the last weekend in January. Its
seasonal amusements include a giant ferris wheel,
dodgems, trampolines and miniature boats.
There's also a circus. The area is chock-a-block
with stands serving candy floss and *farturas* –
fried doughnuts dipped in sugar and cinnamon.

Beyond the traffic snarl of Entrecampos
roundabout is leafy Campo Grande, home of
the **Biblioteca Nacional** (no.83, 21 798 2000,
www.bnportugal.pt), Portugal's main copyright
library. To consult any publication, bring ID.

Further up Campo Grande as it widens out to
form a proper park are astounding ceramics in
the **Museu Rafael Bordalo Pinheiro** and, at
its northern end, historic exhibits in the **Museu
de Lisboa**. Contemporary art is often on show
in the latter's Pavilhão Branco annexe. Behind
the museum grounds is the Hipódromo do Campo
Grande, home of the **Sociedade Hípica
Portuguesa** (21 781 7410, www.sociedadehipica.
pt), which organises show-jumping competitions
and riding lessons for local kids. On the other side
of Lisbon's main ring road, the Segunda Circular,
is the striking football stadium of **Sporting
Clube de Portugal** (*see p121* **Football Crazy**).

A few blocks east from Campo Grande,
Avenida da Roma cuts through Alvalade, a smart
residential and shopping area. To the north,
again beyond the ring road, is the city's airport.

Sights & Museums

Casa-Museu José Anastácio Gonçalves
*Avenida 5 de Outubro 8 (21 354 0823, www.cmag.
imc-ip.pt). Metro Picoas.* **Open** 10am-6pm Tue-Sun.
Admission €3; €1.50 reductions; free under-13s & all
1st Sun of mth. **No credit cards. Map** p118 D6 ⓫
Originally commissioned by painter José Malhoa,
who had his atelier upstairs, this house was bought by
art enthusiast Dr Gonçalves. He favoured landscapes
and portraits by Mário Augusto, Bordalo Pinheiro
and his chum Silva Porto. Gonçalves also amassed
a collection of Chinese porcelain from the Ming and
Transition periods, as well as 18th- and 19th-century
English, French and Portuguese furniture.

Culturgest
*Edifício Caixa Geral de Depósitos, Rua Arco do
Cego 1 (21 790 5155, www.culturgest.pt). Metro
Campo Pequeno.* **Open** Gallery 11am-7pm Mon,
Wed-Fri; 2-8pm Sat, Sun. Last entry 30mins before
closing. **Admission** €2; €1.20-€1.40 reductions;
free under-17s & all Sun. **Map** p119 E5 ⓬
The programming at this bank-owned foundation is
the most avant-garde of Lisbon's major art institutions. Its auditoria are used to stage everything from
showcases of foreign film to jazz concerts.

★ Museu de Lisboa

Campo Grande 245 (21 751 3200, www.museu dacidade.pt). Metro Campo Grande. **Open** 10am-1pm, 2-6pm Tue-Sun. **Admission** €2; €1 reductions; free under-13s & all Sun 10am-1pm. **No credit cards. Map** p118 D1 ⑱

The 18th-century Pimenta Palace houses this city-run museum charting Lisbon's history. Some displays are skimpy, but they cover the ground as best they can, starting with the Stone Age and working through Roman times to the Visigoths and Moors and into modern times. The highlights, though, are a scale model of Lisbon before the 1755 Earthquake, the fabulous kitchens and the formal garden with its peacocks. One area harbours a display of giant ceramic works by Bordalo Pinheiro. Also in the garden, the modern Pavilhão Branco is an important contemporary art space.

Museu Rafael Bordalo Pinheiro

Campo Grande 382 (21 817 0667, http://museu bordalopinheiro.cm-lisboa.pt). Metro Campo Grande. **Open** 10am-6pm Tue-Sun. **Admission** €1.50; €0.75 reductions. Free to all Sun 10am-2pm. **No credit cards. Map** p118 D1 ⑭

Portuguese architect and artist Rafael Bordalo Pinheiro (1846-1905) had his own ceramics factory in Caldas da Rainha, where he produced fantastic designs. Examples include a pig's head on a platter, lobsters in baskets and frogs sat on plates or climbing vases and poles. He was a prolific caricaturist, using his everyman character Zé Povinho to puncture the pomposity of public figures.

Restaurants

Portugália

Avenida Almirante Reis 117 (21 314 0002, www.portugalia.pt). Metro Arroios. **Open** noon-midnight Mon-Fri, Sun; noon-1am Fri, Sat. **Main courses** €7.40-€18.95. **Map** p119 F6 ⑮ **Beer hall**

This old brewery, originally called Germania (a name hastily changed when Portugal entered World War I on the Allied side), has morphed into a chain.

FOOTBALL CRAZY

From Benfica to Belenenses, Lisboetas love the beautiful game.

Stadium attendances in Portugal lag behind the European average – most people simply can't afford the tickets – but there's no doubt that the locals are football mad. In these difficult times for newspapers, Portugal still has three that are pretty much entirely devoted to the sport. A sure-fire way to start up a conversation in a café or taxi is to ask how things are going for Benfica, a club supported by one-third of the country's population. Its revival in recent years after a long period of dominance by FC Porto has given many Lisboetas a lift.

Both Benfica and its main rival, Sporting, are based in northern Lisbon. The former's Estádio da Luz, an imposing bowl of 65,000 red seats in four tiers, was built in time to host the final of Euro 2004 and has hosted a string of big matches since – most recently the 2014 Champions League Final. Its red arches and half-translucent roof let natural light flood in (although the 'Stadium of Light' moniker actually comes from the neighbourhood, Luz). It's a truly 21st-century complex, with nine panoramic restaurants (21 712 5180, open noon-midnight Mon-Sat, noon-5pm Sun), a health club and a museum – along with a statue of revered 1960s star Eusébio. The pre-match ritual, in which an eagle swoops above the crowd to land on its handler's glove, makes it worth arriving early.

Sporting's renowned training school may have spawned the global phenomenon that is Cristiano Ronaldo, but since winning the league in 2000 and 2002 (after an 18-year drought) the club has mostly been mired in mediocrity. Its ground, built in time for Euro 2004 to a design by Tomás Taveira, was dubbed 'the bathroom' by Benfica fans because of its external tiling. The compact shape adds atmosphere, though.

The most scenically located club is Belenenses. It's one of only two other than the Big Three to have won the Portuguese league, in 1946. No one expects that to happen again soon, but the river views from its Restelo stadium are lovely, so a match can make for a good end to a day's sightseeing in Belém, even if crowd atmosphere is lacking.

The season runs from late August until the May/June final of the Taça de Portugal at the Estádio Nacional in Cruz Quebrada.

TALKING BULL

Fighting over tradition.

To Portuguese aficionados bullfighting is definitely not sport, except in the Shakespearean sense. It may not be your idea of fun (or the bull's) but many locals are passionate about a tradition that, as they point out, goes back at least two millennia. A complex subculture has grown up around it, linked with a rural world that's losing its influence in society and is intertwined with notions of class.

That will surely ring a few bells with Brits – and British campaigners against fox hunting have indeed been among the handful of demonstrators outside Lisbon's 19th-century Praça de Touros at the start of recent bullfighting seasons.

In Portugal, it's illegal to kill the bull in the ring – but it's butchered afterwards. While Portuguese *touradas* might have disappointed Hemingway, they're still bloody affairs. The spectacle starts with a rider in 18th-century costume, mounted on an elegant Lusitano horse, sticking small spears into the bull to irk it. Then the *forcados* take over: half-a-dozen unarmed catchers on foot who wrestle the bull after enticing it to charge. For many, these amateurs are the real heroes (even if the bull's horns are tipped).

The reopening in 2006 of the revamped Campo Pequeno bullring heralded a bullfighting revival. The €50 million overhaul added a shopping centre and Lisbon's largest car park, and the arena now also hosts concerts and other events. The spectacle no longer has the mass appeal it did before the advent of TV, even if there are places where it remains a huge deal, such as the south-bank town of Montijo and, to the north of the capital, Vila Franca de Xira. Here, fighting bulls and Lusitano horses are bred, and the town has a full season of events, ending with an October fair with lashings of music, food and drink, and a Pamplona-style running of the bulls.

Campo Pequeno
21 799 8450, www.campopequenotauro maquia.com. Metro Campo Pequeno. **Open** *Box office* 11am-7pm Mon-Fri; 2-7pm Sat, Sun or until show starts. **Bullfights** *Easter-Sept* 10pm Thur. **Admission** *Bullfights* €15-€75. **No credit cards. Map** p119 E4.

But there's nothing like going to the original beer hall. It's atmospheric and refreshingly simple: pretty much just shellfish, steaks and lots of beer, served up with brusque efficiency. Of the other branches, the best located is the one on the river in Santos. **Other locations** throughout the city.

★ Spazio Buondi – Nobre
Avenida Sacadura Cabral 53B (21 797 0760, www. justanobre.pt). Metro Campo Pequeno. **Open** noon-3pm, 7.30-11pm Tue-Fri, Sun; 7.30-11pm Sat. **Main courses** €15-€35. **Map** p119 E4 ⑯ **Portuguese**
Don't let the name fool you: though it's bankrolled by an Italian coffee company and decorated in a modern style, this is a showcase for the rural cuisine of Justina Nobre, who learned her tricks growing up in rural Trás-os-Montes. Try one of her specialities such as shellfish soup, baked *robalo* (sea bass) or stewed partridge: none of it comes cheap but you won't find better in Lisbon. The range of desserts runs from ultra-light egg *farófias* to a filling chestnut-and-hazelnut tart. On Sundays, locals make a special trip for the *cozido à portuguesa*. During the afternoon, the space remains open as Buondi's flagship café.

Taberna Maria do Correio
Rua Acácio Paiva 5D (21 406 0970). Metro Alvalade. **Open** noon-10pm Mon-Sat. **Snacks** €3.50-€12.50. **Main courses** €6-€14.50. **Map** p119 F2 ⑰ **Portuguese**
This place serves dainty (and cheap) portions of hearty dishes from Trás-os-Montes in north-eastern Portugal: *entremeada de coentrada* (spare ribs in coriander sauce), mushrooms with *chouriço*, potato-and-onion tortilla and the like, plus of course the divine *posta à Mirandesa* (tender beef from Miranda do Douro). There are also unusual toasted sandwiches such as wild mushrooms, *alheira* sausage with vegetables, or cheese with almonds and honey. You can buy products to take away, including hams and cheeses, *botelo* (a giant pork sausage unique to the region), *licor de abrunho* (sloeberry liqueur), honey from Vimioso and flagons of fine olive oil.

Cafés & Bars

Pastelaria Mexicana
Avenida Guerra Junqueiro 30C (21 848 6117). Metro Alameda. **Open** 8am-midnight daily. **Map** p119 F5 ⑱
This large snack bar – with nothing Mexican about it – is handy for a drink or meal after a show at Culturgest (*see p120*) or Teatro Maria Matos (*see p161*), as it serves food right up until closing time. It was opened in 1946 – and is still owned by the same family – but the striking tiled decor dates from 1962. The cakes, pastries and scones are all made on the premises.

Pastelaria Versailles
Avenida da República 15A (21 354 6340). Metro Saldanha. **Open** 7.30am-10pm daily. **Map** p119 E6 ⑲

How many places are there where you can take afternoon tea or a late-night hot chocolate surrounded by chandeliers, carved wooden display cases and stained glass? This 1922 gem has a huge selection of cakes, meringues and pastries. You can have lunch or dinner here too: the desserts are fantastic.

Shops & Services

Aerosoles
Avenida de Roma 27C (21 797 7032, www. aerosoles.pt). **Open** 10am-7pm Mon-Fri; 10am-1pm Sat. **Map** p119 F4 ⑳ **Fashion**
Aerosoles shoes combine comfort and style, with a range of attractive designs. The company is one of the few Portuguese manufacturers to have built a brand abroad. In Lisbon, there are also branches in Amoreiras and Colombo shopping centres, and inside Alameda Metro station.
Other locations throughout the city.

Flores da Romeira Roma
Avenida de Roma 50C (21 848 8289, www. floresromeira.com). Metro Roma. **Open** 8am-9pm Mon-Sat; 9am-8pm Sun. **Map** p119 F4 ㉑ **Florist**
This warehouse of cut flowers and potted plants has built up an unrivalled reputation for service and efficiency over 50 years. Credit cards may be used in the shop; for telephone orders, payment by cash or cheque must be made first.

★ Galeria 111
Campo Grande 113 (21 797 7418, www.galeria 111.pt). Metro Campo Grande. **Open** 10am-7pm Tue-Sat. **No credit cards. Map** p118 D2 ㉒ **Gallery**
This high-profile gallery, founded before the 1974 Revolution, boasts a huge stock of work by the likes of Paula Rego, Alexandre Pomar and António Dacosta. It has a fine collection of prints and drawings, plus a bookshop. There's overspill round the corner at Rua Dr João Soares 5B (21 781 9907).

Horta do Campo Grande
Campo Grande 171 (21 782 6660, www. hortodocampogrande.com). Metro Campo Grande. **Open** 9am-7pm Mon-Sat; 10am-7pm Sun. **Map** p118 D2 ㉓ **Garden centre**
An enormous garden centre that sells all manner of plants, from bonsai trees to 7m (23ft) palms and giant cacti. Flowers can be sent via Interflora.

Parque de Jogos 1º de Maio
Avenida do Rio de Janeiro (21 845 3470, www. inatel.pt). Metro Roma. **Open** 7am-10.45pm Mon-Fri; 7.30am-10.45pm Sat, Sun. Closed Aug. **Court hire** €7.20-€12.30/hr. **No credit cards. Map** p119 G3 ㉔ **Sports centre**
This affordable sports complex has three outdoor hard tennis courts with floodlights. Beware if you're playing late: they lock up at 11pm. For Sunday, you must book and pay at least a day in advance.

Rita Salazar
Avenida de Roma 16E (21 848 6799, http://anaby herself.com). Metro Areeiro. **Open** 10am-7pm Mon-Sat. **Map** p119 F5 ㉕ **Fashion & accessories**
One of the few places where fashion-lovers can find items by Ana Salazar, one of Portugal's most admired and experienced designers.

LUMIAR

North of Campo Grande, Avenida Padre Cruz winds past Telheiras – where the results of a decade-long building boom are much in evidence – towards Lumiar. Once a sleepy village, it's now a dreary suburb choked with traffic that hasn't been much eased by the recent arrival of the Metro. The **Museu Nacional do Traje** and **Museu Nacional do Teatro** are housed in wings of an 18th-century former palace that overlooks the Parque Monteiro-Mor (€3; €1.50 reductions), a reminder of more bucolic times. The park now has glades dotted with sculptures.

Sights & Museums

Museu Nacional do Teatro
Estrada do Lumiar 10 (21 756 7418, www.museu doteatro.pt). Metro Lumiar. **Open** 10am-6pm Tue-Sun. **Admission** €4; €2 reductions; free under-13s & all 1st Sun of mth. Combined ticket with Museu do Traje & park €6; €3 reductions. **Map** p118 D1 ㉖
Opened in 1985, this theatre museum has more than 300,000 items, including costumes, stage designs, manuscripts and many photographs. The café has a shaded terrace overlooking the overgrown garden.

Museu Nacional do Traje
Largo Júlio Castilho 2, Estrada do Lumiar (21 756 7620, www.museudotraje.pt). Metro Lumiar. **Open** 2-6pm Tue; 10am-6pm Wed-Sun. **Admission** €4; €2 reductions; free under-13s & all 1st Sun of mth. Combined ticket with Museu do Teatro & park €6; €3 reductions. **No credit cards. Map** p118 D1 ㉗
Despite the limited display, the Costume Museum is worth a visit just to see the prettier parts of the former Palácio de Angela-Palmela. Walls are decorated with garlands and musical instruments in pastel colours, and most of the original wall tiles remain. Round the back, in a neo-Gothic pavilion, a fancy restaurant serves lunch only (96 404 1232).

Eastern Lisbon

SANTA APOLÓNIA & MADRE DE DEUS

Santa Apolónia railway station at the foot of Alfama is the terminus for lines going to Oporto, Madrid, Paris and beyond. Long the city's main station, it has lost some of that status to the

EXPLORE

monumental new Gare do Oriente station up the line near Parque das Nações, although it is now finally on the Metro network.

Santa Apolónia was built in the 1860s on the Cais dos Soldados – 'Quay of the Soldiers' – from where troops departed on their way to colonial campaigns in Africa and India, Timor and Macao. Fittingly, the **Museu Militar** is opposite the station. In the 19th century, there was no road to the right of the station; ships would tie up next to the tracks. Nowadays the warehouses that sprang up on landfill across the way have been cleared.

A new cruise ship terminal has been installed – and is being expanded – along with a string of trendy shops, restaurants and clubs, including **Lux** (see p149) and the **Jardim do Tabaco** complex a little nearer to Praça do Comércio. Behind Santa Apolónia station, the **Clube Ferroviário** (see p147) has a rooftop terrace bar that's great for summer nights.

Other old industrial and monumental spaces in eastern Lisbon have been turned over to new uses, such as the award-winning **Museu da Água** in an old pumping station on Rua do Alviela, and the **Museu Nacional do Azulejo**, which took up residence in 1980 in one of the city's most important Manueline landmarks, the 16th-century **Convento da Madre de Deus**. This once stood on the waterfront but is now separated from the river by a bewildering assortment of streets, overpasses, railways and cranes. Upriver, the **Convento do Beato** was built in the 16th century. In the mid 19th century it was annexed to the Nacional biscuit factory, but has now been restored and is occasionally used for special events. Old warehouses and even former churches in the area are also used for theatre and music performances.

Museu da Água

Rua do Alviela 12 (21 810 0263, www.epal.pt). Metro Santa Apolónia or bus 794. **Open** 10am-5.30pm Tue-Sat. **Admission** €5; €2.50 reductions; free under-13s. **No credit cards. Map** p125 C2 ㉘
Like Belém's Museu da Electricidade (see p102), the Water Museum and its contents are important parts of Portugal's industrial archaeology and still run by a utility firm – in this case, state water company EPAL. Housed in the first main pumping station to serve Lisbon, the museum is dominated by four huge steam engines from the 1880s, formerly used as pumps. One is set in motion every month or so. The rest of the displays trace the history of Lisbon's water supply from Roman times to the present.

Museu Militar

Largo do Museu do Artilharia (21 884 2361, www.exercito.pt). Metro Santa Apolónia. **Open** 10am-5pm Tue-Fri; 10am-12.30pm, 1.45-5pm Sat, Sun. **Admission** €3; €1.50 reductions; free under-7s. **No credit cards. Map** p125 A3 ㉙

A former 17th-century weapons factory provides an appropriate setting for the Military Museum. The tour begins upstairs, with two rooms devoted to the Napoleonic invasions, and a display on World War I (the Portuguese suffered heavy losses in the 1918 Battle of Le Lys, known to the British as Estaires). A series of rooms with elaborately carved and gilded decoration leads to a comprehensive display of Portuguese arms up to the 20th century. Downstairs you'll find a plethora of cannons and a mind-boggling variety of weaponry captured from adversaries during the colonial wars of the 1960s and '70s. Labels are in Portuguese, but there's a leaflet in English.

★ Museu Nacional do Azulejo

Rua da Madre de Deus 4 (21 810 0340, www.museudoazulejo.pt). Bus 718, 742, 794. **Open** 10am-6pm Tue-Sun. Last entry 5.30pm daily. **Admission** €5; €2.50 reductions; free under-13s & all 1st Sun of mth. **No credit cards. Map** p125 D1 ㉚
The Tile Museum, housed in a former convent, charts the development of the art of Portuguese *azulejos* since the 15th century, including a panel depicting Lisbon before the 1755 Earthquake and some striking contemporary tiles. The building is a treat, with a tiny Manueline cloister and a barrel-vaulted church. The shop sells superior tiles, and there's a lovely café.

Restaurants

★ Bica do Sapato

Avenida Infante D Henrique, Armazém B (21 881 0320, 91 761 5065, www.bicadosapato.com). Metro Santa Apolónia. **Open** *Restaurant* 5pm-1am Mon; noon-1am Tue-Sat (mid Sept-June 12.30-4pm Sun brunch). *Sushi bar* 7.30pm-1am Mon-Sat. **Main courses** €12.50-€28.50. **Map** p125 B3 ㉛
Portuguese/International
This large dockside space, dotted with designer furniture, features a main restaurant, a large terrace on the river, and an excellent sushi bar upstairs. Its kitchen is now run by one of Portugal's most admired chefs, Alexandre Silva. The menu might offer the likes of poached John Dory with a lentil and fennel stew or Alentejo *presas* (pork shoulder) with a dried fig stuffing. There are always vegetarian options and lovely light desserts. There's also a great Sunday brunch outside high summer.

Cais da Pedra

Avenida Infante D Henrique, Armazém B, Loja 9 (21 887 1651, www.caisdapedra.pt). Metro Santa Apolónia. **Open** noon-midnight Mon-Wed; noon-2am Thur, Fri; 10am-2am Sat; 10am-midnight Sun. **Main courses** €9-€20. **Map** p125 B3 ❸❷ **Burgers**

This may be 'just' a burger bar, but its menu and setting in a cavernous former warehouse with a terrace right on the river ensure that it stands out from the crowd. It serves a wide range of burgers in various types of warmed buns, including *alfarroba* (carob), as well as tasty freshly cooked snacks. The drinks range from unusual herbal teas to great cocktails and there are interesting desserts. Cais da Pedra is overseen by inventive chef Henrique Sá Pessoa.

Casa do Bacalhau

Rua do Grilo 54 (21 862 0000, www.acasado bacalhau.com). Bus 718. **Open** noon-3pm, 7.30-11pm Mon-Sat; noon-3pm Sun. **Main courses** €14-€18. **Map** p125 D1 ❸❸ **Portuguese**

Although there are other fish and meat dishes at the 'House of Bacalhau' – and even some vegetarian fare – the focus here is cod. The range of *bacalhau* dishes is unrivalled: from accessible standards to rarer treats such as *feijoada de sames*. There's a good wine cellar too.

Casanova

Avenida Infante D Henrique, Armazém B, Loja 7 (21 887 7532, www.restaurantecasa nostra.com). Metro Santa Apolónia. **Open** 12.30pm-1.30am daily. **Main courses** €7.50-€15.50 **Map** p125 B3 ❸❹ **Italian**

This offshoot of Casanostra (*see p82*) turns out magnificent pizzas from its huge wood-fired oven. They're all great, from a simple napoletana to the Casanova, laden with cherry tomatoes, rocket and mozzarella di bufala. You can't book, but tables are shared and turnover is fast – diners catch waiters' attention by switching on a red bulb dangling above their table – even on the riverside terrace.

D'Avis

Rua do Grilo 96 (21 868 1354, 96 884 8961, www.davis.com.pt). Bus 718, 742, 759. **Open** noon-3.30pm, 7.30-10.30pm Mon-Sat. **Main courses** €8.80-€14. **Map** p125 D1 ❸❺ **Portuguese**

This rustic tavern attracts a steady stream of fans for its authentic Alentejo regional specialities. These usually include *ensopada de borrego* (lamb stew), *caldeta de cação com poejo* (dogfish soup), *pezinhos de porco de coentrada* (pork trotters with coriander), a slew of dishes involving *migas* (fried breadcrumbs – tastier than they sound and seasoned in many different ways) and lots of *bacalhau*.

EXPLORE

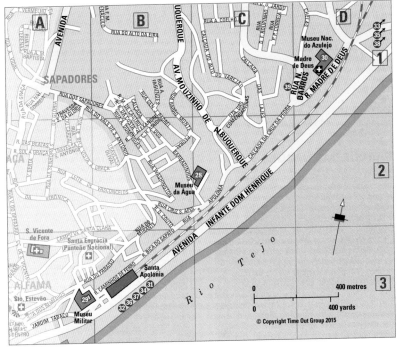

Shops & Services

Deli Delux
*Avenida Infante D Henrique, Armazém B, Loja 8,
(21 886 2070, www.delidelux.pt). Metro Santa
Apolónia.* **Open** *Winter* noon-10pm Mon-Fri;
10am-10pm Sat, Sun. *Summer* noon-midnight
Mon-Fri; 10am-midnight Sat, Sun. **Map** p125 B3
③ **Food & drink**
'O Deli', as devotees call it, caters largely to diplomats
and the local bourgeoisie, who come here to snuffle
for truffles and similarly pricey fare, from fine wines,
hams and cheeses to dried mushrooms and cran-
berry sauce. The café has a healthy gourmet menu.

★ Flur
*Avenida Infante D Henrique, Armazém B, Loja 4
(21 882 1101, www.flur.pt). Metro Santa Apolónia.*
Open 1-8pm Mon-Sat. **Map** p125 B3 ③ **Music**
A magnet for DJs and fans of independent music,
Flur is also one of the best places in town to pick up
flyers for parties and gigs.

Galeria Filomena Soares
*Rua da Manutenção 80 (21 862 4122, www.
gfilomenasoares.com). Metro Santa Apolónia.*
Open 10am-8pm Tue-Sat. Closed Aug. **Map**
p125 D1 ③ **Gallery**
Soares is one of Europe's most influential female art
dealers, representing a roster of local heavyweights
such as Ângela Ferreira and José Pedro Croft, plus
global stars such as Shirin Neshat and Tracey Moffatt.

Kunsthalle Lissabon
*Rua Nelson de Barros 9 (91 204 5650, www.
kunsthalle-lissabon.org). Metro Santa Apolónia.*
Open 3-7pm Thur-Sat. **Map** p125 C1 ③ **Gallery**
The name wrily contrasts this basement gallery's
modest size with Germany's grand 'art halls', but is
also a statement of intent: the Portuguese duo who
run it aim to stoke debate about contemporary art as
well as display it.

PARQUE DAS NAÇÕES

In 1990, the area around Cabo Ruivo was a
wasteland of near-derelict warehouses, the
municipal abattoir, a munitions factory, an oil
refinery and dozens of oil tanks. But it hadn't
always been so. In the area's heyday, the
Companhia dos Diamantes on Avenida Marechal
Gomes da Costa (now the headquarters of state
broadcaster RTP) had overseen Africa's diamond
trade, and Pan-American Clipper seaplanes
docked on the Olivais quay, where the ultra-
modern **Oceanário** (*see right*) now stands.

By the mid 1990s, a site measuring 330 hectares
had been levelled as armies of bulldozers and
workers wrought the transformation that readied
the area for the opening of Expo 98 on 22 May
1998. The four-month World's Fair was timed

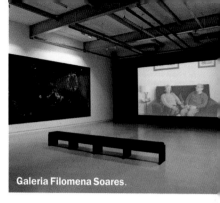

Galeria Filomena Soares.

to coincide with the 500th anniversary of the
discovery of the sea route to India, with oceans as
its theme. It introduced Lisboetas to a different
city that looked east over the Mar de Palha.
A new Metro line was built, with expensive and
impressive artistic imput (*see p202* **Wall-to-
Wall Art**), to shuttle visitors to and from the site.

Expo closed its doors on 30 September 1998,
reopening as an urban district dubbed Parque das
Nações, and the development of hotels, offices
and residential complexes has continued ever
since. The centrepiece is the Oceanário, one of
the world's largest aquariums. Nearby, the cable
cars of Telecabine Lisbon dangle above the
riverside walkway as they travel towards **Torre
Vasco da Gama**, Lisbon's tallest structure.
On the other side of the dock, the **Pavilhão
de Portugal**, designed by Álvaro Siza Vieira,
hosts occasional exhibitions but lacks a
permanent vocation.

The futuristic beetle-shaped building next
door is the Pavilhão Atlântico (now officially
known as the **MEO Arena**, *see p152*). It has
hosted everything from rock concerts to ice
spectaculars. South of the Oceanário, the
Pavilhão do Conhecimento (*see p132*)
continues to delight children and their parents
with hands-on science exhibits. By the river, the
Teatro Camões (*see p160*) is home to the
Companhia Nacional de Bailado.

The **Ponte Vasco da Gama**, completed in
1998, was briefly Europe's longest bridge. The
project was dogged by controversy.

★ Oceanário
*Esplanada Dom Carlos I (21 891 7002, www.
oceanario.pt). Metro Oriente.* **Open** *Summer*
10am-8pm daily (last entry 7pm). *Winter* 10am-
7pm daily (last entry 6pm). **Admission** €14;
€9 reductions; free under-4s. **Map** p127 D3 ④
Europe's largest aquarium, Oceanário has a vast
central tank plus four smaller ones representing the
Antarctic, Indian, Pacific and Atlantic Oceans, each
topped by a room representing the respective coastal
habitat. There are observation decks on two levels,
while mini-aquariums showcase exotic species.

EXPLORE

Restaurants

La Rúcula
Rossio dos Olivais (21 892 2747, www.larucula.com.pt). Metro Oriente. **Open** noon-1am Mon-Sat; noon-3pm Sun. **Main courses** €9-€16. **Map** p127 D2 ⓪ Italian
This airy space with lovely river views is a pleasant choice for lunch in an area short of well-priced dining options. Offerings include tasty carpaccio and decent pizzas cooked in a wood-fired oven.

★ Senhor Peixe
Rua da Pimenta (21 895 5892). Metro Oriente. **Open** noon-3.30pm, 7-10.30pm Tue-Sat; noon-3.30pm Sun. **Main courses** €13-€40. **Map** p127 D2 ⓪ Seafood
At 'Mr Fish', a sign in Portuguese boasts that this is 'Setúbal in Lisbon': their man is in the dockside market each morning to snap up the day's catch when it comes in. There are 15 or so kinds of fish on offer, most served charcoal-grilled, plus various pasta and rice dishes. The house speciality is a lavish *caldeirada* (fish stew) for two, good value at €29.

Shops & Services

Centro Vasco da Gama
Avenida Dom João II (21 893 0600, www.centrovascodagama.pt). Metro Oriente. **Open** 9am-midnight daily. **Map** p127 D2 ⓪ Mall
Stores at this compact, three-floor mall are clustered by genre. There's also a hypermarket and a small multiplex. When you're done, go up to the beer deck and gaze out at the Tagus.

South of the River

CACILHAS & ALMADA

The ferries that criss-cross the Tagus are the equivalent of commuter trains in other cities and are packed at rush hours. The busiest terminal on the south bank is Cacilhas, ten minutes by boat from Cais do Sodré. There's a cluster of seafood restaurants that are full of families at weekends wielding plastic hammers over lobsters and crabs. Cacilhas is the gateway to Almada, a burgeoning metropolis whose cultural life includes Portugal's biggest annual theatre event, the **Festival Internacional de Teatro** (*see p32*); in summer, Lisboetas pack on to buses at Cacilhas, headed for the **Costa da Caparica** beaches (*see p170*).

Further west, on the Cais do Ginjal, are a dirty river beach and the terrace of brilliant seafood restaurant **Atira-te ao Rio** (www.atirateaorio.pt). On the cliff at the end is Almada's cute old town: the Boca do Vento elevator whisks you up to the *miradouro* behind the Câmara Municipal (City Hall) for great views – and a bar and restaurant

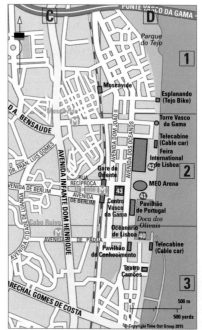

named after the elevator (21 082 0554, open 10.30am-1am daily). There are often free art exhibitions at the nearby **Casa da Cerca** (Rua da Cerca 2, 21 272 4950, open 10am-6pm Tue-Fri, 1-6pm Sat & Sun), a Baroque palace in lovely gardens. West again is the **Cristo Rei** statue.

Sights & Museums

Santuário do Cristo Rei
Almada (21 275 1000, www.cristorei.pt). Ferry to Cacilhas from Cais do Sodré then bus 101. **Open** *Winter* 9.30am-6.15pm daily. *Summer* 9.30am-6.30pm Mon-Fri; 9.30am-7pm Sat, Sun (last entry 15mins before closing). **Admission** €4; €2 reductions; free under-8s. **No credit cards**.
This stiff echo of Rio's statue of Christ the Redeemer, inaugurated in 1959, gazes across at the city from a hill on the south bank. It's worth the trip to take the lift up 75 metres to the observation deck at the 28-metre statue's feet. The ground-floor chapel, remodelled in 2006, is a site of pilgrimage.

ALCOCHETE

Visitors crossing the Ponte Vasco da Gama pass over a large area of old salt pans near Alcochete. This is the start of the **Reserva Natural do Estuário do Tejo** (21 234 8021, www.icnf.pt), a birdwatchers' paradise.

Arts & Entertainment

Children

The Portuguese have always been child-friendly, without that necessarily being translated into organised fun. Nowadays, though, there are more than enough activities to keep families occupied. KidZania and Oceanário are potential highlights of a family visit, the latter one of a cluster of attractions in the Parque das Nações. Getting around town is pretty easy: the inconvenience of Lisbon's hills is offset by affordable public transport and taxis. If the weather is too hot or too lousy, the city's largest mall has bowling and amusement arcades as well as a multiscreen cinema. And if the city itself gets a bit too much, head for one of the many beaches (see pp166-173), which are free and a whole lot more fun than a dusty museum.

ARTS & ENTERTAINMENT

WHAT'S ON WHEN

For event listings, peruse the 'Miúdos' section at www.lazer.publico.pt. Note that in Portugal, to be sure of catching the original version of English-language animated films, you need to look out for the 'VO' tag; most screenings are 'VP', meaning the dubbed Portuguese version. Also worth a look is the city council's *Agenda Cultural*, a Portuguese-only monthly booklet available at most tourist sites and trendier cafés and bars. The regional tourist board site (www.visitlisboa.com) has plenty of suggestions too.

For shows, agency website www.ticketline.sapo.pt has a children's section ('Infantil/Juvenil'). The **Centro Cultural de Belém** (*see p157*) often features performances aimed at children. Both it and the **Gulbenkian** (*see p159*) have educational departments that are active all year round, and the **Museu da Marioneta** (*see p95*) stages shows and workshops for various ages, including mask-making and shadow puppetry. Activities for kids are run by the **Museu do Oriente** (*see p97*), while **Chapitô** (*see p162*) has courses covering everything from cookery to circus arts.

During June's **Festas dos Santos Populares** (*see p32*), there's a plethora of events for kids around town. In the summer holidays, the **Museu do Traje** (*see p123*) has courses for six- to 12-year-olds on theatrical expression, yoga and hip hop, and on gardening in the magical Parque Monteiro-Mor, while **Ciência Viva** (808 200 205, www.cienciaviva.pt) organises free science-related activities in August and September, from peering through telescopes to visiting hydroelectric dams.

EATING OUT

Generally speaking, you'll have nothing to worry about at dinner time as children are welcome and restaurants usually try to cater for everyone's needs. If you eat on an esplanade, such as those overlooking the park in Belém, the kids can run off their meals while you digest yours. Be sensible, not nervous: Lisbon doesn't have a history of children disappearing from the streets and locals confidently let theirs run amok.

Among eateries with indoor play areas are **Noobai** (*see p89*) in the Bica neighbourhood and **Pão de Canela** (*see p110*) in São Bento.

GETTING AROUND

Negotiating Lisbon's hills can be pretty exhausting. Streets are invariably cobbled and often steep, so pushing a pram isn't easy and little legs soon get tired. However, the public transport system is efficient, reliable, well priced and accessible if walking isn't your thing.

Where the terrain is relatively flat, cycle hire is now more widely available (for a list of companies, see p225).

Buses, metros and trams are free for under-fives, then full fare. Trains are free for under-fives, half-price for under-12s, then full fare. If your child looks old for their age, it's best to carry a form of ID. Taxis are plentiful. Seatbelts aren't obligatory in the back but are recommended, particularly as taxi drivers have a tendency to speak over their shoulder while driving.

One of the best ways to see Lisbon's sights – and tackle the rather daunting topography – is the 85-minute **Hills Tramcar Tour**, a comfortable journey across the city's seven hills on a refurbished tram, with a useful English commentary. Though not cheap, it's reasonable value compared with the open-top double-deckers, and there's also a 40-minute **Castle Tramcar Tour**. (If you buy your tour voucher at the airport, you can take the Aerobus shuttle into town for free; the tours also give free travel on ordinary trams and buses for the rest of the day.) There's also a two-hour Tagus boat trip, which offers panoramic views and a refreshing breeze; the commuter ferry is a budget alternative. If you want to combine the two, book a seat on the amphibious HIPPOtrip.

Tours

Cruzeiros no Tejo

21 042 2417, 919 593 761, www.transtejo.pt. **Lisbon seen from the river** *Apr-Oct* 3pm daily. **Discoveries circuit** *Apr-Oct* Terreiro do Paço 11.15am daily; Cais do Sodré 11.30am, 4.15pm daily. Closed Nov-Mar. **Tickets** *Lisbon seen from the river* €20; €10-€15 reductions; free under-6s. *Discoveries circuit* €15; €7.50-€10 reductions; free under-6s. **No credit cards**.

The Transtejo ferry company offers two guided trips with English commentary. 'Lisbon seen from the river' starts and ends at Terreiro do Paço and takes in everything from Parque das Nações to Belém (2hrs 30mins). By contrast, the Discoveries route (1hr 30mins), departing from Terreiro do Paço with a stop at Cais do Sodré, focuses on the city centre and Belém; the afternoon tour from Cais do Sodré is a shorter (1hr) version of this. Water and soft drinks are included in all tours.

HIPPOtrip

21 192 2030, www.hippotrip.com. **Departures** every 2hrs 9am-7pm. **Tickets** €25; €15 reductions. This chunky yellow amphibious vehicle tours the city centre and Belém, where it plunges into the river to give you a different perspective of Lisbon and its history. It's the splashy transition that kids love, of course. In all, it's a 1hr 30min trip, starting from the Associação Naval de Lisboa at the Doca de Santo Amaro in Alcântara.

Tramcar Tours

21 347 8030, 96 629 8558, www.carris.pt. **Hills Tramcar Tour** *Oct-May* every 30mins 9.30am-5.30pm daily. *June-Sept* every 20mins 9.20am-6.20pm daily. **Castle Tramcar Tour** every 40mins 10.30am-4.30pm daily. **Tickets** *Hills Tramcar Tour* €18; €9 4-10s; free under-4s. *Castle Tramcar Tour* €9; €4.50 4-10s; free under-4s. **No credit cards**.

The distinctive red tram sets off from Praça do Comércio for a 1hr 25min tour round Lisbon's hilly centre. It's fun, but definitely on the expensive side for a large family. The green tram does a cheaper 40min run past the castle and up to Graça. Both avoid the queuing and crowding of the city's standard yellow trams.

Yellow Bus

21 347 8030, 96 629 8558, www.carris.pt. **Tagus Tour** *Oct-May* every 20mins 9am-5.30pm daily; *June-Sept* every 15mins 9am-7pm, then 7.30pm & 8pm, daily. **Olisipo Tour** *Oct-May* every 30mins 9.15am-5.45pm daily; *June-Sept* every 30mins 9.15am-7.15pm daily. **Tickets** €15; €7.50 4-10s; free under-4s. **No credit cards**.

Open-top hop-on/hop-off double-decker buses, with English commentary, set off from Praça da Figueira on two different Lisbon circuits. The 1hr 40min Tagus Tour takes in the centre, the shopping hubs of El Corte Inglés and Amoreiras, Estrela, Belém, the docks, and the Museu de Oriente and Museu Nacional de Arte Antiga; the 1hr 45min Olisipo Tour trundles past Alfama and on to the Museu do Azulejo out to Parque das Nações, before looping back via the Museu da Cidade, the bullring and the parliament building. In Belém itself, Carris also runs a hop-on hop-off minibus, setting off at least once an hour from 10am or earlier (with a break for lunch). There are various combination tickets, including a bus tour and river cruise for €29 (€14.50 for 4-12s). Yellow Bus is an offshoot of city transport operator Carris; it has several highly visible private rivals.

SIGHTS & MUSEUMS

Head up to the **Castelo de São Jorge** (see p64) for a memorable experience, with cannons on the ramparts and a bird's-eye view of the city. Those

---

IN THE KNOW FAMILY TRIP

If you're a fan of hop-on/hop-off tours, consider a 3-in-1 Yellow Bus ticket, which gives you 48 hours to do both the main circuits and make use of the Belém minibus. It's good value at €19 per adult plus up to two under-12s. Alternatively, with the €25 'premium' 4-in-1 ticket, you get the Hills Tramcar Tour thrown in too.

who don't fancy the climb can take tram 12 or 28 part of the way up or bus 737 to the Castelo neighbourhood's outer gate. There are more amazing views to be had from the roofs of the **Igreja de São Vicente** and **Panteão de Santa Engrácia** (for both, *see p67*). To the west, the **Torre de Belém** (*see p103*) riverbank has plenty of green for kids to run around. Across the road, the **Mosteiro dos Jerónimos** (*see p100*) has an enchanting medieval feel, particularly the cloisters. Out of town, Sintra, Estoril and Cascais are great for kids tired of the city (*see pp166-181*), including the magical ruins of a Moorish castle and mystery at the Quinta da Regaleira.

As well as the children's champions listed below, other local institutions that might be of interest are the public transport museum, **Museu da Carris** (*see p97*), where kids can clamber on to old buses and trams; and the shipshape **Museu da Marinha** (*see p102*).

Jardim Zoológico de Lisboa

Estrada de Benfica 158-60, Sete Rios (21 723 2910, www.zoolisboa.pt). Metro Jardim Zoológico. **Open** *mid Mar-mid Sept* 10am-8pm daily (last entry 6.45pm). *Mid Sept-mid Mar* 10am-6pm daily (last entry 5.15pm). **Admission** €18.50; €13-€14.50 reductions; free under-3s. **No credit cards. Map** p248 J3.

Lisbon's zoo strikes an excellent balance between fun and conservation, so that everyone is sure to get something out of a visit. Home to some 2,000 creatures of more than 300 different species, from every continent, it also has a botanical garden, pleasant cafés and an amusement park. A miniature train takes the strain on hot days. Check the website for feeding times and shows, which vary by season.

★ KidZania

Dolce Vita Tejo loja 1054, Avenida Cruzeiro Seixas 7, Amadora (21 154 5530, www.kidzania. pt). Metro Pontinha then Rodoviária de Lisboa bus 231 (10mins). **Open** 10am-6pm Wed-Fri; 11am-8pm Sat, Sun. **Admission** €10-€19.50; free under-3s.

It is out in the suburbs and not cheap, but KidZania is a humdinger of an attraction. A city within a city where kids can play at being adults, it has 6,500sq m of avenues and apartments, shops and factories, buses and ambulances. On arrival, kids are fitted with an electronic tag: over-eights may then roam free – perhaps starting with the minibus tour (there's an English audio-guide) and then driving a car, wearing a police uniform, performing 'surgery', making a TV show or flipping a burger (note that brands feature prominently here). Their guardians are free to go off and shop in the mall in which KidZania is located. But if your children are younger – or you want to see how your offspring's career as a fire-fighter, artist, dentist, baker, teacher, model, footballer or carpenter

is going – then join in with their activities, or just relax in the in-house café. (Adults are tagged, too, so you can always be found.) Children of all ages are welcome at KidZania, but four- to 12-year-olds will get the most out of it; there's a nursery and play area for the youngest. For weekends, when the place packs out, you must book ahead via www.ticketline. pt or in Lisbon at El Corte Inglés (*see p120*), Fnac (*see p78*) or any Abreu travel agency.

★ Oceanário

Esplanada Dom Carlos I, Parque das Nações (21 891 7002, www.oceanario.pt). Metro Oriente. **Open** *Summer* 10am-8pm daily (last entry 7pm). *Winter* 10am-7pm daily (last entry 6pm). **Admission** €14; €9 reductions; free under-4s; €36 family ticket.

The Oceanarium, situated at the former Expo site, is one of Europe's largest aquariums, with 8,000 fish, birds and mammals in rooms and tanks that represent the earth's different oceans. The core exhibit is the huge Atlantic tank, containing sharks and rays, but children are just as likely to appreciate the penguins, otters and jellyfish that live elsewhere in the aquarium. It's a terrific day out – or night if you book the popular 'Sleeping with the Sharks' package (€65 child, €60 adult) for your six- to 12-year-old. There are also concerts for under-fours at 9am on Saturdays (€25, with two adults, Oceanarium visit included).

★ Pavilhão do Conhecimento

Alameda dos Oceanos, Parque das Nações (21 891 7100, www.pavconhecimento.pt). Metro Oriente. **Open** 10am-6pm Tue-Fri; 11am-7pm Sat, Sun. **Admission** €8; €3-€5 reductions; free under-3s; €17 family ticket.

The Pavilion of Knowledge, an interactive science and technology centre, also located at the former Expo 98 site, has changing interactive exhibitions that make for an excellent mix of fun and learning for visitors of all ages. The hands-on displays are sure to pique kids' curiosity, with experiences that help to explain the reasons behind natural phenomena. Examples include the chance to start your own tornado or blow a giant soap bubble.

Planetário Calouste Gulbenkian

Praça do Império, Belém (21 362 0002, http:// planetario.online.pt). Train from Cais do Sodré to Belém or tram 15. **Open** times vary; check website for details. **Admission** €5; €2.50 reductions; free to all 1st Sun of mth. **No credit cards. Map** p244 B9.

The 330-seater planetarium is a real buzz for children. Many of the sessions are aimed at Portuguese school groups; the times and themes for the public sessions change periodically, so check the website for details. Various family tickets are available. The Museu da Marinha next door appeals to nautically minded youngsters.

OPEN SPACES

Parque Eduardo VII
Metro Marquês de Pombal or Parque. **Open** 24hrs daily. **Admission** free. **Map** p246 K6.
This park has plenty of greenery, a small playground with structures to clamber on, and greenhouses to explore (*see p56*). Two esplanades offer fine views of Lisbon; the one at the top, the Linha d'Água, overlooks a shallow pool that is as irresistible to dogs as it is – unfortunately – to toddlers.

Parque Florestal de Monsanto
Espaço Monsanto (information centre), Estrada do Barcal, Monte das Perdizes (21 817 0200/1, www. cm-lisboa.pt/monsanto). **Open** *Espaço Monsanto* Apr-Sept 9.30am-5pm Mon-Fri; 9.30am-6pm Sat; 2-6pm Sun. Oct-Mar 9.30am-5pm Mon-Sat; 2-5pm Sun. *Playgrounds* Oct-Mar 9am-6pm daily; Apr-Sept 9am-8pm daily. **Admission** free.
Lisbon's green lung, Monsanto Forest Park, was long dismissed by locals as the haunt of drug dealers and prostitutes, but it has gained huge popularity thanks to substantial municipal investment and regular open-air events. Its 306km (190 miles) of hiking and bike trails now link up with central Lisbon, and it has several playgrounds. The largest and busiest is the hilltop Parque Recreativo do Alto da Serafina, near where the Aqueduto das Águas Livres (*see p112*) enters Monsanto. It has a leafy picnic area, driving circuit for children, climbing wall, boating lake and restaurant – as well as marvellous views; you can reach it by taking bus 770 from Jardim Zoológico metro station. On the eastern side of the forest, the Parque Infantil de Alvito offers three safe play areas for different ages; it's served by bus 774 (running between Calçada da Tapada in Alcântara and Benfica rail station). To the south-west, the Parque Recreativo dos Moinhos de Santana has lawns, a lake and waterfall, a play area and two old windmills. For ecological exhibitions and information, visit the Espaço Monsanto, near the Mata de São Domingos adventure park.

Parque da Quinta das Conchas
Alameda das Linhas das Torres, Lumiar. Metro Quinta das Conchas. **Open** 6am-1am daily. **Admission** free.
This park in northern Lisbon has ample lawns, a playground and – the big attraction – six large slides embedded in a slope, plus two esplanades (open until at least 8pm) for weary parents.

SPORTS

With almost twice the number of sunshine hours of London, the Portuguese capital is a great place for outdoor sports such as tennis. Meanwhile, the vast Tagus estuary (not to mention the Atlantic) affords opportunities to get out on the water, through sailing clubs such as the

Associação Naval de Lisboa (www.anl.pt) and neighbouring Clube Naval de Lisboa.
In town, you can go bowling in the city's largest shopping centre. Or football-mad youngsters will enjoy a night out at Benfica's vast stadium (*see p121* **Football Crazy**).

Bowling City
Centro Colombo, Avenida Lusíada, Piso 2, Loja A 204 (21 716 2382, www.bowling-city.pt). Metro Colégio Militar/Luz. **Open** noon-midnight Mon-Thur; noon-1am Fri; 11am-1am Sat; 11am-midnight Sun (from 11am daily in school hols).
This brash, colourful entertainment hub is set over two floors. On the lower floor are the games machines, some of which take up to six players – children and adults – and a '5D' theatre that screens five- to ten-minute 'interactive' movies designed to appeal to all your senses. A separate gaming arcade is for over-15s only. Upstairs is the bowling alley, with 12 lanes.

Centro de Ténis de Monsanto
Estrada do Alvito (21 364 8741). Bus 724. **Open** 8.30am-9pm Mon-Fri; 8.30am-8.30pm Sat, Sun. **Court hire** *Hard surface* €7.50/hr; *day* €8.50/hr; *covered* €12.50/hr. *Floodlights* €4/hr. **No credit cards**.
In a lovely setting surrounded by eucalyptus and other sweet-smelling trees, this reasonably priced municipal tennis centre has a range of courts on offer. Non-members can't book ahead (you can call an hour before you arrive to find out how busy it is), but during the week you should be able to just roll up. Overlooking the courts are a café and excellent restaurant serving rustic Portuguese food.

Lisboa Racket Centre
Rua Alferes Malheiro, Alvalade (21 846 0232, www.lrc.pt). Metro Alvalade then 10min walk or bus 744. **Open** 8am-11.30pm Mon-Fri; 9am-8pm Sat, Sun. **Court hire** *Tennis* €5-€10/hr per person. *Floodlights* €4/hr. *Squash* €14-€18/hr. **Map** p249 O1.
On the edge of a leafy park, this friendly club is the best in-town option for racket sports, with nine tennis courts (seven of them floodlit), paddle tennis and squash. It also has a gym, sauna and paddling pool, and a cafeteria with esplanade.

Parque de Jogos 1º de Maio
Avenida Rio de Janeiro, Alvalade (21 845 3470/1, www.inatel.pt). Metro Roma. **Open** 8am-10.45pm daily. Closed Aug. **Court hire** €8-€12.70/hr. **No credit cards. Map** p249 N2/3.
This sports complex, owned by workers' institute Inatel, has three outdoor hard tennis courts, with floodlights, available for non-members to hire. Beware if you're playing late: they lock up at 11pm. To play on Sunday, you must book and pay in advance as the booth is closed. A bonus for families is the nearby 18-hole mini-golf (€2.70).

Film

A small domestic market coupled with chronic underfunding means that the local film industry is tiny compared to that of neighbouring Spain – even if its artiest output has long been prized by foreign critics. Locals, for their part, have tended to show themselves to be overwhelmingly indifferent to the meditative fare produced by veteran director Manoel de Oliveira and his followers, and have voted with their feet for Hollywood blockbusters. Still, cinephiles in Lisbon can choose from a healthy supply of European arthouse fare, as well as a varied festival selection. And amid the austerity of recent years, plenty of young Portuguese filmmakers have defied the odds to turn out prize-winning animations, shorts and features.

PORTUGUESE FILM

Lisbon has always been at the heart of Portugal's film industry. In 1922, businessman Raul de Caldevilla bought the Quinta das Conchas estate in Lumiar with plans to build a film city there. After António Oliveira Salazar's Estado Novo regime was installed in 1928, propaganda chief António Ferro oversaw the creation of Cinelândia, housing laboratories and studios. The buildings survive today, dwarfed by high-rise flats.

The first talkie made in Portugal was, fittingly enough, about a fado diva: *A Severa* (1931) by José Leitão de Barros. The next two decades became the golden era of Portuguese cinema, with comedies, musicals and historical dramas aligned with the dictatorship's world view perhaps inevitably dominating.

IN THE KNOW CHEAP SEATS

If you want to cut costs, save your movie-going for Monday, when many cinemas charge up to 30 per cent less for admission (Wednesday is the day for cut-price tickets at UCI). Alternatively, head to Medeia Monumental before 8pm (Tue-Thur) for reduced-price seats.

After the fall of Salazar, the Cinema Novo group was established by the Centro Português de Cinema (with help from the Gulbenkian Foundation), while the government created the Instituto Português de Cinema – now the Instituto do Cinema e Audiovisual (ICA). These twin approaches remain. The 'commercial' school – spearheaded by directors such as João Canijo, Joaquim Leitão, António Pedro Vasconcelos and Leonel Vieira – targets the domestic market. Since the 1974 Revolution, though, Portuguese cinema has been dominated by auteurs, usually living a hand-to-mouth existence. The exception to this is director Manoel de Oliveira: his career began in the silent era and reached an early peak with *Aniki-Bóbó* (1942), whose realist style predated Italy's masters by several years. He's still making movies today and received a lifetime achievement award at Cannes in 2008, at the tender age of 100.

Younger auteurs have looked to follow De Oliveira's lead, exploring themes of colour, space and *saudade* (melancholic nostalgia). This is not, however, the stuff of box-office hits. In the words of one Portuguese critic, local moviegoers 'have a fragile relationship' with their country's cinema. Can audiences saturated by decades of mediocre *telenovelas* really take an interest in film-makers' art? The critic's answer was an emphatic 'no'. But the recent opening of **Cinema Ideal** (*see p135*) shows that at least some in the business disagree.

INFORMATION & TICKETS

All the major shopping centres have cinemas, run by NÓS; for information and credit card booking for these, *see right* **Cinemas NÓS Amoreiras**. Similar fare is offered by **UCI** and **Cinema City**, while **Medeia Monumental** and **Nimas** are the best places for European and US indie films. Listings can be found in national newspapers, weekly magazines such as *Time Out Lisboa* and *Visão*, and at www.cinecartaz.publico.pt – where the original title of foreign films is always given. This isn't always the case with cinemas' own websites (and the Portuguese title attached to a film may bear little or no relation).

Weekly programmes change on a Thursday. Films in languages other than Portuguese are subtitled rather than dubbed, except for children's animation – and even for these, there will be some screenings in the original version ('VO'). At venues other than the Cinemateca, you can reserve over the phone – but tickets need to be collected 30 minutes before the screening.

Foreign cultural institutes, including the British Council, have film libraries. Spain's **Instituto Cervantes** (Rua Santa Marta 43, 21 310 5020, www.lisboa.cervantes.es) has occasional screenings. Retailer **Fnac** (*see p78*) also shows the odd topical film in its café, while **Galeria Zé dos Bois** (*see p85*) in the Bairro Alto screens arthouse and experimental film.

CINEMAS

Cinema City
Campo Pequeno (21 798 1420, www.cinema city.pt). Metro Campo Pequeno. **Admission** €6.70; €5.70 reductions & all Mon. *3D films* €1.80 extra. **Map** p248 M4.
It's mainly commercial fare at this small multiplex located in a mall underneath the Lisbon bullring. Rooms are themed, so you may find yourself watching a drama from a chair stamped with cartoon characters. For some films, extra-comfy VIP seats are available; the €18 ticket (€15 reductions; €14.90 Wednesdays) gives you access to a special lounge with free drinks and snacks. Family tickets (from €4.90 per person) are offered for adventure, comedy and animation films.
Other location Avenida da Roma 100 (21 841 3040/3).

Cinema Ideal
Rua do Loreto 15 (21 099 8295, www.cinema ideal.pt). Metro Baixa-Chiado. **Open** *Box office* from 12.30pm daily. *Café & shop* noon-2am daily. **Admission** €5-€7. **Map** p250 L9.
In a space that once housed one of the world's oldest cinemas (but was for many years given over to porn), this new venue, inaugurated in mid 2014, aims to fill the considerable gap left by the closure of all of Lisbon's neighbourhood cinemas. Programming is varied: in part the aim is to serve as a showcase for contemporary Portuguese cinema. The building – restored by prize-winning architect José Neves – also houses a café, a shop selling DVDs and books, a library, and an area to borrow and watch DVDs.

Cinemas NÓS Amoreiras
Avenida Engenheiro Duarte Pacheco (box office €0.60/min 16996, http://cinemas.nos.pt). Bus 74, 83, 711, 713, 718, 723, 748, 753, 758. **Admission** €6.70; €5.80 reductions & all Mon. *3D films* €2 extra. **Map** p245 J7.
You buy your tickets from a single booth at the Amoreiras shopping centre, but the seven screens are scattered around the complex so look for the overhead signs. The booking line is the same for all the company's multiplexes.
Other locations Centro Colombo (see p120); Centro Vasco da Gama (see p127); Alvaláxia, Estádio José Alvalade, Campo Grande.

Cinemateca Portuguesa/ Museu de Cinema
Rua Barata Salgueiro 39 (box office 21 359 6262, recorded information 21 359 6266, museum 21 359 6200, www.cinemateca.pt). Metro Marquês de Pombal. **Open** *Box office* 2.30-3.30pm, 6-10pm Mon-Sat. Closed Aug. *Museum* 1.30-10pm Mon-Fri. **Admission** *Films* €3.20; €2.15 reductions. *Museum* free. **No credit cards. Map** p246 L7.
Lisbon's equivalent of London's BFI Southbank has two screens showing as many as five different films a day, in themed world cinema retrospectives. Tickets are only sold on the day and non-members can't reserve, so there may be queues for rare or popular classics. The Cinemateca has had museum status since cinephile Dr Felix Ribeiro persuaded the government to found it in 1948. The archive in his former home contains historical gadgets, 19,000 books and 1,500 other publications in European languages,

Cinema Ideal.

Vertical text in right margin: **ARTS & ENTERTAINMENT**

plus posters and other Portuguese film memorabilia. To visit the library (*biblioteca*), bring ID and seek out the helpful English-speaking librarians in the old building. The new building has a restaurant-bar (12.30pm-1am Mon-Sat), a shop selling books, magazines and DVDs (1-10pm Mon-Fri, 2.30-10pm Sat), and space for exhibitions in an atrium with columns made from stacked film reels. Saturday afternoon screenings for kids take place at Palácio Foz on Praça dos Restauradores.

★ Medeia Monumental

Avenida Praia Vitória 72 (21 314 2223, www. medeiafilmes.pt). Metro Saldanha. **Admission** €6.50; €5.50 reductions; €4.50 Mon & before 8pm Tue-Sun. *3D films* €2 extra. **Map** p249 M5.

Four screens show leading indie and European arthouse fare. The cinema has excellent acoustics and sightlines, and attracts the highest audiences per screen in town. The café-bar offers a range of Belgian beers and decent food, and there's a quiet mezzanine area with DVDs, books for sale and free Wi-Fi. Around the corner, small sister cinema Nimas (Avenida 5 de Outubro 42B, 21 357 4362) draws local intellectuals with a mix of premieres, classics and film series. **Other location** Medeia Fonte Nova, Estrada de Benfica 503 (21 714 5088).

UCI El Corte Inglés

Avenida António Augusto Aguiar 31 (box office 707 232 221, www.uciportugal.pt). Metro São Sebastião. **Admission** €6.90; €5.60 reductions; €4.70 Wed. *3D films* €1.50 extra. **No credit cards.** **Map** p248 L5.

This 14-screen multiplex attached to a Spanish-owned department store offers a mix of artsy films and blockbusters, with the same movie often shown on different screens on the same day, at staggered times. Several of its theatres feature larger, more comfortable VIP seats (€8.80).

FESTIVALS & SCREENINGS

The last of the city's old picture palaces, **Cinema São Jorge** (Avenida da Liberdade 175, 21 310 3400), is now council-owned and has established itself as a major venue for film festivals. It has one of Lisbon's largest screens, plus two smaller screens, spacious reception areas and a balcony overlooking the avenue. The council's **Fórum Lisboa** (Avenida da Roma 14, 21 842 0900) and **Culturgest** (*see p120*) also host screenings. The various entities behind most of the festivals listed below now share a home in the Bairro Alto, the **Casa do Cinema** (Rua da Rosa 277).

The festival year kicks off in March, with Monstra (www.monstrafestival.com), an animation festival for adults and children, with competitive sections. That's followed in April by **FESTin** (http://festin-festival.com), which screens films from Portuguese-speaking

countries – with Brazil inevitably supplying the lion's share. At the end of the month and running into May is **IndieLisboa** (www.indielisboa.com), a veritable feast of independent film that has steadily grown in scale and international clout since its modest beginnings in 2004. It features Portuguese and international competitions, plus a parallel event for kids, IndieJúnior, with its own competitive sections. **Panorama** (www. panorama.org.pt), a showcase for Portuguese documentaries, follows later in May.

Out of town in Setúbal, **Festroia** (www. festroia.pt) is the only generalist event of its size in the region, and is usually held in June. Its main competition each year focuses on a nation with an annual output of no more than 30 features; other prizes include best European screenplay, and there are themed sections such as Man and Nature.

After the summer lull, September sees **MotelX** (www.motelx.org), a horror showcase organised by fans, but along increasingly professional lines and now with a competitive section for Portuguese shorts. Later in the same month comes **QueerLisboa** (www.queerlisboa.com), a long-running LGBT competitive festival with international pulling power. **DocLisboa** (www. doclisboa.org) follows in October, with more than 100 documentaries from around the world; it has several competitive sections and features very popular debates and director's workshops.

At November's **Lisbon & Estoril Film Festival** (www.leffest.com), the focus is on European features. But its founder, veteran Portuguese producer Paulo Branco, flies in A-list guests from around the world to take part. In December, Culturgest screens winning films from **Cinanima**, Portugal's leading festival of animated film, held for the past 38 years in the northern town of Espinho.

Lisbon also plays host to film showcases from a number of different nations: German films in **Kino** (www.goethe.de/portugal) and the latest output from Hong Kong in **Mostra de Cinema de Hong Kong**, both in January; Italian movies at **8½ – Festa do Cinema Italiano** (www. festadocinemaitaliano.com) in spring or early summer; French fare at **Festa do Cinema Francês** (www.festadocinemafrances.com) in October, sometimes with the presence of a French star; and **Festa do Cinema Romeno** (Romanian film) in November.

In July, cinemas **Monumental** and **Nimas** (for both, *see left*) may re-run arthouse films from the past year. But for those who like their summer cinema outdoors, more mainstream fare is screened in late June and July in the Quinta das Conchas park, near the metro station of the same name, as part of the city's free **CineConchas** initiative. There are usually other outdoor screenings around town too. Beware, though: Lisbon summer nights can be cool and windy.

REEL LIFE

A new crop of directors are flying the flag for powerful Portuguese cinema.

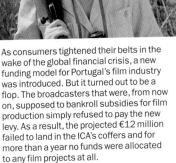

As consumers tightened their belts in the wake of the global financial crisis, a new funding model for Portugal's film industry was introduced. But it turned out to be a flop. The broadcasters that were, from now on, supposed to bankroll subsidies for film production simply refused to pay the new levy. As a result, the projected €12 million failed to land in the ICA's coffers and for more than a year no funds were allocated to any film projects at all.

The crisis prompted Miguel Gomes, one of Portugal's leading young directors, to write an article for *Público* newspaper titled 'Portuguese cinema: the alarm sounds'. He distributed the text in English at the 2013 Venice Film Festival, where his latest work, *Redenção* (Redemption), was being premiered; this short, he noted, used footage from the national film archive, whose funding had also been broken down. Foreign film critics were simultaneously concerned and baffled: the years since 2010, when Portugal's output began to plummet, have brought a string of fascinating films from the troubled country.

Gomes's own breakthrough 2012 feature, *Tabu* (Taboo), was a multi-layered exploration of memory that picked up the FIPRESCI (International Federation of Film Critics) Prize at that year's Berlin Film Festival. Described by reviewers as 'pure magic' and 'wonderfully strange', it showed the kind of playfulness with form hinted at in his 2008 *Aquele Querido Mês de Agosto* (Our Beloved Month of August). Back home, *Tabu* did better at the box office than several so-called 'commercial' Portuguese films released in the same year.

Now, in a project he began shooting in 2014, *As 1001 Noites* (Arabian Nights), Gomes is addressing the crisis head on, blending fact and fiction. Based on real-life stories, he is portraying the pain inflicted by the austerity policies introduced following Portugal's euro-zone bailout.

Joaquim Pinto's *E Agora? Lembra-me* (What Now? Remind Me), which was chosen to inaugurate Lisbon's new Cinema Ideal (*see* p135), is more personal than Gomes's work. This portrait of a year of Pinto's treatment for AIDS and hepatitis secured the Special Jury and FIPRESCI prizes at the 2013 Locarno Film Festival.

In 2014, Pedro Costa picked up the best director prize at the same festival for *Cavalo Dinheiro* (Horse Money), described by *Variety* as 'hauntingly beautiful'. The film, Costa's most visually sumptuous to date, is his latest to focus on Lisbon's down-at-heel Fontainhas neighbourhood, after *Ossos* (Bones) in 1997, *No Quarto de Vanda* (In Vanda's Room) in 2000, and *Juventude em Marcha* (Colossal Youth) in 2006. Once more, it features Ventura, an ageing immigrant from Cape Verde, whose deteriorating physical state is seen as a metaphor for the faded hopes of Portugal's 1974 Revolution.

Like Manoel de Oliveira's work, Costa's is highly culturally specific while having universal resonance. And like a handful of other directors who are somehow managing to work in the current circumstances, he has a growing band of foreign admirers.

Gay & Lesbian

Portugal has come a long way since the 1974 Revolution. Although more traditional family values prevail outside the big cities, live-and-let-live attitudes have spread to this south-western corner of Europe. A major milestone was reached in 2010 when parliament voted to allow marriage between same-sex couples – not the halfway house of civil unions that the conservative opposition had proposed at the last minute. From a visitor's point of view, Lisbon's balmy climate, charming locals and rich nightlife mean it has all the makings of a great LGBT destination.

THE GAY SCENE

Long before the governing Socialist Party included same-sex marriage in its manifesto, gay and lesbian visitors were already getting a warm welcome in a city where mixed bars and clubs often offer the best evening out. But if you do prefer exclusively gay places, there's plenty of choice as well.

Pride (www.portugalpride.org) takes place in late June as part of the **Festas dos Santos Populares** (*see p32*). Film festival **Queer Lisboa** (*see p32*), which has been going for two decades, has the city's active support. Nowadays you'll even find a few themed or fetish bars, and public displays of affection between gay couples are increasingly common even outside core areas. And everywhere in the region, you can make the most of the laid-back atmosphere.

Cruising in Lisbon is usually limited to parks, mainly at weekends, and beaches. Be on the alert for muggers and the occasional police patrols. At Cidade Universitária (University Campus) in Campo Grande there's some car cruising. There's still plenty of activity on the Caparica coast (*see p170*), where there are nudist and gay beaches at mini-train stops 17, 18 and 19. If you want to cruise on summer days, head for the dunes; there's night-time car cruising on access roads and parking areas all year round.

To find out what's on, check out www.portugalgay.pt, an informative site in English, French, Spanish and German about activities throughout Portugal, or chat to staff in bars such as **Portas Largas** (*see p145*) or **Bar 106**. Major events for lesbians are flagged on http://lesboaparty.blogs.sapo.pt.

Information

See also pp226-232 **Resources A-Z**.

Checkpoint LX

Travessa do Monte do Carmo 2 (91 069 3158, www.checkpointlx.com). Metro Rato or bus 758. **Open** noon-8pm Mon-Fri; 2-6pm Sat. **Map** p246 K8.
This free HIV-testing centre in the heart of the Príncipe Real neighbourhood will produce your results in 30 minutes, and also offers advice and health information.

SHOPS

Men Spot

Rua de São Marçal 168A (96 357 7215, www.menspot.pt). Metro Rato or bus 758, 773, 790. **Open** 11am-8pm Mon-Sat. **Map** p246 K8.
This Príncipe Real shop sells underwear, swimming trunks, sportswear and clubbing gear. Men only.

Mr Woof Store

Rua Rúben A Leitão 23 (91 729 4354). Metro Rato or bus 758, 773, 790. **Open** 4pm-midnight Mon-Sat. Map p246 K8.
This fetish and leather specialist in Príncipe Real sells accessories to fulfil a range of fantasies: masks, whips, handcuffs, harnesses, boots, gloves, ropes and the like. It also stocks clothing such as Fred Perry.

HOTELS

As well as the following gay pads, we recommend the **Pensão Londres** (*see p219*), **Hotel Alegria** (*see p214*), **Pensão Globo** (*see p218*, run by the same people as Hotel Anjo Azul) and **York House** (*see p220*). **Residência Mar dos Açores** (*see p216*) also proclaims itself to be gay-friendly.

Hotel Anjo Azul
Rua Luz Soriano 75 (21 347 8069, www.blue angelhotel.com). Metro Baixa-Chiado or tram 28. **Map** p246 K9.
Lisbon's most renowned gay hotel offers great value for money. Doubles start at €40 in low season, and it's clean, friendly and well situated on a quiet street (where poet Fernando Pessoa also lived). The 20 rooms are decorated in a simple, comfortable style; all have en suite bathrooms and some feature jacuzzis. There's no breakfast offered, but there are plenty of nearby cafés.

My Rainbow Rooms
(21 842 1122, www.myrainbowrooms.com). Metro Saldanha.
This bed and breakfast near Praça Duque de Saldanha is out and proud – it describes itself as 'a gay-boy's dream pad' – but the precise address is only revealed once you've booked. Rooms are bright and airy with simple furniture, but there are extras you wouldn't normally find in a *pensão*, such as a DVD/CD player, WiFi, hairdryer and safe. Rates start at €45. The owners can also organise city tours on foot or in a limousine.

Pouso dos Anjos
Rua dos Anjos 31 (21 357 2759, www.pousodos anjos.com). Metro Intendente. **Map** p246 M7.
The 'Angel's Perch', run by the owner of Portas Largas (*see p145*), is situated in the restored home of an 18th-century countess. The 32 rooms, some en suite, range from singles to quadruples, with doubles costing from €45 a night in low season. The back garden is especially pleasant during the summer, when parties are held there. The area isn't within walking distance of the Bairro Alto scene, but it's one of the city's most happening neighbourhoods.

RESTAURANTS & CAFES

Almost all restaurants and cafés in Bairro Alto and Príncipe Real are gay-friendly, but **Pap' açorda** (*see p83*) and **Sinal Vermelho** (*see p84*) are justly renowned. **Café A Brasileira** (*see p76*) gets particularly cruisey in the early evening. The kitchen at the **Gayola** bar (*see p140*) also stays open late.

Frei Contente
Rua de São Marçal 94 (93 821 2749). Metro Rato. **Open** noon-3pm, 7.30-11.30pm Mon-Thur; noon-3pm, 8pm-2am Fri; 8pm-2am Fri, Sat. **Main courses** €7-€11. **Map** p246 K9.
The 'Happy Friar' is by no means an exclusively gay restaurant, but its location and late opening hours have helped to make it something of a hub for those planning an evening out in Príncipe Real. The pretty *calçada a portuguesa* paved floor and traditional Portuguese cuisine add to the atmosphere. The two- and three-course menus are great value.

Põe-te na Bicha
Travessa Água da Flôr 34 (21 342 5924). Metro Baixa-Chiado or tram 28. **Open** 7.30pm-midnight Mon, Tue, Thur-Sun. **Main courses** €10-€16. **Map** p250 L9.
Traditional Portuguese food is creatively presented in a refined but intimate setting at this long-established restaurant with a punningly suggestive name. ('*bicha*' means queue but is also Brazilian slang for gay, in a phrase that starts 'Put yourself in the…'). On Thursdays a pianist provides the soundtrack.

Frei Contente.

ARTS & ENTERTAINMENT

Stasha

Rua das Gáveas 33 (21 343 1131). Metro Baixa-Chiado or tram 28. **Open** 12.30-3pm, 7.30-11pm Tue-Sun. **Main courses** €7.50-€16.50. **No credit cards.** **Map** p250 L9.

Traditional Portuguese cuisine, plus a decent selection of pasta dishes and salads, are on the menu at this colourfully decorated place run by the owner of Bar 106. It tends to stay open an hour later on Fridays and Saturdays.

NIGHTLIFE

Nights out in Lisbon don't get going until after 11pm. Most places are in and around Príncipe Real – where you'll find a couple of clubs and the most established gay bars – and the eternally trendy Bairro Alto. **Portas Largas** (*see p145*) remains a popular starting point, but a crowd also gathers at the *esquina cor-de-rosa* (the 'pink corner') – the crossroads between Rua da Barroca, Travessa dos Fiéis de Deus, Travessa da Espera and Rua das Salgadeiras. Here you'll find several key bars popular with the gay crowd: **Clube da Esquina** (Rua da Barroca 30, 92 909 2742), **Purex** and **Sétimo Céu**, among others. There are often hundreds of people filling the street. In summer, it's the place to be after dinner.

Just before Bairro Alto bars close at 2am (3am on weekends) people head off to gay venues such as **Trumps** and **Finalmente**, or major clubs such as **Lux** (*see p149*), where the far left end of the bar downstairs is a gay area. **Baliza** (*see p145*) in Bica, on the way down to Cais do Sodré, is also very gay-friendly. At venues listed below, there's no admission charge unless stated.

There has been a flurry of bear venues opening lately, including **WoofLX**, **TR3S Lisboa** (Rua Rubén A Leitão 2, 21 346 3012) and **Ursus Bar** (Praça das Flores 8, 21 397 0360). Also keep an eye out for the kitsch parties organised by **Conga Club**, where anything goes. They tend to be on the first Saturday of the month (details on the Facebook page), most often at the Faktory Club in **LX Factory** (www.lxfactory.com).

Bars

Bairru's Bodega

Rua da Barroca 3 (no phone, www.bairrusbodega. com). Metro Baixa-Chiado or tram 28. **Open** 10pm-2am Tue-Thur; 10pm-3am Fri, Sat. **No credit cards.** **Map** p250 L9.

This large, sociable corner wine bar welcomes all-comers, but its location round the corner from Purex (*see p141*) has helped to make it something of a hub for gays and, especially, lesbians. There's a good range of Portuguese wines on offer, as well as fine hams, cheeses and other snacks. There are also occasional fado sessions.

★ Bar 106

Rua da São Marçal 106 (21 342 7373, 96 663 5616, www.bar106.com). Metro Rato or bus 758, 773, 790. **Open** 9pm-2am Mon-Thur; 9pm-3am Fri, Sat. **No credit cards.** **Map** p246 K8.

This stylish, modern bar has a fun, friendly atmosphere and attracts a wide range of punters with its various themed nights. Owner José will fill you in on what's hot (and not) on the Lisbon gay scene.

Bar Cru

Rua de São Marçal 170 (www.barcru.eu). Metro Rato or bus 758, 773, 790. **Open** 5pm-3am Tue-Thur, Sun; 5pm-4am Fri, Sat. **Map** p246 K8.

As the name hints, this place is an out-and-out cruising bar. Open six days a week, it organises themed underwear and fetish parties, which progress to nude (including staff) after 10pm.

Etílico

Rua do Grémio Lusitano 8 (21 347 0359). Metro Baixa-Chiado or bus 757, 773, 790. **Open** 8pm-2am Mon-Thur; 8pm-3am Fri, Sat. **Map** p250 L9.

This sizeable bar stages a steady stream of events, from exhibitions to pole dancing, transvestite and strip shows. There's also karaoke.

Gayola

Rua da Imprensa Nacional 116B (21 397 4493). Metro Rato. **Open** 6pm-3am Tue-Sun. **Map** p246 K8.

The name is a punning homage to the film *La Cage aux Folles* ('A Gaiola das Malucas'), but this bar in Príncipe Real is far from exclusively queer. Furnished in colonial style, with old tables and armchairs, it features an installation by the artist Bassanti (Ivo Moreira) – and manages to be both cosy and contemporary. The kitchen turns out great steaks until closing time.

Le Marais

Rua de Santa Catarina 28 (21 346 7355). Metro Baixa-Chiado or tram 28. **Open** *Winter* 5.30pm-2am Mon-Thur, Sun; 6pm-4am Fri, Sat. *Summer* 5.30pm-2am Tue-Thur, Sun; 6pm-4am Fri, Sat. **No credit cards.** **Map** p246 K8.

The Parisian influence at this welcoming bar south of Bairro Alto is felt not just in the name, but also in the decor and ambience. It stages monthly art shows and its champagne cocktails are the talk of the town (happy hour 6-8pm weekdays). The bar was used in the making of the 2013 film *Night Train to Lisbon*.

Salto Alto

Rua da Rosa 159 (no phone). Metro Baixa-Chiado or Rato or bus 758, 773, 790. **Open** 10pm-2am Tue-Thur; 11pm-3am Fri, Sat. **Map** p250 L9.

One of a wave of new lesbian-run bars, the 'High Heel' welcomes a diverse crowd. Weekend nights are busy, with crowds drawn by the regular DJ sets. There are special drinks prices during the week.

WoofLX.

★ Sétimo Céu

Travessa da Espera 54 (no phone). Metro Baixa-Chiado or tram 28. **Open** 10pm-2am Mon-Thur; 9pm-3am Fri, Sat. **No credit cards.** **Map** p250 L9.
After a year's hiatus, 'Seventh Heaven' reopened in early 2013 with a more intimate feel – and a dark room. It remains at the heart of the Bairro Alto scene, almost two decades after it first opened. In warm weather, the crowd spills on to the street and mixes with punters from other bars, in a street party with something for every taste.

WoofLX

Rua da Palmeira 44B (21 347 0302, www.wooflx.com). Metro Rato or bus 758, 773, 790. **Open** 10pm-4am daily. **Map** p246 K8.
Opened in 2008 to fill a gap in the market, WoofLX has become the focus of a thriving bear sub-culture, but everyone's welcome. The management runs events away from the bar too.

Clubs

Construction

Rua Cecílio de Sousa 84 (21 343 0040, www.constructionlisbon.com). Metro Rato. **Open** 11.45pm-6am Fri, Sat. **Admission** €10. **Map** p246 K8.
This self-declared bear venue is welcoming to all. It has pumping house music, well-built dancers on raised platforms and a very popular dark room. The themed nights, with erotic performances, are fun.

Finalmente

Rua da Palmeira 33 (21 347 9923, www.finalmente club.com). Metro Rato or bus 758, 773, 790. **Open** midnight-6am daily. **Admission** (incl drink) €7 (free before 2am). **Map** p246 K8.
The kitsch drag shows here, which start at around 2am, are a Lisbon institution, and the place is packed at weekends. After the acts, it's dark, clubby and cruisey, with the younger punters on the raised dancefloor almost as entertaining as the show itself. Monday is open-mic night for up-and-coming performers. The place was renovated a couple of years ago but retains a pleasingly decadent feel.

Ponto G

Rua da Madalena 106 (no phone). Metro Baixa-Chiado. **Open** noon-6am Fri, Sat. **Admission** €5. **Map** p251 M9.
This club, located on the border between Baixa and Alfama, is one of the few in Lisbon aimed squarely at a female clientele. Lesbians should certainly feel at home at 'G Spot', though there are usually plenty of men here too. The soundtrack ranges from house to hip hop, with the occasional dubstep or afro-beat night thrown in for good measure.

★ Purex

Rua das Salgadeiras 28 (no phone). Metro Baixa-Chiado or tram 28. **Open** *Winter* 10.30pm-2am Tue-Thur, Sun; 10.30pm-3am Fri, Sat. *Summer* 10.30pm-2am Mon-Thur, Sun; 10.30pm-3am Fri, Sat. **No credit cards.** **Map** p250 L9.
A trendy, mixed bar (these days, gay men mostly outnumber women) that combines arty decor with a cosy, friendly feel. The place is particularly busy at weekends, when a DJ ensures the small dancefloor packs out, making this one of the area's buzziest clubs. The cocktails are worth trying too.

Trumps

Rua Imprensa Nacional 104B (91 593 8266, www.trumps.pt). Metro Rato or bus 758, 773, 790. **Open** 11.45pm-6am Fri, Sat. **Admission** (incl drinks) €10. **Map** p246 K8.
Two dancefloors and three bars help to make Trumps the place where most clubbers end their night. There's techno and house in the main space, and pop and Brazilian music elsewhere, plus drag shows and scantily clad go-go boys. It gets busy from 2am, after the Bairro Alto bars close.

SAUNAS

SaunApolo 56

Rua Luciano Cordeiro 56 (21 828 2854, 92 613 6808, www.saunapolo56.pt). Metro Marquês de Pombal. **Open** 3pm-3am daily. **Admission** €15-€80. **Map** p246 L7.
This sauna prides itself on welcoming everyone, gay or straight. As well as the normal price of €30 for eight hours, there are special afternoon and off-peak deals. Various massage packages are available, and there are snacks and a buffet for guests.

Trombeta Bath

Rua do Trombeta 1C (21 609 5626, www.trombetabath.com). Metro Baixa-Chiado or tram 28. **Open** noon-6am Mon-Thur; non-stop noon Fri-6am Mon. **Admission** €10 Mon; €14 Tue-Sun (€9 noon-2pm Tue-Fri; midnight-6am Mon-Thur); €9 students. **Map** p250 L9.
When this slick sauna opened in 2010 in the heart of the Bairro Alto it raised the bar in terms of quality and cleanliness. It has private booths, a Turkish bath, an area to watch porn and a dark room.

Nightlife

Lisbon is an outdoors city and at weekends it can seem as if every partygoer in the country has come to town to let their hair down. Thankfully, even when people are milling around the alleyways of Bairro Alto or sitting in a 3am traffic jam, the atmosphere remains refreshingly relaxed. Still, there are some serious clubbers around, and no shortage of well-versed DJ crews to serve them. There's plenty of variety in the city's music-driven bars and clubs, from style palaces whose snooty doormen enforce strict no-trainers rules to sweaty African dancehalls where you'll hear Cape Verdean and Angolan rhythms.

BAR OR CLUB?

In this city, the dividing line between bars and clubs is so fine that it often disappears. You may not even have to pay to dance the night away: for all places listed below, admission is free unless otherwise stated. Where a fee is listed, most or all of it goes towards your drinks bill. The bar-club continuum is partly how Lisbon earned its justified fame as a non-stop party town. In theory, you can go out on a Friday night and return home on a Monday without interrupting the fun for longer than it takes to catch a cab along the river. The scene is best in summer, when things gets going later (once people have had time to come back from the beach and change). By the time you resurface, the sun is up and the buses are running.

While there are many good nights to be had, few venues have a consistent music policy. **Lux**, long established as Lisbon's premier club, may hog the limelight, but the scene belongs to the crews that make it: established DJs such as Rui Vargas and Zé Pedro Moura, and newer ones such as Xinobi and other members of the Discotexas collective and its offshoot Rooster. These and others pop up in clubs and DJ-driven bars around town. All year round, there are one-off parties in locations that range from old warehouses in Alcântara to bars on the Caparica coast.

For the latest listings, check *Time Out Lisboa* or *Dance Club* magazine (on Facebook), or pick up flyers from music store **Flur** (*see p126*), near Lux. Most venues tend to let their website lapse, while updating their Facebook page fairly regularly.

In terms of neighbourhoods, the cheap bars of Santos are a magnet for students, and the Bairro Alto attracts many youngsters at weekends too. But for now most of the action is in Cais do Sodré, where revellers pack the 'pink street', Rua Nova de Carvalho, and the surrounding area until the early hours. The scene has become so popular – and noisy – that residents' complaints have finally borne fruit: opening restrictions already in place in the Bairro Alto (to 2am during the week, 3am at weekends) are now to be applied in Cais do Sodré too. The Intendente area, meanwhile, is emerging as a low-profile rival to Cais do Sodré as Lisbon's hippest area, especially in summer when the large square hosts live performances.

African clubs are dotted around town, inhabiting their own parallel nightlife universe. **B.Leza** (*see p153* **The Beauty of B.Leza**) is the largest, most famous and most accessible. South of the river in Caparica town, the beach crowd stays on for Cape Verdean *kizomba* and pop at **Ondix Beach** (Praia da Vila 26, 96 919 1035, www.ondeando.com) during the summer months.

But it's in regular clubs and at parties that the happening 'African' sound – actually a Lisbon sound as it emerged from the city's own musical mix – looms large. Electronic or progressive *kuduro* is a breakbeat/hip hop makeover of the Angolan rhythm of the same name, and Buraka Som Sistema have taken it from the Lisbon suburbs 'to the world', to quote from the name of their first release (in 2006). DJ Mobuku, DJ Marfox and other rising stars who have made their names at block parties in the suburbs can now be found spinning *batida*, *funaná* and Afro house sounds at mainstream clubs. Meanwhile, dance classes in *kizomba*, a softer Angolan rhythm, are also multiplying, including at B.Leza.

Club bars

BAIXA

Ministerium
Praça do Comércio, Ala Nascente 72/73 (21 888 8454, www.ministerium.pt). **Open** times vary (usually midnight-4am Fri, Sat). **Admission** free-€15 (incl 1 drink). **Map** p251 M10.
This large central venue in a former government ministry has mostly one-off parties, so check first that there's something on. The attached restaurant and terrace, Ministerium Cantina (21 888 8454), is good for a late-night snack in summer.

Primeiro Andar
Ateneu Comercial de Lisboa, Rua das Portas de Santo Antão 110 (21 346 1327). Metro Restauradores. **Open** 7pm-2am Mon-Sat. **Map** p250 L8.
There's a pleasing DIY feel to this warren of a bar on the first floor of a decaying sports and social club. To find it, climb the ramp along the right-hand side of the building and enter the black door on your left. Once inside, you can order a cheap beer or cocktail and sample tasty home-made snacks or light meals. At the weekend, stay on for late-night DJ sets. If it's a warm night, climb the flight of stairs in the corner of the basketball court to see what's on in the garden space – a film screening, maybe, or a themed party.

CASTELO, ALFAMA & GRAÇA

Although this side of town has plenty of congenial spots for an *aperitivo* before dinner or an *aguardente* to wind up the night – such as **Cerca Moura** on Largo das Portas do Sol and the **Esplanada da Graça** (*see p67*) – it lacks a major nightlife scene.

Chapitô
Costa do Castelo 7 (21 885 5550). Tram 12, 28 or bus 37. **Open** *Winter* 10pm-2am Tue-Sun. *Summer* 10pm-2am daily. **No credit cards**. **Map** p251 M9.
This bar attached to the Chapitô circus school has a broad terrace from which visitors can enjoy one of the best views in Lisbon. There's also a restaurant upstairs with an international menu. A separately run basement space, Bartô (*see p154*), has exhibitions, poetry recitals and regular live music.

Tejo Bar
Beco do Vigário 1A (no phone). Metro Santo Apolónia. **Open** 10pm-2am daily. **No credit cards**. **Map** p247 N9.

An alternative, informal place with a handful of tables with low seats and shelves loaded with books and board games. Its Brazilian owner, nicknamed Mané do Café, is an amateur artist, novelist and poet, and presides over daily readings. Anyone may strum the house guitar (don't applaud: patrons instead rub their hands together to show their appreciation, thus minimising noise). The bar has many regulars – who help themselves to drinks, noting down what they've taken – but it's also a magnet for students and musicians. Mané is incapable of throwing people out, so the place sometimes closes after 5am.

INTENDENTE

Lisbon's newest nightlife hub. In summer, the square hosts large-scale concerts of world music or Portuguese rock, while cheap pop-up bars appear in the surrounding streets. Opening hours are more restricted in this residential area than in the Bairro Alto or Cais do Sodré: to midnight during the week and 2am at weekends.

Casa Independente
Largo do Intendente 45 (21 887 5143, http:// casaindependente.com). Metro Intendente. **Open** 2pm-midnight Tue-Thur; 2pm-2am Fri; noon-2am Sat. **Map** p246 M8.
In a decaying mansion that has housed all manner of clubs and associations over the past century or so, this is the latest (and probably the liveliest) incarnation. The large front 'Tiger Room' hosts gigs and DJ sets, there are various small rooms that are good for a chat or a spot of work on your tablet, and the café and back patio are great places to relax. The bar serves a good range of teas, fresh juices and cocktails, while finger food is served until midnight.

IN THE KNOW GIN JOINTS

Portugal's neighbour, Spain, has had gin fever for ages, and in the past couple of years it has hit Lisbon. The ailment takes the form of an obsession with drinking the stuff before, during and after dinner, invariably from a balloon glass. The pioneer, in Alfama, was **Taberna Moderna** (see *p62*), whose owner is from Galicia in northern Spain. Its Lisbonita Gin Bar stocks 70 varieties from around Europe and the US, in five categories: classic (distilled with juniper), citric, spiced, floral and herbal. Up in Chiado, gourmet restaurant **Largo** (see *p75*) also has a long list of gins (and tonic waters) at its newish bar. Then there's **Gin Club** (91 088 2025, www.ginclub.pt). Not only do they stock dozens of premium gins, they also have workshops on how to select, mix and serve them.

▶ *A few doors down at no.52, Sport Clube do Intendente (open 8.30pm-midnight Tue-Fri, 2.30pm-midnight Sat, Sun) is an unreconstructed local social club – complete with pool tables – where non-members are welcome.*

CHIADO & BAIRRO ALTO

New cafés and bars seem to open in Chiado every week, although few stand out and the most popular meeting place for friends planning a night out in Bairro Alto remains **A Brasileira** (*see p76*). **Fábulas** (*see p77*) is another good option. Some local bars are part of the gay scene but all have a loungey atmosphere.

The Bairro Alto was an area of whorehouses and fado for two centuries, but for the past couple of decades it has teemed with more bars than you could handle in one night. Some gay-run places are often very mixed and worth anyone checking out: **Purex** (*see p141*) is one of the best. In line with strict rules brought in by the council to safeguard residents' sanity, bars here close by 2am, except on Fridays and Saturdays when those with a dancefloor carry on until 3am.

For a civilised start to the night, visit a local wine bar (*see right* **In the Know**) or **Solar do Vinho do Porto** (*see p84*), handily located at the top of the Ascensor da Glória. Indeed, this funicular is a good alternative to Baixa-Chiado metro station and tram 28 as a way to approach the Bairro Alto; alternatively, for the upper end of the neighbourhood, you could walk the ten minutes or so from Rato metro.

A Capela
Rua da Atalaia 45 (21 347 0072). Metro Baixa-Chiado or tram 28. **Open** 8pm-2am Mon-Thur, Sun; 8pm-3am Fri, Sat. **No credit cards.** **Map** p250 L9.
With a bar in front and a few tables at the back, the small, atmospheric 'Chapel' can get overcrowded. It's often even more packed after 2am at weekends, when some other local bars close and revellers who are not going clubbing somewhere else pile in to continue the party, to the sound of dance and electronic music. If you need a break, there's a pleasingly old-fashioned pool hall across the street.

Estádio
Rua São Pedro de Alcântara 11 (21 342 2756). Metro Baixa-Chiado or tram 28. **Open** 7pm-2am daily. Closed Aug. **No credit cards.** **Map** p250 L9.
There's no name outside but you can recognise this bar by the paintings of Roman-style stadiums – *estádios* – around the walls. It's a pleasingly scruffy place with rudimentary snacks and the tackiest jukebox in Lisbon, with a diet of fado lightened by the odd 1970s pop tune. Young bohos mix with garrulous old geezers around Formica-topped tables, served by a famously gruff old waiter who's a

sweetie at heart. A perennial early-evening meeting point for foreign students, and anyone who wants to nurse a beer while watching football.

★ Majong
Rua da Atalaia 3-5 (no phone). Metro Baixa-Chiado or tram 28. **Open** 5pm-2am Mon-Thur, Sun; 5pm-3am Fri, Sat. **No credit cards.** **Map** p250 L9.
Majong, a busy corner watering hole, is a key Bairro Alto bar, with cool decor and a well-judged DJ-driven soundtrack. It's favoured by a self-consciously avant-garde crowd, but don't let that put you off. After 11pm it can get absurdly crowded. Smoking is allowed here.

★ Maria Caxuxa
Rua da Barroca 12 (93 866 1134). Metro Baixa-Chiado or tram 28. **Open** 7pm-2am Mon-Sat; 9pm-2am Sun. **Map** p250 L9.
The phrase '*do tempo da Maria Caxuxa*' means old and old-fashioned, but this café-bar in a barely renovated former bakery packs in hip folk in their twenties and thirties. During the week it's an ideal place to wind down to a loungey soundtrack. DJs spin dub and house music from Thursday to Saturday, when space is at a premium and drinkers spill out on to the street.

Mezcal
Travessa Água da Flor 20 (21 343 1863). Metro Baixa-Chiado or tram 28. **Open** 8pm-2am Mon-Thur, Sun; 9pm-3am Fri, Sat. **No credit cards.** **Map** p250 L9.

IN THE KNOW
WINNING WINE BARS

Lisbon's handful of *enotecas* (wine bars) offer a fast route to enlightenment. **Chafariz do Vinho** (Rua da Mãe d'Água, 21 342 2079, www.chafarizdovinho.com), run by wine writer João Paulo Martins, offers some 200 Portuguese and foreign wines, decent food and a terrace. Downhill at no.9, tiny **Goliardos** (21 346 2156, www.osgoliardos. com), with its even tinier patio, is only open Thursday to Saturday as the owners spend much of their time scouring the country for new liquid delights. In Bairro Alto, **Garrafeira Alfaia** (Rua Diário de Notícias 125, 21 343 3079, www.garrafeiraalfaia. com) is a bar-cum-shop where wine tastings are accompanied by delicious cheeses, hams and sausages. Nearby **Artis** (Rua Diário de Notícias 95, 21 342 4795, www.artisbairroalto.blogspot.com) takes a similar approach. Lisbon's *enotecas* are open from late afternoon to around 2am (and to 3am Fri & Sat in Bairro Alto).

Park.

Don't be put off by the kids hanging around outside, lured to Mezcal by the cheap takeaway beer and cloying shots such as *pastél da nata*; this bar is the ideal place for fans of tequila. The tacos are pretty decent and the music is mainly Mexican.

Park

Calçado do Combro 58 (21 591 4011). Tram 28. **Open** 1pm-2am Tue-Sat; 1-8pm Sun. **Map** p246 K9.

A relative newcomer, this sprawling rooftop bar on a multi-storey car park at the south-western corner of the Bairro Alto gets packed on warm evenings. Beautiful young things chat amid giant pot plants, swaying to a DJ-driven soundtrack of jazz, soul and funk. The view out over the river and Ponte 25 de Abril is stunning. Snacks and light meals are available until 3pm, and then again from 8pm to 11pm.

Portas Largas

Rua da Atalaia 103-105 (no phone). Metro Baixa-Chiado or tram 28. **Open** 8pm-2am Mon-Thur; 8pm-3am Fri, Sat. **No credit cards. Map** p250 L9.

Its location in the centre of the Bairro Alto makes this place a real hub, and on summer nights the street outside is packed. Gay-owned and -run, it's nevertheless quite mixed, particularly early on. The decor is unchanged from when it was a scruffy *tasca* before the in-crowd's arrival: same marble tables, same peanut-littered floor and same music split between fado and dance (unless a Latin band takes over).

PRÍNCIPE REAL

Príncipe Real is essentially an extension of Bairro Alto, with fewer bars and a greater gay focus (*see also pp138-141*).

★ Cinco Lounge

Rua Ruben António Leitão 17A (21 342 4033, www.cincolounge.com). Metro Rato or bus 773. **Open** 9pm-2am daily. **No credit cards. Map** p246 L8.

This New York-style cocktail bar is a colourful haven in a bit of a nightlife no-man's-land. Its British owners have built up a loyal clientele, who come to lounge on low sofas and savour some of the 100 drinks on

offer: from classic martinis through fruity mocktails to sophisticated devils such as Madagascar Bourbon and Madeline Hays. Alcoholic cocktails start from €7, non-alcoholic from €5.

Pavilhão Chinês

Rua Dom Pedro V 89 (21 342 4729). Metro Baixa-Chiado or Rato, or bus 790. **Open** 6pm-2am Mon-Sat; 9pm-2am Sun. **Map** p250 L8.

Undoubtedly Lisbon's best bar decor, courtesy of Luís Pinto Coelho. The warren of rooms is lined with floor-to-ceiling glass cases stuffed with toy battleships, eastern European army officers' hats and other grim ornaments. This museum of kitsch is not cheap, but it's definitely worth a look. The back room is an atmospheric setting for a frame of pool. Another bar designed by the same man, Procópio (Alto de São Francisco 21A, 21 385 2851) near Amoreiras, has an extraordinary Wild West saloon-meets-musty museum feel.

SANTA CATARINA & BICA

Places here are also really part of the Bairro Alto scene. The **Esplanada do Adamastor** (*see p89*), with its simple café and fine river view, has a laid-back vibe and fills up on warm nights. **Noobai** (*see p89*), next door, is more secluded.

Baliza

Rua da Bica de Duarte Belo 51A (no phone). Metro Baixa-Chiado or tram 28. **Open** 10pm-2am Mon-Thur; 8pm-2am Fri, Sat. **Map** p250 L9.

This corner bar recently celebrated its 15th anniversary. It's a tiny former football *tasca* (the name means 'goal') that now boasts wild berry vodkas, great *tostas* and a bubbly gay/straight clientele. It serves as a handy stop on the late-night pilgrimage from the Bairro Alto down to Cais do Sodré and Santos.

A Bicaense

Rua da Bica de Duarte Belo 42 (21 015 6040). Metro Baixa-Chiado or tram 28. **Open** noon-2am Wed-Sat. **No credit cards. Map** p250 L9.

This large converted *tasca* is the hub of the Bica neighbourhood, best enjoyed away from the rush and push of weekends. It's basically one large room with a long bar and stools for perching plus a few tables. Fine sounds – dub, electro, funk and reggae from resident DJs, plus the odd bit of live jazz – indomitable staff and a large range of spirits attract a creative crowd. Smoking is allowed.

CAIS DO SODRÉ

During the Salazar years, the area by the harbour was the only place where visiting foreigners were able to find late-night drinking or any lowlife action. The latter remains in and around Rua Nova de Carvalho, where prostitutes solicit openly and seedy bars are named after distant port cities. Many retain their tacky 1970s decor, although one has now been transformed into a live music venue, **MusicBox** (*see p154*), and another into **Europa** (*see p147*). **O'Gilins** (*see p155*), with regular live music, is Lisbon's only authentic Irish bar, though Hennessy's round the corner has all the trappings. There are sometimes concerts at **Armazém F** (www.armazemf.com), but on the way there you'll also find riverfront terrace bar **Meninos do Rio** (*see p94*), which keeps going until 4am in summer.

Bar da Velha Senhora
Rua Nova do Carvalho 40 (21 346 8479). Metro Cais do Sodré. **Open** 6pm-3am Tue-Sat. **Map** p250 L10.
The name is a sly reference to a nickname for the dictator Salazar, 'the old lady' in power for four decades to 1968. Picking up on the area's louche traditions back then, this bar hosts burlesque shows from 11pm to midnight on Thursdays, Fridays and Saturdays. The small stage is at the far end of what is little more than a brick-lined tunnel, and space is at a premium – though there's room to breathe on the terrace. On Tuesdays and Wednesdays there's live music – flamenco and jazz respectively – from 10.30pm. This is a good place to head for if you've skipped dinner: they serve quite elaborate snacks until midnight.

O Bom, O Mau e o Vilão
Rua do Alecrim 21 (96 795 0287). Metro Cais do Sodré. **Open** 7pm-2am Mon-Wed; 6pm-4am Thur-Sat. **Map** p250 L10.
The Portuguese title for the Sergio Leone film *The Good, the Bad and the Ugly* provided the name for this ambitious project, hinting at its multifaceted nature: bar, restaurant, film club and music venue, with concerts or DJ sets daily. Check the Facebook page for details. In contrast to most Lisbon bars, where house and electronica rule, here soul, funk, Afrobeat and jazz dominate. Several rooms feature striking murals by local artists.

British Bar
Rua Bernardino Costa 52 (21 342 2367). Metro Cais do Sodré or tram 15, 18, 25. **Open** 10am-2am Mon-Wed; 10am-4am Thur-Sat. **Map** p250 L10.

With a long bar and wooden floor, the British Bar is designed like an English pub, but you'll rarely find a native of the isles here. A classic Lisbon establishment, it has carried on in its own dignified way since 1919, offering a great selection of beers, aperitifs and a digestif of its own. It also has a famous clock that marks the time with Swiss precision, only in reverse.

Copenhagen
Rua de São Paulo 8 (91 711 4670). Metro Cais do Sodré or tram 15, 18, 25. **Open** 10pm-4am Tue-Sat. **Map** p250 L10.
Recently reopened after a lengthy period of renovation, this legendary Cais do Sodré bar is back with a new look and pulls in a young crowd, including many students. The decor has a definite nautical theme: lots of timber (befitting what is an old port district) and a mural featuring cartoons of recognisable local types. On Thursdays (and some Tuesdays) there's live music; on Wednesdays, Fridays and Saturdays DJ sets – mainly hip hop and R&B, filling a gap in the local market – run from 11pm to closing time.

★ Lounge
Rua da Moeda 1 (no phone). Metro Cais do Sodré or tram 15, 18, 25. **Open** 10pm-4am daily. **No credit cards. Map** p246 K9.
Lounge, a roomy Bairro Alto-style bar, has moderate prices, an unkempt and youngish crowd, and interesting musical events. On regular nights, decent DJs spin an underground mix of electro and minimal techno, and there's the occasional themed party. It's packed inside and out at weekends, when ordering a drink can be a challenge.

Pensão Amor
Rua Nova do Carvalho 36 (21 314 3399, www.artbuilding.eu). Metro Cais do Sodré. **Open** noon-2am Mon-Wed; noon-4am Thur, Fri; 6pm-4am Sat. **Map** p250 L10.

O Bom, O Mau e o Vilão.

The name means 'Love Boarding House' – a nod to the building's past as a place of business for sex workers and their clients. Trendy locals now flock here to see and be seen in the over-the-top lounge bar – a sort of decadent tearoom, open from late afternoon – and attached rooms, which include an old-style disco. There are occasional concerts and the background music is eclectic.

Sol e Pesca
Rua Nova do Carvalho 44 (21 346 7203, www. solepesca.com). Metro Cais do Sodré. **Open** noon-2am Tue, Wed; noon-3am Thur-Sat. **Map** p250 L10.
This little place has metamorphosed from fishing equipment store to trendy snack bar with only the lightest of makeovers. It has kept the original name ('Sun and Fishing') and decor, but now sells canned fish and other delicacies to accompany the well-priced beer. You can also buy a tin to take away – some of them have lovely designs.

SANTOS & AVENIDA 24 DE JULHO

The scene in Santos and along Avenida 24 de Julho opened up, in part, for one obvious reason: cars can drive along here, whereas in the Bairro Alto there's no parking at all. As a result, cruising the Avenida has become a popular nocturnal pastime. The area bristles with bars, though few deserve a special mention. Sometimes the best way to enjoy a night down here is simply to drink a few beers at a fast-food van or on the terrace of a scruffy café and watch the world sweep by. **Main Lisbon** (Avenida 24 de Julho 68, 96 155 3745, www.mainlisbon.pt) – formerly Kapital – is a cavernous nightclub on three floors that hosts parties, often using minor local celebs as a draw.

Estado Líquido
Largo de Santos 5A (21 395 5820, www. estadoliquido.com). Tram 15, 18, 25, 28. **Open** 8pm-midnight Mon, Sun; 8pm-2am Tue, Wed; 8pm-3am Thur; 8pm-4am Fri, Sat. **Map** p245 J10.
A laid-back bar where established local DJs (from 11pm Thur-Sat) supply chilled dance music, with the selection at times quite eclectic. Upstairs restaurant Sushi Lounge is worth a look too.

SANTA APOLÓNIA

Clube Ferroviário
Rua de Santa Apolónia 59 (92 534 608, 21 815 3196). Metro Santa Apolónia. **Open** 6pm-2am Tue-Thur; 6pm-4am Fri; 4pm-4am Sat; 4pm-midnight Sun. **Map** p247 O9.
On warm summer nights the rooftop terrace at the 'Railworker Club' heaves with yuppies and trendies, sharing the tattered old train seats that serve as sofas. The building still houses a social club that goes about its business downstairs, where the

fab decoration, complete with trophy cabinets, has barely changed. Now, though, the place also hosts dance classes, open-air cinema, concerts and DJs – check the Facebook page for what's on. The terrace affords amazing river views.

Clubs

CHIADO

Silk
Rua da Misericórdia 14, 6th floor (91 300 9193, www.silk-club.com). Metro Baixa-Chiado or tram 28. **Open** 7pm-2am Tue-Thur (last entry 1am Tue, Wed; 1.30am Thur); 7pm-4am Fri, Sat (last entry 2.30am). **Map** p250 L9.
Located on top of the Espaço Chiado shopping mall, with a 270° view of the city and river, Silk originally aimed to replicate the model of a London club, granting entry only to members and their guests. Now, though, you're all but guaranteed entry if you phone ahead (and, on less busy nights, even if you don't). The effort is worth it for the 300 or so who can fit in, for the views and swish decor. In summer, the terrace is the big draw. Food is served until midnight.

SÃO BENTO

Incógnito Bar
Rua dos Poiais de São Bento 37 (21 390 8755, www.incognitobar.com). Tram 28. **Open** 11pm-4am Wed-Sat. **Admission** (incl drink) free-€20. **Map** p246 K9.
An established 'alternative dance bar', Incógnito offers a discerning mix of music from across the indie-rock-dance spectrum. A decent small venue, it covers all ages, is low on posers and permits smoking. Swashbuckling doorman D'Artagnan is a famous figure on the local scene.

A Lontra
Rua de São Bento 157 (96 192 8100, 96 551 3827). Bus 706, 749 or tram 28. **Open** 11.30pm-6am Tue-Thur, Sun; 11.30pm-7am Fri, Sat. **Admission** free, except Fri (€10 for men) & Sat (€20 for men, €4 for women). **Map** p246 K9.
'The Otter' is a venerable African disco with a funky vibe and intimate dancefloor. There's live music on Thursdays and the occasional DJ set with dub, techno and *kuduro*, but regular nights offer a pretty cheesy mix of Angolan *kizomba* and Cape Verdean *funaná*, with the odd (hetero) strip show. Whether you get in or not is at the doorman's whim.

CAIS DO SODRÉ

Europa
Rua Nova do Carvalho 18 (91 848 9595, www. europabar.pt). Metro Cais do Sodré or tram 15, 18, 25. **Open** 11pm-4am Wed, Thur; midnight-4am

Downtown, **Solmar** (Rua das Portas de Santo Antão 106) serves snacks and **Café no Chiado** (see *p76*) light meals, both until 2am; in summer, the posh snack bar attached to **Ministerium** (see *p143*) on Praça do Comércio is open until at least 1am. Up in Príncipe Real, **Snob** (Rua do Século 178, 21 395 2911) serves steak until 2am; as does **Café de São Bento** (see *p107*) on Fridays and Saturdays. In Santos, old clubbers' favourite **A Merendeira** (Avenida 24 de Julho 54) serves nourishing *caldo verde* (cabbage soup) and *pão chouriço* (sausage bread) hot from its impressive brick ovens until dawn.

Fri, Sat. **Admission** free to 1.30am, then €5-€10 (incl €3 drink). **No credit cards. Map** p246 L10. In a scruffy street that's now one of Lisbon's busiest, doors open on to a brightly coloured, modern club that buzzes with life most nights, hosting a healthy mix of DJs spinning various genres (from midnight) including cutting-edge electro. It regularly hosts music launches, slam poetry events and exhibitions. Smoking is allowed. Due to new local restrictions on opening hours, the club's legendary after-hours parties now take place at Europa Sunrise (Pátio do Pinzaleira 26, open 5-10am Sat, Sun & hols) in an alley off Avenida 24 de Julho (nos.68 & 70) in Santos.

Jamaica
Rua Nova de Carvalho 8 (21 342 1859). Metro Cais do Sodré or tram 15, 18, 25. **Open** midnight-6am Tue-Sat. **Admission** free-€6 (incl drink). **No credit cards. Map** p246 L10. Still going after some 35 years, Jamaica is a world unto itself. The DJs are the nostalgic kind, whether they're spinning rock, soul or reggae, but they know their stuff and unfailingly get the mixed crowd jumping. Bob Marley is always heard at some point in the evening. Smoking is allowed.

ALCÂNTARA, DOCAS & BELÉM

Docas is a veritable mall of docklands nightlife, with all manner of Cuban-themed bars and the like, but there's little to attract serious clubbers. More authentic Alcântara is doing better, not least by becoming something of a centre for African music.

Belém Bar Café
Avenida Brasília, Pavilhão Poente (21 362 4232, www.belembarcafe.com). Train to Belém from Cais do Sodré or tram 15. **Open** midnight-6am Fri, Sat. **Admission** from €5. **Map** p244 A10.

Belém Bar Café is a flashy place that attracts packs of women hunting its hunky owner, model-turned-actor Paulo Pires. Although styled as a lounge bar, the place is far from casual; you'll be asked to pay a silly admission price if the place is busy and they don't like your look.

Funky
LX Factory (Edifício H, Espaço 0.09), Rua Rodrigues Faria 103 (no phone). Tram 15, 18. **Open** 10pm-4am Tue-Sun. To have a drink while listening to cool music, either live or a DJ set, head for Funky, the latest project from legendary nightlife figure Hernâni Miguel. As well as the inevitable funk, you can catch soul, Latin and Cape Verdean sounds.

Gossip
Rua da Cintura do Porto, Armazém H, Naves A & B (96 509 0435). Tram 15, 18. **Open** midnight-6am Fri, Sat. **Admission** free-€15 (incl drink). Currently Lisbon's temple to techno, with parties that draw a young crowd and keep the energy going until morning. Top local DJs are likely to be on duty, and there's plenty of space on the large dancefloor to make the most of it. The venue tends to host a lot of student parties.

Luanda
Travessa Teixeira Júnior 6 (96 207 7898). Tram 15, 18. **Open** 11pm-6am Thur-Sat. **Admission** €8 women (incl drink); €16 men (incl 2 drinks). The success of Luanda has drawn other African enterprises to Alcântara, where techno once reigned. The club attracts a young, laid-back crowd for *kizomba* and *zouk* on Friday and Saturday nights; Thursday is ladies' night. Things can get heavy later on in the evening, when the doormen can be edgy.

★ Op Art Café
Doca de Santo Amaro (21 395 6787, www.opart cafe.com). Tram 15, 18. **Open** 12.30pm-4am Tue-Thur, Sun; noon-6am Fri, Sat. **Admission** free-€12 (incl drink). A riverside café-restaurant-club in a glass box, Op Art looks like an aquarium. But even without its in-your-face architecture it would stand out from the identikit bars of Docas. Op Art is still a top spot for electro fans, with Fridays and Saturdays (after 2am) devoted to it; jazz and chillout dominate during the week. The dockside location makes for a lovely summer venue.

SANTA APOLÓNIA

★ Lux
Avenida Infante Dom Henrique, Armazém A (21 882 0890, www.luxfragil.com). Metro Santa Apolónia. **Open** 11pm-6am Thur-Sat. **Admission** €12 (incl drink). **Map** p247 O9.

Lisbon's best club, with two dancefloors (one loungey, one sweaty) and a roof terrace overlooking the river. As the hip furniture indicates, it's a see-and-be-seen place, but the crowd is friendly and the measures Lisbon-large. House and guest DJs offer everything from electro and hip hop to bursts of '80s music. Thursdays are popular with locals keen on leftfield names; on Saturdays the place is mobbed by out-of-towners. Lux's programme – which includes live bands and the odd Sunday afternoon event, as well as big international DJs – and its catch-all social role remain unrivalled. Exude photogenic importance at the door if you arrive after 2am.

Fado

Fado means 'fate' and is often regarded as an expression of a supposed national trait of fatalism. Whatever the truth of this, many songs, whether performed by men or women, do touch on betrayal, jealousy and disappointed love. Fado is also linked with the notion of *saudade*, a longing for something impossible to attain. However, fado can be upbeat in tone. In the more informal venues, audiences tend to be less reverential and may interrupt the singer with repartee. In the *desgarrada*, a conversation in song, singers challenge each other, often with caustic remarks.

In fado, conveying sentiment is more important than technical perfection (some amateurs may sound a little harsh on the ear). The *fadista* is accompanied by a *guitarra* (a mandolin-shaped Portuguese guitar) and a *viola* (an acoustic Spanish guitar). The 12 strings of the *guitarra* are arranged in pairs, producing a resonant sound that at times highlights the singer's melody and at others plays solo, while the *viola* provides a rhythmic accompaniment.

In the mid 1800s, fado was performed in the seedy taverns of working-class *bairros*, notably Alfama and Mouraria, where legendary *fadista* Maria Severa Onofriana – known as 'A Severa' – lived and loved until her death at the age of 26. But it was taken up by members of the aristocracy – the first in a series of transformations that took fado beyond its humble origins. Another was the interest shown by intellectuals in the 20th century; as poets wrote lyrics for fado, they made it more sophisticated.

Radio, the gramophone and then television helped fado become a truly national music style – as did the Salazar regime's bid to mythologise it as an element of identity. Perhaps this couldn't have happened without Amália. Born in 1920 to a poor family and possessed of a uniquely expressive voice ('I don't sing fado – it sings in me,' she said), Amália Rodrigues became fado's biggest star, taking it from the taverns to the stage and then screen in *Capas Negras*, a film that broke national

box office records in 1947. She was the first *fadista* to gain international recognition, singing at the Paris Olympia and appearing on Broadway, and going on to develop a repertoire that went far beyond Portuguese music.

Fado fell out of favour after the 1974 Revolution but has since been fully rehabilitated. When Amália died in 1999, she was mourned by the nation; her remains were eventually transferred to the Panteão Nacional (*see p67*). Today, her passing can be seen to have marked the end of an era. While most of the fado sung in Lisbon restaurants is in the tradition she embodied, today's vibrant scene has taken a step forward.

CASAS DE FADO

Fado needs the right setting to work its magic, and the convention is to stop talking during the performance. There are always several singers, so don't worry if you don't like the first performance. At a proper *casa de fado* ('fado house') – a restaurant where professional musicians perform – the standard of music is good, but remember that people who sing (sometimes daily) for a living can get jaded.

This doesn't happen in the taverns specialising in *fado vadio* ('vagabond fado'), where a more laid-back attitude prevails and anyone may get up and sing (*see below* In the Know). Another difference is that, while admission to *fado vadio* places is invariably free, restaurants require customers to dine (at prices higher than equivalent eateries) or to stump up a *consumo mínimo* ('minimum spend'). On less busy nights, they may allow you to come in later and nurse a drink; do check first. We give average dinner prices or those of set

ARTS & ENTERTAINMENT

IN THE KNOW FADO VADIO

In *fado vadio* venues, don't expect quality food or quality singing – or any singing, for that matter, if you go on an odd day. The best bets are **O Jaime** in Graça (Rua da Graça 91, 21 888 1560, fado 4-8pm Sat, Sun & hols), and **Tasca do Chico** in Bairro Alto (Rua Diário de Notícias 39, 96 505 9670, fado 8pm-1am Mon & Wed). In both cases, you can just poke your head in the door; in fact, that's all you can do unless you arrive early. **Baiuca** in Alfama (Rua de São Miguel 20, 21 886 7284, fado 8pm-midnight Mon, Thur-Sun) is unusual in that you must dine, but you won't spend much over €25 for a fun evening. At nearby **Bela** (Rua dos Remédios 190, 96 467 0964, fado from 9pm Sun), owner Anabela is a local legend; the snacks are tasty and the fado seriously good.

Adega Machado.

menus where these exist (but are not obligatory). In general, kitchens close around midnight – but when the *casa de fado* itself closes depends on how much business there is. In touristy places, folk dancing may be on offer; this usually winds up around 10pm, to get to the serious business.

Adega Machado

Rua do Norte 91 (21 322 4640). Metro Baixa-Chiado or tram 28. **Open** *Mid Nov-mid Mar* 7pm-2am Tue-Sun. *Mid Mar-mid Nov* 7pm-2am daily. *Fado* 8.30pm. **Admission** minimum spend €27 until 10.30pm, then €17. **Map** p250 L9.

This long-established fado house has had a tasteful facelift and, most importantly, cut out the folk dancing to focus on good-quality fado. The restaurant's large size means it still attracts tour groups, yet it retains atmosphere. The black-and-white photos of Amália are still here too. Performers include Isabel de Noronha, Pedro Viana, Joana Viega and Marco Rodrigues. Accompanying them is a double-bass, as well as the traditional Spanish and Portuguese guitars. You'll pay between €40 and €50 a head for a full meal here.

Adega do Ribatejo

Rua do Diário de Notícias 23 (21 346 8343). Metro Baixa-Chiado or tram 28. **Open** *Nov-Feb* 6pm-midnight Mon-Sat. *Mar-Oct* 6pm-midnight daily. *Fado* from 8pm. **Admission** minimum spend €10. **Map** p250 L9.

If you want decent food and proper table service without paying through the nose, this long-established *tasca* at the bottom of the Bairro Alto is a good option, since most of the main dishes cost less than €10. As well as the official singers, at some point in the evening your waitress is likely to burst into song, which adds to the fun.

Café Luso

Travessa da Queimada 10 (21 342 2281, www. cafeluso.pt). Metro Baixa-Chiado or bus 758, 790. **Open** 7.30pm-2am daily. *Fado & folk dancing*

8.30pm. *Fado only* 10.30pm-2am. **Admission** minimum spend €25 until 10.30pm, then €16. **Map** p250 L9.

This is the oldest fado joint in Bairro Alto, where Amália started out. Opened in the 1920s in the former stables of the Palácio de São Roque, it's looking better than it has for years after a recent makeover. Four or five *fadistas* perform each night, with highlights including Catarina Rosa and veteran singer-manager Filipe Acácio. As in many places these days, a double-bass accompanies the singers as well as Spanish and Portuguese guitars. The folk dances – which are squarely aimed at tourists – come from across the country, including Lisbon. The minimum spend is one of the lowest in the area; there are also various set menus that offer reasonable value compared with the competition.

Clube de Fado

Rua São João da Praça 92-94 (21 885 2704, 21 888 2694, www.clube-de-fado.com). Tram 28. **Open** 8pm-2am daily. *Fado* 9.30pm. **Admission** €7.50 plus dinner (average €50) until 11pm, then €10 plus drinks. **Map** p251 M10.

Owned by talented *guitarrista* Mário Pacheco, this club attracts his friends, some of whom may perform, and features sessions by leading traditional *fadistas* such as Cuca Roseta (when she's not touring, as she's now something of a star), Miguel Capucho, Ana Maria and Cristiana Águas. The place has a lovely atmosphere, with stone arches dividing the room into nooks.

O Faia

Rua da Barroca 54-56 (21 342 6742, www.ofaia. com). Metro Baixa-Chiado or tram 28. **Open** 8pm-2am Mon-Sat. *Fado* 9.30pm. **Admission** dinner only (average €55) until 11pm; after 11pm minimum spend €25. **Map** p250 L9.

An upmarket and slightly antiseptic venue, but an excellent place to hear good-quality *fadistas*. The daily roster includes Anita Guerreiro, who had a successful career in *revista* (music hall) before

ARTS & ENTERTAINMENT

focusing on fado; António Rocha, known for his classic style; and Lenita Gentil. If he's not on tour, you should also get to hear one of fado's top young stars, Ricardo Ribeiro. There's a proper bar area if you just want to look in later on and hear some fine fado over a couple of drinks.

Maria da Mouraria

Largo da Severa 2 (21 886 0165, 96 476 6056, www.casadasevera.pt). Metro Martim Moniz. **Open** 5pm-2am Wed-Sun. *Fado* from 8pm. **Admission** varies. **Map** p251 M9.

Housed in the Casa da Severa – the building where 19th-century fado diva Maria da Severa is said to have lived out her last years, and now redone in sleek contemporary style – this relatively new venue is an offshoot of the Museu do Fado. Well-known *fadista* Hélder Moutinho manages the place and regularly performs; other musicians and singers are of equally high quality.

Marquês da Sé

Largo Marquês do Lavradio (21 888 0234, www.marquesdase.com). Metro Terreiro do Paço. **Open** 8pm-2am Tue-Sun. *Fado* from 9pm. **Admission** minimum spend €20. **Map** p245 J9.

Located in a former heavy rock venue, the Marquês is a classy place to hear fado in luxurious and spacious surroundings. The food and service are also better than in most fado joints. There are no big-name resident stars, but the quality of the singing is reliably good.

★ Mesa de Frades

Rua dos Remédios 139 (91 702 9436). Metro Santa Apolónia. **Open** 8.30pm-2am Mon-Sat. *Fado* from 11pm. **Admission** dinner only (set menu €45) until 11pm. **Map** p245 J9.

This *azulejo*-lined former chapel of the Quinta da Dona Rosa, a palace built by Dom João V for one of his lovers, is owned by *guitarra*-player Pedro de Castro. It has a reputation as the *fadistas'* canteen, and you never know who might roll up in the wee hours and do an impromptu performance. The food is Portuguese, prettified – *bacalhau com natas* with parmesan and the like – but really not up to the quality of the fado. Booking is a must for dinner. If you drop in later (and can squeeze in) there's no minimum spend.

★ A Parreirinha de Alfama

Beco do Espírito Santo 1 (21 886 8209). Metro Santa Apolónia. **Open** 8pm-2am. *Fado* from 9.15pm. **Admission** dinner only (average €35) until 10.30pm; after 10.30pm minimum spend €15. **Map** p251 N10.

This low-ceilinged, atmospheric restaurant in an alley off Largo do Chafariz de Dentro is owned by fado legend Argentina Santos. She doesn't unleash her thrilling, husky voice every night, but invariably monitors the quality of both singing and audience from her seat near the door.

A Severa

Rua das Gáveas 51 (21 346 4006, www.asevera. com). Metro Baixa-Chiado or tram 28. **Open** 7.30pm-2am Mon, Tue, Thur-Sun. *Fado* from 9pm. **Admission** minimum spend €25. **Map** p250 L9.

This family-owned fado house has been in the same hands since 1955 and has hosted many fine *fadistas* over the years. Current resident performers are Aina Santos, Natalino de Jésus, Fernando Sousa and Alzira de Sá. The minimum spend applies at any time and there are €49 fixed menus – it may sound a lot, but don't forget you're paying for the show too.

Sr Vinho

Rua do Meio à Lapa 18 (21 397 2681, www. restsrvinho.com). Tram 25. **Open** 8pm-2am daily. *Fado* 9.15pm. **Admission** minimum spend €25. **Map** p245 J9.

This classic Lisbon venue has helped to launch countless *fadistas*, including Mariza and Camané. The best known of the current crop are Joana Amendoeira and Aldina Duarte – whose recordings have been selling well – but Duarte, Francisco Salvação Barreto and Liliana Silva are also expert singers. 'Mr Wine' is owned by a grande dame of fado, Maria da Fé, but she herself performs rarely these days. The food here is good (albeit with slow service) and booking is essential.

Rock, Pop, Jazz & Roots

Keep your ears open as you walk around town and you'll soon realise you're in a very diverse musical environment. A balmy climate and tolerant attitude mean that pop and samba, fado and Cape Verdean mornas, chilly northern European techno and feisty local rap all spill on to the beaches of Caparica and the streets of Bairro Alto and Santos. In addition, big global names regularly include Lisbon in their European tours and well-priced festivals abound.

Dailies *Público* and *Diário de Notícias* have music sections with listings, plus a showbiz magazine on Fridays, but *Time Out Lisboa* is one of the most informative sources. Online, the Música section of http://lazer.publico.clix.pt is pretty comprehensive. Tickets can be obtained downtown from **ABEP** (*see p156*) and branches of **Fnac** (*see p78*) – whose cafés often showcase local talent – or from **Ticketline** (*see p156*). In general, tickets are still cheap compared with most of Europe.

Concerts at major venues usually start at 9pm, but doors open an hour earlier. At smaller, alternative venues shows start at 10pm or later. Programming is irregular, so check listings or pick up fliers.

MAJOR VENUES

The stadium of Lisbon football club **Sporting** (*see p120*) hosts occasional big concerts by U2 and the like, and a number of Lisbon concert halls are used for rock as well as classical music: the Coliseu dos Recreios; **Culturgest** (*see p120*), whose programming leans towards jazz and global; and the **Centro Cultural de Belém** (*see p157*). The CCB's main auditorium makes audiences feel like they should be on their best behaviour, but there are more relaxed free concerts at 7pm most weekdays in the terrace bar. **Paradise Garage** (Rua João de Oliveira Miguens 38, 21 393 0216, www.paradisegarage. pt) is an atmospheric place for metal and indie.

Aula Magna
Alameda da Universidade, Cidade Universitária (21 796 7624). Metro Cidade Universitária. **Admission** €20-€30. **No credit cards.** **Map** p248 L2.
With its wide and steeply banked seating area, this university amphitheatre doesn't really lend itself to rock gigs. Given the right act, however, it can pull off a great show.

Casino Lisboa
Alameda dos Oceanos, Parque das Nações (21 892 9000, www.casinolisboa.pt). Metro Oriente. **Open** 3pm-3am Mon-Thur, Sun; 4pm-4am Fri, Sat. **Admission** €12-€35.
This slick glass complex contains several restaurants and bars, hundreds of slot machines and a 634-seat auditorium with the latest equipment. It often stages concerts by leading Portuguese and foreign artists – jazz in particular. There are also free gigs by local and foreign musicians and singers in the atrium bar (for dates, see www.arenalounge.ws), where aerial acrobats also regularly perform above the rotating bar on weekend nights.

★ Coliseu dos Recreios
Rua das Portas de Santo Antão 96 (21 324 0585, www.coliseulisboa.com). Metro Restauradores or Rossio. **Open** *Box office* 1-7.30pm Mon-Sat or until 30mins after start of performance. **Admission** €10-€60. **No credit cards. Map** p250 L8.
Lisbon's coliseum was completed in 1890 and stages everything from circus acts to rock concerts and classic operas. Acoustics vary; some maintain that the left side is best.

Espaço Armazém F
Rua da Cintura, Armazém 65, Cais do Gás (21 322 0160, www.armazemf.com). Metro Cais do Sodré. **Admission** €8-€25. **Map** p246 K10.
This cavernous riverside warehouse is a popular venue for rock and pop gigs or DJ parties. Access to Espaço Armazém F is along the riverbank behind Cais do Sodré station.

MEO Arena (Pavilhão Atlântico)
Rossio dos Olivais, Parque das Nações (21 891 8409, http://arena.meo.pt). Metro Oriente. **Admission** €20-€55.
Built for Expo 98 to an impressive design by Regino Cruz, this UFO-shaped riverside arena – whose new official name reflects a major sponsorship deal – is Lisbon's premier indoor rock venue, if not always the most atmospheric. It also hosts tennis and other sports tournaments, ice spectaculars and the like.

Santiago Alquimista
Rua de Santiago 19 (21 888 4503, 91 851 2114, www.santiagoalquimista.com). Tram 28 or bus 734. **Admission** from €5. **Map** p251 M10.
An elegant and intimate space, with a balcony on three sides overlooking a low stage and bar area, Santiago Alquimista hosts indie bands (local and foreign), DJ parties, stand-up comedy and theatre.

★ Teatro Municipal de São Luíz
Rua António Maria Cardoso 40 (21 325 7650 box office, www.teatrosaoluiz.pt). Metro Baixa-Chiado. **Open** *Box office* 1-8pm daily or until 30mins after start of performance. Closed Aug. **Tickets** €8-€22. **No credit cards. Map** p250 L10.
The 1,000-seat main auditorium stages everything from world music to theatre. The glass-walled Jardim de Inverno (Winter Garden) hosts talks and concerts, including a mini jazz festival in early April. There's a studio theatre downstairs.

MUSIC BARS

As well as the venues listed below, the **Hard Rock Café** (Avenida da Liberdade 2, 21 324 5280, www.hardrock.com) programmes bands at the beginning and end of the week (11pm-1am Mon, Sun). **Hennessy's** (Rua Cais do Sodré 32, 21 343 1064, www.hennessys-pub.com), a large 'Irish pub' down by the river, has an open mic night on Wednesdays and live bands on Fridays and Saturdays (all from 11.30pm). **Rock in Chiado Café** (Rua Paiva de Andrade 7, 21 346 4859, www.rockinchiado.com) is a 100-seat café-restaurant in Chiado that attracts a varied crowd with free pop and rock performed by tribute and cover bands (from 11.30pm Fri & Sat).

At **Café Tati** (*see p94*) there's live jazz or African music on Wednesdays from 10pm to 11.30pm, and jam sessions on Sundays from 5pm to 8pm. In Rua Nova de Carvalho, **O Bom, o Mau e o Vilão** normally has live jazz on Mondays, while **Bar da Velha Senhora** (for both, *see p146*) has live flamenco music or jazz on Tuesdays and Wednesdays (when its burlesque performers take the night off). At other Cais do Sodré bars, nights may vary, so it's best to check. In Bica, **Belo o Nós** (Rua da Bica Duarte Belo 23, 92 759 6239, open midnight-4am Thur-Sat) has Cape Verdean music from around 11pm or midnight to 3am.

Central Lisbon

★ Hot Clube de Portugal

Praça da Alegria 48 (21 346 0305, www.hcp.pt).
Metro Avenida. **Open** 10pm-2am Tue-Sat. *Live*
music 10.30pm Tue, Wed; 10.30pm & midnight
Thur-Sat. **Admission** *Jam sessions* free. *Concerts*
€7.50-€10. **No credit cards.** **Map** p246 L8.
The city's only dedicated jazz venue, this is one of
Europe's most venerable clubs and it consistently
draws the best local and foreign performers. It's
actually now next door to its original premises,
after a fire a few years ago, but the spirit is just as
strong. There are jam sessions on Tuesdays and
Wednesdays and paying concerts on other nights.
The club has its own jazz school and the best students (and professors) often perform, sometimes
as an orchestra, which is worth catching. All in all,
musical satisfaction is pretty much guaranteed and
the suitably laid-back atmosphere is helped by the
pouffes scattered about.

Sé, Castelo & Alfama

At the atmospheric if touristy **Duetos da Sé**
(Travessa do Almargem 1B, 21 885 0041, www.
duetosdase.com), a Brazilian duo play standards
from their country as well as blues and jazz

THE BEAUTY OF B.LEZA
Celebrate the sounds of Africa.

Lisbon has always been a great place to hear
music from the former colonies. But there's
never been a venue as spacious and slick as
the new **B.Leza**, in a prime riverfront location
near Cais do Sodré.

For many years this legendary club was
housed in a dilapidated palace in São Bento.
The old place witnessed many a memorable
night of live music from Cape Verde, Guinea-
Bissau and other African countries. Close
dancing – often with total strangers – was
the norm, and the cheap drink flowed.

In 2007, with the building in a perilous
state and after several spells out of action,
the club was forced to close. A petition to
save it gathered hundreds of signatures, but
in the years that followed the club led a virtual
existence, with 'B.Leza nights' staged at
assorted venues around town.

Finally, in 2012, B.Leza moved into its new
home. There's a long bar and plenty of space
to bump and grind to the mornas and sembas
turned out by the likes of Cape Verdean
veterans Tito Paris and Dany Silva, or Calú
Moreira and the house band. On Sundays at
6pm there are dance classes (mainly Angolan
kizomba; information 963 612 816) followed
by a danceable DJ set. As at the old B.Leza,
unattached women won't want for attention
or dance partners.

B.Leza, by the way, was the quirkily spelled
stage name of renowned Cape Verdean
musician Francisco Xavier da Cruz (*beleza*
means beauty), who was celebrated for the
Brazilian-influenced innovations he made in
the morna. For a real taste of old Africa, this
is the place to come.

B.Leza

Cais da Ribeira Nova, Rua Cintura do Porto
de Lisboa 16, Armazém B (no phone). **Open**
10.30pm-4am Wed-Sun. *Live music* from
10.30pm or 11pm Wed-Sat. **Admission**
free-€7.50. **Map** p246 K10.

classics nightly from 9.30pm. **Voz do Operário** (Rua da Voz do Operário 13, 21 886 2155, www. vozoperario.pt), a venerable workers' club at the foot of Graça, has a magnificent top-floor hall that's often used by African performers. The downstairs café sometimes hosts folk gigs too. Up the street, the **Caixa Económica Operária** (no.64, 21 886 2836) is a social club that makes for an atmospheric venue. Live music (check the Facebook page) starts at 11pm (doors open 10pm).

Bartô

Costa do Castelo 7 (no phone). Tram 12, 28. **Open** Live music from 10pm Thur-Sat. **Admission** free-€3. **No credit cards. Map** p251 M9.

Its full name is Bartô do Chapitô: this tiny space is actually underneath the popular bar and restaurant of the Chapitô circus school (*see p162*). Descend the spiral staircase to encounter anything from fado or Brazilian music to free jazz or electronica. Or someone might be reciting poetry. (Check the Facebook page.) The stage in this former laundry is cramped but the bar has reasonable acoustics.

Bairro Alto

Caipirinhas and Brazilian music are consumed in quantity in the area's bars, but community centre **Casa do Brasil** (Rua Luz Soriano 42, 21 340 0000, www.casadobrasil.info) is as authentic as it gets, with dance lessons several days a week: forró (9pm Tue) and samba (8pm Tue & Thur) usually followed by a party. The mood is informal and floor space at a premium.

Bibo Bar

Travessa Água da Flor 43 (21 137 3237, 91 978 7195). Metro Baixo Chiado. **Open** 4pm-2am Tue-Thur, Sun; 4pm-3am Fri, Sat. *Live music* 9.30pm Tue; 11pm Thur, Fri; 11.45pm Sat. **No credit cards. Map** p250 L9.

In a small space long known for its live music, this relative newcomer continues the tradition with fado on Tuesdays, rock and blues on Thursdays, and jazz on Fridays – played for a thirtysomething crowd. This is a place for real music lovers: when shows are on, head for a side room if you want to chat. There's stand-up on Wednesdays and DJs on Saturdays; every first Sunday there's poetry from 5pm. At other times the place has a loungey feel, with film screenings, photography exhibitions and workshops.

Espalhafato Bar

Rua da Atalaia 85 (96 231 0731). Metro Baixa-Chiado. **Open** 9pm-2am Tue-Thur; 9pm-3am Fri, Sat. *Live music* from 10.30pm. **No credit cards. Map** p250 L9.

This bar is little more than a corridor but it manages to squeeze in a tiny stage on which a three-man combo belts out soul and funk standards until closing time. On Sundays there's samba – complete with

MusicBox.

cavaquinho and *pandeiro*. The beer is cheap and there are various cocktails and shots, as well as burgers and *bifanas* (pork sandwich). Down the street, Spot (no.25) caters to a young crowd with cheap beer and cocktails, plus live pop and rock covers.

★ Galeria Zé dos Bois

Rua da Barroca 59 (21 343 0205, www.zedosbois. org). Metro Baixa-Chiado or tram 28. **Open** 6pm-2am Mon-Thur, Sun; 6pm-3am Fri, Sat. *Live music* from 10pm Wed-Sat. **Map** p250 L9.

ZDB, as this alternative arts space is also known, has provided a stage for far-out music for nigh on two decades now. Its main performance space has the feeling of a fish tank, with large floor-to-ceiling windows looking out on to the street along the back of the building. There's a roof terrace for lounging on warm evenings. *See also p85.*

Páginas Tantas

Rua do Diário de Notícias 85-87 (21 346 5495, 96 624 9005). Metro Baixa-Chiado or tram 28. **Open** 8.30pm-2am Mon-Thur; 8.30pm-3am Fri, Sat; 8.30pm-2am Sun. *Live music* 10pm-1.30am Tue-Thur; 10pm-2.15am Fri, Sat. **No credit cards. Map** p250 L9.

A spacious bar that's a good post-dinner destination if you want to wind down rather than rage, with trad jazz, blues and the occasional bit of bossa nova. There's live music from Tuesday to Saturday, including a guest musician or singer at weekends. It's supposedly a journalists' hangout – hence the name 'so many pages' – but attracts all types.

Cais do Sodré

★ MusicBox

Rua Nova do Carvalho 24 (21 347 3188, www. musicboxlisboa.com). Metro Cais do Sodré. **Open** 11pm-4am Mon-Sat. *Live music* from 10.30pm Wed, Thur; 11pm or midnight Sat. **Admission** free-€10. **No credit cards. Map** p250 L10.

The managers of this key club in Cais do Sodré have music industry connections and exploit them creditably. It's one of the city's most interesting venues, with a regular programme of rock bands, electronic live acts, singer-songwriters and DJ sets (all night on Fridays). Note that some shows may start as late as 2am; for details, check the website, which is comprehensive. The space has an underground feel and look (it's literally beneath steep Rua do Alecrim) and is located in what was once one of Lisbon's seediest streets – and is now one of its buzziest at night.

O'Gilins

Rua dos Remolares 8 (21 342 1899). Metro Cais do Sodré or tram 15, 18, 25. **Open** 11am-2am daily. *Live music* 11pm-2am Mon, Fri, Sat. **No credit cards. Map** p250 L10.

This low-key authentic Irish pub offers pints of Guinness (always), Sky Sports (occasionally) and hearty Irish breakfasts until 4pm on Sundays. It attracts a mix of locals and expats. So far as live music goes, Mondays are jam sessions, with a band on Fridays and Saturdays; landlord Conor occasionally steps in to sing or play the spoons.

Tokyo

Rua Nova do Carvalho 12 (21 347 2429, www. tokyo.com.pt). Metro Cais do Sodré or tram 12, 15, 25. **Open** 10pm-4am Tue-Sat. *Live music* 11pm Tue-Sat. **Admission** free-€3. **Map** p250 L10.

Formerly one of the area's sleaziest bars, this joint has gained a new lease of life as a rock bar, with local bands pumping out mainstream standards, and the odd night of funk thrown in.

Alcântara

Speakeasy

Cais das Oficinas, Armazém 115, Rocha Conde d'Obidos (21 396 4257, www.speakeasy-bar.com). Train to Santos from Cais do Sodré; tram 15, 18, or bus 714, 728, 732, 743. **Open** 8pm-4am Wed-Sat. *Live music* 11pm Wed, Thur; midnight Fri, Sat. **Map** p245 H10.

This slick bar and restaurant, owned by a son of fado singer Carlos do Carmo, aims to cater to both the Cascais jet set and music enthusiasts. If you're one of the latter, you should book a table right at the front to be able to hear the live rock, jazz, blues, Brazilian (and even classical) music above all the background chatter.

Northern Lisbon

Templários

Rua Flores do Lima 8A (21 797 0177, 21 407 0817, www.templarios.pt). Metro Roma or Entrecampos. **Open** 10.30pm-3am Mon-Thur; 10.30pm-3.30am Fri, Sat. *Live music* midnight-2am Mon-Thur; 12.30-2.30am Fri, Sat. **Admission** €7 (incl drink). **Map** p248 M3.

A bar where punters of all ages knock back beer and caipirinhas while listening to Portuguese and international standards, as well as the odd original set. There are smoking and non-smoking areas. Phone reservations (call 2.30-3.30pm or during opening hours) are guaranteed only until 11.30pm.

Eastern Lisbon

★ Fábrica Braço de Prata

Rua da Fábrica do Material de Guerra 1 (96 551 8068, www.bracodeprata.com). Bus 718, 728, 755, 781, 782. **Open** 6pm-2am Wed, Thur; 6pm-4am Fri, Sat. *Live music* from 11pm Wed-Sat. **Admission** free, except €3 from 10pm Wed; €5 from 10pm Fri, Sat.

On the city's eastern fringe, on the road to Parque das Nações, the hulking former headquarters of an arms manufacturer now houses this thriving cultural centre. As well as nightly dance classes, it hosts concerts of everything from fado to classical music on Wednesdays, Fridays (normally jazz night) and Saturdays. On Thursdays there are free jam sessions and at other times anyone can play the bar piano. There are also film screenings and talks on philosophy, and exhibitions by local artists. The restaurant serves tasty snacks and does well-priced set menus.

FESTIVALS

Every other year (next in 2016), the season starts in late May with **Rock in Rio Lisboa** (*see p30*). Spread over two long weekends and two stages, it hosts Portuguese, Brazilian and global names (Shakira, Robbie Williams, Megadeth).

June's **Festas dos Santos Populares** (*see p32*) usually include free jazz and fado concerts around town, listed on council website www. egeac.pt, but the first big music festival of the year, in July, is **Nós Alive!** (*see p32*). Brewer Super Bock always organises a summer bash too.

Late July is also the time for Portugal's leading world music event, **Festival Musicas do Mundo** (*see p32*), a couple of hours south of Lisbon in Sines. **Festival Sudoeste** (Herdade da Casa Branca, www.musicanocoracao.pt or www.meosudoeste.pt), takes place in August further down the coast at Zambujeira do Mar. Now into its second decade, it packs an unrivalled range of music into four litter-strewn days.

Back in the Lisbon area, in early September the communist **Festa do Avante** (*see p32*) runs the gamut of styles south of the river.

There are numerous jazz events throughout the year: from **Festa de Jazz do São Luíz** in early April and **Estoril Jazz** in mid-May to **Cool Jazz** in June and July, **Jazz em Agosto** in August and **Seixal Jazz** in September. For all, *see pp28-33*.

Experimental music takes centre stage in **Música Viva** (date varies), organised by promoter Miso Music (www.misomusic.com).

ARTS & ENTERTAINMENT

Performing Arts

The city's performing arts scene has always been characterised by creativity in the face of adversity – and at times a struggle to identify and attract the audiences to appreciate it. Portuguese composers aren't particularly well known abroad. But the country has strong classical music traditions, underpinned by centuries of royal patronage. Many concerts take place in churches, palaces and monasteries, and summer festivals attract international artists. Funding for opera and ballet – despite or perhaps because of their elite status – can never be entirely cut for reasons of national pride, but theatre and dance in general are chronically short of funding. Yet after a lengthy hangover following the post-Revolution party of the 1970s, both have emerged artistically vibrant, if far from financially stable.

Classical Music & Opera

Although Lisbon isn't renowned for classical excellence, and music snobs may be dismayed by the faulty etiquette of the city's less-than-sophisticated local audiences, the range and quality of performances on offer, from home-grown musicians as much as visiting artists, is improving – and prices are still below what you'd pay in many other European capitals.

Portugal's early classical repertoire has been rediscovered of late, and a browse through the CD racks at **Fnac** (*see p78*) will throw up excellent recordings of works penned by Dom Dinis, the medieval troubadour king; early Renaissance composers such as Pedro de Escobar; and later ones such as Manuel Cardoso and João Rebelo. Modern musicians have also tackled the 'colossal Baroque' *Te Deum* of António Teixeira, the virtuoso harpsichord sonatas of Carlos Seixas and the rococo elegance of Sousa Carvalho.

From the 18th century, royal initiatives to send Portuguese composers to study in Italy, and to bring Domenico Scarlatti to teach in Lisbon, bore fruit through the likes of Domingos Bomtempo

(1775-1842); Viana da Mota (1868-1948), a pupil of Liszt; and Luís de Freitas Branco (1890-1955).

Contemporary Portuguese composers include Luís Tinoco and the challenging Eurico Carrapatoso; performers of note include pianists Maria João Pires, Artur Pizarro, Pedro Burmester and António Rosado, as well as Portuguese-born soprano Jennifer Smith. Elisabete Matos, also a soprano, is the country's best-known opera singer.

INFORMATION & TICKETS

Newspapers have daily listings; the *Público* cultural supplement on Fridays and *Expresso* on Saturdays are also worth a look. Municipal monthly *Agenda Cultural* is available from tourist offices and hotels, and online at www.lisboacultural.pt, while our sister magazine *Time Out Lisboa* also has information and reviews.

You can buy tickets for some shows at **Multibanco** (ATM) cash machines, but people mostly pick them up at the venue, often after reserving by phone. Tickets can also be bought in person for a fee at the **ABEP** booth on the south-eastern corner of Praça dos Restauradores (21 347 0768, open 9am-8pm Mon-Sat, 9am-6pm Sun), or by phone or online at **Ticketline** (24hr booking line 1820, from abroad +351 21 794 14 00, www.ticketline.sapo.pt).

ORCHESTRAS & ENSEMBLES

The **Orquestra Gulbenkian** (*see p158* **Prospecting for Culture**) is Portugal's oldest orchestral group; British and other foreign musicians are well represented. The state **Orquestra Sinfónica Portuguesa**, founded just 20 years ago, is based at the **Teatro Nacional de São Carlos** (*see p159*) but also plays at the **Centro Cultural de Belém** (*see right*). Its repertoire includes major symphonies and operas. Since the beginning of 2014, its resident conductor has been Joana Carneiro, back from a successful spell in the US and herself a product of the Gulbenkian.

Lisbon's third orchestra, the **Orquestra Metropolitana de Lisboa** (21 361 7320, www.metropolitana.pt) was founded in 1992 and, despite a difficult period financially, takes its role as a municipal orchestra extremely seriously, putting on literally hundreds of concerts in Lisbon and the surrounding region every year, many of them free. These range from full-blown orchestral concerts, presided over by conductor-composer Pedro Amaral, to solo and chamber performances at the downtown **Palácio Foz** (*see p159*), **Museu do Oriente** (*see p97*) and other venues. The orchestra is also very unusual in having three music schools attached. Every now and then it and its student offshoot, the Orquestra Académica Metropolitana, join forces to form a full symphony orchestra, the **Orquestra Sinfónica Metropolitana**, which has been a resident performer at the CCB's **Dias da Música** (*see p30*) for the last three years.

VENUES

Among its many other cultural functions, the **Centro Cultural de Belém** hosts classical concerts on a regular basis: its Grande Auditório has fine acoustics. The **Coliseu dos Recreios** (*see p152*) is more of a rock venue but is also used for the occasional classical concert and even opera. Acoustics vary; some maintain that the left side is best. At **Culturgest** (*see p120*), the Grande Auditório (tickets €15-€20) has a capacity of 618 and reasonable acoustics. **Teatro da Trindade** (*see p161*) has been known to stage light opera, while the **Pavilhão Atlântico** (*see p152*) is used for musical spectaculars. There are regular free concerts at the **Palácio Foz**, and the **Conservatório Nacional** (Rua dos Caetanos 29, 21 342 5922, www.emcn.edu.pt) occasionally hosts performances by its students or teachers.

Lisbon is blessed – or perhaps cursed, given their ruinous maintenance costs – with some lovely 18th-century church organs. Those in the **Igreja de São Vicente** (*see p67*), **Igreja da Graça** (*see p66*) and **Sé** (*see p62*) are used fairly frequently to give free concerts.

★ Centro Cultural de Belém

Praça do Império (21 361 2878, www.museu berardo.pt). Train to Belém from Cais do Sodré, tram 15, or bus 714, 727, 728, 751. **Open** *Box office* 11am-8pm daily (or until 30mins after start of performance). **Tickets** €5-€60. **Map** p244 B10.

The CCB's two auditoriums are sometimes used for classical concerts: the Grande Auditório has excellent acoustics for large-scale works and opera, while

Teatro Nacional de São Carlos.
See p159.

ARTS & ENTERTAINMENT

PROSPECTING FOR CULTURE

Sweet music at the Gulbenkian Foundation.

Sixty years after its founder's passing, the **Fundação Calouste Gulbenkian** (see p159) remains Lisbon's most important cultural institution, as well as funding research and other initiatives in the fields of education and science. Created in 1956, it's constantly reinventing itself.

Calouste Gulbenkian was born in Istanbul in 1869, into a family of Armenian traders, though he later was naturalised British. He made his fortune in oil – his deal-making earning him the nickname 'Mr Five Per Cent' and helping to open up the reserves in the Middle East to Western companies. From Paris, where he was living at the oubreak of World War II, he fled to Vichy and then Lisbon, where he lived the rest of his life.

Gulbenkian is said to have been bitten by the collecting bug in his teens, after picking up some coins in a bazaar. By the time he died in 1955, he had amassed one of the most valuable collections in private hands, and unrivalled in Europe for Islamic and Oriental art. He left it all to the foundation created by a clause in his will and endowed it with his fortune. It was only 14 years after his death, following wrangles over the return of art on loan to institutions around the world, that the Museu Calouste Gulbenkian (see p116) finally opened its doors.

Well before that, 'the Gulbenkian' – as the foundation is invariably known – had already started to fill the considerable gap in Portugal left by feeble state funding. Today, as well as the museum, it runs a Centro de Arte Moderna (see p116), provides grants to students, publishes arts-related material and runs a specialist central library and nationwide network that puts the state's efforts to shame. Its funds aren't limitless, but in the field of music in particular the foundation remains unrivalled.

Founded as a chamber group in 1962, the Orquestra Gulbenkian developed its own distinctive sound, though with 60 players the orchestra falls short of symphonic dimensions. While its size makes it flexible, and its repertoire is vast, the end result depends upon the inspiration provided by the conductor. In 2013, Englishman Paul McCreesh took over as principal conductor and artistic adviser from long-time American maestro Lawrence Foster, who retains emeritus status. Guest conductors are also a feature of the October to May seasons; one of the current crop, Portugal's own Joana Carneiro, has worked extensively with orchestras abroad and is now the first woman to conduct the Gulbenkian.

The Foundation's concert series bring major world orchestras, chamber groups and soloists to the Grande Auditório and other spaces, including the outdoor amphitheatre in the foundation's gardens, as well as various other local venues.

The 100-strong Coro Gulbenkian celebrated its 50th anniversary in 2014, having been founded two years after the orchestra. The choir marked the big date with the national première of a specially commissioned work by leading Portuguese composer Eurico Carrapatoso. For almost the whole of its existence it has been under the baton of Michel Corboz, and has won plaudits for its work with the Orchestra of the 18th Century, founded by Frans Brüggen.

ARTS & ENTERTAINMENT

the Pequeno Auditório is more intimate. The still smaller Sala de Ensaio (Rehearsing Room) is occasionally used for alternative music. The CCB also hosts special events throughout the year, such as the Dias da Música festival in May (*see p30*), and has various workshops for children.

★ Fundação Calouste Gulbenkian

Avenida de Berna 45A (21 782 3700 information, 21 782 3030 box office, www.musica.gulbenkian. pt). Metro Praça de Espanha. **Open** *Box office* 10am-7pm Mon-Fri; 10am-5.30pm Sat (10am-7pm concert nights); 1-7pm Sun (concert nights only). **Tickets** €5-€60. **Map** p248 K4.
See p158 **Prospecting for Culture**.

Palácio Foz

Praça dos Restauradores (21 322 1237, www. gmcs.pt/palaciofoz). Metro Restauradores. **Admission** free. **Map** p250 L8.
At this grand former private residence, free concerts by members of the Orquestra Metropolitana de Lisboa and visiting international musicians are staged on weekdays and the odd Saturday in the opulent first-floor Sala de Espelhos (Mirror Room). Enter via the door at the far right of the imposing 18th-century façade. The building now houses government departments, including the Gabinete para os Meios de Comunicação Social (media unit), whose website lists upcoming concerts and notice of occasional tours of the palace, including a basement whose decor is charged with Masonic symbolism.

★ Teatro Nacional de São Carlos

Rua Serpa Pinto 9 (21 325 3045, www.saocarlos.pt). Metro Baixa-Chiado or tram 28. **Open** *Box office* 10am-7pm Mon-Fri; 10am-5pm Sat, Sun (or until 30mins after start of performance). **Tickets** *Opera* €20-€50. *Orchestral/choral* €10-€20. **Map** p250 L10.
A grand 18th-century opera house inspired by the likes of Milan's La Scala, with a rococo interior, excellent acoustics and good sightlines. Despite chronic under-investment, its artistic profile has been raised over the past decade by a well-connected Italian director, Paolo Pinamonti – now officially with consultant status but still actively involved. As well as the Orquestra Sinfónica Portuguesa (*see p157*), the theatre is home to the Coro do Teatro Nacional de São Carlos, headed by Giovanni Andreoli, while its well-respected former director João Paulo Santos now oversees musical and dramatic production. Note that reservations are accepted only up to 48 hours before a show. *Photo p157.*

FESTIVALS

The CCB has an annual festival, **Dias da Música** (*see p30*); this is preceded in late March by a one-day **Festa de Primavera**, which includes some free concerts. The **Festival de Sintra** (*see p32*)

is a summer highlight for classical buffs, with concerts by international artists. Almada, a culturally vibrant municipality on the south bank of the River Tagus, has a Mês da Música in October that encompasses music from hip hop to fado and classical, the latter in the form of **Os Sons de Almada Velha** with concerts staged in lovely old churches. In November in Lisbon, look out for **Música em São Roque** (*see p33*); and then, in December, **Concertos de Natal**.

Música Viva

Various venues (21 457 5068, www.misomusic. com). **Tickets** €10; €2-€5 reductions. **Date** varies.
Música Viva is a series of experimental music concerts that invariably includes several world premières and provides an important forum for local musical creativity. Dates vary, as do venues: in past years, concerts have been held in places ranging from the Gulbenkian (*see left*) to the Mosteiro dos Jerónimos.

Os Sons de Almada Velha

Various venues, Almada (21 294 5807, 21 272 4008, www.cm-almada.pt). Ferry to Cacilhas from Cais do Sodré boat station then TST buses. **Admission** free. **Date** late Sept-late Oct.
The Sounds of Old Almada is a council-run festival in which churches and former convents in the old town and the dockside neighbourhood of Cacilhas host concerts of music above all composed in Europe in the first half of the 17th century. For buses to these south-bank venues, check the TST website (21 112 6200, www.tsuldotejo.pt).

Dance

A generation of choreographers was nurtured at the Ballet Gulbenkian – for 40 years Portugal's strongest contemporary dance company. It was wound up in 2005, when officials at the **Fundação Calouste Gulbenkian** (*see p158* **Prospecting for Culture**) decided resources could be better used to fund burgeoning independents, which has produced some promising results. Classical ballet has a short history in Portugal. The **Companhia Nacional de Bailado** (21 347 4048, www.cnb.pt), based at the Teatro Camões, was set up in 1977.

Away from the big institutions, Lisbon's dance community is good at collaborating with umbrella projects such as **Forum Dança** (21 342 8985, www.forumdanca.pt), **c.e.m. centro em movimento** (21 887 1763, www.c-e-m.org) and **Alkantara** (*see p160*). Few companies have their own performance space, but most tour regularly abroad. The **Companhia Portuguesa de Bailado Contemporâneo** (21 394 0460, www. cpbc.pt), founded in 1998 by Gulbenkian veteran Vasco Wellencamp, is among the more accessible.

Olga Roriz and her eponymous company (21 887 2383, www.olgaroriz.com) tackle provocative

ARTS & ENTERTAINMENT

social, political or religious themes. João Fiadeiro's **RE.AL** company (21 390 9255, www.re-al.org) collaborates with other groups such as Artistas Unidos, freely mixing in text and drama. Vera Mantero, seen by many as Portugal's most important choreographer, heads **O Rumo do Fumo** (21 343 1646, www.orumodofumo.com). **Clara Andermatt** (21 590 3105, http://clara-andermatt.com) has overseen some interesting work with Cape Verdean artists. Also well-known abroad is **Rui Horta**, another Gulbenkian alumni who has tried his hand in areas from film to circus, but now runs a dance research centre (26 689 9856, www.oespacodotempo.pt) in the Alentejo.

If you want to dance yourself, a plethora of courses are advertised in *Agenda Cultural*, including at **Chapitô** (*see p162*). There are also periodic open dances (tango, samba and so on) at the **Teatro Municipal de São Luíz** (*see p152*), while the **CCB** (*see p157*) runs regular workshops. Workshops at **c.e.m.** (*see p159*) are also open to amateurs.

VENUES

The **Coliseu** (*see p152*) hosts visiting ballet companies, as well as circuses and rock concerts. But the **CCB** (*see p157*) is a better place to catch up-and-coming local dancers and choreographers: its Box Nova series offers the chance for works that are selected to be put on in its Sala de Ensaio (rehearsal room) for two consecutive nights.

Teatro Camões

Passeio de Neptuno, Parque das Nações (21 892 3477, www.cnb.pt). Metro Oriente. **Open** *Box office* Nov-Apr 1-6pm Wed-Sun. May-Oct 2-7pm (or until 30mins after start of performance). **Tickets** €5-€25.
Built for Expo 98, this big, blue glass-and-metal cube seats 890 amid state-of-the-art acoustics. It's home to the Companhia Nacional de Bailado (*see p159*). Bookings may also be made via the Teatro Nacional de São Carlos (*see p159*), but reservations are only accepted until 48 hours before the performance. The theatre also hosts a variety of other shows and workshops for all ages.

FESTIVALS

Portugal's **Festival Internacional de Teatro** (*see p34*), held in July, now includes dance too.

★ Alkantara Festival

Various venues (information 21 315 2267, www.alkantara.pt). **Tickets** €5-€12. **Date** mid May-early June.
What was once a small-scale dance event has blossomed into a major biennial multi-disciplinary festival, with performers from around the globe. Alkantara, the name of a neighbourhood in western

Alkantara Festival.

Lisbon, means 'bridge' in Arabic, and the festival seeks to foster links between different cultures and disciplines. Multi-show tickets are available.

Quinzena da Dança de Almada

Various venues (information 21 258 3175, www.cdanca-almada.pt. **Tickets** €6-€10. **Date** Sep-Oct.
This contemporary dance festival has been staged annually since 1993, largely showcasing Portuguese groups. Shows take place mostly on the south bank, but some are at the CCB and other Lisbon venues.

Theatre

As with the visual arts scene, Lisbon's relative isolation can spawn both hackneyed pretension and shining originality. There's now at least plenty of choice: both state and independent companies abound, offering ballet and street theatre, Brecht and Gil Vicente (the 16th-century father of Portuguese drama). There's a growing commercial sector, too, embracing comedy and musicals. If you speak little or no Portuguese, then **Estrela Hall** (English-language theatre), **Chapitô** (mainly physical theatre) and **Teatro Politeama** (with subtitles) will generally be your best bets, although **Teatro Nacional Dona Maria II** and other major theatres – as well as festivals – occasionally host foreign troupes, which may perform in a language you can follow.

INFORMATION & TICKETS

Newspaper listings cover the big theatres and some independents and have reviews, as does our sister publication *Time Out Lisboa*. Poster-spotting, leaflet-gathering and word-of-mouth should do the rest, and even alternative groups such as **Teatro do Vão** (96 661 5453, www.teatrodovao.com) and Palmela-based **O Bando** (21 233 6850, www.obando.pt) now have websites. Shows are usually at 9pm from Wednesday or Thursday to Saturday; there may be a Sunday matinée. Whatever a box office's normal hours, on performance days it will be open at least until showtime. Most locals buy tickets at the theatre, after reserving by phone or email, but agencies sell tickets for big shows.

ESTABLISHMENT THEATRES

With Lisbon's largest auditorium, another medium-sized one and a studio theatre, all with machinery, the **Centro Cultural de Belém** (*see p157*) has the best facilities. Its programme encompasses national and foreign groups, offering everything from puppet theatre to Hofesh Shechter. Founded back in 1993, **Culturgest** (*see p120*) usually has more adventurous programming. The **Pavilhão Atlântico** (*see p152*) hosts musical and ice spectaculars. The **Teatro Municipal de São Luíz** (*see p152*) has some musicals and drama, though it more often hosts jazz and rock concerts.

Teatro da Trindade
Largo da Trindade 7 (21 342 3200, http:// teatrotrindade.inatel.pt). Metro Baixa-Chiado. **Open** *Box office* 2-8pm Tue-Sat; 2-6pm Sun (or until 30mins after start of performance). **Tickets** €6.50-€15. **Map** p250 L9.
Teatro da Trindade is a 19th-century gilded jewel that specialises in high-profile one-off shows and new plays with a strong political theme. The theatre is now striking out in a fresh musical direction, too, bringing light opera to the masses. There's also a studio theatre and a smoky basement bar that offers music and comedy.

Teatro Municipal Maria Matos
Avenida Miguel Frei Contreiras 52 (21 843 8801, www.teatromariamatos.pt). Metro Roma. **Open** *Box office* 3-8pm Tue-Sun (or until 30mins after start of peformance). Closed Aug. **Tickets** €5-€15. **No credit cards. Map** p249 N3.
This 500-seat theatre, owned by the council, hosts an eclectic range of shows, from contemporary plays to children's theatre, jazz and other concerts. The upstairs café has a small stage.

★ Teatro Nacional Dona Maria II
Praça Dom Pedro IV (800 213 250, www. teatro-dmaria.pt). Metro Rossio. **Open** *Box office* 2-7pm Tue, Sun; 11am-10pm Wed-Fri; 2-10pm Sat. **Tickets** €2.50-€16. **No credit cards. Map** p250 M9.
Inaugurated in 1846, this is Lisbon's leading national theatre. The 320-seat Sala Garrett (named after the founder) and 52-seat studio stage in-house produc- tions, some in partnership with independents, and

periodically host foreign groups. There are work- shops for children, literary readings and talks, Lisbon's only thespian bookshop and a café with great cakes. A few tickets are sold on the day (2-3pm) at €6. You can also book a guided tour of the theatre (11.30am Mon, closed Aug). The website is one of the few where you can buy tickets (but only if you have access to a printer).

COMMERCIAL THEATRES

Teatro Maria Vitória
Parque Mayer, Avenida da Liberdade (21 346 1740, www.teatromariavitoria.com). Metro Avenida. **Open** *Box office* 1-9.30pm Tue-Sun. **Tickets** €12.50-€90. **No credit cards. Map** p246 L8.
The only theatre not to have gone dark in Parque Mayer – Lisbon's old theatreland and the home of *revista*, the authentically Portuguese-style music hall that provided an escape valve under Salazar. It stages two shows a night with a trademark mix of slapstick, glittery camp and mild satire.

Teatro Politeama
Rua das Portas de Santo Antão 109 (21 324 5700, www.teatro-politeama.com). Metro Restauradores. **Open** *Box office* 2-7pm Mon, Tue; 2-9.30pm Wed- Fri; 3.30-9.30pm Sat; 3.30-5pm Sun. **Tickets** €10- €30. **No credit cards. Map** p250 L8.
This 700-seat theatre puts on slick musicals and cabaret-style *revistas* masterminded by impresario Filipe La Feria. One major advantage over just about every other local venue is that shows have English subtitles. The latest long-running production is

Teatro Nacional Dona Maria II.

ARTS & ENTERTAINMENT

Teatro do Bairro.

Portugal à Gargalhada (meaning 'Portugal laughing out loud') – a prime example of Portuguese *revista* of the kind also to be found at Teatro Maria Vitória (*see p161*). You can buy tickets for shows via the theatre's website.

Teatro Tivoli BBVA

Avenida da Liberdade 182 (21 357 2025, www. teatrotivolibbva.pt). Metro Avenida. **Open** *Box office* 1-2.30pm, 3.30-8pm Tue, Wed; 1-2.30pm, 3.30-7.30pm, 8-9.30pm Thur, Fri; 2-10pm Sat; 2-5pm Sun. **Tickets** €10-€60. **No credit cards**. **Map** p246 L8.

This central venue, with more than 1,000 seats, opened in 1924. It was acquired by promoter UAU (www.uau.pt) in 2012, and now relies on local and imported (Brazilian) TV stars to pull in the punters. The theatre also hosts some rock concerts. The in-house restaurant serves mainly Portuguese fare.

Teatro Villaret

Avenida Fontes Pereira de Melo 30A (21 353 8586, http://teatrovillaret.com). Open 2-10pm Wed-Sun. **Tickets** €8-€20. **No credit cards**. **Map** p246 L6.

This 384-seat theatre, named after comic actor João Villaret, has been associated with comedy since its inauguration in 1964 by Raúl Solnado, a major influence on today's alternative comedians. Now managed by the Teatro Nacional Dona Maria II, it hosts a confusing mix of commercial comedies, challenging contemporary works and shows for children – plus the occasional stand-up comedy show in the downstairs bar.

ALTERNATIVE THEATRES

★ Chapitô

Costa do Castelo 1-7 (21 885 5550, www.chapito. org). Tram 12, 28 or bus 37. **Open** *Box office* 2hrs before performance; phone bookings 10am-8pm daily. **Tickets** €5-€12. **No credit cards**. **Map** p251 M9.

This venue has a unique atmosphere, with students from the circus school and tourists rubbing shoulders on a restaurant patio that has fabulous views. It's home to the Companhia do Chapitô, a troupe known

for inspired comic physical theatre and overseen by London-based director John Mowat. Chapitô also plays host to an annual female clowns' convention.

Estrela Hall

Rua Saraiva de Carvalho (21 396 1946, www. lisbonplayers.com.pt). Tram 28 or bus 9. **Open** *Box office* 1hr 30mins before performance; book online or by leaving message. **Tickets** €8-€10. **No credit cards**. **Map** p245 J8.

Once attached to the Anglican church round the corner, this is home to the Lisbon Players, a long-established amateur group (formed in 1947) that performs regularly in English. The focus is firmly on the classics, but comedy and musicals get a look-in. The venue was recently given an overhaul but don't expect luxury.

Teatro Aberto

Praça de Espanha (21 388 0089, www.teatro aberto.com). Metro São Sebastião or Praça de Espanha. **Open** *Box office* 2-10pm Wed-Sat; 2-6.30pm Sun. **Tickets** €7.50-€15. **No credit cards**. **Map** p248 K4.

Now working in this modern building with two plush auditoriums (one with 400 seats, the other half that), the O Novo Grupo company is the successor of the cutting-edge 1970s Grupo 4. Under João Lourenço and his partner, playwright and Germanist Vera San Payo de Lemos, its repertoire was in the past slanted towards heavyweights such as Brecht, but in recent years has produced more modern fare such as Neil LaBute and Caryl Churchill.

Teatro do Bairro

Rua Luz Soriano 63 (21 347 3358, 91 321 1263, www.teatrodobairro.org). Metro Baixa-Chiado or tram 28. **Open** *Box office* 8pm to start of performance (phone bookings 4-8pm). **Tickets** €7-€10. **Map** p250 L9.

This relatively new neighbourhood theatre housed in an old newspaper printing press started out professing to offer a distinctive artistic project, but seems to have lapsed into staging mainly light comedies. Still, it's a stylish venue that's as much bar and social club as theatre, and has regular live music and screenings of European films.

Teatro Cinearte

*Largo dos Santos 2 (21 396 5275, 21 396 5360,
www.abarraca.com). Tram 15, 25.* **Open** *Box office*
1hr30mins before performance; phone bookings
10am-7pm daily. **Tickets** €5-€20. **No credit
cards.** Map p245 J10.

Cinearte is the showcase for A Barraca, a troupe
founded 30 years ago and led by Maria do Céu
Guerra, one of Portugal's handful of established
female directors. It stages productions of modern
Portuguese and European classics. There are two
auditoriums, and the upstairs café-bar has an offbeat
programme of concerts, poetry and stand-up comedy, as well as workshops for children.

Teatro da Comuna

*Praça de Espanha (21 722 1770, www.comuna
teatropesquisa.pt). Metro Praça de Espanha.*
Open *Box office* 8-9.30pm on performance days;
phone bookings 10am-7pm Mon-Sat. **Tickets**
€5-€10. **No credit cards.** Map p248 K4.

Resident company Comuna – Teatro de Pesquisa
(Research Theatre) has a history of experimentation
dating from the early 1970s, but today the theatre
also plays host to mainstream pieces. Its four show
spaces include a café that hosts mainly comedy.

Teatro da Cornucópia

*Rua Tenente Raul Cascais 1A (21 396 1515,
www.teatro-cornucopia.pt). Metro Rato.* **Open**
Box office 3-9.30pm Thur-Sat. **Tickets** €5-€15.
No credit cards. Map p246 K8.

Tucked away in a quiet corner is this well-equipped
theatre with a 135-seat auditorium where respected
group Teatro do Bairro Alto presents challenging
productions, often in Portuguese, as well as the occasional Greek classic. It's run by Luís Miguel Cintra, a
fine actor much used over the years by veteran director Manoel de Oliveira (*see p134*).

IN THE KNOW CHEAP SEATS

Theatre in Lisbon can be very cheap, if you're
free on the right night. At Teatro da Trindade,
tickets for Wednesday performances bought
at the theatre on the day cost just €5,
while at Teatro Cinearte that applies on
Thursdays; at Teatro Comuna and Teatro da
Politécnica, tickets for both these days cost
€5. At Teatro Nacional Dona Maria II, tickets
to Thursday performances of shows with
a run of at least three weeks are half price,
and every day a limited number of €6 tickets
go on sale for an hour from 2pm (max two
per person). And if you're too disorganised to
manage any of the above, Teatro Municipal
de São Luíz, Teatro Municipal Mário Matos
and Teatro Cinearte are among venues that
offer €5 tickets to under-30s most nights.

Teatro Meridional

*Rua do Açúcar 64, Poço do Bispo (91 999 1213,
www.teatromeridional.net). Bus 28, 718.* **Open**
Box office 1hr before performance; phone bookings
2-8pm Tue, 2-9.30pm Wed-Sat, 2-4pm Sun. **Tickets**
€5-€10. **No credit cards.**

A converted warehouse in eastern Lisbon is the base
for Teatro Meridional, a Portuguese-Spanish group
that focuses on comic and physical drama. It often
stages works by African authors. Shows may start
as late as 10pm.

★ Teatro da Politécnica

*Rua da Escola Politécnica 56 (21 391 6750, box
office 96 196 0281, www.artistasunidos.pt). Metro
Rato.* **Open** *Box office* from 5pm Tue-Fri until end
of performance, from 3pm Sat; phone bookings
3-6pm daily. **Tickets** €5-€10. **No credit cards.**
Map p247 M9.

The latest home of Artistas Unidos, which despite
its status as one of Lisbon's most vibrant companies has been forced to move four times in a decade.
Shows may also be staged at larger venues such as
the CCB (*see p157*) or taken on national tour. As well
as a core of talented young actors, the group draws
on a wider 'family' – including well-known figures
from local television and cinema. The whole project
is overseen by founder-director Jorge Silva Melo,
himself a fine actor. The company also publishes
Portuguese translations of the contemporary foreign
plays it produces.

Teatro Taborda

*Costa do Castelo 75 (21 885 4190, www.teatro
dagaragem.com). Tram 12, 28 or bus 37.* **Open**
Box office from 30mins before to 30mins after
start of performance; phone bookings 10am-
6pm daily. **Tickets** €5-€10. **No credit cards.**
Map p247 M9.

This late 19th-century, council-owned theatre is now
home to long-established troupe Teatro da Garagem.
It has a 150-seat auditorium, a small room for low-
budget performances, an exhibition space, and a
cosy rear café and terrace with spectacular views
(open 6pm-midnight Mon, 3pm-midnight Tue-Thur,
3pm-2am Fri, Sat, 3pm-midnight Sun). You can book
tickets by email (geral@teatrodagaragem.com).

FESTIVALS

The Almada-based **Festival International
de Teatro** (*see p32*) is firmly established as
Portugal's biggest festival of drama, with
performances staged both south and north of
the River Tagus. Almada also has a smaller
Mostra de Teatro (21 273 8102, www.
mostradeteatrodealmada.blogspot.pt) in
February. In early summer in Lisbon, there's a
veritable orgy of puppet shows at the **FIMFA
Festival Internacional de Marionetas
e Formas Animadas** (*see p30*).

Escapes & Excursions

Escapes & Excursions

One of the best things about a visit to Lisbon is that you can enjoy a city break – complete with historical sights, fine food and drink, and great nightlife – with a beach holiday thrown in for good measure. Or, if you have an extra day, head for wonderfully romantic Sintra, with its hilltop castle, palaces and gardens; the picture-postcard walled village of Óbidos; the palaces of Queluz and Mafra; continental Europe's westernmost point at Cabo da Roca; or one of the countless other charming destinations in the region. All are within reach of the capital by public transport.

Beaches

The Algarve may be the country's best-known beach destination, but the Lisbon region offers plenty of opportunities for sunbathing and beachcombing. West of the city, the Estoril coast is dotted with sheltered beaches. Continue on round the cape to windswept Guincho and beyond for more spectacular cliffs and coves. South of the Tagus, Caparica is the gateway to miles of dune-backed sands, served by bars that cater to every kind of style tribe. More solitary souls can head further south, where you'll find more isolated beaches.

There are currently 16 Blue Flag beaches in the Lisbon region, but water quality varies, particularly on the Estoril coast. As for safety, beaches as far as Cascais are fairly sheltered, but take care elsewhere; drownings occur off Portugal's coast every year. Where lifeguards are on duty in the bathing season (June-mid Sept), check the colour of the flag flying on the beach: if it's red, limit yourself to paddling. Note also that the ocean, particularly north of Cascais, can be chilly. Portugal increasingly draws leading surfers and windsurfers (*see p171* **Wave Riders**), but wetsuits are de rigueur.

LISBON TO CASCAIS

Catch the Cascais train from Cais do Sodré (every 15-30mins, €2.15 on a €0.50 electronic card) and you can be on your towel in 45 mins. The furthest you'll have to walk to a beach is 10mins, at Carcavelos. The further down the line you go, the more resort-like the surroundings. The return journey offers fine sunset views. When travelling to smaller stations, buy a return or keep coins handy: counters may close as early as 4.30pm, leaving only machines to sell tickets. But trains run as late as 1.30am both ways. Note that some trains out of Cais do Sodré don't stop at every station, and some terminate at Oeiras.

By car, the A5 toll motorway between Lisbon and Cascais, which is well signposted around Praça de Espanha and Praça Marquês de Pombal, closes in on the coast around Estoril. The N6 'Marginal' hugs the coastline all the way along, but is prone to traffic congestion.

At Estoril and on some other beaches, sun shades and loungers can be rented from €6 per item. A continuous promenade runs from São João do Estoril to Cascais; restaurants and bars with esplanades abound, some with showers. There's also fitness equipment at regular intervals between Estoril and Cascais.

Carcavelos

We wouldn't recommend any of the beaches up to the São Julião da Barra headland, 20km west of Lisbon, for swimming. But just before it, a 20-minute walk from Santo Amaro or Oeiras rail stations, is a fun seawater pool, the **Piscina Oceânica** (21 446 2552, http://piscinaoceanica. oeirasviva.pt; open June 10am-7pm daily, July & Aug 9.30am-8pm daily, Sept 10am-7pm daily; from €4.10/half-day, €3.20 under-17s, €14.40 family) that posts water quality daily. It costs more at weekends, but come two hours before closing and the price plummets. Or carry on past the São Julião headland to Praia de Carcavelos, whose broad sands are unmatched along this coast. It's packed in summer, attracting hordes of local youngsters. There are volleyball nets and the beach is popular with surfers all year round. At the **Windsurf Café** (21 457 8965) you can rent kayaks or book lessons with top local experts in surfing, bodyboarding and windsurfing. For eats, **A Pastorinha** (21 457 1892, main courses €25, closed Tue) is a good fish restaurant, while **Sun 7 Bar** serves fajitas and chicken. At the far eastern end of the beach, craggy rocks mark off a middle-class hangout. **Bar Moinho** (21 458 0194, closed Wed), the larger of two bars, is open until 2am, with deckchairs and chillout music.

Parede

At the next major beach west of Carcavelos, the peeling promenade may not exude the elegance of Estoril or Cascais, but the sheltered patch of sand is quieter than both of those beaches and good for bathing (it has a Blue Flag). Older Portuguese flock here for the high iodine content in the waters – it supposedly helps against rheumatism. West from Parede, shelves of rock reach out into the sea, creating pools where waves break low. Further on, Praia das Avencas, reached on foot via a subway, is served year round by the cosy **Bar das Avencas** (21 457 2717, closed Tue).

São Pedro do Estoril

An attractive beach, little used by tourists but crowded on summer weekends. A narrow strip of sand slips into clear waters, where rock slabs create shades of blue and green: a big draw for divers, but it makes for a dodgy dip at low tide. If you're coming by car, drive round the roundabout to the beach side and enter the clifftop car park. Below is Praia de Bafureira, its bars popular with local youngsters. The **Peixe na Linha** restaurant (Praia da Bafureira, 21 468 5388, main courses €19) has a varied menu and giddy sea views.

São João do Estoril

Heading further west, above the tidal Praia da Forte, funky clifftop shack **Alcatruz** (Rua Vasco da Gama, 21 195 7792) serves snacks and drinks from noon until the wee hours. A little further on are the area's two main beaches, linked by a promenade: first the pretty and peaceful Praia da Azarujinha, and then, after a headland, the larger Praia da Poça, a 'locals' beach that offers respite from the crowds elsewhere on the coast. At its western end is a large seawater pool; at the other, **Bar Atlantis** is good for watching the sunset.

Carcavelos.

Guincho.

Estoril

The narrow strand at Tamariz beach, next to Estoril station, is occupied by tourists and locals. The promenade is filled with the tables of adjoining bars and restaurants (some doubling as noisy nightspots). If you want the seclusion of a private seawater pool, **Piscinas de Tamariz** (open June-mid Sept 10am-7pm daily, from €9, reductions after 2pm) keeps the mob at bay. Towards Cascais is **Bar Jonas** (closed Nov & Dec), where you can sip sangria and listen to ambient music, and beyond it another beach with its own station, Monte Estoril. At the Cascais end, **Escotilha Bar** tempts Brits with fish and chips. Further on is a seawater pool; take care – the waves lap over with force. For more on Estoril away from the beach, *see p174*.

Cascais

The first Cascais beach is only a frisbee throw from the train station: Praia da Conceição, which is separated by a strip of sand from Praia da Duquesa. **John David's Café**, at the east end of the beach by the station, panders to Anglo-Saxon palates, while the attached **Cascais Watersport Centre** offers visitors diving, waterskiing, windsurfing or pedal boats. Like other bars, it has showers, changing rooms and sunbeds for hire. Beyond the **Albatroz Hotel** (*see p222*) you'll find the tiny Praia da Rainha. In front of Praça do 5 de Outubro, Praia da Ribeira is bigger but geared to fishing rather than sunbathing. For more on Cascais town, *see p174*.

GUINCHO & THE SINTRA COAST

The sea crashes into the rocks with a new violence beyond Cascais. **Boca do Inferno** (*see p175*) marks the change. At Guincho, cliffs give way to a great bank of sand, which is ringed by heath and woodland. Further to the north, the Sintra hills

end in the cliffs of **Cabo da Roca** (*see p176*). Beyond here the beaches are smaller, tucked between dramatic headlands and linked by clifftop trails as far north as Magoito.

Getting to these beaches by public transport is a bit more of a performance, but Scotturb buses (www.scotturb.com) cover the whole region. As well as individual tickets, there's a €12 day pass (or a €15 one that includes train travel to and from Lisbon, and can be bought in town). Alternatively, taxis from Cascais (21 466 0101, 21 465 9500) are relatively cheap; to Guincho the trip should cost no more than €10.

If you're driving from Cascais, for Praia do Guincho take the Estrada do Guincho coast road, or the inland route through Birre and Areia villages. The latter is the route you'll pick up if you come on the A5 motorway straight from Lisbon. If you're headed instead for the Sintra coast, from the A5 head north on the N9-1 and at Malveira pick up the N247 Sintra road; each beach is signposted off this road.

Guincho

Some 6km (four miles) from Cascais, the open sands of Praia Grande do Guincho stretch back, forming dunes that reach up the hillside beyond the main road. To the north, the Sintra hills form a craggy horizon, and fresh pine scents mix with the salty ocean tang. Dismissed in the 1940s by *Life* magazine as a beach with no future, Guincho is now a prime destination. But take heed. A breeze in Cascais probably means a gale here. Bathers should be wary of powerful waves and currents; note that there are no lifeguards in the middle of the beach.

Guincho is among Europe's top spots for windsurfing, but is no place for beginners. It can also offer good surfing, mainly early and late in the day when the wind dies down. At the southern end, the long-established **Guincho Surf School** (91 753 5719, www.guinchosurfschool.com) caters for everyone from rookies to advanced surfers with lessons and week-long 'clinics'. **Estalagem do Muchaxo**, a hotel built around an old fort, has an excellent restaurant and its own sheltered seawater pool (mid May-Sept, non-guests €15 Mon-Fri, €17.50 Sat, Sun). Just to the south are two smaller, more sheltered beaches, with showers. At the opposite, northern end (a 20min walk from where the 405 bus turns inland; turn left after the picnic site), **Bar do Guincho** (91 850 0043, closed Mon) draws watersports enthusiasts. The bar's restaurant has a decent menu (main courses €12) and is cosy in winter. To reach tiny, sheltered Praia do Abano follow the track past Bar do Guincho car park for another 1.3km (one mile).

Fine dining options dot the coast road between Cascais and Guincho: fish restaurants where you can divide your attention between the sunset and the seafood. **Mestre Zé** (21 487 0275, main courses €23) offers excellent fare. Overlooking the beach, there's the Michelin-starred **Fortaleza do Guincho** (21 487 0491, main courses €30).

Guincho is a smooth 20- to 30-minute bike ride from Cascais and you can borrow bikes for free from four strategically located booths – one right by the train station – run by BiCas (information 21 482 5000, May-Sept 8am-5.30pm daily, Oct-Apr 9am-5pm daily, last pick-up 90mins before closing). You'll need a passport or ID card; under-16s must be accompanied by parents. If you don't fancy cycling, Scotturb buses (www.scotturb.com) leave from downtown Cascais about every hour (€3.25), plying a circular route in opposite directions and stopping at the sights and restaurants. For sea views on the outward journey, take bus 405; for the same on the return leg catch bus 415.

Praia da Adraga

Off the N247 Sintra road 15km north of Guincho, a road winds downhill from Almoçageme to a near-perfect beach wedged between tall cliffs. At one end, an arch has formed through the rocks, and at low tide you can discover a string of caves. A beachfront bar and restaurant complete the picture. Public transport is limited (bus 403 to Almoçageme from either Cascais or Portela de Sintra, or bus 439 from Portela de Sintra then a 20min walk). The narrow road down to the beach can get congested.

Praia Grande

Just north of Praia da Adraga, this larger beach is also signposted from the Sintra road. It's less secluded, with several restaurants and, at its northern end, the **Hotel Arribas** (21 928 9050) with an Olympic-sized pool (mid June-Sept, €8 Mon-Fri, €9.80 Sat & Sun). Surf competitions are held at Praia Grande and the southern end attracts a young, sporty crowd. A track leads to Praia Pequena, a smaller beach accessible at low tide. Near Bar do Fundo, 338 steps lead to clifftop trails running north and south. Praia Grande is served by bus 439 from Portela de Sintra.

Praia das Maçãs

This is a medium-sized family beach by a village with lots of seafood restaurants. It has changing rooms and showers, plus municipal sports facilities and a swimming pool nearby, as well as *tiralôs* for the disabled (July, Aug 10am-6pm daily; *see p172* **In the Know**).

ESCAPES & EXCURSIONS

Praia da Adraga.

From mid June to mid September, you can take a fun antique tram to Praia das Maçãs from Sintra. It runs down the leafy hills past Colares village, with its ancient vineyards. Friday is the best day to go, as locals tend to mob the beach at weekends. Trams leave roughly hourly (9am-6pm Fri-Sun; €3, €2 reductions) from a stop next to the MU.SA art museum (*see p178*), about a 10min walk from Sintra or Portela de Sintra rail stations. Scotturb bus 441 also does the trip from Portela de Sintra, before continuing on to Azenhas do Mar.

There's no shortage of restaurants at Praia das Maçãs, but during the summer you'll need to book ahead for the better ones. Near the bus stop, **Búzio** (Avenida Eugéne Levy 56, 21 929 2172, main courses €13) has a loyal local clientele. Another friendly place, with a beach view, is **O Loureiro** (21 929 2581, main courses €13), not to be confused with the snack bar of the same name. It serves everything from *carapau* (mackerel) to roast kid goat.

Azenhas do Mar

This picturesque village clings to a headland north of Praia das Maçãs. There's a 2km marked footpath between the two. Open-air cafés (one in a Moorish watermill) and the **Azenhas do Mar** restaurant (21 928 0379, main courses €16) with picture windows overlook a minute beach. The place is renowned for its seafood and location – it feels as though the waves are about to crash on to your plate – and it's best to book ahead. Down below, steps lead to a rock-cut seawater pool (free) that's refilled by the tide. As well as bus 441 that goes through Praia das Maçãs, bus 440 also goes to Azenhas.

THE CAPARICA COAST

The Caparica coast begins near the mouth of the River Tagus, where a huge maritime grain silo dominates Trafaria village. Although it's one enormous strand, each stretch has its own feel, with the tone set by beach bars.

North from Caparica town, a broad promenade has been laid out with plenty of room to walk, run or cycle. South from the town, dunes rise up a short distance from the sea, and beyond them thickets of green reach inland to the base of a tree-crowned sandstone cliff. In spring, this area is all yellow flowers. The density of the beach population fluctuates with the popularity of the bars spaced along the dunes. The bars are reached by wooden walkways from the mini-train stops and car parks. Many have showers and first-aid posts, some have music and dancing, and most are closed out of season.

Provided you avoid rush hour, you can get from Lisbon to anywhere on the Caparica coast in less than an hour. Take the Ponte 25 de Abril suspension bridge then follow signs to Caparica. From there, the road south gives access to 12km (7.5 miles) of beaches; these are signposted off the road down dusty tracks and each has parking. On summer weekends, either pack up early or stay on until very late, as the traffic on the way back can be horrendous.

To reach Caparica from Lisbon by public transport, catch the ferry to Cacilhas from Cais do Sodré boat station (€1.20 on a €0.50 card, every 10-40mins), and from there a 135 TST bus (€3.25, 30min; you can buy cheaper multiple tickets at the booth in Cacilhas, which also has timetables). The last ferry back is around 2am, but the last bus to Cacilhas is usually at 8pm. There's also bus 153

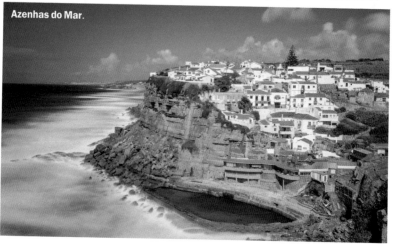

Azenhas do Mar.

WAVE RIDERS

Surf's up on the Portuguese coast.

Pure Emocean.

Older children can take advantage of the deep ocean rollers by learning how to surf or bodyboard. Or they can opt for kitesurfing or windsurfing, or the newly fashionable stand up paddle (SUP). All the beaches that are good for these activities have centres offering individual or cheaper group lessons (or a bundle of group lessons, which works out even cheaper) and equipment hire.

On the Estoril coast, Praia de Carcavelos is a vast beach with several good spots for surfing. At the **Windsurf Café** (21 457 8965, www.windsurfcafe.com) you can sign up for kayak, banana-boat or jet-ski outings. It also has links with the long-established **Carcavelos Surf School** (96 285 0497, 96 613 1203, www.carcavelossurfschool.com), which offers group lessons and individual lessons. You can bodyboard here for most of the year with specialists **Pure Emocean** (91 659 9466, 91 483 1659, www.puremocean. com); between July and September they work out of a shack on Praia Grande, near Sintra.

A little further west is São Pedro do Estoril, a beach that is particularly good for beginners, served by **Surf in São Pedro** (91 636 2559). With no set beach but based in Cascais, and variously making use of beaches at Carcavelos, Guincho and Praia Grande (depending on weather and waves), the **Cascais Surf School** (912 156 654,

www.surfcascais.com) does group lessons, with equipment and transport included. Also in Cascais, you can try SUP and surfing with the **Surf'n'Paddle School** (93 325 8114, www.surfnpaddle.com) at Praia da Duquesa. Or, if you know what you're doing, just hire a board, paddle and wetsuit.

Beyond Cascais, at Praia do Guincho, you can learn to surf with veteran instructors at **Guincho Surf School** (91 753 5719, www. guinchosurfschool.com). Or make the most of the strong north wind with **Guincho Kitesurf Adventures** (91 312 1606, 96 226 2879, www.kitesurfadventures.com.pt); they also offer SUP lessons. They have another base at Fonte da Telha at the southern end of the Costa da Caparica and, in winter, kitesurf on the Lagoa de Albufeira, a lagoon still further south. *See also p173.*

Also in Caparica, the **Carcavelos Surf School** (*see left*) has surfing lessons at the Praia do Infante. The more sparsely populated Praia da Nova Vaga, known for its wind and good waves, is another good place to try kitesurfing, with lessons from the **Boarder Club** school (21 214 1392, 93 418 4065, www.boarderclubportugal.com). You can also do SUP here.

For more on surfing in Portugal, featuring videos with veteran US professional Garrett McNamara, see www.portuguesewaves.com.

ESCAPES & EXCURSIONS

IN THE KNOW TIRALÔS

During the official bathing season (June-mid Sept) visitors with physical limitations can take advantage of free *tiralôs*, chair-cum-beach vehicles to help them into the water at the spot of their choice. No need to book; just turn up. On the Estoril coast (91 825 2302) participating beaches are Praia de Carcavelos, Praia do Tamariz at Estoril and Praia da Conceição at Cascais (all 9am-7pm daily), with trained physiotherapy students on hand. In the Sintra area (21 923 6021/08), there are *tiralôs* at Praia da Adraga and Praia das Maças in July and August only (10am-7pm daily), overseen by trained monitors.

direct from Lisbon's Praça de Espanha (40mins; €3.25); it drops you in Praça da Liberdade, next to Caparica market, a 5min walk from the mini-train. The last bus back to Lisbon (from round the corner) is at midnight. There's also bus 161 from Lisbon's Praça do Areeiro (€4.10). In summer, Lisbon bus company Carris usually lays on at least one beach service too.

An alternative route is the ferry from Belém to Trafaria (€1.15, about every hour), at the mouth of the Tagus. From there, bus 129 takes you to Caparica town (€2.25, 30mins); or hop off at São João when you see the sign 'Praias'. The last boat back is at 9.30pm on weekdays, 9pm at weekends. If you want to walk to the beach, it's 30mins to the nearest – or a 10min cycle ride if you've thought to hire a bike in Lisbon.

São João de Caparica

Liked by locals but relatively unknown to tourists, this beach north of Caparica town is backed by campsites and has a large shaded car park. There are several bars, some serving food, and a crèche. It's highly regarded by surfers and windsurfers, but currents nearer the northern end can be treacherous.

Caparica

Caparica town is not for those seeking sophistication or seclusion. There are several good seafood restaurants on the promenade, notably the bustling **O Barbas** (Praia do CDS, 21 291 3089, main courses €11). Access to the beach is via busy Rua dos Pescadores, near where buses from Lisbon unload. The approach is a jumble of restaurants and stalls, before you reach the **Transpraia** (21 290 0706, June-Sept), a small open-top train that stops at beaches all the way to Fonte da Telha (*see p173*). Departing at least

half-hourly between 9am and 8pm, the train scoots between the dunes: ring the bell to get off; stops are numbered. There are two zones; the most you'll pay is €2.10 single/€4 return, and there are reductions. The last train back leaves Fonte da Telha at 7.30pm.

A less quaint alternative is the TST 130 bus, which runs parallel to the coast from Caparica town as far as the dirt track that leads to Praia do Rei/da Morena/da Sereia (look out for the blue signs), before turning inland. Stops are a 5-15min walk from the beaches.

Praia Nova

The first stretches served by the Transpraia mini-train are a rag-bag of wooden beach huts and bars, with families entrenched in the dunes. At train stop 5, **Bar Golfinho** is a popular hangout, with a stoned surfer feel and live bands on summer evenings.

Praia da Mata

The true beauty of this coast reveals itself around train stop 8. This area tends to be busy, as it's the closest point to town where you can enjoy the beauty of the landscape with nothing more than an occasional bar to block the view. **Bar Praia** has a reasonably priced restaurant serving fish and meat dishes.

Praia da Riviera to Praia do Rei

This stretch attracts a younger, more middle-class crowd with wheels. At Praia da Riviera (stop 9) an eponymous restaurant offers grilled fish in cramped surroundings, but it's fresh and cheaper than Queen's Beach Club at stop 10. Between the two is **Jamming**, a beach club with a surf school (96 602 5252, www.essencia-surf.com) attached. At Praia do Castelo (stop 11), where volleyball nets dot the beach in summer, bars serve fish, salads, shots and cocktails. The **Cabana do Pescador** (Praia do Pescador, 21 296 2152, main courses €10), right by stop 12, is a more traditional eaterie that attracts lunch crowds even in winter.

Praia do Rei to Praia da Sereia

At Praia do Rei (stop 13) another eponymous restaurant offers good fish and seafood. **Hula Hula** bar attracts a younger crowd, serving all the salads, juices and cocktails you'd expect. On Praia da Morena (stop 14), **Borda d'Água** (21 297 5213) draws an older middle-class crowd, thanks to discreetly placed sun loungers. At Praia da Sereia (stop 15), a Blue Flag beach, **Bar Waikiki** (21 296 2129) is where young poseurs hang out. During the day drinks are served to sun loungers on the beach.

Meco.

Praia da Nova Vaga to Fonte da Telha

The sands are less crowded from Praia da Nova Vaga (stop 16), a kitesurfing favourite. **Tartaruga Bar** is on hand with juices and snacks. After Praia da Bela Vista (stop 17), the beach bars disappear. The final 3km (two-mile) stretch to Fonte da Telha is for male nudists and the site of much gay cruising – the dunes are very active, though the beach is fairly quiet. There are peaceful spots on the fringes and things get mixed again soon after stop 19.

Fonte da Telha

The Transpraia train line ends just before the village. The beach is busy here, with music bars such as **Cabana** (21 297 7711) pulling in younger customers. Its diving centre functions year round. **Restaurant O Camões** (Avenida 1° de Maio, Lote 94, 21 296 3865, main courses €10, closed Thur) serves fish caught by the owners. Further on, **Beira Mar** (Rua 1° de Maio C-105, 21 296 9504, main courses €13) is trendier, with a beach-facing terrace. **Inéditu's Bar** (91 724 0460) has good hamburgers for €2.

A walk up to the wooded hilltop (where buses to and from the Cacilhas ferries stop) yields wonderful views and access to clifftop paths. You can also go direct to Fonte da Telha from Cacilhas on the TST 127 bus (€4.10, 50mins then a 15min walk). There are buses back until at least 11.30pm.

LAGOA DE ALBUFEIRA & MECO

South of Fonte da Telha only the first tiny stretch of beach is accessible by car. Walking this way, you're unlikely to see another soul – apart from an occasional misanthropic nudist. The isolation increases the further you go, until you near Albufeira lagoon and then Meco. Here, the sea seems bluer, the shrubbery greener and the air fresher.

By car, follow the A2 motorway from the Ponte 25 de Abril, then take the N378 Sesimbra road. At a roundabout some 8km (5 miles) further on, the turning to Lagoa de Albufeira and Meco is signposted. Day-tripping in these parts by public transport is challenging, to say the least: set off early, armed with a timetable. Catch a TST bus to Sesimbra from Praça de Espanha or Cacilhas; from there, there are several buses to Meco village.

Lagoa de Albufeira

A tree-lined lagoon winds inland, cut off from the sea by a sandbar. The constant breeze and smooth waters make it ideal to try out windsurfing and there's lakeside **Escola Rui Meira** (21 268 4527, 96 918 6859, www.escolaruimeira.com) for windsurf, surf and kitesurf lessons or equipment hire. There are two beach restaurants, and a restaurant and café by the lake.

Meco

A kilometre or so south of Lagoa de Albufeira, a big sandstone rock marks Praia Moinho de Baixo. Here you'll find a good seafood restaurant and, thanks to the road link with Meco village, more people. The stretch beyond is nudist. Don't be alarmed if mud-caked natives sway into view; water trickling down the cliffside forms a clay that makes an ideal all-over mud pack. Walking round the headland at low tide gets you to Praia das Bicas, where there's another restaurant and a clifftop campsite. Meco itself has several bars and restaurants, plus trendy shops.

Casino Estoril.

Day Trips

If you want to get out of town and don't fancy a day at the beach, there are plenty of alternative day or half-day trips that will supply fresh air and fun. Any visit of more than a couple of days to the Portuguese capital should take in **Sintra**. It's best known for its palaces, which have earned it UNESCO World Heritage status as the 'first centre of European Romantic architecture', but there are also wonderful gardens. Other options include the old casino resort of **Estoril**, the palaces at **Queluz** and **Mafra**, and **Cascais**, an ancient fishing port that's also home to a fine museum dedicated to artist Paula Rego.

Casa das Histórias Paula Rego.

WEST OF LISBON

Estoril

Estoril was once a grand resort for titled Europeans, though its lustre has faded a little. Portugal was neutral during World War II and the resort attracted both spies, including Graham Greene, and exiled royals, such as Umberto of Italy and Juan Carlos of Spain. The **Casino Estoril** (21 466 7700, www.casino-estoril.pt) was the inspiration for Ian Fleming's *Casino Royale*. Now owned by Macao-based tycoon Stanley Ho, it draws legions of slot-machine addicts and has glitzy floor shows and the occasional free concert by Portuguese bands. Over the road, from June to September, there's a craft fair every evening. For more on local beaches, *see p166*.

The train is undoubtedly the most scenic, and the simplest, way to get to Estoril from Lisbon. There are generally three trains per hour Mon-Fri (5.30am-1.30am) from Cais do Sodré station (about 30mins; €1.25), with a less frequent service at weekends.

Where fine dining is concerned, the casino's **Estoril Mandarim** (closed Mon & Tue, main courses €30-€60) remains the undisputed regional champion, with more than 100 Cantonese dishes to choose from. It also has an excellent choice of Portuguese wines, elegant decor and ultra-efficient service, as well as a nice view of the fountains and garden. It's pricey, but you can just drop in for the juicy dim sum at lunchtime. There's also a cheaper Italian option, **Al Fresco** (Galerías do Estoril, Rua de Lisboa, 21 467 6770, main courses €13), opposite the casino's main entrance.

Cascais

This ancient fishing port at the end of the rail line from Cais do Sodré (4mins by train or 20mins on foot from Estoril) is also a busy modern town and resort. Around the Baia de Cascais are lobster pots, gaily painted boats and old fishermen talking football. In the winding streets to the north you'll find the **Museu do Mar** (Rua Júlio

Pereira de Mello, 21 481 5906, closed Mon), which pays tribute to fisherfolk and shipwrecks. Just beyond it is the **Casa das Histórias Paula Rego** (*see below* **Every Picture Tells a Story**), a striking building by Portuguese architect Eduardo Souto de Moura that showcases the intriguing narrative art of local girl Paula Rego. Across from the Cidadela, a 16th-century fort that now houses a fancy hotel and a trendy *taberna* for wine and snacks, the modern **Centro Cultural** (Avenida Rei Humberto II de Itália, 21 481 5660, closed Mon) hosts free art exhibits. Past the entrance to the marina, with its bars and restaurants, the **Casa de Santa Maria** (Rua do Farol, 21 481 5382, closed Mon) is an early work by Portuguese architect Raúl Lino with

a fine interior. Further on is the **Museu Conde de Castro Guimarães**, a lavish mansion containing Indo-Portuguese furniture, paintings and porcelain – left to the town by the Count of Guimarães and his wife when they died in 1892.

A 15-minute walk beyond this is **Boca do Inferno** (Hell's Mouth) where great columns of water shoot up at high tide. It was here in 1930 that Aleister Crowley faked his own death. En route is a palace where the Duke of Windsor and Mrs Simpson stayed after the abdication. At the start of the road to the beach at **Guincho** (*see p168*) is the **Casa da Guia** (21 484 3215), a 19th-century *palacete* – now a chic shopping centre – surrounded by esplanades with sea views. The BusCas shuttle, which starts at the

EVERY PICTURE TELLS A STORY
Paula Rego's brilliance on display.

Lisbon-born Paula Rego fled to London during the 1950s to study, and to escape the restrictions imposed on women in ultra-conservative Portugal. But the artist always made regular visits to her homeland, and particularly the Estoril coast where she grew up. So it's appropriate that Cascais was chosen as the location for the **Casa das Histórias Paula Rego** (*see p176*), which provides an in-depth introduction to her work. The inauguration of the museum in 2009 by Portugal's president confirmed her status as a national treasure, in a country that hasn't always celebrated the achievements of go-ahead women.

Rego has never shied away from supporting women's causes, such as the campaign against Portugal's strict abortion laws that for years saw tens of thousands risk their health – and lives – in illegal clinics or worse. Her contribution was a viscerating series of works depicting the tribulations of a victim of the prevailing law. In a 2007 referendum, voters approved the legalisation of abortion.

In much of Rego's art, women appear in less harrowing circumstances, often emanating energy and determination as much as pathos. As Germaine Greer has written of her works: 'It is not often given to women to recognise themselves in painting, still less to see their private world, their dreams, the insides of their heads, projected on such a scale and so immediately, with such depth and colour.'

The seeds of Rego's mature style can be found in a 1954 nude portrait that, while obeying academic rules, contains raw

emotion. After experimenting with collages and abstraction, she returned to figurative work, but with a theatrical element. Clothes are often key: in *The Moth*, a little girl wears a dress that belonged to the artist's mother.

The name Casa das Histórias (House of Stories) was at Rego's suggestion, because nursery rhymes, folk tales and stories in general are central to her work. She harks back to the narrative tradition of Jan Van Eyck, William Hogarth, Zurbarran and others, whose works she often quotes, but reinvents by manipulating the relations between figures and their setting to create new psychological drama. Some critics argue that she's currently the world's leading narrative painter; she's certainly Portugal's best-known female artist.

railway station, is the cheapest form of transport on this route (€0.85 one way), but Scotturb day passes are not valid for this bus.

For more on Cascais and the surrounding area, contact the **tourist office** (Rua Visconde da Luz 14, 21 482 2327, open 10am-1pm, 2-6pm daily) or the **nature tourism office** opposite Parque Marechal Carmona (Avenida da República, 21 460 42 30, open May-Sept 8am-8pm Mon-Fri, Oct-Apr 9am-4pm Mon-Fri), which has information on the nearby Parque Natural de Sintra-Cascais.

Beer, chips and TV football are available at pubs around Largo de Camões. Nearby, **Dom Manolo** (Via Visconde da Luz 6, 21 483 1126, main courses €9) does good, cheap grilled chicken. There are several fine fish restaurants in the pedestrianised centre, such as **Beira Mar** (Rua das Flores 6, 21 482 7380, www.restaurante beiramar.pt, main courses €12, closed Tue), and on the coast road to Guincho, starting with **Furnas** (21 486 9243, mains €20). The **Porto de Santa Maria** (21 487 9450, 91 444 4482, www. portosantamaria.com) is a great place to try the freshest local seafood, but the pick of the bunch is the **Fortaleza do Guincho** (21 487 0491, www. guinchotel.pt), which has been Michelin-starred since 2001 thanks to fine Portuguese ingredients prepared in classic French style. Sommelier Inácio Loureiro has won awards in his field too.

In late July, Cascais fishermen organise the **Festa do Mar** (Festival of the Sea), which includes a parade of boats, fado singing, fireworks and the procession of Nossa Senhora dos Navegantes (Our Lady of the Seafarers).

Casa das Histórias Paula Rego

Avenida da República 300 (21 482 6970, www. casadashistoriaspaularego.com). **Open** 10am-8pm Tue-Sun. **Admission** €3; free under-11s, over-65s.

Museu Condes de Castro Guimarães

Avenida Rei Humberto II de Itália (21 481 5308). **Open** 10am-5pm Tue-Fri; 10am-1pm, 2-5pm Sat, Sun. **Admission** free (but charges planned).

Cabo da Roca

West of Cascais, the coast road rolls past rocky bays, wild dunes and windswept Guincho beach (*see p168*), then climbs up over a series of craggy cliffs, eventually reaching Cabo da Roca, continental Europe's westernmost point – Promontorium Magnum to the Romans. A wall protects the central area around the raised stone cross but take care elsewhere: there's a flimsy wooden fence or nothing at all stopping you from plunging hundreds of metres down on to the rocks below.

By bus, Scotturb 403 leaves Cascais (22mins) or Sintra (37mins) hourly. The fare is €3.25 but you can buy cheaper pre-paid tickets or passes, with or without rail travel from Lisbon.

Just after the turning off the N247 towards Cabo da Roca, a dirt track on the left leads to an old windmill, **Moinho Dom Quixote** (21 929 2523, main courses €9), now a cosy bar open until 2am that also serves food. Its *azulejo*-lined terrace affords breathtaking views of Guincho.

Sintra

Lord Byron called Sintra and its surroundings 'Glorious Eden' and that's only a minor exaggeration. If you take one day trip from Lisbon, this should be it. Described by UNESCO, which made Sintra a World Heritage Site in 1995, as 'the first centre of European Romantic architecture', it's a magical (literally, early inhabitants believed) place of lush forests and turreted palaces. Invariably several degrees cooler than Lisbon, it was once the royal family's summer retreat. That made it a magnet for Portuguese and foreign aristocrats and social climbers alike, who built wonderfully fancy houses and laid out fine gardens mixing native and exotic plants, greatly influencing landscape architecture across Europe.

Sintra is easily reached by train from Lisbon's Rossio or Oriente stations (39mins or 51mins, €2.15 on a rechargable €0.50 card), leaving at least half-hourly. From Estoril, you can take Scotturb bus 418; from Cascais, the 403 (via Cabo da Roca) or 417. You'll need to put aside a full day to get the most out of the town; there are various combination tickets available.

Few visitors are up to taking in all the sights on foot. A one-day Scotturb bus pass (€12) lets you roam the region, but if you're focusing on Sintra, a €5 hop-on hop-off ticket for the 434 service linking the old town and the hilltop sights should do (a one-way ticket costs €3). Alternatively, hire a **horse-drawn carriage** in Largo Rainha Dona Amélia (21 924 1238, www.sintratur.com).

By car or bus, you might head first for the **Castelo dos Mouros**, the Moorish castle ruins whose dragontooth walls creep over the Serra de

Sintra.

Sintra (known to the Romans as the Mountains of the Moon). On a clear day there are spectacular views to the sea, and the pink-and-yellow **Palácio Nacional da Pena** on the next hill. Built by German-born Dom Fernando II at the end of the 19th century around a ruined monastery, it's a pastiche of various styles. The exterior is covered with gargoyles and has an incredible bay window, held up by a huge stone Triton. The palace is entered through an impressive portcullis and set in acres of rolling gardens – a wonderful place to walk and picnic, particularly by the swan lake. Buses and cars can only go as far as the main entrance to the grounds; there's a shuttle (€3) up to the palace itself.

After the death of the queen, Fernando had a private chalet built in the palace's wooded grounds for the woman who would become his second wife, Elise Hensler. The **Chalet da Condessa d'Edla** and its elaborate garden – which in recent decades had been swallowed up by undergrowth – have now been expertly and sensitively renovated. The Chalet is signposted off the main road up to the Palácio da Pena.

Sintra's other highlight is the **Palácio Nacional de Sintra** – the building in the old town centre with two massive white chimneys. It was built in the 14th century by Dom João I, who lived here with his wife, Philippa of Lancaster, daughter of John of Gaunt. The tiled Arab room is striking, as is the Swan room. The hexagonal Sala

dos Brasões ('coats of arms room') is also lined with *azulejos*, while its domed ceilings are painted with the emblems of nobles of the court. One of the oldest parts of the palace is the Magpie room, painted with 136 of the birds, each bearing a rose and a scroll marked '*Por bem*'. The story goes that Dom João I proffered a rose to a lady-in-waiting when Queen Philippa wasn't looking and a magpie snatched it. The king excused himself by saying '*Por bem*' – 'all to the good'.

Dotted in and around the old town are various pricey antiques and lace shops. The **Museu de História Natural** (Rua do Paço 20, 21 923 8563, closed Mon) boasts a fascinating and well-presented collection that includes fossilised dinosaurs' eggs and a unique flying reptile. Beyond the main **tourist office** (Praça da República, 21 923 1157, open Sept-July 9.30am-6pm daily, Aug 9.30am-7pm daily) is **Lawrence's Hotel** (Rua Consiglieri Pedroso 38, 21 910 5500, www.lawrenceshotel.com), where Byron began writing *Childe Harold's Pilgrimage*. Said to be the oldest hotel on the Iberian peninsula, it has a pleasant esplanade and a copious wine list. Further on is **Quinta da Regaleira**, a neo-Manueline fantasy with a garden full of grottos and a secret passage from a well. You can wander the grounds yourself with a detailed map or take a guided tour. There are at least six a day (eight in summer); book well ahead as numbers are limited.

ESCAPES & EXCURSIONS

SUGAR CLUB
Sweet treats in Sintra.

Locals associate Sintra as much with pastries as with palaces. The oldest documented ones, dating back to the 13th century (when apparently they were used to pay local taxes) are *queijadas de Sintra* – tartlets that today are sold in prettily wrapped six-packs at football matches in Portugal. Some of the best – with a filling of cottage cheese, egg and sugar in a flour-and-water case – are at **Fábrica das Verdadeiras Queijadas da Sapa** (Volta do Duche 12, closed Mon), on the road that links Sintra station to the old town. The business has been here a mere 125 years; it was founded in 1756 in the village of Ranholas.

In town, **Piriquita** (Rua das Padarias 1, 21 923 0626) has also been turning out *queijadas* for 150 years. But nowadays the big draw for its Portuguese regulars are *travesseiros* – 'pillows' of flaky pastry with

an ultra-sweet filling of egg, almond and gila pumpkin. Unsurprisingly, there is now a larger Piriquita Dois up the street (no.18, closed Tue). Piriquita also makes the simpler *pastéis de Sintra* – with an egg-and-almond filling – to an old recipe.

For some of the many other traditional local treats, drop in at **Pastelaria Gregório** (Avenida Dom Francisco de Almeida 35), in the new town on the other side of Sintra station, which sells fine *queijadas*, famous *broas de mel* (honey-and-cinnamon cornbread), and *areias* (butter biscuits flavoured with cinnamon and lemon zest). If you have a really sweet tooth, head for the village of Colares (catch the 403 bus from Sintra station), where **Pastelaria Moinho** (Avenia Dr Brandão Vasconcelos, 21 929 0267, closed Mon) has revived an old recipe from nearby Galamares for *nozes douradas* – 'golden walnuts' with egg and caramel.

Queijadas de Sintra.

There are more grand houses up the hill, starting with the **Tivoli Palácio de Seteais** (21 923 3200), a luxury hotel with a terrace overlooking the grounds. The **Palácio de Montserrate**, once the Gothic home of English writer and eccentric William Beckford, was later turned into a Moorish fantasy with subtropical gardens. Both house and gardens have been extensively renovated. Up in the Sintra hills, the **Convento dos Capuchos** is an eerie place, where monks lived in tiny, cork-lined cells. For more on Montserrate and Capuchos, as well as the Pena Palace and Moorish castle, check out www.parquesdesintra.pt.

The only attraction in the new town centre (beyond the rail station) is **MU.SA** (Museu das Artes de Sintra, open 10am-6pm Tue-Sun), in a former 1920s casino. It has mainly 19th-century Romantic art by painters such as Columbano Bordalo Pinheiro and Alfredo Keil, but also more recent works by the likes of Vitor Pi and Júlio Pomar, and stages temporary exhibitions of photography and contemporary art. In summer, beach parties catch the vintage tram for Praia de Maçãs from a stop next to the building. Behind MU.SA is the **Centro Cultural Olga Cadaval** (21 910 7110, www.ccolgacadaval.pt), which hosts the Festival de Sintra (*see p32*) and other shows.

At Odrinhas, 12 kilometres (8 miles) north of Sintra on the road to Ericeira, the **Museu Arqueológico** (21 960 9520, closed Mon & Sun) showcases artefacts of the many peoples who have inhabited this enchanted region.

Touristy restaurants abound in Sintra, plus cafés serving great pastries (*see above* **Sugar Club**). The **Dom Lopo** teahouse (Largo Ferreira de Castro 2, 96 614 0492, open noon-2am Tue, Thur-Sun) is a welcome recent arrival. Housed in a former hotel, it features rooms decorated with lovely landscape frescoes, and has views of the ocean on one side and Castelo dos Mouros on the other. **Orixás** (Avenida Adriano Júlio Coelho 7, 21 924 1672, www.restauranteorixas.com, main courses €20, closed Mon), stands out for a different reason: it's a Brazilian restaurant and art gallery. Worth a detour if you're going to the beach at Praia das Maçãs (*see p169*) is **Colares Velho** (Largo Dr Carlos França, 21 929 2727, main courses €17, closed Mon, Sun eve), next to Colares parish church (Igreja Matriz). It serves inventive fish and veggie dishes, fine desserts, and tea and scones at weekends.

Castelo dos Mouros
2710 Sintra. **Open** *Winter* 10am-6pm (last entry 5pm). *Summer* 9.30am-8pm (last entry

7pm). **Admission** €6.50; €5-€5.50 reductions; free under-6s.

Chalet da Condessa d'Edla
Estrada da Pena (21 923 7300). **Open** *Winter* 10am-6pm (last entry 5pm). *Summer* 9.30am-8pm (last entry 7pm). **Admission** €8.50; €7-€7.50 reductions; free under-6s.

Convento dos Capuchos
Rua dos Capuchos, N247-3 (21 923 7300). **Open** *Winter* 9.30am-8pm (last entry 7pm). **Admission** €5; €4-€4.50 reductions; free under-6s.

Palácio de Montserrate
Rua Barbosa do Bocage (21 923 7300). **Open** *Winter* 10am-5pm (last entry 4.30pm). *Summer* 9.30am-7pm (last entry 6.15pm). **Admission** €6.50; €5-€5.50 reductions; free under-6s.

Palácio Nacional da Pena
Estrada da Pena (21 923 7300). **Open** 10am-6pm daily (last entry 5pm). **Admission** €11.50; €9-€10 reductions; free under-6s. *Park only* €6.50; €5 reductions.

Palácio Nacional de Sintra
Largo da Rainha D Amélia (21 923 7300). **Open** *Winter* 9.30am-6pm daily. *Summer* 9.30am-7pm daily. Last entry 30mins before closing. **Admission** €8.50; €7-€8 reductions; free under-6s.

Quinta da Regaleira.

Quinta da Regaleira
Rua Barbosa do Bocage (information 21 910 6656, reservations 21 910 6650). **Open** *Nov-Jan* 10am-5.30pm daily (last entry 5pm). *Feb, Mar, Oct* 10am-6.30pm daily (last entry 6pm). *Apr-Sept* 10am-8pm daily (last entry 7pm). **Admission** €6; €3-€4 reductions. *Guided tours* €10; €5-€8 reductions.

Queluz

The shabby town of Queluz has little to recommend it beyond the **Palácio**, which is very much worth a visit. This pink edifice was a royal hunting lodge until, in 1747, Prince Dom Pedro decided he fancied it as a home and had it converted into a rococo palace with delightful gardens. In 1760, when he married his niece, the future Queen Maria I, he organised operas and chamber concerts here for her. But in 1788, after the death of their son, she went mad, wandering the corridors tearing her hair and shrieking.

When the royal family fled to Brazil to escape the 1807 French invasion, they took most of the furniture with them, but the palace has been carefully refurbished. One wing accommodates visiting heads of state, and the music room, with its superb acoustics, is still used for concerts.

From Lisbon, catch a Sintra train from Rossio or Oriente, but get off at Queluz-Belas (13mins from Rossio), then 15mins walk; €1.55).

From April to mid November, the **Escola Portuguesa de Arte Equestre** (21 435 8915) stages weekly dressage shows (11am Wed, €6, €3 reductions, free under-6s) in the palace grounds, displaying the talent of the Lusitano breed.

Cozinha Velha (21 435 6158, main courses €19), in the old palace kitchens across the road, serves fine food. There's also a basic café by the main palace entrance.

Palácio de Queluz
2745 Queluz (21 434 3860). **Open** *Winter* 9am-5.30pm daily (last entry 5pm). *Summer* 9am-7pm daily (last entry 6pm). **Admission** €8.50; €7-€8 reductions; free under-6s.

NORTH OF LISBON
Mafra & Ericeira

The enormous marble **Palácio Nacional de Mafra** was begun in 1717 by Dom João V, and financed by gold from Brazil. The project – a combined palace and convent – became ever more elaborate, taking 38 years to finish and employing more than 50,000 builders. The 880 rooms and 300 monks' cells have been fully restored. The dome is one of the world's largest, and the rococo library has a chequered marble floor and more than 38,000 leather-bound books. The monks' pharmacy is quaint with its old jars and bizarre

ESCAPES & EXCURSIONS

instruments. Each of the chapel's belltowers has a carillon; the working one has 114 bells – the world's largest assemblage – used for concerts on summer Sundays. The chapel's organs are also used; indeed, after lengthy renovation, all six have been played together for the first time since the 1834 dissolution of Portugal's monasteries. The palace lost its royal status in 1910, after Portugal's last king, Dom Manuel II, escaped his republican persecutors from here. The local tourist office (261 817 170) is in the building.

From Lisbon, there are half a dozen direct trains from Sete Rios station to Mafra station, but the latter is eight kilometres from town. Instead, catch a Mafrense bus from Lisbon's Campo Grande bus station (45mins, €4.10). From Sintra, buses also go from Portela station.

The **Tapada Nacional de Mafra** former hunting grounds (261 817 050, www.tapada demafra.pt), whose main entrance is eight kilometres from Mafra at Codeçal, can be explored on foot (€4.50) or, if you book ahead, on a mini-train tour (2hrs, €12, various reductions).

Near the village of Malveira is an interesting wolf conservation project, the **Centro de Recuperação do Lobo Ibérico**, which has guided visits at weekends (May-Sept 4.30pm & 6pm, Oct-Apr 3pm & 4.30pm) if you book in advance (261 785 037, 91 753 2312, crloboiberico@ ciencias.ulisboa.pt, €6, €4 reductions).

The town has places to eat, but if you're driving, detour to the village of Negrais – 15 minutes south-east – which is famed for its *leitão* (suckling pig). Locals favour **O Caneira** (Avenida General Barnabe António Ferreira 171, Pêro Pinheiro, 21 967 0853, www.caneira.com, main courses €13, closed Sun eve).

For fresh fish, visit Ericeira, a laidback fishing village some 10km from Mafra, where the best restaurants are in side streets. It's a magnet for surf freaks: with seven world-class breaks in a few kilometres of coastline, it was named a World Surfing Reserve by the Save the Waves Coalition in 2011. There are several local schools that can teach you a few tricks. The **tourist office** (Rua Dr Eduardo Burnay 46, 261 863 122) can help out with information.

Palácio Nacional de Mafra

Terreiro Dom João V (261 817 550). **Open** 9am-6pm Mon, Wed-Sun (last entry 5pm). **Admission** €6; €3 reductions; free under-13s.

Óbidos

This picture-postcard walled village on a hill was a wedding gift from Dom Dinis to his bride, Isabel of Aragon, in 1282. Its whitewashed houses have terracotta roofs and trademark ochre or blue bands painted around their base, and sport window boxes of geraniums.

Pick up a map at the **tourist office** (26 295 9231, www.obidos.pt) at the entrance to town; you can also hire a bike for €5 per half day. Then pass through the tiled main gate and search out the old **pillory** with the town's arms – a fishing net with a drowned person inside (Isabel and Dinis's son drowned in the Tagus before being fished out) – and the **Igreja de Santa Maria**, where ten-year-old Dom Afonso V married his eight-year-old wife in 1444. The church has 17th-century tilework, wooden painted ceilings, and panels by Josefa de Óbidos, a Spanish-born artist (1634-84) whose dark still lifes are enjoying a revival. She's

Palácio Nacional de Mafra.

Óbidos.

buried in the Igreja de São Pedro; there are works by her in the **Museu Municipal** (Rua Direita, 262 959 299, closed Mon). The castle is a *pousada* but you can walk the walls and try to spot the sea in the distance.

The annual **Chocolate Festival** (www. obidos.pt) in March is great fun but a crush at weekends. At other times of the year, café **Porta da Vila** near the main gate serves local pastries. For first-rate Portuguese cuisine, search out **Alcaide** (Rua Direita, 262 959 220, www. restaurantealcaide.com, closed Wed, main courses €15); in summer, book ahead.

From Lisbon, Rodoviário do Tejo runs at least five direct fast buses (Rápidas) daily from Campo Grande bus station (1hr, €7.60). There are half a dozen direct trains a day from Sete Rios (1hr 58mins, €8.30); it's then a 15-minute walk into town from Óbidos station. Taxis aren't always standing by; phone the tourist office for local cabbies' mobile numbers.

SOUTH OF LISBON
Sesimbra

Overlooked by a fairytale castle, Sesimbra is a busy fishing village-cum-resort with white-washed streets leading up from the harbour. Not surprisingly for a place that supplies fresh fish to a number of posh Lisbon eateries, it has great seafood. The **tourist office** (93 740 5902, 93 740 5904) is in a renovated 17th-century fort, the Fortaleza de Santiago.

Sesimbra is reached by crossing the Ponte 25 de Abril and then traversing the Serra da Arrábida (Transportes do Sul do Tejo buses

leave Praça de Espanha more or less hourly and take an hour; a one-way ticket costs €4.10.) This beautiful protected area of sandy coves and towering limestone cliffs is covered with pines and thickets of green Mediterranean-style vegetation, which thrive thanks to Arrábida's microclimate. From Sesimbra you can hire a boat to take you to one of the beaches or drive to the sheltered **Praia do Portinho da Arrábida**, whose warm waters attract snorkellers.

With a car at your disposal, you can also head west to **Cabo Espichel**, where the **Santuário da Nossa Senhora do Cabo** (21 268 0565, open 10am-1.30pm, 2.30-4pm Mon-Sat, 10am-1.30pm, 2.30-5pm Sun) stands on a windswept cliff, the approach lined with derelict pilgrims' cells. The 18th-century church contains candles lit by fishermen before their favourite saints. On the last weekend in September there's a mass to pray for a good (and safe) year, and a procession of the image of the Virgin.

IN THE KNOW
MONASTIC LIFESTYLE

Phone ahead for a guided tour of the **Convento da Arrábida** (21 219 7620, www.foriente.pt), a beautifully preserved 16th-century Franciscan monastery in a breathtaking hillside setting overlooking the Atlantic. The convent's owner, Fundação Oriente, uses it as a conference venue: at the annual Arrábida Meetings, bigwigs from around the world discuss security and international affairs.

History

*From Phoenician outpost
to European mainstream.*

TEXT: BRAD CHERRY & ALISON ROBERTS

Before it reaches Lisbon, the River Tagus broadens into one of the world's largest natural harbours. It then narrows again and empties into the Atlantic. Its south bank is flat, with inlets famed for millennia for rich oyster beds and fisheries; salt pans still exist around Alcochete and Montijo. On its north bank, freshwater streams flow in from surrounding hills, with the city growing up on the most prominent of these, near where the current runs fastest and deepest. Lisbon owes its eminence largely to the river, the longest in the Iberian peninsula, with a basin stretching beyond Madrid. One tradition has it that Ulysses founded the city and that its name is a corruption of his. More credible is the story that Phoenician mariners dubbed the place 'Alis Ubbo' – 'peaceful harbour' – which mutated to Olisipo, then Lisbon.

Teatro Romano.

ANCIENT ORIGINS

The region has been populated for millennia. Nomadic hunting societies left their mark, while later agricultural populations settled on small tributaries of the Tagus, and the estuary harboured primitive shell-gathering cultures. The area was a crossroads of late Bronze Age trade, and from the eighth to the sixth centuries BC the Phoenicians extended their trade up from Cádiz to the Tagus estuary, where they established an entrepôt for tin coming from Cornwall. Lisbon was a Mediterranean port many centuries before it became the first Atlantic one.

The Roman presence in Iberia dates to the Second Punic War in the late third century BC, which ended half a century of Carthaginian domination. Putting down restive locals proved more difficult, and it took two centuries to establish the Pax Romana across the peninsula. One local chieftain – Viriatus – gained renown as a resistance leader between 147 BC and 139 BC, harrying Roman legions from the Smerra da Estrela. His Lusitani tribe gave its name to the Roman province of Lusitania, which encompassed most of present-day Portugal.

Lisbon fell in 138 BC and was occupied by the governor Decimus Junius Brutus. He fortified the emergent city, though it's not clear where he built his walls. Lisbon became a district capital under the provincial capital Mérida in what is now Spain. By 30 BC, the city was renamed Felicitas Julia Olisipo after Julius Caesar, then a peninsula commander. The city spread down from today's **Castelo de São Jorge** (see p64) to the Tagus and westwards towards what is now Rossio – then a hippodrome. The main exports via its port

were the fish paste known as garum, salt and local horses; Pliny the Elder described mares from the Tagus as 'fine, docile and impregnated by the west wind, [which] brought forth offspring of surprising fleetness'.

The principal Roman remains in Lisbon are the **Teatro Romano** (see p60), an amphitheatre built under Emperor Augustus that is only part-excavated. The Forum was probably near an arch that stood by today's Largo da Madalena. In the middle of Rua da Conceição is the entrance to vaulted cellars – probably the foundations of a waterfront temple or similar building, not fish-conserving tanks as once thought. The elongated shape of Rossio, the city's central square, is believed by some historians to follow the perimeter of a Roman hippodrome.

Olisipo prospered for four centuries, ruling a district that extended northwards towards present-day Torres Vedras and Alenquer. Rich farmland was dotted with estates known as *villae*; remains have been found near the airport and around Cascais. Waterfront activity centred on salting fish and maritime commerce. Christianity was established by the middle of the fourth century. There's a persistent legend of three Christians – Verissimus, Maximus and Julia – martyred during the persecution by Emperor Diocletian on a river beach later named Santos. (Much later, Portugal's first king was to address his prayers to them before conquering Lisbon.) The city's first bishop was later canonised as St Gens.

Roman rule in Iberia crashed in 409 when hordes of Suevi, Alans and Vandals swept over the Pyrenees. The Suevi swung north, one group of Vandals headed up to Galicia and the other south, and the Alans settled between the Douro and the Tagus. Lisbon fell to this Iranian people, who left few traces. In 418, the Romans called in the Visigoths to kick out the other tribes. The Alans joined with the Vandals in the south (in Vandalusia, later Andalusia), before they all retreated to North Africa. The Visigoths, based in Toledo, soon dominated the peninsula, taking over Olisipo in 469.

MOORISH INVASION
AND BIRTH OF A NATION

In 711, Muslim armies hit southern Spain and within five years conquered most of the peninsula, with Lisbon – now much reduced in size after three centuries of sacking and pillaging – falling in 714. Iberian Christendom regrouped in northern Spain and began the Reconquista. By the mid 800s, northern Portugal was Christian again. The area around Oporto was called Portucale, the 'gateway to Cale'. Although forays were made as far as the Tagus, Lisbon remained in Muslim hands for three centuries. Moorish traveller al-Idrisi wrote of the city then called al-Ushbuna: 'This lovely city is defended by a ring of walls and a powerful castle'. That castle was built over the earlier Roman fortification where the Castelo now stands. The Moorish siege walls – Cerca Moura – enclosed about 15 hectares in all, from the Castelo to the present-day Portas do Sol, where one tower houses the

Cerca Moura café. From there the line can be traced through Alfama, or over to Largo da Madalena where the Roman arch had become the city gate.

Much of the city stood outside the walls, including most of Alfama. Its name (al-Hama, 'springs') refers to the abundance of water – later medieval fountains on Largo do Chafariz de Dentro and Chafariz d'el Rei are extant.

Moorish Lisbon at its ninth-century height was a major city of al-Andalus, with 30,000 residents. Immigrants, from Yemenis to newly converted Moroccan Berbers, flooded in and Arabic predominated. Christians (known as *moçárabes*) and Jews could practise their religions, within the strict limits prescribed by their rulers.

In 1128, Afonso Henriques wrested control of Portucale from his mother, Teresa, after the death of his father, Henrique. In 1139, he trounced the Moors at Ourique and a year later proclaimed himself king of Portugal. (The pope approved the new nation's foundation in 1179, in exchange for 1,000 gold coins). Aided by northern European crusaders, in 1147 Afonso Henriques attacked Lisbon. On St Crispin's Day, 25 October, a soldier called Martim Moniz led the invading force into the city, where they ran amok.

Later, Afonso Henriques heard of a shrine in the Algarve where relics of St Vincent were guarded by ravens. An expedition of *moçarabes* was sent to retrieve the remains.

IN CONTEXT

The 1755 Lisbon earthquake.
See p191.

According to myth, a boat bearing the corpse, circled by ravens, reached Lisbon in September 1173. The image of a boat and ravens duly became the city's symbol.

CAPITAL CITY

The last Moorish bastions in the Algarve fell in 1249 and Lisbon established itself as the capital, replacing Coimbra. The city huddled within the old walls, with the royal palace in the castle. The **Sé Catedral** (see p62) was built soon after. Other houses of worship included the primitive chapels of Santos and St Gens (now Nossa Senhora do Monte, see p66). Moors and Jews were permitted to stay on outside the walls – in Mouraria and the Judiarias in the Baixa and Alfama.

For centuries a provincial outpost, Lisbon was now becoming a political and business centre. Portuguese ships plied routes as far as the Baltic and south into the Mediterranean. Medieval Portugal reached its height under poet-king Dom Dinis (1279-1325). He founded the University of Lisbon in 1290 (later moved to Coimbra), planted coastal pine forests to prevent erosion, and built castles to keep out Castilians and Moors. The national borders formalised in the 1297 Treaty of Alcanices with Castile are almost unchanged today.

By the late 1400s, Lisbon's population was back above 14,000 and the walls expanded to enclose 60 hectares (148 acres). Commerce had moved downhill to the Baixa, with the diagonal Rua Nova (now disappeared) the main street and Rossio a busy open market.

Lisbon suffered several earthquakes during this period. Tremors in 1321 and 1344 damaged the Sé, while another in 1356 set church bells ringing. And the Black Death struck in 1348 and 1349. Despite quakes, plague and persistent grain shortages, Lisbon outgrew its walls once more, creeping up hills north and west of Rossio. When a Castilian raiding party laid waste to much of extramural Lisbon in 1373, Dom Fernando I had new walls built. The Cerca Fernandina was just over five kilometres long with 77 towers and 38 gates and circled Rossio, the Baixa and part of today's Chiado, enclosing 50,000 residents. The Portas de Santa Catarina stood where two churches now face each other in Largo do Chiado. There are remnants of these walls just uphill in the atrium of the Espaço Chiado and downhill on Rua do Alecrim.

When Fernando died in 1383, war broke out between his widow Leonor Teles and João, master of the Military Order of Aviz. Leonor sought support in Castile. When the two opposing sides met in 1385 at Aljubarrota, a vastly outnumbered Portuguese force, assisted by English archers, trounced the invaders, cementing Portuguese independence. João I thus founded Portugal's second ruling house, the Avis dynasty. In gratitude, he ordered the construction of the magnificent monastery of Batalha. He also signed the Treaty of Windsor with England, forging an alliance that stands to this day.

THE DISCOVERIES

Portugal's first maritime foray was the 1415 conquest of Ceuta in North Africa. Key to organising and financing this assault was João I's wife, English princess Philippa of Lancaster. Among the participants was João's son, Henriques. Known as Infante Dom Henriques or Prince Henry the Navigator, he soon began training mariners. In 1415 and 1416, expeditions sailed to the Canary Islands; next Madeira was discovered around 1419; the Azores in the 1430s. Ships were dispatched to explore the African coast. The psychological barrier of Cape Bojador – people thought they'd fall off the edge of the world – was overcome and charted by Gil Eanes in 1434.

What prompted this sudden burst of activity? Portugal's identity was forged in battle, but it could not expand on land. So it went to sea, driven by greed, adventure and religious fervour – Prince Henry was a master of the Order of Christ, successor to the Knights Templar and a sworn enemy of Islam. After Ceuta, Portugal took Alcacer-Ceguer in 1458, and Arzila and Tangier in 1471.

Madeira and the Azores were by now settled and a brisk trade grew up with these additions to the 'Kingdom of Portugal, the Algarve and the Ocean Seas and Beyond in Africa'. Henry died in 1460, but by the mid 1470s Portuguese squadrons were active in the Gulf of Guinea and had crossed the equator.

Trade with Asia was at this point in history controlled by Venice, Genoa and Cairo; the only way to reach Asia while avoiding these competitors was to sail all the way south around Africa. Later royals took up this fundamental challenge. Dom João II was

Tile depicting a ship from the Discoveries.

nicknamed the Perfect Prince for his Machiavellian talents – he had his rival the Duke of Braganza beheaded in Évora and personally stabbed to death his brother-in-law, the Duke of Viseu. Sailing under the orders of this magnificent schemer, navigator Diogo Cão reached the Zaire river in 1482 and later explored the coast to Angola. Meanwhile, Bartholomew Dias rounded the Cape of Good Hope in 1488 and reported that Africa was circumnavigable. In 1497, Vasco da Gama set out from Restelo (now Belém) with three caravels and a supply ship. Rounding the Cape in November, he sailed up the East African coast and across to India, putting in at Calicut on 20 May 1498. Portugal could now control Indian Ocean trade.

Its only rival at this time was Spain. The 1479 Treaty of Alcáçovas was the two countries' first attempt to carve up the world. The 1494 Treaty of Tordesillas divided the world along a line 370 leagues west of Cape Verde. Portugal could take anything to the east (with the exception of the Canary Islands, already ruled by Spain). This division puts much of present-day Brazil within the Portuguese sphere. There is evidence that, in fact, the Portuguese knew of the South American land mass well before Pedro Álvares Cabral 'discovered' it in 1500.

A FORTUNATE SON

Dom Manuel I was dubbed 'the Fortunate' because he came to the throne in 1495, just before Portugal won the India lottery jackpot, which he greedily controlled through royal monopolies. After Vasco da Gama returned with his cargo of spices, the city was overwhelmed by the 'vapours of India', an irresistible force that drew young and old overseas. Many did not return, victims of shipwreck, piracy or disease.

Lisbon's population was now 40,000; it grew west along the river as convents and palaces sprang up. Traders, moneychangers and booksellers jostled along the Rua Nova. The opulence in Europe's richest city was unrivalled – as was its depravity, as caricatured by Gil Vicente in his play *Auto da Índia*, depicting a wife at play while her husband travelled.

Dom Manuel spent part of his new-found fortune on two important monuments: the **Torre de Belém** (*see p103*) to guard the harbour entrance, and the **Mosteiro dos Jerónimos** (*see p100*) to thank God for his unexpected wealth. Both are masterpieces of the Portuguese late Gothic style that is known as Manueline, replete with oriental and maritime motifs.

In 1492, Ferdinand and Isabel of Spain had expelled all non-Christians after conquering Moorish Granada. Portugal at first welcomed fugitive Jews, but in 1496 expelled all Moors and Jews who refused baptism. Those who stayed were to form an underclass of 'New Christians'. In 1506, thousands were massacred in a riot that lasted for days. Not surprisingly, after this, most of the Jews fled to North Africa and northern Europe.

Lisbon's population grew fitfully, to 72,000 in 1527 – another plague year. The city had its glories – Renaissance man Damião de Goís described seven of its buildings as wonders of the world, among them the Palácio de Estaus and Hospital de Todos-os-Santos on Rossio, but none survived the 1755 earthquake. Other travellers complained of the stench of slaves' corpses cast into pits such as the Poço dos Negros, and crime was rampant.

PORTUGAL RULES THE WAVES, THEN THE SPANISH MOVE IN

The Indian Ocean, for centuries traversed by Roman, Arab, Indian and Chinese merchants, was lined with prosperous cities and states where standards of living and literacy were often higher than in Europe. The Portuguese sailed in like fundamentalist terrorists armed with bronze cannons – previously unknown in

THE MAKING OF THE MARQUÊS

A visionary but autocratic statesman.

A towering figure in Portugal – literally so in Lisbon, where his statue dominates its main traffic intersection – the man known in posterity as the Marquês de Pombal was graced with that title only towards the end of his long career as a minister. For most of it he was plain Sebastião José Carvalho e Melo.

Born in Lisbon in 1699, in a house that still stands today (at Rua do Século 79), Carvalho was the son of a rich squire and cavalry officer from the provinces. After studying at the University of Coimbra and a spell in the army, he eloped with an aristocratic widow; this caused problems initially but was a useful bit of social climbing. From 1738, he served as ambassador in London and then Vienna, before being recalled in 1749. The following year, he was appointed foreign secretary by the newly crowned Dom José I. By the time he was named Secretary of the State of the Kingdom (the top job), he had amassed the unprecedented power that enabled him to govern practically alone for almost three decades.

Carvalho showed his mettle above all after the 1755 earthquake, and central Lisbon is his most visible legacy. But his deeds were many and varied. A visionary and forceful leader, he made at least as many foes as friends. Some of the latter, young noblemen handpicked by Carvalho for his personal guard who were known as the Capotes Brancos for their part-white capes, roamed the Bairro Alto looking for excuses to clash with their black-clad adversaries, the Capotes Negros, who were backed by prominent aristocrats. After all, Carvalho was not only not one of them, he was also an *estrangeirado*: full of strange foreign ideas that he had picked up above all in England.

During his time in power, he abolished slavery in Portugal (but not its colonies), revoked official discrimination against New Christians (descendants of converted Jews) and Freemasons (many believe he himself became one in London), and ended autos-da-fé. He didn't dismantle the Inquisition itself, though, not least because he found it to be a handy instrument for his ends. (It was only abolished in 1821.)

The earthquake gave Carvalho the chance to raze the damaged palaces of aristocratic rivals and cut down powerful opponents such as the Society of Jesus (Jesuits). Priests were thrown into prison by the dozen, and one, Gabriel Malagrida, was sentenced to death by the Inquisition (conveniently headed at the time by Carvalho's brother) for heresy. Among other offences, he had attacked a book on public health distributed to public officials after the earthquake, for explaining the disaster in terms of natural causes rather than as God's wrath.

Carvalho also accused the Jesuits of being involved in the conspiracy to assassinate the king in 1758. A year later, he expelled the order from Portugal and its colonies, and was among those who persuaded Pope Clement XIV to suppress the order worldwide. Back home, he instituted reforms at his alma mater in Coimbra, which the Jesuits had dominated for two centuries.

On the economic front, his regime created new industries and fostered existing ones, including the important but abuse-ridden port wine business. He created the world's first properly regulated wine region.

For all this and more, a grateful Dom José I ennobled Carvalho in 1759, issuing a royal decree that made him Conde de Oeiras. But it was the title of marquess, conferred a decade later and identifying him with the town near Leiria where much of his family's lands were located, that labelled him for the rest of time as the Marquês de Pombal.

the region – and prepared to use violence on a scale that staggered the locals.

In 1502, Vasco da Gama returned to Calicut in response to the massacre of Portuguese expatriates by local Hindus, a slaughter that had been incited by Muslims. He took terrible revenge, bombarding the city for three days, before he cut off the ears, noses and hands of prisoners he had taken and burned them alive. Elsewhere, he sank a ship of 700 Muslim pilgrims and sent longboats to spear survivors. Other prisoners were rigged up and used for crossbow practice.

In 1510, Viceroy Afonso de Albuquerque conquered Goa, which became the sumptuous seat of the 'pepper empire'. The taking of Malacca in 1511 opened the way to the Far East: caravels soon reached the Spice Islands (Moluccas) and Timor, and by 1513 were trading with China. In 1542, caravels reached Japan, and in 1557 Portugal won the right to administer Macao on the southern coast of China. The poet Luís Vaz de Camões spent time here, as well as in Africa, Goa and the East Indies, during 17 years of travel. At one point he almost lost his epic poem, *The Lusiads*, in a shipwreck, but made it ashore with the poem and later completed it. Published in 1572, it chronicles Vasco da Gama's first voyage to India. Inspired by the origins of empire, Camões saw it come to an end. Young, heirless Dom Sebastião I led a disastrous expedition to Morocco in 1578, where he perished along with much of Portugal's nobility. In 1582, Philip II of Spain snatched the Portuguese crown.

The Habsburg Philip backed his claim to the throne by landing an army outside Lisbon and routing the Portuguese in the Alcântara district. As Philip I, he ruled from 1581 to 1598. After modernising the bureaucracy along Spanish lines, he cast his eyes further afield. In 1588, he assembled a fleet of 130 ships and 27,000 men in Lisbon and sent it to attack England. The invincible Armada lost to both the elements and the English, scuttling Spain's ambitions of global domination. Nonetheless, construction of the imposing **Igreja de São Vicente de Fora** (*see p67*) started in 1590, under Juan de Herrera of Escorial fame.

The Inquisition, an agent of state rather than church, had been in Lisbon since 1537, and in 1570 it took over the Estaus Palace on Rossio, where the Teatro Nacional Dona Maria II is now. The inquisitors requested more funds to expand crowded dungeons and organised the notorious autos-da-fé, which began with processions from the **Igreja de São Domingos** (*see p49*) and ended with the condemned being burned.

The Portuguese chafed under Spanish rule – especially when Philip IV (III of Portugal) began appointing Spanish nobles to positions reserved for locals and ignoring the welfare of Portuguese overseas possessions. On 1 December 1640, conspirators overpowered the authorities in Lisbon and proclaimed the Duke of Braganza Dom João IV of Portugal. After a war of secession in 1668, Spain recognised Portugal's independence and possessions, except Ceuta, Ceylon and Malacca. To bolster its position, Portugal matched Catherine of Braganza with England's King Charles II; her dowry included the ports of Bombay and Tangier.

WEALTH AND RECONSTRUCTION

Portugal's new-found confidence was soon displayed in the reconstruction of the Igreja do Loreto in Chiado – finished in 1663 – and a start to the building of the **Panteão Nacional de Santa Engrácia** (*see p67*). Then, in 1699, gold was discovered in Brazil. The flagship of the ensuing construction boom was the massive monastery-palace started by Dom João V in 1717 at **Mafra** (*see p179*). Elsewhere, artisans created gilded Baroque masterpieces behind the altars of churches of **Madre de Deus** (at the Museu Nacional do Azulejo, *see p124*), **Santa Catarina** (*see p88*) and **São Roque** (*see p82*), and ornate private carriages, some now on display at the Museu Nacional dos Coches (*see p102*). The 1730s also saw construction of the indestructible **Aqueduto das Águas Livres** (*see p112*). But Lisbon was still mostly a medieval city of narrow lanes. The Bairro Alto became an entertainment centre, as popular theatres staged farces and comedies for plebeians. By 1755, the population had reached 190,000.

On 1 November 1755, Lisbon was struck by a devastating earthquake that lasted six minutes and brought buildings crashing down. It was All Saints' Day, so the churches were packed, while at home candles had been lit in memory of the dead. Panic-stricken citizens racing down to the river were met by a tidal

IN CONTEXT

wave that engulfed the Baixa, and a dry north-east wind fanned fires for days.

Dom José I's chief minister, Sebastião José de Carvalho e Melo, threw himself into recovery work. Seen by some as an enlightened despot, by others as high-handed and dictatorial, he is known today as the Marquês de Pombal, a title awarded in 1769. The dust had barely settled when Pombal decreed: 'Bury the dead, feed the living'. Teams searched the rubble for bodies, while taxes on food were dropped and grain was requisitioned: no one starved and no major epidemics followed a disaster that had killed some 15,000.

In the Baixa, hit by the triple scourge of earthquake, tidal wave and fire, Pombal opted to build a new city. The plan, drawn up by Eugénio dos Santos and Hungarian-born Carlos Mardel, was based on the grid scheme of a military encampment, the city's medieval maze overlain by straight roads earmarked for use by distinct trades. Rubble was used as landfill to prevent flooding. Rossio was neatened into a rectangle, and the wide Rua Augusta cut down to the riverside Terreiro do Paço, renamed Praça do Comércio, where Lisbon's rebirth was celebrated 20 years on. The equestrian statue of Dom José I was unveiled in an incomplete square, with wooden façades arranged to fill in the gaps.

Pombal's authoritarianism brought him results and enemies (see p190 **The Making of the Marquês**). He cowed the aristocracy by executing nobles accused of plotting to kill the king in 1758. But when José I was succeeded in 1777 by his daughter, Dona Maria I, she dismissed Pombal and cultivated links with France, a policy that had to be reversed after the 1789 revolution there. Her fragile health degenerated into insanity in 1791 and the prince regent, later Dom João VI, took over. She left one important legacy, the **Basílica da Estrela** (see p110), built between 1779 and 1789, while her consort, Pedro, oversaw the building of the **Palácio de Queluz** (see p179), often called the Portuguese Versailles.

In Lisbon, the superintendent of police – or *intendente* – Diogo Inácio de Pina Manique held sway from 1780. A social reformer, he was instrumental in founding the Casa Pia in 1780, which even now is doing good work for orphans and the poor, despite being buffeted by scandals over child abuse. He introduced Lisbon's first widespread street lamp-lighting scheme, oversaw the paving of streets, the laying of sewers and the collecting of rubbish, and subjected prostitutes to regular health inspections. He also oversaw the construction of the neoclassical **Teatro Nacional de São Carlos** (see p159) in 1793 and planted 40,000 trees in 1799. Meanwhile the population continued to grow: in 1801 it was near 170,000.

PENINSULAR WARS

In 1801, France and Spain joined forces and invaded Portugal. After a brief campaign, the country was forced into submission, ceding to Spain the town of Olivenza (Olivença in Portuguese) near Badajoz; it remains a bone of contention to this day. During Napoleon's rise, Portugal tried quietly to maintain trade with England. But in 1806, he decreed a continental embargo. Portugal faced an unhappy choice: accede and see Britain take over its overseas possessions; or refuse and be invaded. Napoleon gave the Portuguese until September 1807 to declare war on England. Portugal stalled, France invaded and the royal family fled to Brazil, staying for 14 years. Many followed their example: 11,000 passports were issued in short order.

The French invaded three times. In 1808, a British force led by General Arthur Wellesley (better known as the Duke of Wellington) sent them packing after the battles of Roliça and Vimeiro. The French returned under Marshal Soult the following year, but were ejected by Portuguese and British forces. In summer 1810, Marshal Masséna arrived, and after initial setbacks his forces marched on Lisbon. Wellington stopped them with fortifications (the Torres Vedras Lines) stretching north of Lisbon from the Tagus to the sea. The French fled. By 1814, they were back in Toulouse.

The Peninsular Wars left Portugal a wreck. Lisbon's population dipped to 150,000, regaining its turn-of-the-century peak only in 1860. Under the post-war British regency (read, occupation) of Marshal Beresford, unrest was never far from the surface. New ideas took root and words such as 'liberal' and 'constitution' entered the dissident vocabulary. In 1820, Beresford went to Brazil to coax home Dom João VI, who was loath to trade the comforts of Rio for devastated Portugal. In Beresford's absence, the regency was overthrown and liberal rule installed. Elections were held and the Cortes, or parliament, approved a constitution in March 1821.

Now João VI returned and swore allegiance to the new constitution. Crown Prince Pedro, however, stayed in Brazil. In 1822, when the Cortes threatened to strip Brazil of its status as a kingdom, it declared itself independent, and Portugal lost her largest source of overseas income. An ensuing constitutional conflict split the royals. The Absolutists were led by Prince Miguel. The Liberals championed his brother Pedro, whom they proclaimed Dom Pedro IV when João VI died in 1826. Pedro, content as Emperor of Brazil, abdicated the Portuguese throne in favour of his seven-year-old daughter. When she was crowned Dona Maria II in 1828, Miguel declared himself king. So Pedro abdicated the Brazilian throne and returned to head a Liberal counter-revolt.

The war lasted from 1832 – with Lisbon captured by a Liberal army on 24 July 1833 – to 1834, when Miguel was forced into exile. Pedro died months after taking over as regent for the now 13-year-old Maria II, but oversaw the 1834 abolition of religious orders. Monks and nuns were turned out from their cloisters, which were annexed by public and private institutions. Parliament set up in the Mosteiro de São Bento, renamed the **Palácio da Assembléia da República** (see p107), while the monastery up in Graça was among religious foundations that became barracks. In 1836, Maria II married Ferdinand of Saxe-Coburg-Gotha, responsible for the fantasy Palácio da Pena on a hilltop at Sintra (see p177), which spawned a fashion for Romantic mansions and gardens.

ROMANTICISM, REFORM AND THE NEW REPUBLIC

In Lisbon, the era saw fado music and military uprisings. Maria Severa Onofriana, the prostitute known as 'A Severa', kept open house in Mouraria, her soprano voice attracting lovers, including the bullfighting Count of Vimioso. She died in 1846, at the age of 26.

Meanwhile there was a series of revolts, the bloodiest occurring on 13 March 1838 when government troops fought rebellious national guardsmen in Rossio. Rossio itself underwent a major facelift in the following

years. Black-and-white cobblestones were laid in 1840, and in 1846 the new **Teatro Nacional** (see p161) was inaugurated by Dona Maria II. The driving force behind it was Romantic author Almeida Garrett, one of many intellectual former exiles.

By the middle of the 19th century, political stability made possible a major building programme. The grand arch on Praça do Comércio was completed in 1873. Railways had arrived in the 1850s; by the 1860s trains steamed from Santa Apolónia station to Oporto and Madrid, and by the 1890s from neo-Manueline Rossio station towards Sintra. Prosperity fuelled public entertainment: the **Coliseu dos Recreios** (see p152) opened in 1890, followed by the **Campo Pequeno** bullring (see p122) in 1892. During Pombaline reconstruction, a green space had been opened north-west of Rossio. The Passeio Público, as it was called, was not a hit at first – the idea of both sexes strolling in a public garden grated with contemporary mores. In the 1830s, it was remodelled as a Romantic garden and became popular with the emergent bourgeoisie. It was extended in the 1880s, becoming the tree-lined Avenida da Liberdade. At its southern end, at Praça dos Restauradores, a monument was raised to the 1640 restoration. The park laid out to the north was named after Britain's King Edward VII.

Other urban projects of the late monarchy period included the introduction of the first funiculars in 1884, using the water gravity system – a tram filled a tank of water at the top of the hill, and on the downhill run that provided enough counterweight to pull up another car from the bottom. Electrification began in 1901, and the city soon filled with electric trams.

In the 1870s, a group known as the Cenáculo dominated literary Lisbon. Among its number were storyteller Teófilo Braga, later President of the Republic; historian Oliveira Martins, whose pan-Iberian vision was to shape future generations; and Eça de Queiroz, whose novels The Maias and Cousin Bazilio offer an unrivalled and at times satirical portrait of Lisbon life. Politically, intellectuals favoured republicanism, especially after the monarchy gave in to the 1890 British ultimatum that demanded Portugal withdraw from much of south-central Africa.

IN CONTEXT

In 1905, Dom Carlos I appointed João Franco as chief minister. Stepping up censorship and persecution of republicans, Franco only inflamed the situation.

On 1 February 1908, Dom Carlos, his wife Amélia and princes Luís Filipe and Manuel returned from a visit to the Alentejo. Their procession had reached the north-west corner of Praça do Comércio when a black-cloaked figure circled behind the carriage and opened fire. Another conspirator ran out from the arcade. Yet another fired from the central statue. The horseguards rampaged, killing two of the assassins and several bystanders. But the king and crown prince lay dead.

Carlos's second son lasted as Dom Manuel II only until the Republican revolution of 4-5 October 1910. When warships shelled his Palácio das Necessidades, he fled to Ericeira and into exile. From the balcony of the Câmara Municipal (City Hall), the Republic was proclaimed.

'During the war, Portugal settled into uneasy neutrality, providing tungsten for the Nazi war effort while lending Azores air bases to the Allies.'

NASCENT FASCISM AND DICTATORSHIP

The optimism accompanying the provisional government set up on 5 October 1910 was soon betrayed by battles over the constitution. A persistent concern was how to hang on to the African colonies, prompting Portugal to enter World War I on the side of the Allies. The Portuguese Expeditionary Force was virtually wiped out in the April 1918 battle of La Lys.

Back in Lisbon, an army major named Sidónio Pais had led a revolt on 5 December 1917, taking the heights around Parque Eduardo VII and bombarding the Praça do Comércio ministries. Loyalists counter-attacked and hundreds of soldiers died in

a brief, bloody fight at Largo do Rato before Sidónio prevailed. What was arguably Europe's first fascist regime saw huge rallies, mass arrests of opposition leaders and heavy censorship. However, Sidónio's chaotic rule lost him allies, and he was assassinated in December 1918.

Competing local powers threatened to rip Portugal apart. In January 1919, the monarchy was proclaimed in the north; Republican forces took a month to quell the rebellion. In Lisbon, the National Republican Guard (GNR) was heavily armed and often influenced government. On 19 October 1921 – the Noite Sangrenta or 'bloody night' – members of the GNR and navy revolted; several politicians were massacred, including Prime Minister António Granjo. The next government – the 31st since 1910 – lasted two weeks; 45 Republican administrations would fall before the military definitively took over in 1926.

Meanwhile, despite the political turmoil, intellectual life was thriving. In 1915, the only two issues of the magazine *Orfeu* appeared, introducing painter José de Almeida Negreiros and poets Fernando Pessoa and Mário de Sá Carneiro. In 1924, the Tivoli cinema (now theatres, *see p162*) opened on Avenida da Liberdade; the Teatro Municipal de São Luíz in Chiado followed in 1928.

This cultural awakening was stifled by the Estado Novo ('New State') regime that prevailed after the May 1926 coup d'état led by Marshal Gomes da Costa. Two years later, a conservative Coimbra professor, António Oliveira Salazar, was named finance minister. In 1932, Salazar became prime minister and was to rule for almost four decades, backed by the infamous PIDE political police. In the early years the regime styled itself as a dictatorship without a dictator, because it eschewed personality cults. But Salazar cracked down on the left and played right-wing rivals off against each other. In 1940, the regime mounted the Exhibition of the Portuguese World in Belém, glorifying national achievements while ignoring World War II and the miserable conditions of rural and industrial workers.

During the war, Portugal was once more forced into a balancing act. When the threat of an Axis invasion evaporated in 1940, Portugal settled into uneasy neutrality, providing tungsten for the Nazi war effort while lending Azores air bases to the Allies. British and

REVOLUTIONARY ROAD

Forty years on, the Revolution remains firmly on the political agenda.

For an event that forged contemporary Portugal and is recalled fondly by so many, the 1974 Revolution has left surprisingly few visual clues for the visitor. The last of the colourful political murals from the period have now faded – or the walls themselves have been bulldozed for redevelopment.

The date of the coup that brought down the dictatorship, 25 April, remains a national holiday, marked by both official and popular celebrations. Over the years, there have been many attempts by politicians to appropriate the Revolution for their own purposes. One of the most glaring – and unsuccessful – examples was in the run-up to the 30th anniversary, when the right-of-centre government led by José Manuel Durão Barroso launched a poster campaign proclaiming that 'Abril é Evolução' – that is, Evolution not Revolution – and citing social and economic statistics to show how Portugal has advanced in three decades.

Barroso's own journey in that time from Maoist firebrand to conservative (some would say neo-liberal) leader may represent a kind of evolution. But the slogan predictably triggered an outcry from the opposition – and many historians – and embarrassment in his own camp. As for the hoardings, leftists diligently painted a large red 'R' in front of the word 'Evolução' on most of them.

Ten years after that, the 40th anniversary in 2014 coincided with the harsh austerity ushered in by the global financial crisis and resulting euro-zone bailout. As usual, tens of thousands marched to recall the events of 1974, but this time many were shouting anti-austerity slogans too.

At a special session in parliament, Portugal's conservative president, Aníbal Cavaco Silva, was among speakers who hailed the 1974 coup and the mid-ranking officers who staged it. But he also focused on the present, calling on the parties to work together to improve state finances. And despite the praise lavished on the former coup leaders, they were not invited to speak. So they held their own ceremony in Largo do Carmo, the square where the dictatorship had surrendered, complete with the (now antique) armoured cars used to besiege it. They were joined by thousands of citizens.

In speeches to the crowd, the now-retired officers accused politicians of losing sight of the principles of the Revolution – which included not only the right to vote, but universal healthcare, quality education, decent pensions and employment rights. They also questioned whether Portugal should remain in the euro, or even the EU, if it carried on as it was. Their words were met with cheers and a sea of upraised carnations, the symbol of the Revolution. Meanwhile, there's still no museum telling the story of the Revolution, or documenting the misdeeds of the dictatorship. The former headquarters of the PIDE, the secret police of the Salazar-Caetano regime (see *p50* **Walk**), was converted into luxury flats a few years ago despite a campaign for it to be turned into a memorial to the regime's opponents, some of whom were interrogated and tortured in cells there. Meanwhile, a museum project in the former Aljube prison, opposite the Sé cathedral, has been repeatedly delayed.

But the charged atmosphere of the 40th anniversary did prompt some youngsters to set to with pots of paint and brushes, drawing on the iconography of 1974. The most impressive of the new murals, by the Underdogs art group, is outside Universidade Nova on Avenida da Berna, its centrepiece a portrait of the most admired of the 1974 coup leaders, the late Salgueiro Maia. In general, though, the Revolution is best preserved in the wellspring of memories that locals are only too delighted to share.

German diplomats avoided one another at receptions, and Sintra airport was alone in Europe in offering scheduled flights to both London and Berlin.

Lisbon's cafés were crowded with refugees. Even the king of Romania passed through. *Casablanca* was to have been set here, and Lisbon remained the hoped-for destination in the finished film. French airman-author Antoine de Saint-Exupéry whiled away hours at the Estoril Casino in December 1940, awaiting passage to America; he eventually made it with refugee film director Jean Renoir. Ian Fleming also visited the casino, gleaning ideas for his protagonist by watching Yugoslav spy Darko Popov at the gaming tables.

The Allies' victory in 1945 put Portugal's right-wing dictatorship in a tricky position: celebrating the victory of democracy and communism over its natural allies. The Cold War came to the rescue. After some cosmetic concessions, Portugal aligned with the West in 1949, as a founding member of NATO. Salazar had a scare in 1958 when General Humberto Delgado garnered support and enthused the opposition in show elections for the presidency. Delgado was forced into exile (and assassinated by PIDE agents in 1965) and internal repression was stepped up. Revolts across the African colonies in 1960 and 1961 became full-blown wars that were only resolved after the 1974 Revolution.

During the 1950s and 1960s, Salazar kept Portugal closed to outside influences. Lisbon was one of the cleanest, quietest cities in Europe: you could chat in the middle of Avenida da Liberdade during rush hour. In the older neighbourhoods, poverty was rampant. Keeping order were the police, who fined citizens for cursing or letting their laundry drip.

Many emigrated. The rest hunkered down and swallowed the regime's three Fs: Fátima, Football, Fado. In 1917, the Virgin Mary supposedly appeared to three shepherd children at Fátima, north of Lisbon. The church had doubts at first, but the regime adopted the cult, building an enormous shrine that became a pilgrimage destination on the 13th of each month from May to October. Football had always been a national passion, but **Benfica** (*see p121* **Football Crazy**) reached the heights of European football in the 1960s thanks to the peerless Eusébio, and the national team, inspired by him, finished third in the 1966

Revolution of the Carnations, 1974.

World Cup. The 1950s and '60s were also a golden age of fado, dominated by Amália Rodrigues. Down on Praça de Alegria, the **Hot Clube** (*see p153*) turned Lisbon on to jazz.

Major public works were undertaken by the Estado Novo, not least the bridge over the Tagus (Ponte Salazar, later renamed Ponte 25 de Abril after the date of the 1974 Revolution). Linking Lisbon to Almada and its Cristo Rei statue, it was erected in 1958 in thanks for keeping Portugal out of World War II. The Metro was inaugurated in 1959. The city spread outwards. Art nouveau buildings on Avenida da República were demolished and replaced by the first concrete office blocks.

THE REVOLUTION

In 1968, Salazar was incapacitated by a stroke after his deckchair collapsed. No one had the heart to tell him President Américo Tomás had appointed the reformist Marcello Caetano in his place; until his death in 1970, ministers held sham meetings at his bedside. Caetano proved unable to unravel the Estado Novo or answer the colonial question. Student demonstrations had been common in the 1960s; now the army joined in. On 25 April 1974, a military coup was masterminded by Otelo Saraiva de Carvalho. Caetano, holed up in the GNR barracks on Largo do Carmo, surrendered after a young captain, Salgueiro

Maia, threatened the GNR with tanks, supported by a cheering populace. The only bloodshed came as crowds massed outside the PIDE headquarters on Rua António Cardoso. Shots fired from inside killed three. A plaque marks the spot (see p50 **Walk**).

General António Spínola headed a Junta de Salvação Nacional, and on 1 May hundreds of thousands demonstrated on Avenida Almirante Reis to back the Revolução dos Cravos – Revolution of the Carnations – as it became known after citizens stuffed soldiers' rifles with the red flowers. Spínola was out by September, and for 14 months right and left, military and civilians, tussled for power. After the 'hot summer' of 1975, when the Communist Party led by Álvaro Cunhal seemed to gain the upper hand, Portugal became a parliamentary democracy.

In the Revolution's aftermath, the colonies won independence, prompting an exodus of hundreds of thousands of Portuguese citizens. These *retornados*, as the white and mixed-race 'returnees' were called (though many had been born in Africa and never seen Portugal), flooded into a post-revolutionary shambles. Later waves of African immigrants came too, for economic or political reasons. Many found low-paid, insecure work in the construction industry, and settled in homes in the shanty towns on the edge of the city.

CATCHING UP

In the early 1980s, Lisbon's image was one of genteel decay. Money was scarce, public works were at a standstill, and emigration to northern Europe or the US continued. But, after Portugal joined the European Community in 1986, an inflow of funds provided stability for sustained development. The opening of the Amoreiras shopping centre in 1986 marked the arrival of mass shopping culture.

The once quiet streets of Lisbon became clogged with motor vehicles. The Ponte 25 de Abril is notorious for rush-hour jams, barely eased by the newer rail service beneath its carriageway. Another bridge, the Ponte Vasco da Gama, opened in 1998, draining off some weekend traffic. Road-dependent dormitory communities have mushroomed on the outskirts. But in the old city at least, a few more streets are barred to traffic each year.

On 25 August 1988, fire broke out in the Chiado, ripping the heart out of the classy shopping district and ending its outdoor café culture. Renowned Oporto architect Ávaro Siza Vieira was called in, and in the face of sloth-like city administration, his sensitive vision of reconstruction was realised.

Further redevelopment took place on the waterfront, where parks, promenades and marinas emerged from Belém to Santa Apolónia station. Upriver, the 1998 Expo was held on former industrial wasteland. Its stated purpose was to mark the 500th anniversary of Vasco da Gama's discovery of the sea route to India, and its hallmark a giant aquarium, the **Oceanário** (see p126). After Expo ended on 30 September 1998, the site reopened as **Parque das Nações** (see p126), a residential and business district with extensive parkland stretching along the river. Another legacy was Portugal's confidence in its ability to organise big events, including football's Euro 2004.

Portugal's entry into the EU monetary union on 1 January 1999 underscored its European identity. It handed over its last colony, Macao, to China at the end of the year. Yet a few months earlier, when government-backed militias in Indonesian-ruled East Timor terrorised civilians who had voted for independence, ordinary Portuguese mobilised on behalf of this far-flung former colony with a fervour that recalled revolutionary times.

Recent years have been difficult for many Portuguese. The economy has struggled as EU regional funds and foreign investment switched to Eastern Europe. Politicians lost credibility after three prime ministers departed in quick succession, having failed to tackle deep-rooted problems. The election in 2005 of the first ever majority Socialist administration was seen as a mandate for reform, but after its return to power without a majority, it became mired in accusations of corruption and finally fell after being forced in 2011 to seek a euro-zone bailout.

Since then, disenchantment with monetary union and the austerity policies that it seems to entail has prompted many to question long-held assumptions about Portugal's place in Europe. Add to that the growing importance of links with former colonies such as Angola and Brazil – and the emergence of Portuguese as 'the new language of power and trade', in the words of *Monocle* magazine – and people here are once more starting to see the world through a global prism.

IN CONTEXT

Architecture

From the Moors to a
magnificent metro.

Though Moorish elements linger, it's the period of the maritime Discoveries that left the first lasting mark on Lisbon's architecture, reflecting the city's prosperity and global links. Later, the devastation of the 1755 earthquake was followed by a pioneering example of Enlightenment town planning that still structures the city's life today. Decorative elements came to loom large, above all *azulejos* – the famous Portuguese ceramic tiles that appear both individually and in ambitious panels.

In more recent times, a great deal of harm was done to the urban fabric. The focus has now shifted to much-needed preservation and rehabilitation work, and away from flagship projects.

Torre de Belém.

EARLY ORIGINS

Although Lisbon's origins are lost in legend, its days as a Roman provincial city are recalled by the ruins that dot the centre in subterranean (but visitable) pockets. The **Teatro Romano** (see p60) is one of these. The centuries after the fall of Rome left little mark and the earliest physical evidence of urban civic life still found in the modern city is of Moorish rule between the eighth and 12th centuries. Surrounded by the Cerca Moura, the Moorish siege walls that skirt the Castelo de São Jorge, Alfama was the city's core. Latticed window shutters to shield women from the glances of passers-by can still be seen on some houses, and the quarter retains the feel of a North African port. Popular style has changed little over the centuries, with the traditional *casa portuguesa* based on simple lines and whitewashed walls with small windows.

Portuguese architecture advanced in the 15th century when Dom Manuel I began putting to use the riches gleaned from the sea route to the Indies. Palaces and churches were built, and royal architects such as Francisco de Arruda devised the new, late Gothic Manueline style. This featured plain walls with extravagant windows and portals decorated with flora and fauna, maritime motifs, the king's seal and the Vera Cruz, or True Cross. Structures still visible today include the **Torre de Belém** (see p103), the **Mosteiro dos Jerónimos** (see p100), with its spectacular cloister and nave, and the Madre de Deus church, now the **Museu Nacional do Azulejo** (see p124). *Lioz*, a local limestone, lent these massive buildings a light, airy look.

SPANISH STYLE

Philip II of Spain's ascension to the Portuguese throne in 1582 as Philip I brought a more monumental style, sombre on the outside but gilded within. Still visible are the **Igreja de São Vicente da Fora** (see p67), the **Igreja de São Roque** (see p82), the Mercês church on Largo do Chiado and the Convento do Beato on Alameda do Beato out east in Xabregas. São Vicente, white and imposing on the hill above Alfama, is a prime example. It typifies the mannerist style of the Counter Reformation, rich in ideology and imagery, and its twin bell towers served as models for local architects for two centuries. The interior houses some of Lisbon's most elaborate panels of *azulejos* (tiles). Once imported from Seville, but long since made in Portugal, these tiles remain a consistent presence (see p202 **Wall-to-Wall Art**).

This period also saw the first attempts at planning. In 1580, the **Bairro Alto** ('Upper Town'; see p80) was laid out on a grid of streets that were perceived as wide and regular at the time – now they seem cramped and maze-like.

SOBERING UP AND REBUILDING

Following the restoration in 1640, a sober style known as the Estilo Chão (Flat or Plain Style) developed, in which massive corner pillars framed horizontally organised façades, with simple balconies topped by stone balustrades or plain railings. Larger country houses and palaces began to mimic the French U-shaped style. Most surviving Lisbon palaces from this period are in Estilo Chão, including the Palácio Galveias

Basílica da Estrela.

Hungarian Carlos Mardel and Eugénio dos Santos. They plotted out a new Baixa of 200,000 square metres, on a grid of seven streets running north–south, christened after the trades that would operate on them, and eight streets running east–west.

Pombaline style is characterised by scant exterior decoration, although façades were given a glossy finish by pressing the fresh stucco with tin plates – a process known as *estanhado*. The mainly four-storey houses were built around a *gaiola*, or cage – a flexible structure with wooden joists filled with brick, stone and plaster, intended to withstand earthquakes. Another innovation was to raise the walls separating houses to a level higher than the roof joists, to act as a firewall. Fully equipped with modern sanitation, these blocks were at the very cutting edge of urban planning.

As soon as Pombal fell from grace, Lisbon resumed its haphazard growth. Dom José's daughter, who became Dona Maria I, was a pious woman responsible for two beautiful churches – the **Igreja da Memória** (*see p100*) and the **Basílica da Estrela** (*see p110*). The latter is an imposing building in white stone, topped by an ornate dome that, when illuminated, dominates the western skyline. Inside is a finely crafted profusion of pink and black marble. The Igreja da Memória is reminiscent of the Basílica – both are mostly the work of Mateus Vicente – but more intimate. Also of note are the 1792 **Teatro Nacional de São Carlos** (*see p159*), perhaps Lisbon's first neoclassical building, and the **Palácio da Ajuda** (*see p103*).

(Campo Pequeno), now a library, and **Palácio dos Marqueses da Fronteira** (*see p117*).

Artistry and engineering flourished: the **Aqueduto das Águas Livres** (*see p112*) was completed; fancy wood carving and sculpture became de rigueur in royal, church and public interiors; and façades with intricately painted blue-and-white *azulejos* multiplied.

Under Dom João V, the Magnificent, Baroque triumphed in palaces such as the Paço de Bemposta (off Campo dos Mártires da Pátria, now a military academy), the **Igreja da Graça** (*see p66*) and the Palácio das Necessidades (on Largo das Necessidades, today's Foreign Ministry). Many were inspired by the palace and convent at Mafra, north-west of Lisbon, designed by German architect João Frederico Ludovice.

The Great Earthquake of 1 November 1755 left a score of churches, the royal palace and dozens of other noble dwellings, and two thirds of the city's medieval housing in rubble. In the aftermath of the ensuing tidal wave and fires, the all-powerful minister of Dom José I, later known as the Marquês de Pombal, sought to impose modernity. He began by forbidding construction outside the city limits and reconstruction inside them until his plans were concluded, and drafted in three bright architects – Manuel da Maia, newly arrived

STAGNATION AND INDUSTRY

The first half of the 19th century was a turbulent time, and urban planning languished, although the **Teatro Nacional Dona Maria II** (*see p161*) was built between Rossio and the Passeio Público. The industrial revolution brought a new age of engineering (and Romantic nostalgia), epitomised in the neo-Manueline Rossio station and the more French neo-Gothic of the **Elevador de Santa Justa** (*see p43*), designed by Raul Mesnier du Ponsard. The Campo Pequeno bullring (*see p122* **Talking Bull**) and the Casa do Alentejo in Baixa (Rua das Portas de Santo Antão 58) reflect the neo-Moorish trend that emerged during the 1890s.

IN CONTEXT

WALL-TO-WALL ART

Lisbon's azulejos constitute the city's largest permanent exhibition.

The Portuguese ornamental element that most catches visitors' fancy is the *azulejo*, or tile. These are everywhere: from palaces to the façades of the humblest houses, from butcher's shops to Metro stations. There's a **Museu Nacional do Azulejo** (*see p124*) in a former convent, but sometimes the whole city seems like one big tile museum.

The word *azulejo* comes either from *zulej*, 'blue' in Persian, or from *al-zuleycha*, Arabic for polished stone. Tiles from Islamic Asia are on show at the **Museu Calouste Gulbenkian** (*see p116*), but the tradition has deep roots in Iberia. Tiles produced in Seville by Muslim craftsmen were first imported in large numbers during the 14th century; Sintra's **Palácio Nacional** (*see p177*) has some fine examples. But the craze really took off a century later, with the

arrival of Italian majolica techniques. After Spain expelled all *mudéjars* (local Muslims) in 1610, new factories in Portugal produced flat painted tiles rather than the old relief designs. Made mainly for religious buildings, such as the **Igreja de São Roque** (*see p82*), they depicted biblical landscapes or popular saints.

Larger 'tile tapestries' appeared in the 17th century. Splendid examples survive in the **Igreja de São Vicente** (*see p67*) and the **Palácio dos Marqueses da Fronteira** (*see p117*), whose Sala das Batalhas – full of panels representing battles of the Portuguese Restoration War – has been called 'the Sistine Chapel of tilework'. Mass production began in 1767 when the Marquês de Pombal founded the Real Fábrica do Rato to serve post-earthquake reconstruction. Tiles were used increasingly in façades, in a more restrained, neoclassical style.

The popularity of *azulejos* declined in the early 19th century thanks to the Peninsular War, the court's departure to Brazil and the dissolution of the monasteries; the Real Fábrica closed in 1835. The industrial age heralded a comeback: examples include the 1865 façade of **Fábrica Viúva Lamego** on Largo do Intendente (now vintage store A Vida Portuguesa, *see p69*), and the façade on Rua da Trindade facing Largo Rafael Bordalo Pinheiro, depicting Progress and Science. Three firms from the period survive today, selling mostly to northern Europe.

The craft moved on. Particularly in Lapa, Campo de Ourique and Saldanha, colourful art nouveau tiles frame doors, windows and balconies. Artists such as Rafael Bordalo Pinheiro and Jorge Colaço created lavish façades and interiors. In later decades, run-of-the-mill tiles were too often slapped on to façades to provide colour or protect against

Museu Nacional do Azulejo.

Igreja de São Vicente.

rain. But the latter part of the 20th century saw a revival, with Portuguese and foreign artists designing *azulejos* for sale in specialist shops – and, of course, for Lisbon's Metro.

Campo Grande station is graced by Eduardo Néry's 'deconstructions' of traditional blue and white *azulejo* panels; Campo Pequeno, two stops away, has fight scenes that recall the nearby bullring. Parque station was clad in cobalt blue by Belgium's Françoise Schein and France's Federica Matta, with designs alluding to Portugal's maritime history and noble quotations from poets, philosophers and the Universal Declaration of Human Rights. Out at Carnide, José de Guimarães's inimitable style finds expression in neon and stone renditions of wobbly animal forms. At bustling commuter terminal Cais do Sodré, António da Costa's giant versions of the White Rabbit from *Alice in Wonderland* announce 'I'm late'.

Olaias station.

The Linha Vermelha line, inaugurated to coincide with Expo 98, has been the biggest publicly funded showcase of recent times. At brash **Olaias**, love-him-or-hate-him architect Tomás Taveira produced a dizzying mosaic of primary colours and restless patterns. For the next station, Bela Vista, Querubim Lapa mixed geometric patterns and naïve designs. Chelas integrates architecture by Ana Nascimento and decoration by Jorge Martins: tunnels plunge into blue limestone walls with no visible support, slashed by bold rents and asymmetric windows. Olivais is one of the network's deepest stations, with fittingly profound artwork by Nuno de Siqueira: panels with images of adversity, war and revolution hint at Portugal's contribution to modernity, while phrases such as 'a thing is not only what we see but also what it signifies' comment obliquely on the artist's own work. At Cabo Ruivo, David de Almeida set white Stone Age hunting images on black walls. As your train passes, these flash between pale blue arches, creating a moving-image effect.

The line originally terminated at Oriente, designed by Sanchez Jorge. It's a gallery of huge panels on maritime themes by renowned Portuguese and international artists, including Hundertwasser and Erró, more of whose work can also be found in the patio of the nearby VIP Art's hotel on Avenida Dom João II. In 2013, the line was finally extended to the airport – tunnels in the new Aeroporto terminus are dotted with mosaic cartoons of Portuguese cultural icons by António Antunes.

IN CONTEXT

Lisbon's distinctive *calçada à portuguesa* (Portuguese paving) came into its own in 1849 with the completion of the dizzy-looking Rossio Square – restored at the end of the 20th century after decades of being eaten into by asphalt. Even today, *calcário* (limestone) is hewn into tiny blocks to decorate walkways with traditional and modern designs, with each stone cut and laid by hand. In 1986, the city set up a vocational school to keep these old skills alive.

Portugal's early 20th-century experiment in democracy produced the first district of social housing in Arco do Cego (now dwarfed by state bank Caixa Geral de Depósitos, sponsor of Culturgest; see *p120*), as well as the **Parque Mayer** (see *p53*), a cluster of variety theatres off Avenida da Liberdade. The ultra-modern Teatro Capitólio, built between 1925 and 1931, was one such theatre. Technical innovations included reinforced concrete, a naturally lit auditorium and Portugal's first escalator. Long derelict, the theatre was saved from demolition after a vigorous campaign, but it's yet to be restored.

With the rise of Salazar, architecture took on a pseudo-fascist look, with monumental buildings such as the Palácio da Justiça at the top of Parque Eduardo VII and the **Biblioteca Nacional** (see *p120*). Modernism struggled on – examples include Cassiano Branco's **Eden** theatre on Praça dos Restauradores and his **Hotel Victoria** on Avenida da Liberdade (for both, see *p53*), as well as the Instituto Superior Técnico, an 'acropolis' of learning by Porfírio Pardal Monteiro that was Portugal's first campus. But the regime favoured the Portuguese Modern Traditional style, which featured galleries with round arches and bas-reliefs. The Igreja da Nossa Senhora da Fátima on Avenida da Berna and the twin-towered Igreja São João de Deus on Praça de Londres are outstanding examples.

By 1940, nationalism was in full flow and the Exposição do Mundo Português (Exhibition of the Portuguese World) was held in Belém. It centred on the chauvinistic **Padrão dos Descobrimentos** monument (see *p103*), featuring giant statues of Henry the Navigator and his courtiers, map-makers and sailors advancing along a plinth towards unknown seas. Also part of the Exposição, the building nearby will soon house a revamped **Museu Nacional de Arte Popular**, while the fountain

Eden theatre.

on Alameda Dom Afonso Henriques, with its Tagus nymphs and mythical creatures from Camões's *Lusiads*, is from the same period.

However, it would be simplistic to write off the Salazar era. It saw the construction of Pardal Monteiro's impressive modernist Gare Marítima de Alcântara (1943), with murals by José de Almada Negreiros, while the hyperactive minister of public works Duarte Pacheco was a visionary, laying out three large residential neighbourhoods – Alvalade, Restelo and Olivais – and starting the first dual carriageway. By the 1960s, Portugal could no longer avoid international trends: the first Metro line opened in 1960, the Ponte Salazar (now Ponte 25 de Abril) was built in 1966 and the **Fundação Calouste Gulbenkian** (see *p159*) opened in 1969.

MODERN TIMES

Much harm was done to the city's fabric after the 1974 Revolution. In the 1970s and '80s, corrugated-iron shanty towns sprang up and dormitory suburbs were built, largely illegally. Portugal's 1986 entry into the EU generated wealth at a time of minimal public awareness of urban planning, and city officials permitted the rape of several historic zones. On Largo de Martim Moniz, a shopping centre was built on the back of a tiny, ancient chapel; architect Tomás Taveira tested local humour with his pink and smoked-glass **Amoreiras** mall (see *p113*), which juts out from an old hilltop district, and an office block that echoes the form of a Portuguese guitar (Avenida de Berna 175).

After the 1988 Chiado fire, reconstruction was handed to Portugal's leading architect, Álvaro Siza Vieira. He rescued 18 of the 20

Champalimaud Center for the Unknown.

damaged façades and rebuilt the gutted insides, restoring the Armazéns do Chiado department store as a shopping centre and luxury hotel. It was above all this project that secured him the 1992 Pritzker Prize, seen as architecture's equivalent of the Nobel Prize.

That same year, Portugal inaugurated the **Centro Cultural de Belém** (see p157) to host the EU presidency. Put opposite the Mosteiro dos Jerónimos, Vittorio Gregotti and Manuel Salgado's *lioz* block was controversial at the time but has come to be accepted, if not loved.

The most important urban project of the late 20th century, though, was Expo 98, which rehabilitated a stretch of eastern waterfront polluted by oil refineries, munitions factories and a slaughterhouse. Now called **Parque das Nações** (see p126), its architectural highlights are Peter Chermayev's Oceanário, Regino Cruz's UFO-like Pavilhão Atlântico, Siza's Pavilhão de Portugal with its concave concrete canopy, and Santiago Calatrava's soaring Gare do Oriente. Built in conjunction with Expo were the 17km (10.5-mile) Ponte Vasco da Gama and a Metro line with some remarkable stations (see p202 **Wall-to-Wall Art**). Recent years have seen big international names bandied about – Renzo Piano, Jean Nouvel and Norman Foster among them – in plans to provide the city with architectural pizzazz, particularly along the neglected riverfront. None has come to fruition except, in 2010, the **Champalimaud Center for the Unknown** (see p100) in Belém, designed by Indian architect Charles Correa.

These days, not only is there no public money for new flagship projects; there isn't always the cash to open those already built. A design by Brazil's Pritzker laureate, Paulo Mendes da Rocha, for a new 16,000sq m home for Portugal's most visited museum, the **Museu dos Coches** (see p102), was approved in 2006 and work began three years later. By mid 2012, the giant raised hangar for exhibits and the reception block were both virtually complete. But the site then went silent for more than two years – funds were lacking for making crucial finishing touches and the big move itself. Even closed, the building costs hundreds of thousands of euros a year to maintain. Open, it will cost ten times as much.

In the meantime, public and private investment is being ploughed almost solely into urban rehabilitation – no bad thing when so much of the built fabric needs repair. Siza Vieira oversaw the overhaul of an old warehouse in São Bento to create the **Atelier-Museu Júlio Pomar** (see p106), a project praised for the elegance and simplicity of its 'almost invisible' architecture – as Mayor António Costa put it at the 2013 inauguration – in this densely packed neighbourhood.

Another Pritzker Prize-winner, Eduardo Souto Moura from Oporto, has meanwhile been working on a cluster of projects in the Príncipe Real area to turn old mansions into upscale residential and commercial spaces. **Embaixada** and **Entre Tanto** (for both, see p86) were the first, but there should be more to come.

IN CONTEXT

Essential Information

Hotels

The tourism boom of the past couple of years has triggered a building bonanza: new hotels, hostels and tourist apartment complexes have been opening on a monthly, if not weekly, basis as the capital extends its lead over the Algarve in terms of visitor numbers. Crumbling mansions in the old central neighbourhoods have emerged as boutique hotels, sometimes with the aid of city funding, while glass towers have multiplied in business hubs such as the Parque das Nações. Lisbon caters ever more abundantly for the well-heeled, but continues to welcome the mid-market tourists and backpackers who were for so long a speciality. Out on the coast, meanwhile, you can find everything from palaces to campsites.

ESSENTIAL INFORMATION

PRICES AND INFORMATION

Listings in this chapter are divided into areas that correspond to those used elsewhere in this guide – although hotels often cluster in rather different areas to sights and entertainment venues. In any case, bear in mind that in a small city such as Lisbon, such geographical divisions are rather artificial. We have also provided a few options in Cascais and Estoril, as some visitors may prefer to be based nearer to local beaches.

In town, much of the accommodation is found between the Baixa and Parque Eduardo VII, but scattered throughout the city are cheap hotels – invariably still with *pensão* in their name, although the official classification for non-hotel accommodation now is *alojamento local*. It's harder to find rock-bottom prices these days, since even downmarket *pensões* have been forced to upgrade their facilities to compete with a wave of hostels (*see p210* **Budget Beds**), which has resulted in higher rates to pay for the investment. Still, prices remain cheap compared with much of Europe; in some mid-range and lower-priced hotels, rates may be negotiable. Even in fancier establishments, there are often bargains to be had if you book ahead or online.

Area sections are subdivided by price: Deluxe, Expensive, Moderate and Budget. A double room in a **Deluxe** hotel will cost upwards of around €250, **Expensive** is €150-€250, **Moderate** €70-€150 and **Budget** under €70. Campsites (*see p223* **Perfect Pitch**) and hostels (*see p210* **Budget Beds**) – defined as anywhere whose rooms are mostly in dorms – are set apart from the main hotel listings, although note that hostels invariably have a double room or two. Note also that they're not always cheaper per head than *pensões* – some of which have triple and quadruple rooms or, in the case of **Residencial Saldanha** (*see p221*), a quintuple. But they do have kitchen and other facilities such as sociable lounges; towels, on the other hand, may not be provided or might cost extra. Almost all budget lodgings tend to have free Wi-Fi throughout, whereas some fancier hotels make you pay extra in your room. And in general, even budget accommodation is clean, partly because the authorities are strict.

Several of the places listed in this chapter proclaim themselves to be gay-friendly, including **Pensão Globo** (*see p218*), **Residência Mar dos Açores** (*see p216*) and **Internacional Design Hotel** (*see p209*). For more gay-friendly accommodation, *see p139*.

In hotels that serve tourists rather than the business trade, prices can as much as double during the summer, particularly along the Estoril coast. Book a fortnight in advance in July and August, especially if you want to be near a beach.

In Lisbon lodgings, rates can depend on the size of the room, the view and whether there's a bathroom. Prices generally include breakfast, but not with all online deals.

Where booking is concerned, most specialist online sites have a fair range of Lisbon hotels, but sometimes your best bet is to go direct, since even budget places often have online as well as phone/email reservations. Once in town, tourist offices provide only limited help with finding accommodation; there's a comprehensive listing on the **Turismo de Lisboa** website (www.visitlisboa.com) but they have no advance reservation service. Hostellers should note that the **YHA** has a central booking service (*see p210* **Budget Beds**), but privately run hostels are not covered.

For longer stays, renting an apartment is an increasingly popular option. There are no particularly helpful local databases; such accommodation tends to be publicised on global search sites such as **Airbnb** (www.airbnb.co.uk).

All of our hotel listings feature a full postal address (including the seven-digit postcode); note that in the Portuguese format, where the house number after the street name is followed by a comma and a single digit, this single digit denotes the floor – this applies above all to downtown *pensões*.

BAIXA & ROSSIO

Expensive

Hotel Mundial
Praça Martim Moniz 2, 1100-341 (21 884 2000, www.hotel-mundial.pt). Metro Martim Moniz or Rossio, or tram 12, 15, 28. **Rooms** 350. **Map** p251 M9.
Featuring 350 guest rooms, the Mundial is by far the largest hotel in the heart of town, but staff work very hard to ensure you don't feel like just another tourist. The functional rooms have decent views and are quiet thanks to double glazing. Parking is free, but the Wi-Fi isn't. The hotel has two restaurants; the one on the eighth floor has panoramic views. As well as a cosy ground-floor bar, there's another on the rooftop where you almost feel you could reach out and touch the castle.

★ Internacional Design Hotel
Rua da Betesga 2, 1100-090 (21 324 0990, www.idesignhotel.com). Metro Rossio. **Rooms** 55. **Map** p250 M9.
Strategically located on a corner of the city's main square, this modern boutique hotel makes up in style, service and amenities what it inevitably lacks in terms of other facilities. The 55 guest rooms come in varying sizes but all are spacious enough, and are decorated with one of four striking themes: Urban, Tribal, Zen and Pop Art. Each has an espresso machine and free Wi-Fi. An airport transfer service is also included. The recently opened restaurant has been a big hit with local foodies.

Moderate

Beautique Hotels Figueira
Praça da Figueira 16, 1100-241 (21 049 2940, www.thebeautiquehotels.com). Metro Rossio or tram 12, 15. **Rooms** 50. **Map** p250 M9.
The olive-green façade of this relatively new hotel in a refurbished 18th-century building (it opened in early 2013) is a taster for the darkly handsome contemporary interiors dreamed up by leading Portuguese designer Nini Andrade e Silva. The rooms have a lighter touch, with creams and whites balancing out the browns and blacks that prevail elsewhere. All rooms have iPod docking stations and free Wi-Fi. The golden ground-floor bar is a glamorous place for a cocktail. The tiny gym has two machines and an exercise ball, and there's a spa

Beautique Hotels Figueira.

BUDGET BEDS
Hostels to head for in Lisbon.

Travellers House.

The tourism boom of the past couple of decades has encouraged many traditional *pensões* (guesthouses) to hike their prices and upgrade to hotel status, which has left a gap at the bottom of the market. This has been filled by a plethora of enterprising privately run hostels, which have become renowned not just as great places to meet other travellers, but also for combining quality, service and style on a shoestring (dorm beds start from around €16).

Among those long-established hostels that have kept standards high over the years is **Travellers House** (Rua Augusta 89, 21 011 5922, www.travellershouse.com). Set right in the middle of the Baixa, it offers lovely airy dormitories and a few en suites for those who want to mix the privacy of a hotel with the sociability of a hostel.

Round the corner is the goofily named **Yes! Lisbon Hostel** (Rua de Sao Juliao 148, 21 342 7171, www.yeshostels.com). It has lockers, laundry facilities, free Wi-Fi and internet PCs, as well as extras such as a reading light for your bed and free walking tours. The common areas are vast and staff hand out free shots to help break the ice. Yes! Lisbon Hostel also has its own restaurant with a €10 menu.

Another central hostel aimed squarely at backpackers is the **Rossio Hostel** (Calçada do Carmo 6, 21 342 6004, www.rossio hostel.com), located on the upper floors of a beautifully restored 18th-century building. It's right in the heart of the action with a supermarket just steps away.

For something a little artier, head uphill to the fifth-floor **Lisbon Poets Hostel** in Chiado (Rua Nova da Trindade 2, 21 346 12 41, www. lisbonpoetshostel.com), where the rooms and dorms are all named after Portuguese writers, and there's a good choice of books and DVDs in the lounge. Continental breakfast is included and free city walking tours are available.

The tiny **Lisbon Lounge Hostel** (Rua São Nicolau 41, 21 346 2061, www.lisbon loungehostel.com) is known as much for its three-course dinners as for its graffiti-daubed walls, while the meals at the larger **Home Lisbon Hostel** just down the street (no.13, 21 888 5312, www.homelisbonhostel.com) – dubbed 'Mamma's dinners' – are another backpackers' favourite.

For something a bit special, the **Oasis Hostel** (Rua de Santa Catarina 24, 21 347 8044, www.oasislisboa.com), up beyond the Bairro Alto area, organises a fortnightly gastronomic tour and a weekly *petiscos* (snacks) tour as well as free walking and fado tours. If you like the area, it's worth noting that the **Evidência Light Santa Catarina Hotel** (see *p218*) also has a dormitory.

Another option if cash is really tight are the state-run *pousadas de juventude*, where beds tend to be several euros cheaper than at private hostels. The best of the four in the region is the **Pousada de Juventude do Parque das Nações** (Rua de Moscavide, Lote 47, 21 892 0890, www.pousadasjuventude. pt), right next to Moscavide rail station and a ten-minute walk from the sights and shops of the Expo 98 site.

The downtown offices of the Instituto Português da Juventude (Rua Rodrigo da Fonseca 55, 21 047 0000, open 9am-6pm Mon-Fri) can help you with booking *pousadas de juventude*, as well as providing information and tips for young travellers, including how and where to get discounts. Private hostels, meanwhile, are listed on websites such as www.hostelworld.com and www. hostelbookers.com.

(€10 for guests, waived if you book a treatment) and a sauna with a view of the castle.

Hotel Metrópole

Praça Dom Pedro IV (Rossio) 30, 1100-200 (21 321 9030, www.metropole-lisbon.com). Metro Rossio or Restauradores. **Rooms** 36. **Map** p250 L9.
Located above famous Café Nicola, the Metrópole combines art nouveau style with modern comforts (including free Wi-Fi) and a friendly vibe. The interior is a throwback to the 1920s, with individually decorated rooms containing period furniture; compared to other hotels in the area, the room rates have thankfully marked time too. Bathrooms are spacious and decorated in white marble. The lounge bar overlooks Rossio; it was from these windows that political leaders such as Mário Soares addressed the people during the 1974 Revolution. It's peaceful now, though: rooms are double-glazed and quiet at night.

Hotel Portugal

Rua João das Regras 4, 1100-294 (21 884 2120, www.hotelportugal.com). Metro Rossio or tram 12, 15. **Rooms** 53. **Map** p251 M9.
Located one block east of Praça da Figueira, this recently upgraded hotel now has four stars and a striking new look, with gold and white dominating in the lobby, and violet and white in the guest rooms. There are ultra-modern touches – the TV is built into the mirror – and bathrooms are spacious and loaded with amenities. The hotel has an inner patio where guests can take breakfast in summer. Free parking is another bonus.

Lisboa Tejo Hotel

Rua dos Condes de Monsanto 2, 1100-059 (21 886 6182, www.lisboatejohotel.com). Metro Rossio or tram 12, 15. **Rooms** 58. **Map** p251 M9.
The Lisboa Tejo offers stylish digs at reasonable prices. Rooms feature brightly coloured walls that contrast with the white-painted furniture, while modern furniture in the common areas is arranged under old stone arches. The lobby bar is a cheerful place for a drink even if you're not staying here. Don't miss the Poço de Borratém on one corner – the water from this ancient well was long used to cure itching and liver ailments, and it's topped with a handsome *azulejo* panel.

Budget

For more budget accommodation, *see p210* **Budget Beds**.

Hotel Duas Nações

Rua da Vitória 41, 1100-618 (21 346 0710, www.duasnacoes.com). Metro Baixa-Chiado or tram 12, 28. **Rooms** 73. **Map** p250 M9.
Now rated as a two-star hotel, this former *pensão* remains one of the best bargains in the Baixa. Rooms are simple and comfortable, and some have

been renovated in the past year; the more expensive ones have private bathrooms with showers. Try to avoid those along Rua Augusta, which can be noisy; the rest are fairly quiet. You can even order a basic continental breakfast in bed. The hotel has no bar, but you can buy chilled soft drinks at reception. There's a charge for Wi-Fi.

★ Pensão Praça da Figueira

Travessa Nova de São Domingos 9, 2D, 1100-372 (21 342 4323, www.pensaopracadafigueira.com). Metro Rossio or tram 12, 15. **Rooms** 32. **No credit cards. Map** p250 M9.
This popular place has chosen to go down the *alojamento local* (*see p208*) route to keep prices low, meaning it still offers some of the best value in the area. Service is good and the atmosphere friendly. The rooms – each painted a different colour during a recent refurbishment – are large with decent views of the square and the ruins of the Carmo church on the hillside; some have a balcony too. Not all rooms have a shower and barely half have their own toilet, but all offer free Wi-Fi and TV.

Pensão Prata

Rua da Prata 71, 3, 1100-414 (21 346 8908, www.pensaoprata.net). Metro Baixa-Chiado or Terreiro do Paço. **Rooms** 12. **No credit cards. Map** p250 M10.
This central *pensão* has decent-sized rooms with shower, sink and bidet; toilets are just outside the rooms. All have TV and free Wi-Fi. The owner speaks little English but her son, Pedro, is fluent. Breakfast isn't available, but there are plenty of cafés nearby. There's also a kitchen for guests' use.

Residencial Rossio

Rua dos Sapateiros 173, 2E, 1100-577 (21 342 7204, www.pensaorossio.com). Metro Rossio or tram 12, 15. **Rooms** 8. **No credit cards. Map** p250 M9.
If you're travelling on a shoestring, this basic residence is safe, clean and friendly. Half the rooms have their own bathrooms; others have basins and share other facilities. Wi-Fi is free throughout. Be aware that it's on the edge of one of Lisbon's red-light areas, so hanging around alone late at night may not be a great idea.

RESTAURADORES & AVENIDA DA LIBERDADE

Deluxe

Hotel Heritage Avenida Liberdade

Avenida da Liberdade 28, 1250-145 (21 340 4040, www.heritage.pt). Metro Avenida. **Rooms** 42. **Map** p246 L7.
A judicious combination of old and new, this compact hotel was opened a decade ago by the same company that owns As Janelas Verdes (*see p219*),

IN THE KNOW SPA STARS

Several giant spas have opened or been revamped of late, including at the renovated **Altis Grand** (*see right*) and **Sheraton** (*see p220*), and the newer **Altis Belém** (*see p219*) and **EPIC SANA** (*see p215*), which has a botanical garden to help you unwind. Elsewhere, serious pampering is on offer at the **Olissippo Lapa Palace** (*see p219*), **Pestana Palace** (*see p219*), **Four Seasons Ritz** (*see p214*) and **Grande Real Villa Itália** (*see p221*). But for the best view while you stew, head for the **Myriad SANA** (*see p221*).

Solar do Castelo (*see p216*) and Hotel Lisboa Plaza (*see p213*). The old comes courtesy of the late 18th-century mansion that houses the hotel, the new from the interiors dreamed up by star Portuguese designer Miguel Câncio Martins. All the rooms have plasma TVs, DVD/CD players and free Wi-Fi; there are also a number of suites. There's no restaurant, but somehow the hotel manages to squeeze in a gym and pool. Guests may also use the more spacious Holmes Place gyms (there's one just up the road).

Hotel Tivoli Lisboa
Avenida da Liberdade 185, 1269-050 (21 319 8900, www.tivolihotels.com). Metro Avenida.
Rooms 306. **Map** p246 L8.
Situated halfway up Avenida da Liberdade, this landmark hotel combines convenience and creature comforts, attracting a steady stream of business-people, honeymooners, families and tour groups to enjoy the spacious public areas and plush rooms. It opened in 1933, but the interior is swish 1950s. The rooftop Terrace Grill has great views and traditional cuisine, while the Beatriz Costa buffet restaurant honours the Portuguese actress who lived in the hotel for years. At the rear, far from the city bustle, a secluded tropical garden (closed during winter) with an oval pool makes an ideal sunbathing spot, and a tennis court and cocktail bar are also on hand. Round the back is the slightly cheaper Tivoli Jardim, while the newer Tivoli Oriente is out at Parque das Nações.

Expensive

★ Altis Avenida Hotel
Rua 1° de Dezembro 120, 1200-360 (21 044 0000, www.altishotels.com). Metro Restauradores.
Rooms 70. **Map** p250 L9.
Despite its monolithic exterior (the hotel is housed in a former government building), the Altis Avenida offers plenty of comfort and style, drawing on a 1940s aesthetic. The cheaper Classic rooms over-look the interior patio, while the more expensive Superior and Deluxe rooms have views of Praça dos Restauradores (double glazing blocks out the

traffic noise). There are also two light-filled suites with views up the Avenida; the esplanade of the top-floor Rossio restaurant and bar affords a similar panorama. There's no on-site gym, but guests have free use of the indoor pool, spa and 24-hour gym at the Altis Grand (*see below*) and discounts at the Altis Belém (*see p219*) spa.

Altis Grand Hotel
Rua Castilho 11, 1269-072 (21 310 6000, www.altishotels.com). Metro Avenida. **Rooms** 300. **Map** p246 K7.
Halfway between the offices and shops of Avenida da Liberdade and trendy Príncipe Real, this iconic hotel caters to a mix of tourists and, thanks to its large conference centre, business travellers. Guests are drawn by modern comforts – including free in-room Wi-Fi – and competitive prices. The hotel has been given a facelift recently, with the rather sombre wood panelling now offset by furnishings in cream, gold and primary colours. There's also a new spa and fitness area with a heated indoor pool, sauna and Turkish bath, treatment rooms and a gym that's open round the clock. Aside from the generous buffet breakfast in the Rio de Janeiro restaurant, the 12th-floor Grill Dom Fernando serves up traditional cuisine and stunning panoramic views, while the new Rendez Vous coffee shop whips up light meals throughout the day. The chain has three other hotels in Lisbon: the glamorous Altis Avenida (*see left*); the riverside Altis Belém (*see p219*) with its renowned

Valverde Hotel.

Inspira Santa Marta Hotel.

restaurant, Feitoria; and the four-star Altis Park Hotel (Avenida Engenheiro Arantes e Oliveira 9, 21 843 4200) near the airport.

Hotel Lisboa Plaza
Travessa do Salitre 7, 1269-066 (21 321 8218, www.heritage.pt). Metro Avenida. **Rooms** 112. **Map** p246 L8.
Opened in the early 1950s, this grand hotel was designed by architect Lucínio Cruz in bold neoclassical style. Graça Viterbo, one of Portugal's best-known interior designers, was let loose on the foyer, where a cream-coloured marble floor blends with the soft pastels of the carpets and furniture. The spacious rooms also show her style, with comfortable furnishings and light, airy bathrooms. A fantastic buffet breakfast is served in the restaurant, which also has a very good à la carte menu. Wi-Fi is free throughout. There's no gym, but guests can use the Holmes Place on Avenida da Liberdade.

Valverde Hotel
Avenida da Liberdade 164, 1250-146 (21 094 0300, www.valverdehotel.com). Metro Avenida. **Rooms** 25. **Map** p246 L8.
There could hardly be a better base for luxury shopping on the Avenida than this drop-dead gorgeous five-star boutique hotel, whose stated aim is to serve as a home from home. Its interiors are a well-judged blend of 1950s and contemporary. Service is attentive but discreet. Some of the rooms only have a shower, but even the singles feature pretty spacious bathrooms. Only the more expensive rooms have espresso machines and free Wi-Fi, but all overlook the Avenida. Breakfast (available up to the civilised hour of 11.30am) may be taken in the winter garden, which also has a small pool. There's a small restaurant and a tiny private cinema that's ideal for canoodling couples.

Moderate

★ Ever Lisboa
Avenida da Liberdade 189, 1250-141 (21 352 2618, www.everhotels.com). Metro Avenida. **Rooms** 37. **Map** p246 L7.
Formerly known as Hotel Veneza, this 1886 edifice built by Portuguese lawyer Adriano Antão Barata Salgueiro has a fabulously over-the-top interior. A colourful mural of Lisbon ascends the elegant spiral staircase. The large rooms aren't quite so kitsch, with beige, brown and cream predominating since the 2014 refurbishment. While the hotel offers few services (there's no Wi-Fi in the rooms, though it is free in the common areas), its location makes it a bargain.

Hotel Britania
Rua Rodrigues Sampaio 17, 1150-278 (21 315 5016, www.heritage.pt). Metro Marquês de Pombal or Avenida. **Rooms** 33. **Map** p246 L7.
The Britania is housed in a carefully restored building from the 1940s that was designed by leading Portuguese architect Cassiano Branco. It attracts a mixture of media business types and city-break couples. Rooms are generously sized with marble bathrooms and classical furniture, and offer five-star comforts at three-star prices, including room service and free Wi-Fi. There's a generous buffet breakfast, the receptionists speak good English and there's a concierge service. Parking is relatively cheap at €9 a day. The Britania is part of the Heritage chain, so guests can use Holmes Place gyms; there's one on Avenida da Liberdade.

★ Inspira Santa Marta Hotel
Rua de Santa Marta 48, 1150-297 (21 044 0900, www.inspirahotels.com). Metro Marquês de Pombal. **Rooms** 89. **Map** p246 L7.

An entire block is taken up by this 'urban oasis' tucked behind a period façade just off Avenida da Liberdade. The Santa Marta, winner of Green Hotel of the Year at the 2014 European Hospitality Awards, employs sleek Scandinavian-style design across five colour themes, as well as feng shui principles to soothe and energise. There's a similar vibe in the rooms: next to the espresso machine and a range of organic teas stands bottled water that comes from the tap but is filtered on site (if you choose to pay, the money goes to the charity Pump Aid), and virtually all furniture and textiles are made locally. Your complimentary newspaper comes via Wi-Fi to your mobile device, from a selection of more than 1,800, and desks are ergonomically designed to make the most of the space. Downstairs, the hotel's compact spa is utterly Zen – you'd never guess that you were right in the city centre – and its jacuzzi, sauna and Turkish bath are free to guests. There's a stylish bar and a modern Mediterranean restaurant.

Turim Suisso Atlântico Hotel

Rua da Glória 9, 1250-114 (21 340 0270, www.turim-hotels.com). Metro Restauradores. **Rooms** 92. **Map** p250 L8.

Located next door to the Elevador da Glória heading up to the Bairro Alto neighbourhood, this three-star hotel is a stone's throw from Praça dos Restauradores and its main tourist office. Long a scruffy Lisbon standard, albeit with friendly staff, the place has now had a complete overhaul but kept room rates reasonable. Note, though, that you have to pay to use the Wi-Fi. There's a small TV lounge off the main foyer but no restaurant (there are plenty of options nearby). The area can get pretty noisy and seedy at night-time, but the hotel itself is peaceful.

Budget

Hotel Alegria

Praça da Alegria 12, 1250-004 (21 322 0670, www.alegrianet.com). Metro Avenida or Restauradores. **Rooms** 35. **Map** p246 L8.

This good-value former *pensão* has upgraded to one-star hotel status but retains a warm and welcoming feel, despite its location in a rather seedy area. All rooms feature TV, air-conditioning and large en suite bathrooms. The best rooms are the spacious doubles at the back, overlooking a square lined with palm trees. There's no in-room Wi-Fi – just a shared internet terminal.

★ Pensão Portuense

Rua das Portas de Santo Antão 151-153, 1150-167 (21 346 4197, www.pensaoportuense.com) Metro Restauradores. **Rooms** 36. **Map** p250 L8.

A first-floor *pensão* run very efficiently by an upbeat, helpful family. The location is fine if you want to be on a street full of restaurants, but it can get noisy at night. Rooms – from single to quadruple – are well furnished and comfortable, and all have

clean, modern bathrooms with decent high-pressure showers. Wi-Fi is restricted to the reception, but the rooms do have TVs.

Residencial Dom Sancho I

Avenida da Liberdade 202, 1250-147 (21 351 3160, www.domsancho.com). Metro Avenida. **Rooms** 40. **Map** p246 L7.

Another well-priced, well-run central guesthouse that's now classed as a hotel (with two stars). The decor is nothing special, but the Dom Sancho offers a decent array of services – hairdryers in the rooms, round-the-clock laundry service, theatre and concert bookings, and excursions. All rooms are en suite and there's free Wi-Fi throughout.

Residencial Florescente

Rua Porta de Santo Antão 99, 1150-266 (21 342 6609, www.residencialflorescente.com). Metro Restauradores. **Rooms** 68. **Map** p250 L8.

Across from one of Lisbon's most important live music venues, the Coliseu (*see p152*), this friendly place has decent-sized rooms (including twins) that are chintzy but immaculate, with bright bathrooms. Rooms have free Wi-Fi; for guests without a laptop, there's an internet PC. They also have TVs but the lounge doesn't, making it a place to read or just relax. The walls of the lounge and breakfast room are hung with naïve-style paintings of Portuguese scenes. Parking costs €15.

MARQUÊS DE POMBAL & PARQUE EDUARDO VII

Deluxe

★ Four Seasons Hotel Ritz Lisbon

Rua Rodrigues da Fonseca 88, 1099-039 (21 381 1400, www.fourseasons.com/lisbon). Metro Marquês de Pombal. **Rooms** 282. **Map** p246 K6.

An art collection worthy of a museum adorns the lounge and lobby areas of this perennial favourite of visiting statesmen, nowadays run by an international chain. Guest rooms are understatedly luxurious: even the smallest have a dressing area with two walk-in closets and all have private terraces. Even though the less expensive rooms are on lower floors, all afford views of the greenery of Parque Eduardo VII thanks to the hotel's elevated position. Wi-Fi is now free, as is parking for guests. The Ritz also boasts the most impressive spa in central Lisbon, with an indoor lap pool, solarium, steam room and sauna. There are wonderful treatments on offer, and a snack and drinks menu to add relish to relaxation. Meanwhile, the penthouse fitness centre – complete with a 400-metre outdoor running track – has breathtaking views over the park and city. Downstairs, the contemporary cuisine turned out by Pascal Meynard and his team in the Varanda restaurant attracts lots of outside custom – as does the renowned breakfast buffet. There's also a sushi bar (Wed-Fri) and a bar with an extensive gin menu and signature cocktails.

Expensive

★ EPIC SANA Lisboa Hotel

Avenida Engenheiro Duarte Pacheco 15, 1070-100 (21 159 7300, www.lisboa.epic.sanahotels. com). Metro Marquês de Pombal. **Rooms** 311. **Map** p245 J6.

There's no doubt that the rooftop pool and sundeck, plus the huge spa with its view of a lovely botanical garden, are the big draws here. But this newish hotel's location – halfway between Praça Marquês de Pombal and the Amoreiras mall – also has its attractions, especially if you're planning to drive out to the beaches along the Estoril coast or magical Sintra (for both, *see pp166-181*). Inside, the understated modern decor and furnishings, all cream and brown, are offset by silvery hues in the common areas and turquoise in the 291 rooms and 20 suites.

Hotel Marquês de Pombal

Avenida da Liberdade 243, 1250-143 (21 319 7900, www.hotel-marquesdepombal.pt). Metro Marquês de Pombal. **Rooms** 123. **Map** p246 L7.

This four-star hotel a few steps from the metro station of the same name has soundproofed rooms that include three suites on the top floor. The understated contemporary decor provides a foil for reproductions of emblematic local architectural features. The hotel is aimed squarely at the business market: all rooms have a large desk, free broadband internet and direct-dial phone with voicemail, and there's PC and printer rental as well as ample meeting facilities.

Families aren't forgotten, though: cots are free on request and there are discounts on extra beds for kids. The health club, with sauna, steam bath and a personal trainer on hand, is free to all guests.

Moderate

Hotel Dom Carlos Park

Avenida Duque de Loulé 121, 1050-089 (21 351 2590, www.domcarloshoteis.com). Metro Marquês de Pombal. **Rooms** 76. **Map** p246 L7.

Despite the location, right by Praça Marquês de Pombal, this spacious and comfortable three-star hotel is surprisingly secluded, overlooking a leafy square. It offers good value, too. Bedrooms are comfortable and quiet with roomy en suite marble bathrooms and free Wi-Fi; in most doubles, an extra bed can be added for a small extra charge. The cosy lounge has TV and free internet, and an honesty bar with drinks and snacks. Round the corner, the slightly smaller Dom Carlos Liberty (Rua Alexandre Herculano 13, 21 317 3570) has a rooftop terrace and small gym; there are also rental flats available in the Chiado for long-stay visitors.

Hotel Jorge V

Rua Mouzinho da Silveira 3, 1250-165 (21 356 2525, www.hoteljorgev.com). Metro Marquês de Pombal. **Rooms** 49. **Map** p246 K7.

Run by friendly staff, the Jorge V offers simple, modern services and compact but well-organised en suite rooms, half of which feature private terraces offering great views. An extra bed can be added to rooms from as little as €20. There's a garish TV lounge with a nondescript adjoining bar serving light snacks. Wi-Fi is free for guests throughout the hotel.

ESSENTIAL INFORMATION

EPIC SANA Lisboa Hotel.

Hotel Miraparque
Avenida Sidónio Pais 12, 1050-214 (21 352 4286, www.miraparque.com). Metro Parque. **Rooms** 96. **Map** p246 L6.
The three-star 1950s 'Parkview' is set in a tranquil location overlooking Parque Eduardo VII, near the El Corte Inglés shopping complex. Rooms are on the cramped side and plainly furnished – the recent refurbishment only went as far as the reception and bar – but a friendly atmosphere and English-speaking staff go some way to making up for that. Internet access is free. Aside from breakfast there's no meal service. Local handicrafts are on sale at reception.

Budget

Residencial Horizonte Hotel
Avenida António Augusto Aguiar 42, 1050-017 (21 353 9526, www.hotelhorizonte.com). Metro Parque. **Rooms** 53. **Map** p246 L6.
This former *pensão* is now a hotel with concierge, laundry and newspaper services. Its location has long made it popular with young business types on a budget (though be warned that the Wi-Fi isn't free). Each room has a TV and a modern bathroom with powerful shower and hairdryer, and breakfast can be served in your room at no extra cost. There's no restaurant on site, but a bar serves drinks and snacks.

Residência Mar dos Açores
Rua Bernadim Ribeiro 14, 1150-071 (21 357 7085). Metro Marquês de Pombal or Picoas. **Rooms** 31. **Map** p246 M6.
Away from Lisbon's busiest avenues, but only five minutes from two metro stations, this *pensão*'s neat and clean rooms were all recently refurbished and now come with TV and free Wi-Fi. You can book a wheelchair-accessible en suite room for a few extra euros. Breakfast is no longer provided, but there are plenty of cafés in the area. The Azorean owners are friendly (and gay-friendly too) and transmit their can-do attitude to the staff. Pets are also allowed. There are also three nearby apartments available to rent from €60 for three beds – even better value.

EAST OF BAIXA
Deluxe

★ Palácio Belmonte
Pátio Dom Fradique 14, 1100-624 (21 881 6600, www.palaciobelmonte.com). Tram 12, 28 or bus 737. **Suites** 11. **Map** p251 M9.
Just a small plaque gives away the presence of this boutique hotel in a patio near the castle. The result of the drive and imagination of French ecological entrepreneur Frédéric Coustols, the Belmonte is a 15th-century palace (itself built into Roman and Moorish walls) that has been painstakingly renovated using modern methods and materials. Fifty-nine tile panels commissioned by the palace's owners

in the 18th century, comprising some 30,000 *azulejos* in total, were restored and remounted. The garden contains native plants and vegetables, as well as a stylish black granite pool, and the hotel's library has 4,000 books, publications and papers in a variety of languages. Service is discreet and efficient. The suites are individually designed and furnished with antiques and contemporary art. The smaller suites have the prices listed; of the larger ones, the Amadeo Souza Cardoso (named after the Portuguese modernist painter) has an *azulejo*-lined grand hall, a balcony and its own terrace, and costs €2,500 a night. There's no restaurant – just a café in the courtyard that's open to the public – but room service is competent and efficient; breakfast is served in your room.

Expensive

★ Memmo Alfama Hotel
Travessa das Merceeiras 27, 1100-348 (21 049 5660, www.memmohotels.com). Tram 12, 28 or bus 737. **Rooms** 42. **Map** p251 M10.
Housed in a 19th-century former bakery and its *vila operária* (workers' housing), this boutique hotel retains traces of its past, such as the original ovens. Outside is a mural by Portuguese artist Vhils in his unique chip-away style, commissioned for the hotel's opening in 2013. The guest rooms – all with free Wi-Fi – are white and minimalist; some have river views while others overlook an inner patio. The hotel has a delightful split-level terrace with a small pool and wine bar (open 6-11pm daily), and fabulous views over Alfama and the river. On warm days, you can take breakfast up here. There's also a tiny gym with three machines (although you're likely to get plenty of exercise negotiating the hills in this part of town). The young staff are friendly and helpful.

Solar do Castelo
Rua das Cozinhas 2, 1100-181 (21 887 0909, www.heritage.pt). Tram 12, 28 or bus 737. **Rooms** 20. **Map** p251 M9.
This bijou hotel is one of the finest properties in the family-run Heritage chain: an 18th-century Pombaline building within the castle walls that once housed the Alcáçova Palace kitchens. The designers preserved the feeling of living inside the castle walls, but not at the expense of a comfortable night's sleep (there's even a disabled-adapted room). A courtyard with a medieval fountain serves as a sunny patio for the honesty bar (there's no restaurant), and all is serenity as cars are kept out of the castle. (Alert staff to your arrival and they'll send a golf cart to pick you and your luggage up from the outer gate.)

Moderate

Albergaria Senhora do Monte
Calçada do Monte 39, 1170-250 (21 886 6002, www.senhoramonte.blogspot.com). Tram 28. **Rooms** 28. **Map** p251 N8.

Bairro Alto Hotel.

Set on one of Lisbon's seven hills, with the old town at its feet and the castle and the river beyond, this place is totally removed from the bustle of the city. It's great for romantic night-time views – so long as you don't mind skimping on modern facilities. The rooms are simple, decorated in pink and white, and have free Wi-Fi. The pricier air-conditioned ones have balconies with beautiful views, but breakfast for all guests is in the top-floor café-bar and terrace, which boasts a heart-stopping vista. The hotel lacks a restaurant, but there's a range of dining options close by, including Via Graça and Haweli Tandoori (for both, *see p69*), plus room service is available.

★ Olissippo Castelo
Rua Costa do Castelo 112-126, 1100-179 (21 882 0190, www.olissippohotels.com). Metro Martim Moniz or tram 12, 28. **Rooms** 24. **Map** p251 N9.
Tucked away on a cobbled street, this four-star hotel below the castle walls has won prizes from local conservationists and plaudits from foreign visitors. The rooms (and two suites) are plush and elegant, and some have balconies with fabulous views. Space elsewhere is at a premium – breakfast is included but there's no restaurant, just a lobby bar. The hotel is a steep walk up from the Baixa, but of the other Olissippo hotels in the city – at Saldanha, in Parque das Nações and in Lapa (*see p219*) – only the latter can beat it for sheer charm, and it looks more and more of a bargain as nearby rivals hike their rates.

Budget

The Keep
Costa do Castelo 74, 1100-179 (21 885 4070, www.thekeep-lisbon.com). Tram 12, 28.
Rooms 18. **No credit cards**. **Map** p251 M9.

Nestling below the castle, far from both nightlife and traffic, this turreted guesthouse offers simple lodgings with five-star panoramas. From a cobbled street high above the Baixa, you climb further up a spiral staircase to a precipitous patio dotted with sunshades. Inside, the rooms are clean but spartan; most share bathrooms. Wi-Fi is free but patchy. At the top of another spiral stairway is an octagonal tower with rickety seats where you can admire the view on three sides. Try to get Room 12 in the northern corner of the *pensão* if you want to feel really on top of the world. Cold soft drinks and crisps are on sale at reception, and there's a kitchen with fridge and microwave for guests' use.

WEST OF BAIXA
Deluxe

★ Bairro Alto Hotel
Praça Luís de Camões 2, 1200-243 (21 340 8288, www.bairroaltohotel.com). Metro Baixa-Chiado.
Rooms 55. **Map** p250 L9.
The decor of this boutique hotel, opened in 2005 in what was once the Grande Hotel Europa, recalls that establishment's 19th-century heyday – when opera divas and thespians such as Sarah Bernhardt stayed here between performances at the nearby Teatro de São Carlos – but with modern touches. The rooms (including four suites) are in tones of blue, red, yellow or ivory, with hand-painted designs of native birds; all have plasma TVs and free Wi-Fi. Bathrooms are done out in bourgeois style; those in the suites have freestanding tubs. There's a small gym on site. The rooftop bar and terrace have fine river views and are popular with locals, while the ground-floor Igloo lounge is a cosy refuge and the Flores do Bairro restaurant serves authentic Portuguese snacks and light meals in a sophisticated but informal atmosphere. A member of the Leading Hotels of the World, this prize-winning place dances to an international beat – sometimes literally, thanks to the house DJ.

Expensive

Hotel do Chiado
Rua Nova do Almada 114, 1200-290 (21 325 6100, www.hoteldochiado.com). Metro Baixa-Chiado. **Rooms** 39. **Map** p250 L9.
One of Lisbon's best-located hotels, right in the middle of the elegant shopping district of the same name and with postcard views. Designed, like much of the area, by Álvaro Siza Vieira, its success is most apparent in the morning, when a tall window frames the best breakfast backdrop in the city. The interior is on clean lines, with hip furniture. Rooms have Oriental and Western furnishings; they're spacious and light, with touches of luxury such as fresh flowers, and some have private terraces that look across to the castle. All have free Wi-Fi. The restaurant

ESSENTIAL INFORMATION

serves dishes created by talented young chef Igor Martinho, loosely based on traditional Portuguese cuisine. The seventh-floor Bar Panorâmico (open 11am-midnight daily) has a view to match its name – taking in the Baixa, castle and river – making it perfect for a romantic aperitif.

Moderate

Hotel Borges
Rua Garret 108, 1200-205 (21 045 6400, www. hotelborges.com). Metro Baixa-Chiado or tram 28. **Rooms** 92. **Map** p250 L9.
One of Lisbon's oldest hotels, the Borges was recently given the latest in a series of renovations. Service has never been the Borges's strong point, but the sheer history of the location makes a stay worthwhile. The best rooms look out on to Rua Garrett, so you can window-shop from bed. Room service is available, including a decent breakfast in your room if you want it, but you do have to pay for Wi-Fi.

Hotel Casa de São Mamede
Rua da Escola Politécnica 159, 1250-100 (21 396 3166, www.casadesaomamede.pt). Metro Rato. **Rooms** 28. **Map** p246 K8.
Convenience is the main selling point here, midway between Príncipe Real and Rato, but this religiously austere 18th-century *pensão* – now officially a three-star hotel – is also as good as it gets for the price. Rooms are large – some even larger after a recent renovation – and reasonably comfortable, with decent bathrooms. The place is ideal if you want somewhere calm and family-oriented: in a superior double (from €20 more than a standard double) up to two under-13s can share for free, and two of the rooms have connecting doors. There's even a special room rate for accompanying grandparents. By contrast, if you plan to stagger in at 4am after a bar crawl, then you should head elsewhere. (The friendly but no-nonsense receptionists are there to make sure guests behave.) A basic breakfast is served and there's free Wi-Fi in the rooms.

Lisboa Carmo Hotel
Rua da Oliveira ao Carmo 1-3, 1200-307 (21 326 4710, www.lisboacarmohotel.com). Metro Baixa-Chiado or Rossio. **Rooms** 45. **Map** p250 L9.
On the corner of a lovely leafy square just up from the main drag of Chiado, this elegant little hotel is staffed by a friendly, helpful team. Some of the rooms are rather small, but all are prettily decorated in pastel colours and floral motifs, with wood floors and classic or contemporary furniture, and have air-conditioning. Those on the top floors have stunning panoramic views; lower ones overlook the square. There is a stylish hotel restaurant, though you won't want for dining options in this part of town. The Carmo is part of the LuxHotels group, which also has several hotels in Fátima: they can advise on packages for pilgrims.

Hotel do Chiado. See p217.

Budget

★ Evidência Light Santa Catarina Hotel
Rua Dr Luís de Almeida 6, 1200-059 (21 346 1009, www.evidenciahoteis.com). Metro Baixa-Chiado or tram 28. **Rooms** 16. **Map** p250 K9.
This no-frills place a short walk from the nightlife of the Bairro Alto features modern design throughout, and offers basic lodgings (no wardrobe, just a rack, and you make your own bed) in doubles and triples. No discount is given for single use, but there's an attic dorm: a little cramped, but the only part of the hotel with air conditioning. Here each curtained-off bed (rates from €15) has its own light, plug and locker, women have their own bathroom, and there is even a small roof terrace for smokers. Downstairs, you'll find a comfy bar (open Wed-Sun) and lounge area, as well as two esplanades out the back. In theory, free Wi-Fi is available throughout, but it's patchy; there are also two internet PCs for guest use. No breakfast is served, but there are plenty of neighbourhood cafés.

★ Pensão Globo
Rua do Teixeira 37, 1200-459 (21 346 2279, www.pensaoglobo.com.pt). Metro Baixa-Chiado or Restauradores then Elevador da Glória. **Rooms** 15. **No credit cards**. **Map** p250 L9.
One of the best choices for value and proximity to trendy restaurants and clubs, this well-run, friendly guesthouse is tucked away on a quiet street, thus avoiding night-time noise. More expensive rooms have en suites with showers; cheaper interior rooms are windowless and share facilities. Rooms are clean and offer free Wi-Fi. There's no breakfast, but cafés abound in the area. The Globo is gay-friendly; sister establishment Hotel Anjo Azul (*see p139*) is squarely aimed at a gay clientele.

Pensão Londres

Rua Dom Pedro V 53, 1250-092 (21 346 2203, www.pensaolondres.com.pt). Metro Baixa-Chiado or Rato. **Rooms** 36. **Map** p250 L8.

A decent option, given that prices haven't kept up with those of local rivals (though neither have the facilities). Londres' location at the Príncipe Real end of Bairro Alto is its trump card: not too noisy, but still close to the city's nightlife. Get a room with a view across Lisbon; the alternative is a distant view of the river or – for those on the lower floor – a busy street. Some of the more expensive rooms have en suites and satellite TV; Wi-Fi is only free in common areas. Staff are friendly, though not all of them speak fluent English.

Pensão Residencial Camões

Travessa do Poço da Cidade 38, 1E, 1200-334 (21 346 7510, www.pensaoresidencialcamoes. com). Metro Baixa-Chiado. **Rooms** 16. **No credit cards.** Map p250 L9.

Popular with backpackers, the Residencial Camões is well located and offers large, comfortable, clean rooms – some en suite, others sharing. Breakfast is included in the price. The chirpy family that run the place speak good English. The main drawbacks are noise from the streets below on weekend nights (although double-glazing helps) and the somewhat unreliable Wi-Fi.

WESTERN WATERFRONT & AJUDA

Deluxe

Altis Belém Hotel & Spa

Doca de Bom Sucesso, 1400-038 (21 040 0200, www.altishotels.com). Train to Belém or tram 15. **Rooms** 50. **Map** p244 B10.

The Altis Belém's prime riverside location guarantees lovely views from all the guest rooms; the more expensive ones even have a jacuzzi on the balcony. There's also a sundeck with pool and a luxurious spa. The hotel's decoration recalls the age of maritime Discoveries, with each wing representing a different continent, and the Michelin-starred Feitoria restaurant picks up on the same theme: ingredients and dishes from Asia, Africa and the Americas complement more traditional Portuguese flavours.

★ Pestana Palace

Rua Jau 54, 1300-314 (21 361 5600, www.pestana. com). Tram 18. **Rooms** 194. **Map** p244 E9.

You'd never guess that this early 19th-century palace had been abandoned for more than 50 years before it was lovingly restored by Portugal's Pestana Group at the beginning of this century. Once home to the Marquês Valle Flor, this national monument now houses a vast collection of rare Portuguese 19th-century paintings, sculpture, frescoes, tapestries and furniture – although most guests stay in

the large modern wings. From its hilltop in Alto de Ajuda, the hotel commands fine views of the Tagus. There are sumptuous gardens (also a listed monument), a health spa that does amazing things with hot stones, and an exquisite chapel. The restaurant is also housed in the splendour of the palace. All in all, a good place to spot visiting celebs.

Moderate

Vila Galé Ópera

Travessa do Conde da Ponte, 1300-141 (21 360 5400, www.vilagale.com). Train to Alcântara Mar or tram 15. **Rooms** 259.

This opera-themed hotel (each room is named after a singer) is a good option in terms of location, price and facilities. Right under the Ponte 25 Abril, it's between the sights of Belém and the bars of Docas, and has easy access to the riverfront via a nearby footbridge. There's live jazz on Tuesday and Thursday evenings in the river-facing Falstaff restaurant, which has an excellent à la carte menu. A well-equipped gym, indoor pool, jacuzzi and sauna are further attractions. Wi-Fi is free in common areas and the more expensive guest rooms.

SÃO BENTO & BEYOND

Deluxe

★ Olissippo Lapa Palace

Rua Pau da Bandeira 4, 1249-021 (21 394 9494, www.olissippohotels.com). Tram 25 or 28. **Rooms** 109. **Map** p245 H9.

Set in tranquil gardens with wonderful views, this former aristocratic residence is one of Lisbon's classiest hotels and is frequented by the likes of Robbie Williams, Sting and Heidi Klum. The interior is positively opulent and there are excellent health and beauty facilities, including a sizzling hot stone therapy and sizeable indoor pool. Each room has a terrace or balcony overlooking the lush garden and outdoor pool or the dome of the nearby Basílica de Estrela (*see p110*). There's an amazing breakfast buffet, including champagne. The hotel has two bars, and one of the two restaurants, the Cipriani, offers outstanding food and views.

Expensive

★ As Janelas Verdes

Rua das Janelas Verdes 47, 1200-690 (21 396 8143, www.heritage.pt). Tram 25. **Rooms** 29. **Map** p245 J10.

It's said that this charming late 18th-century mansion was once the home of Portuguese novelist Eça de Queiroz, inspiring his magical novels *O Ramalhete* and *Os Maias* (recently made into a popular film). As well as examples of his books and paintings, the place is cluttered with antiques. But there's nothing fusty about it: as well as flatscreen

ESSENTIAL INFORMATION

TVs, guest rooms all have CD/DVD players and free Wi-Fi. There's a lovely leafy back yard with an ivy-clad patio, and a reading room with river views. There's no restaurant but the hotel does offer room service and an honesty bar. The Museu Nacional de Arte Antiga is right next door.

Moderate

York House
Rua das Janelas Verdes 32, 1200-691 (21 396 2435, www.yorkhouselisboa.com). Tram 25.
Rooms 32. **Map** p245 J10.
With Graham Greene and John le Carré among past guests, there can't be many better places to find literary inspiration. Behind a wall at the top of a flight of stairs is a courtyard full of flowers, trees and plants. Arranged around it are the guest rooms, a dining room, café and bar. Solid furnishings give it the air of a country retreat, but the cool corridors and ecclesiastical artefacts betray a pious past – this was a Carmelite convent until 1834. The name came in 1880, when a pair of Yorkshirewomen turned it into a guesthouse. Rooms vary from deluxe modern boutique style, refurbished by celebrated interior designer Filipa Lacerda, to the original opulence of gilt mirrors and 19th-century artworks. All have free Wi-Fi. The gourmet restaurant serves Mediterranean fusion dishes based on traditional Portuguese cuisine. During the summer, you can dine in the courtyard. Excellent value all round.

NORTHERN LISBON
Expensive

★ Real Palácio Hotel
Rua Tomás Ribeiro 115, 1050-228 (21 319 9500, www.hoteisreal.com). Metro Picoas. **Rooms** 147.
Map p248 L5.
This charming five-star hotel is built into a 17th-century palace and the neighbouring building. The palace's features are still clearly visible and this part of the hotel is decorated in period style, while the transition between here and the other spaces is sensitively managed. Despite the large number of guest rooms (including four suites), the place still feels cosy, and small artworks dotted about add an air of sophistication. The main restaurant opens on to an inner courtyard, and the health club – to which guests have access – has a lovely jacuzzi, sauna and Turkish bath. Children are well provided for with special furniture, toys and menus. Wi-Fi is free in all rooms and parking is reasonable. Reservations also handle bookings for the four-star Real Parque Hotel round the corner and a nearby aparthotel, the Real Residência.

Sheraton Lisboa Hotel & Spa
Rua Latino Coelho 1, 1069-025 (21 312 0000, www.sheraton.com/lisboa). Metro Picoas.
Rooms 369. **Map** p246 L6.

The Sheraton is a popular choice with foreign business travellers, with all the essentials for mobile office work (even if Wi-Fi is only free in the lobby), which means it can be a good deal for families at the weekends. The outside is rather ugly, but inside is luxury itself: spacious bedrooms with super-snug beds and gleaming marble bathrooms. The 26th floor Panorama Restaurant (dinner only) and Panorama Bar (open 3pm-2am daily) command fine views of the city and river. On the upscale Towers floor, rooms and suites come with their own butler, but service is excellent throughout. The new Spirito spa (€12.50 for guests, though in practice many room rates include free access) encompasses both an outdoor pool and an indoor Vitality pool, sauna and Turkish bath, plus a wide range of massages and therapies including Vichy showers, dished out in spacious treatment rooms.

Budget

Lisbon's downtown *pousada de juventude* (youth hostel) is in this area; *see p210* **Budget Beds**.

★ Pensão Residencial Estrela dos Santos
Avenida Almirante Reis 53, 1150-011 (21 317 1030, www.estreladossantos.residencial. com.pt) Metro Anjos or tram 28. **Rooms** 20.
Map p246 M7.
This homely, family-run guesthouse with spacious rooms, all with private bathrooms and free Wi-Fi, was given an overhaul in 2013. The location is good (it's next to Anjos Metro station and you can be in central Lisbon in ten minutes), but traffic can be noisy. Reception functions 24 hours a day and staff can provide hairdryers, robes, ironing kits and more on request, as well as arranging car hire. There's no bar – just a soft-drinks machine in the lobby; nearby is a gym with a health club and sauna. The *pensão* now shares its entrance with a new (and slightly pricier) stablemate, Lisbon Style Guesthouse (21 317 1035, www.lisbonstyle.pt), which has a funkier vibe and a pleasant patio.

Pensão Residencial do Sul
Avenida Almirante Reis 34, 1150-018 (21 814 7253, www.lisbonsulhostels.com). Metro Anjos or tram 28. **Rooms** 43. **Map** p246 M8.
This first-floor *pensão* compares favourably with the area's other budget options. The decor is fairly austere and Wi-Fi is restricted to the lounge area, but the rooms are large, comfortable and mostly en suite, and the welcome is friendly. Breakfast isn't included but there are plenty of good cafés nearby (there's also a machine selling soft drinks and crisps in the lobby). Nearby sister *pensões* Castro Mira I and Castro Mira II (same phone number) have 15 rooms each, some of which can accommodate up to five people.

Hotel Palácio Estoril.

★ **Residencial Saldanha**
*Avenida da República 17, 1050-185 (21 354
6429, www.residencialsaldanha.pt). Metro
Saldanha.* **Rooms** 12. **Map** p249 M5.
Residencial Saldanha, a plush guesthouse with reasonable rates, is handily located for the cinemas and shops dotted around Praça Duque de Saldanha. All the bedrooms are simply but attractively decorated, with spacious bathrooms, heating, fans and free Wi-Fi. They run the gamut from singles to quintuples; the latter offer unbeatable value.

PARQUE DAS NAÇÕES

This area has a plethora of hotels targeted mainly at business travellers; for a full list, see www.visitlisbon.com. The only budget option is the state-run youth hostel (*see p210* **Budget Beds**).

Deluxe

★ **Myriad by SANA Hotels**
*Cais das Naus Lote 2.21.01, 1990-173 (21 110
7600, www.myriad.pt). Metro Oriente.* **Rooms** 186.
Built right up against the Torre Vasco da Gama – a towering legacy of Expo 98 – the Myriad has incomparable views of the River Tagus at its widest point and the Parque das Nações, as the area is now known. The decor is minimalist white, with splashes of red; furnishings are ultra-modern. The cheaper rooms could do with a bit more space (no more than a child's cot can be added), but they all have espresso machines and free Wi-Fi, plus a whirlpool bath or hydromassage shower, not to mention those

fabulous views. The 23rd-floor spa is a wonderful place to relax still further, with a pool, sauna and treatment rooms.

CASCAIS & ESTORIL COAST

Deluxe

★ **Grande Real Villa Itália Hotel & Spa**
*Rua Frei Nicolau de Oliveira 100, 2750-319
Cascais (21 096 6000, www.hoteisreal.com).
Train to Cascais from Cais do Sodré then bus 405,
415.* **Rooms** 124.
The Grande Real Villa is housed in the former residence of exiled King Umberto II of Italy and a neighbouring mansion, near the Boca do Inferno. It's the most upmarket link in the chain that runs Lisbon's Real Palácio (*see p220*), with a name that signals what much of the €25 million budget was spent on: a spa that claims to be the only one of its kind in Cascais, with a thalassotherapy treatment pool, Turkish bath, sauna, massage, hydromassage, ice fountain and jet, and Vichy showers. Interior decoration is by Graça Viterbo in a 'classical revisited' style with lots of marble and Venetian mosaics, and traditional and modern Portuguese tiling. Most rooms are in blue and grey, giving a nautical feel, but suites and penthouses are in warmer colours. All have views of the sea or garden and free Wi-Fi. Two of the penthouses have a jacuzzi, the third an outdoor pool.

Hotel Palácio Estoril
*Avenida Clotilde, 2769-504 Estoril (21 464 8000,
www.palacioestorilhotel.com). Train to Estoril
from Cais do Sodré.* **Rooms** 160.
This grand pile facing the Casino Estoril has a cream-painted 1930s exterior and lavish interior – marble halls, high stucco ceilings decorated with crystal chandeliers – that has been tastefully restored and filled with classic 19th-century French and English furniture. It's pure luxury with none of the stuffiness that's often found in establishments of

---

IN THE KNOW TEEING OFF

There are two dozen decent golf courses within an hour of the capital, most of them reasonably priced (www.visitlisbon.com lists almost all of them, but the anaylsis on www.golf-portugal.net is more informative). Major Lisbon hotels will make bookings for guests, and some such as the **Tivoli** (see p212) arrange special deals on green fees and bespoke packages. Out of town, the **Cascais Miragem** (see p222) and **Albatroz** (see p222) also offer special rates, while the **Palácio Estoril** (see above) owns one of Portugal's most famous courses, Golf do Estoril, designed by Philip Mackenzie Ross.

ESSENTIAL INFORMATION

Farol Design Hotel.

this kind, and its 'grand and cosy' slogan suits it well. Wi-Fi is free throughout, as is the parking. There are two in-house restaurants. If you don't fancy the beach or the casino, note that the hotel owns the Golfe do Estoril course and guests can play a round at special rates (from €28). In addition to the hotel's own pool, guests have free access to two indoor pools at the luxury spa next door.

Expensive

Albatroz Seafront Hotel

Rua Frederico Arouca 100, 2750-353 Cascais (21 484 7380, www.albatrozhotels.com). Train to Cascais from Cais do Sodré. **Rooms** 52.

Overlooking the Conceição beach, this luxurious gem is small enough to offer truly personalised service. The interior has a relaxed, oriental flavour that makes you just want to sit on the floor and meditate. A stylish mosaic oval pool looks on to the harbour. Room rates vary according to view, but all have lots of amenities and free Wi-Fi. The beachside restaurant specialises in sophisticated seafood dishes; you can also book cooking classes with the chef, preceded by a visit to the local market. The Albatroz Bayside Villa Guesthouse overlooking the nearby fishermen's beach is smaller, with fewer facilities and cheaper rates, but an equally stunning location; its penthouse has terraces on three sides.

Farol Design Hotel

Avenida Rei Humberto II de Itália 7, 2750-800 Cascais (21 482 3490, www.farol.com.pt). Train to Cascais from Cais do Sodré then bus 405, 415. **Rooms** 33.

Architect Carlos Miguel Dias and celebrity room designers – among them fashionistas Ana Salazar, Augustus, Fátima Lopes and João Rôlo – have made this a unique, stylish place to stay. Rates remain fair (varying according to room and view) and everyone gets a jacuzzi and free Wi-Fi. The Farol is well placed

if you want to explore Cascais (it's next to the marina, walking distance from the town centre) and the coast to the north. Kitsch decoration means the common areas look a little like a sci-fi movie set, but you won't find a robot chef in The Mix restaurant, just smooth service and modern Portuguese/Mediterranean cuisine. A deck terrace overlooks the pool, and prompt waiter service makes it ideal for lounging.

★ Fortaleza do Guincho

Estrada do Guincho, 2750-642 Cascais (21 487 0491, www.guinchotel.pt). Train to Cascais from Cais do Sodré then bus 405, 415. **Rooms** 27.

A sprawling coastal fort dating back to the 17th century has been transformed into this characterful yet comfortable hotel, part of the Relais & Châteaux chain. Some rooms have a balcony and all have a jacuzzi; complimentary foreign newspapers and bikes for guests' use are among the many services on offer. The only drawback is that the fort's thick walls mean Wi-Fi is only accessible in the common areas. These include a cosy reading room and a large inner patio that's covered in winter and open in summer. The Michelin-starred restaurant (*see p176*), serving French-influenced food, is now overseen by chef Vincent Farges; its wine cellar is arguably the best of any restaurant in the country. The dining room has views of the Atlantic and the beaches on either side; breakfast is taken in this same gorgeous setting.

Hotel Cascais Miragem Health & Spa

Avenida Marginal 8554, 2754-536 Cascais (21 006 0600, www.cascaismirage.com). Train to Monte Estoril from Cais do Sodré. **Rooms** 192.

The gleaming Miragem is a favourite with visiting showbiz stars, who can choose from 15 suites, each decorated in a different style, and all with 'oversize' marble bathrooms and a balcony. The hotel's outstanding feature is a giant raised terrace with pool framed by cafés and restaurants (three in all), from which you can see the Atlantic but not the busy coast road below. Inside, rooms are large and plush; most have balconies with an ocean view and all have free Wi-Fi. Children are properly spoiled: as well as a play area, there's PlayStation, cartoon DVDs, toys available on request and a free extra bed for under-nines.

Moderate

Hotel Baía
Avenida Marginal, 2754-509 Cascais (21 483 1033, www.hotelbaia.com). Train to Cascais from Cais do Sodré. **Rooms** 113.

Popular with Brits due to its location near a string of pubs, the 'Bay Hotel' is just a stone's throw from the beach (although swimming here isn't recommended) and also has an indoor rooftop pool for cooling down in summer. Modestly priced for what it offers, the hotel has spacious, double-glazed rooms and suites, some with a balcony overlooking the sea. Wi-Fi is only available in the public spaces, including the spacious ground-floor lounge area. The Baía Grill restaurant is worth a visit and the rooftop Blue Bar (open in summer only) is a great place for a sundowner.

PERFECT PITCH

Our pick of the best places to stay in the great outdoors.

There are a number of campsites in the region – including half a dozen on the Caparica coast – but facilities can leave much to be desired. There are, however, a couple of outstanding ones north of the Tagus, in lovely settings.

Just west of Lisbon, **Lisboa Camping** (www.lisboacamping.com) nestles amid the pines of Monsanto forest park and has seen a lot of investment in recent years. It now boasts a hard-surface football pitch, mini-golf, two tennis courts, a pool with diving area, solarium and terrace, two baby pools and children's playgrounds. The campsite can accommodate up to 1,800 guests in all, with tent and caravan pitches, plus 70 furnished bungalows sleeping up to six. There are buses into town and Belém, and if you're here to attend one of the big rock festivals there are usually direct shuttles.

Further west is the **Orbitur-Guincho** campsite (www.orbitur.com), also surrounded by low pine trees but just ten minutes from Guincho, one of Europe's best windsurfing beaches, and five kilometres outside

Cascais. Facilities range from a tennis court and games room to a mini-market. There's a multi-sports court, too, and the swimming pool has fun slides. It can get busy in high season, but the crowd usually creates a good party atmosphere. An open area is available for motorhomes and there are different-sized bungalows – some with kitchen and bathroom, some without – with prices varying according to the number of guests (two to seven). Bed linen and towels can be supplied if you book ahead online.

For more information on sites around Lisbon, as well as further afield, check out www.campingportugal.org and www.roteiro-campista.pt, or visit the Orbitur website (www.orbitur.com); they also run one of the Caparica sites. Also in Caparica – and right next to the beach – you'll find one of the unglamorous but well-located campsites run by workers' leisure foundation **Inatel** (www.inatel.pt; on the English version of the website, click 'Tourism' then 'Hotel Units' and finally, at the bottom of the page, 'Camping').

ESSENTIAL INFORMATION

Lisboa Camping.

Getting Around

ESSENTIAL INFORMATION

ARRIVING & LEAVING

By air

Lisbon's main international airport, **Portela**, is in the north-east of the city. There are two **Aerobus** shuttles run by Carris (*see right*), costing €3.50 (€2 4-10s) or €5.50 for two (€3 4-10s). Tickets give you 24hrs of travel on both Aerobus routes and there are discounts if you buy online. Line 1, running via the city centre (Entre Campos, Saldanha, Marquês de Pombal, Restauradores and Praça do Comércio) to Cais do Sodré, departs every 20mins 7am-11.20pm on weekdays and every 25 mins 7am-10.50pm on weekends. Line 2, running via Entre Campos, Sete Rios and Praça de Espanha to the financial institutions of Avenida José Malhoa, departs every 40mins 7.30am-8pm, then hourly to 11pm, daily.

A cheaper option is to take the new extension of the **Metro** (*see right*), which loops out east to Parque das Nações before heading downtown; for most city-centre hotels, you must then change. Alternatively, catch a regular Carris bus (705 or 722) to Areeiro, then pick up the Metro, or take bus 783 all the way to Marquês de Pombal/Amoreiras.

A **taxi** into the centre should be about €10 (plus €1.60 for luggage). There are some dodgy operators, so check the meter is on. You can pay in advance at the Turismo de Lisboa booth in the arrivals hall: they give you a voucher that you can use in taxis with the relevant sticker. For central Lisbon, this costs €16 during the day (€19.20 9pm-6am). It might work out slightly more expensive (though the voucher cost includes tip and baggage fee) but you'll know you're not getting ripped off. The airport has a 24hr information line (800 201 201), and both staffed and automated bureaux de change.

By rail

Trains from Spain, France or north Portugal end at **Santa Apolónia** station; it has a tourist information booth, bureau de change, taxi rank and a range of bus services, and is on the Metro. Most trains also call at Gare do Oriente station at Parque das Nações, which is about a 20min Metro ride into town. Trains from the Algarve use the rail link under the Ponte 25 de Abril, stop at Entre Campos (another Metro station) and terminate at Gare do Oriente.

PUBLIC TRANSPORT

Information

Maps of the bus and tram system are available at Carris booths and maps of the Metro at major Metro stations. For **Carris** information, call 21 361 3000 (9.30am-12.30pm, 2.30-5.30pm Mon-Fri) or visit www.carris.pt; there's also a customer service office at Avenida Duque d'Ávila 12 (9am-5pm Mon-Fri). For information on the **Metro**, call 21 350 0115 (8.30am-7pm Mon-Fri) or visit www.metrolisboa.pt.

Fares & tickets

You can buy tickets when boarding a bus (€1.80) or tram (€2.85), but for the Metro you must first get a 7 Colinas or Viva Viagem electronic card, chargeable at Metro vending machines or Carris booths, or in post offices or PayShop agents. The card costs €0.50 and is valid for a year; you can either load a €1.40 ticket (for 1hr unlimited Metro and Carris travel) or a 24hr pass (€6) on to it, or instead use 'Zapping'. This means charging it up with €2-€15, after which a single Metro or Carris trip costs €1.25. (Note that if you want to recharge it with a different kind of ticket, you must first use up the original kind.) At Metro gates and on entering buses, hold your card against the electronic pad to validate it.

Lisbon's tourist pass, the **Lisboa Card** (*see p232*), allows the bearer unlimited travel on Metro, buses, trams and trains to Cascais and Sintra, as well as free entry to or reductions at sights and museums.

Metro

This is the speediest way around Lisbon, though many sights aren't covered by the network. Trains run about every 5mins 6.30am-1am daily, or more frequently during rush hour. If you don't have a valid ticket the fine is €125-€187.50 (plus fare). The lost property office for the network is at Marquês de Pombal.

Buses

Carris buses provide good services way out into the suburbs. Stops are indicated by a yellow sign.

Tickets can be bought from the driver, but a smart card is better value (*see left*). The fine for not having a ticket is €210.

Trams

The more traditional *elétricos*, or trams, on the 12, 15, 18, 25 and 28 routes have been joined on the 15 route by modern rapid transport models. All are run by Carris, fares are integrated with the bus system and stops are marked by a yellow sign – often hanging from overhead wires. Don't leave Lisbon without riding the no.28, which passes through historic neighbourhoods, from Graça and Alfama through the Baixa, Chiado and Estrela. Beware of pickpockets on this route.

A pricier tourist tram plies much the same route. The circular no.12, starting in Praça da Figueira, coincides with the no.28 on part of the Alfama stretch; again, a pricier tourist tram covers the same ground. The no.25, meanwhile, runs from the bottom of Alfama to Cais do Sodré and then through Lapa and Estrela to Campo de Ourique. The no.15, starting downtown at Praça da Figueira, is handy for the sights of Belém, while the no.18 coincides with its route for much of the way but starts only at Cais do Sodré and after Alcântara turns uphill to Ajuda.

Funiculars

The city's three funicular trams – officially called *ascensores* but more often known locally as *elevadores* – and the Elevador de Santa Justa, which really is a lift, are run by Carris and integrated with its fare system. Note that tickets bought on board these services are much more expensive than those on buses, so you save a lot if you buy a charge card in advance (*see left*). They all run from 7am, or an hour or two later on weekends. For the closing hours of the Elevador de Santa Justa, *see p43*; the Ascensor da Glória, which runs from Praça dos Restauradores up to the Bairro Alto, keeps going until midnight, while the Ascensor da Bica stops at 9pm and the Ascensor do Lavra at 7.55pm.

Local trains

Local train services are mostly run by branches of national rail operator

CP-Caminhos de Ferro Portugueses (80 820 8208, www.cp.pt). Trains run along the Estoril coast from Cais do Sodré station (which is on the Metro) as far as Cascais every 20-30mins (€1.25-€3.40). Here, too, smart cards (*see p224*) are the norm; you can use your Zapping credit on this route.

Rail services to Queluz and Sintra leave from Rossio, Sete Rios, Entre Campos and Roma-Areeiro – all on the Metro. There are periodic scares about muggings on this line, but it's used by thousands of locals and tourists every day and transport police patrol most trains. A combined train and Scotturb bus pass for the Sintra-Cascais region could be a good option if you're planning several trips out.

Fertagus trains serving Almada and Setúbal cross the Tagus using the line beneath the Ponte 25 de Abril.

Ferries

Transtejo ferries (808 203 050, www.transtejo.pt) link the city with the south bank of the Tagus. They are packed with commuters in rush hour, but offer unrivalled views. Boats to Barreiro leave from shabby Terreiro do Paço boat station, near Praça do Comércio; those to Cacilhas, Montijo and Seixal from the ugly new Cais do Sodré boat station, where car ferries also ply the Cacilhas route; and passenger services to Trafaria depart from Belém. Each station has an information office. Fares cost €1.20 to €2.75 – again, loaded on to a Viva Viagem electronic card (€0.50).

TAXIS

Taxis in Lisbon are common and inexpensive. There's a minimum charge of €3.25 (€3.90 9pm-6am Mon-Fri, all day Sat & Sun). Tipping is optional and even a small amount is appreciated. You are rarely far from a taxi stand: Rossio, Largo do Chiado and Largo de Trindade Coelho/Largo da Misericórdia in the Bairro Alto are reliable. There are several 24hr dial-a-cab services, such as on 21 811 9000 (Retális) and 21 811 1100 (Teletáxis); the booking charge is €0.80.

DRIVING

The Portuguese leave their fabled manners behind when they get behind the wheel. Traffic is chaotic and many streets are narrow, winding and one-way. Police can issue on-the-spot fines for minor driving offences – don't argue. Speed limits are 90km/hr (60km/hr

in built-up areas; 120km/hr on *auto-estradas* – motorways), not that many people take notice. Seat belts are obligatory in front and back, and the limit for alcohol is 0.5g/ml (0.2 if you've had your licence for less than three years) – don't drink and drive. You must be 17 to drive a vehicle in Portugal but may encounter problems if you're under 18.

Parking

Cars are often crammed nose to bumper, half on pavements, reflecting a lack of garages. Be sure to tuck the mirror in on your hire car. Underground car parks (signposted with a white P on blue background) have multiplied of late but are not cheap. On-street parking downtown is on a meter system, for which you need coins. Parking illegally may result in a heavy fine or the vehicle being towed. Even in metered areas, drivers may be met by *arrumadores* – 'fixers' – who will guide you to a place and then, in theory, watch your car. They'll expect an advance tip of about €0.50 for this unsolicited service; refusing to pay will almost certainly trigger no more than unfriendly muttering but you may not want to take the risk.

Car hire

To rent a car in Portugal you must be over 18 (or older for some vehicles) and have had a driving licence for more than one year. All companies listed have a desk at the airport and a free booking number; this is given first, then details of the main downtown office.

Avis
800 201 002 (7am-8pm), www.avis.com; Avenida Praia da Vitória 12C (21 351 4560). Map p249 M5.
Budget
808 25 26 27 (8am-8pm), www.budget.com.pt; Avenida Praia da Vitória 12C (21 351 4560). Map p249 M5.
Europcar
808 204 050 (8.30am-7.30pm Mon-Fri, 9am-6pm Sat), www.europcar.com; Avenida António Augusto Aguiar 24 C/D (21 353 5115). Map p246 L6.
Hertz
808 202 038 (24hr), www.hertz.com; Rua Castilho 72 (21 942 6300). Map p246 K7.

CYCLING

Lisbon's streets are unfriendly to cyclists, with cobbles, tyre-trapping tram lines and bad driving, but there

are now several dedicated cycle routes, including along the river from downtown to Belém. The Estoril and Sintra areas offer the most scenic cycling. You can hire bikes in Lisbon and Sintra; in Cascais they're free under the council-sponsored BiCas scheme. For BiCas and the rental firms, you'll need photo ID.

Belém Bike
Next to Museu de Electricidade, Avenida de Brasília, Belém (96 378 0233, www.belembike.com). Train to Belém from Cais do Sodré or bus 728. **Open** 10.30am-7pm Mon-Fri; 9.30am-7pm Sat, Sun. **Hire** from €2.50/30mins. **No credit cards.**
This riverside shack is the cheapest place in town to hire a bicycle for short periods. Does repairs too.
BiCas
21 460 6250. Train to Cascais from Cais do Sodré. **Open** *Apr-Sept* 8am-7pm daily. *Oct-Mar* 9am-5pm daily. **Hire** free.
This council-funded outfit has three booths in Cascais: one right by the station, one by the nature tourism booth on Avenida da República, and one on the coast road at Guia. The bikes are free; just hand over credible photo ID. Make use of 16km of cycle tracks, including a route along the coast to Guincho beach (20-30mins).
Lisbon Hub
Largo Corpo Santo 5, Baixa (21 347 0347, www.bikeiberia.com). Metro Cais do Sodré or tram 15, 18, 25. **Open** 9.30am-6.30pm daily. **Hire** €4/1hr; €14/day; €45/3 days. **No credit cards.** Map p250 L10.
At this well-stocked outlet for tour company Bike Iberia, rental of a sturdy bicycle includes a lock and key, optional helmet and front basket; also available are child seats, trailers, panniers, tool kits and map cases.
Tejo Bike
Passeio dos Heróis do Mar, Praça do Tejo (91 612 9867). **Open** *Summer* 10am-8pm daily. *Winter* noon-6pm daily. **Hire** from €2/30mins. **No credit cards.**
The Parque das Nações is large enough that hiring a bicycle at the Esplanando café (near the Torre Vasco da Gama/Myriad hotel) could be worth the trouble. There's also the green Parque do Tejo to explore to the north.

WALKING

Our favourite tours are **Inside Tours** (96 841 2612, www.insidelisbon.com), **Lisbon Walker** (96 357 5635, www.lisbonwalker.com) and **Portugal Walks** (96 575 3033, www.portugalwalks.com).

ESSENTIAL INFORMATION

Resources A-Z

ESSENTIAL INFORMATION

ADDRESSES

The name of the road or square comes first, then the number of the building. Numbering starts from the end of the street that is nearest the river. Several major squares have official names and a traditional, more commonly used designation. Prime examples are Praça do Comércio, which is usually known as Terreiro do Paço (also the name of the local Metro station); Praça Dom Pedro IV, which is always known as Rossio (also a Metro station); Largo Trindade Coelho, which is more often known as Largo da Misericórdia; and Campo Mártires da Pátria, invariably referred to as Campo Santana. In the Baixa, Rua Áurea is also known as Rua do Ouro.

AGE RESTRICTIONS

For heterosexuals and homosexuals, the age of consent is 14. You must be 17 to drive a vehicle but you may encounter problems if you're under 18. To hire a car, you must be at least 18; more for some vehicles. The minimum age to purchase cigarettes is 18.

ATTITUDE & ETIQUETTE

The Portuguese are a very courteous people and are sure to say 'com licença' if they want to edge past you, or 'desculpe' if they accidentally bump into you; you should do the same. In shops it's normal to greet the assistant with a 'bom dia' or 'boa tarde', depending on whether it's morning or afternoon. In addressing people, the Portuguese use different forms for 'you' depending on who's being addressed, and are rather more formal than, say, the Spanish. Young people may launch straight in with 'tu', but with strangers you're best sticking with 'você' or even

'o senhor'/'a senhora'. In English, things tend to loosen up.

The Portuguese are also adept at queuing. At bus and tram stops, don't be deceived by the fact that no queue is visible into thinking that one doesn't exist: it almost certainly does, in the heads of the people at the stop. If anyone boards before someone else who's been waiting longer, it's sure to trigger tutting and resentment.

BUSINESS

To start local operations, foreign companies only need to register: to set up as a sole trader, general partnership or limited company, procedures are as for locals. Your embassy's commercial section can advise you, as can the **Centro da Formalidade de Empresas** (*see p227*). When presenting documents, take along the original and two copies, and use the same signature as on your passport. Business people may appear laid-back, but formal address, and dress, are the norm.

Chambers of commerce

British-Portuguese Chamber of Commerce
Rua da Estrela 8, Estrela (21 394 2020, www.bpcc.pt). Tram 25, 28. **Open** 9.30am-4.30pm Mon-Fri. **Map** p245 J8.

Câmara de Comércio Americana em Portugal
Rua da Dona Estefânia 155, 5ºE, Estefânia (21 357 2561, www.amcham.org.pt). Metro Saldanha. **Open** 9.30am-1pm, 2-5pm Mon-Fri. **Map** p246 M6.

There's a very active **American Club of Lisbon**, based at the Sheraton (*see p220*; 21 352 9308,

www.americancluboflisbon.com), which hosts regular lunch addresses by major figures.

Conventions & office hire

The following business centres may be able to help with organising larger events, as will most major hotels.

M76
Rua da Misericórdia 76, 4th floor, Chiado (21 321 0100, www.m76chiado.com). Metro Baixa-Chiado or tram 28. **Open** *Reception* 9am-midnight Mon-Fri; 9am-6pm Sat. **No credit cards. Map** p250 L9. Furnished offices with secretarial support. Meeting rooms for hire.

Regus Business Centre
Avenida da Liberdade 110, Marquês de Pombal (21 340 4501, www.regus.com). Metro Avenida. **Open** 9am-6.30pm Mon-Fri. **Map** p246 L8. Well-staffed, central serviced offices.

Couriers & shippers

EMS, the courier arm of the state postal service (*see p230*), offers a well-priced service, delivering in 48 hours to major European capitals and in two to seven working days elsewhere.

Chronopost
Avenida Infante Dom Henrique, Lote 10, Olivais (21 854 6000, www.chronopost.pt). **Open** 9am-12.30pm, 2-6pm Mon-Fri. **No credit cards.**

DHL
Rua da Cidade de Liverpool 16, Anjos (70 750 5606, www.dhl.pt). **Open** 8.30am-7.30pm Mon-Fri; 9am-2.30pm Sat. **Client service** *Avenida Marechal Gomes da Costa, 27AB.* **Open** 9.30am-noon, 2-8pm Mon-Fri; 10am-2pm Sat. **No credit cards. Other location** Airport, Rua C, Edificio 124 (phone as above).

Secretarial services

Egor Portugal
*Rua Castilho 75, 7th floor, Marquês
de Pombal (21 369 6300, www.egor.
pt). Metro Marquês de Pombal.*
Map p246 K7.

Kelly Services
*Gare do Oriente, Espaço F1 (21
893 30 50, www.kellyservices.pt).
Metro Oriente.*

Translation &
interpretation services

The **British Embassy** (*see right*)
lists translators on its website's
'Living in Portugal' section.

Traducta
*Rua Rodrigo da Fonseca 127-1 Dto,
Marquês de Pombal (21 388 3384,
www.traducta.pt). Metro Marquês
de Pombal.* **Open** 9am-1pm, 2-6pm
Mon-Fri. **No credit cards. Map**
p246 K7.
Traducta is an established
company offering translation
and interpretation services.

Useful organisations

**Centro da Formalidade
de Empresas**
*Rua da Junqueira 39, Alcântara
(21 361 5400, www.cfe.iapmei.pt).
Tram 15.* **Open** 9am-4pm Mon-Fri.
One-stop shop for setting up a
company (*sociedade*). It can get
pretty busy: come early or book
an appointment.

AICEP Portugal Global
*Avenida 5 de Outubro 101, Campo
Pequeno (21 790 9500, www.
portugalglobal.pt). Metro Campo
Pequeno.* **Open** 9am-5.30pm Mon-
Fri. **Map** p248 L5.
The state investment agency is a
good source of information, with
plenty of English speakers.

CONSUMER

All cafés, restaurants, hotels and
other establishments must, by
law, have a *livro de redamações*,
where disgruntled customers may
write their criticism, and which is
periodically inspected by officials.
Merely asking for this 'book of
complaints' is likely to make your
host considerably more emollient. In
general, though, consumer rights are
not very well protected in Portugal.
The most active campaigning
organisation is **Deco** (21 841 0800,
www.deco.proteste.pt), which can
also offer advice.

DISABLED

With cobbled streets and lots of hills,
Lisbon is a challenge for disabled
travellers, though rules for new
buildings are strict. In museums,
hotels and shopping centres, facilities
for the disabled are common, as are
assigned parking spots.
Public transport company **Carris**
has a special minibus service for the
disabled (21 361 2141, 6.30am-10pm
Mon-Fri, 8am-10pm Sat & Sun)
but you need a special card: take a
medical certificate proving disability,
photograph and passport to the
Carris offices in Santo Amaro (Rua
1° de Maio 101). The service must
be booked two days in advance and
confirmed the next day; the cost is
that of an ordinary bus ticket.
Tourism company **Accessible
Portugal** (92 691 0989, www.
accessibleportugal.com) can hunt
down appropriate accommodation
for you, as well as offering tours
and equipment, from wheelchairs
to grab rails.

**Cooperativa Nacional de Apoio
a Deficientes**
*Praça Dr Fernando Amado 566-E,
Chelas (21 895 5332). Metro Chelas.*
Open 10am-1pm, 2.30-6pm Mon-Fri.
This association can provide advice
and information about tourism
services for the disabled.

DRUGS

Since July 2001, consumption or
possession of small amounts of any
drug are no longer crimes punishable
by imprisonment. Offenders are
instead summoned before an
administrative tribunal, which
can impose a fine or compulsory
counselling. Dealing, though, is likely
to result in imprisonment.

ELECTRICITY

Electricity in Portugal runs on 220V.
Plugs have two round pins. To use
UK appliances, purchase an adaptor
(available at UK electrical shops, but
hard to find in Lisbon). US appliances
run on 110V and require a converter,
available at Lisbon's larger specialist
electricity stores.

EMBASSIES &
CONSULATES

Australian Embassy
*Avenida da Liberdade 198, 2°E,
1300 (21 310 1500, www.portugal.
embassy.gov.au). Metro Avenida.*
Open 9am-5pm Mon-Fri. **Map**
p248 L5.

British Embassy
*Rua São Bernardo 33, Estrela, 1249
(21 392 4000, www.gov.uk). Tram
28.* **Open** 9-11.30am, 3-4.30pm
Mon-Thur; 9.30am-12.30pm Fri.
Map p245 J8.
The community site www.bcclisbon.
org also has information.

Canadian Embassy
*Edifício Vitória, Avenida da
Liberdade 196/200-203, 1269 (21
316 4600, www.canadainternational.
gc.ca/portugal). Metro Avenida.*
Open 8.30am-12.30pm, 1-5.15pm
Mon-Thur; 8.30am-1pm Fri. **Map**
p246 L8.

Irish Embassy
*Avenida da Liberdade 200, 4th floor,
1250 (21 392 9440, www.embassy
ofireland.pt). Metro Avenida.* **Open**
9.30am-12.30pm Mon-Fri. **Map**
p246 L7.

US Embassy
*Avenida das Forças Armadas, Sete
Rios, 1600 (21 727 3300, http://
portugal.usembassy.gov). Metro
Jardim Zoológico.* **Open** *Visas*
8-10am Mon-Fri. *Information*
11.30am-4pm Mon-Fri. *Commercial
section* 2-5pm Mon-Fri. **Map** p248 J3.

EMERGENCIES

For emergency services, dial **112**
and specify either **polícia** (police),
ambulância (ambulance service)
or **bombeiros** (fire brigade).

GAY & LESBIAN

Centro LGBT
*Rua dos Fanqueiros 40, Baixa (21
887 3918, www.ilga-portugal.pt).
Metro Terreiro do Paço/Baixa-
Chiado.* **Open** 6-11pm Thur-Sat.
Map p251 M8.
This friendly council-funded
community centre run by the local
ILGA affiliate offers advice,
information and counselling.

Clube Safo
*Mailing address: Apartado
9973, 1911-701 (96 795 7516,
www.clubesafo.com).*
National association defending
lesbian rights.

HEALTH

There are no special threats to
health in Portugal, though strong
suncream and sun hats should be
kept to hand. As for travel elsewhere
in the European Union, UK or
other EU citizens should get a free
European Health Insurance Card

before leaving home. This does not substitute medical and travel insurance, but entitles you to any state-provided treatment that may become necessary during your trip, whether as a result of illness or accident. Any treatment provided is on the same terms as Portuguese nationals – that is, free except for a symbolic fee. Some hospitals offer both free state and paid-for private healthcare; if you're asked to pay anything more than the symbolic fee up front, then you're being presumed to want the latter so you must make clear what you want.

Portugal's public health system is poor by western European standards. Once you reach the specialists, standards are reasonable, but GPs are underfunded and burdened with bureaucracy. Those who have insurance should take advantage of a strong private sector. A visit to a private doctor will cost from €60, but the service is good.

Complementary medicine

Portugal doesn't have a culture of alternative medicine, apart from the use of traditional herbal remedies. Sweet-smelling *ervanárias* still thrive, where customers discuss their ailments in hushed tones with the shopkeeper. Herbs come in 100g (3.5oz) bags and are then made into a tea. There's an enormous variety, used to cure everything from alcoholism to haemorrhoids. The packaging often gives away what's being offered: a large green eye for herbs to ward off jealousy; wads of banknotes to attract money.

Ervanária Rosil

Rua da Madalena 257, Baixa (21 886 5215, www.evanararosil. com). Metro Rossio. **Open** 9am-1.30pm, 2.30-7pm Mon-Fri; 9am-1.30pm Sat. **No credit cards. Map** p250 M9.
This long-established herbalist sells local and imported medicinal herbs and potions, many as blends packaged under its own brand name, for everything from eczema to rheumatism and sexual dysfunctions. Their shop opposite at no.210, which also stocks modern diet products, stays open through lunch. Rival Biototal is at no.150 (21 886 9178, www.biototal.pt). With both companies, you can order online.

Contraception & abortion

Condoms are easily available in supermarkets, from vending machines and in pharmacies, which also sell the 'morning-after' pill. Abortion is legal. *See also right* **Helplines**.

Clínica dos Arcos

Rua Mãe d'Água 15A, Príncipe Real (21 322 0000, www.clinicadosarcos. com). Metro Rato. **Open** 9am-6pm. **Map** p246 L8.
Spanish-owned private abortion clinic; the first to open in Portugal after legalisation.

Hospital de Santa Maria

Avenida Professor Egas Moniz, Campo Grande (21 780 5000, obstetrics ext 1422, information 21 780 5555, www.hsm.min-saude.pt). Metro Cidade Universitária or bus 701, 732, 738, 755, 768. **Open** *Obstetrics* 8am-4pm Mon-Fri. **Map** p248 K2.
This is Lisbon's largest general hospital, with comprehensive emergency services.

Maternidade Dr Alfredo da Costa

Rua Pedro Nunes, Saldanha (21 318 4000, www.chlc.min-saude.pt). Metro Picoas. **Open** *Family planning* 2-6pm Tue-Thur; 8am-noon Fri. *Gynaecology* 8am-2pm Tue; 8am-1pm Wed-Fri.* **Map** p248 L8.
Lisbon's main maternity unit: family planning and counselling. Book in advance.

Dentists

Public health dentists charge a nominal fee, but standards are patchy, so go private if you can. Click through to the list of English-speaking dentists on the 'Living in Portugal' webpage of the British Embassy (*see p227*).

Doctors

Anjos da Noite

Rua Francisco Franco 5-1E, Alvalade (707 507 507, www.anjosdanoite.pt). Bus 705, 721, 722, 791, 708. **Open** *Head office* 8am-10pm daily. **Map** p249 O2.
Members of 'Night Angels' pay a €2.50 monthly fee for a range of (paid) medical services, with clinics and home visits included.

Clínica Médica Internacional de Lisboa

Avenida Sidónio Pais 14, Marquês de Pombal (21 351 3310, www.cmil.pt). Metro Parque. **Open** 9am-8pm Mon-Fri. **No credit cards. Map** p246 L6.
A busy practice where Dr David Ernst and his colleagues are used to dealing with foreigners.

Helplines

Alcoólicos Anónimos

21 716 2969. **Open** 24hrs daily.
The local Alcoholics Anonymous.

Centro SOS Voz Amiga

21 354 4545. **Open** 4pm-midnight daily.
For those suffering from loneliness and depression.

Intoxicações INEM

808 250 143. **Open** 24hrs daily.
Emergency advice on what to do in case of poisoning or overdose.

Linha Verde de Medicamentos

808 202 844. **Open** 9am-6pm daily.
Run by the national medicines authority, fielding questions about medicinal drugs.

Narcóticos Anónimos

Freephone 800 202 013.
Open 8.30-10.30pm Mon, Wed, Fri.
The local Narcotics Anonymous.

Saúde 24

808 24 24 24, www.saude24.pt.
Open 24hrs daily.
Main national health helpline, covering all subjects.

Sexualidade em Linha

808 222 003. **Open** 10am-6pm Mon-Fri.
State-funded helpline aimed mainly at teenagers.

Hospitals: public

For Lisbon's main public hospitals, see www.chlc.min-saude.pt. Hospitals with emergency wards (*serviço de urgência*) that are open 24hrs daily include the **Hospital de Santa Maria** (*see left*) and **Hospital Curry Cabral** (Rua da Beneficência 8; 21 792 4200/2).

Hospitals: private

Hospital CUF

Travessa Castro 3, Avenida Infante Santo, Alcântara (21 392 6100/15, www.saudecuf.pt). Bus 713, 720, 727, 738, 760, 773. **Map** p243 G9.
Other location Hospital CUF Descobertas, Rua Mário Botas, Parque das Nações (21 002 5200).

Opticians

GIL Oculista

Rua da Prata 138-140, Baixa (21 887 9829). Metro Baixa-Chiado or tram 12, 28. **Open** 9.30am-7pm Mon-Fri; 9.30am-1pm Sat. **Map** p246 M9.

Established in 1865, this shop offers personal service and a decent range of glasses and sunglasses.

Multiópticas
Rua do Carmo 102, Chiado (21 323 4500). Metro Baixa-Chiado. **Open** 9am-8pm Mon-Sat. **Map** p246 L9. Modern, efficient chain with a large range of frames and one-hour delivery. The spin-off chain, Sun Planet, specialises in sunglasses. **Other locations** throughout the city.

Pharmacies

Identified by a green cross. Many drugs are available without a prescription and you can get basic advice on the spot. Out of office hours there's at least one pharmacy open in each neighbourhood. A rota is posted in pharmacy windows.

STDs, HIV & AIDS

For most problems, see a GP or use the emergency service of a hospital. AIDS was long aggravated by high levels of needle sharing among addicts, but exchange schemes are now reaching most users. English is spoken at the following HIV/AIDS helplines:

Abraço 21
799 7500. **Open** 10am-7pm Mon-Fri.

Linha SOS Sida
Freephone 80 020 1040. **Open** 5.30-9.30pm daily.
Information, orientation, support.

ID

Legally, you must carry ID at all times; for Britons and non-EU nationals that means a passport. In practice, you'll only need it if you get into trouble.

INSURANCE

The Departamento Legalização de Viaturas of the **Automóvel Clube de Portugal** (www.acp.pt) can help with the paperwork necessary for importing, registering and insuring a car in Portugal – but you'll have to join the organisation.

INTERNET

Internet cafés are easy to find in touristy areas such as Alfama, but for heavy use, head for cheaper joints in neighbourhoods with many South Asian immigrants,

such as Mouraria and Anjos. *See also below* **Libraries**.

LEFT LUGGAGE

Airport

The **Depósito de Bagagem** (21 841 3594) is in the arrivals hall. Cost is according to weight: €3.25 per day for up to 10kg; €4.82 per day for 10-30kg; and €9.55 for 30-60kg. There's no limit on the number of days that you may leave luggage.

LEGAL HELP

If you get into legal difficulties, the **British Embassy** (*see p227;* look on the 'When things go wrong' webpage) can provide a list of English-speaking lawyers. Most big local firms of *advogados* have English speakers.

Centro Nacional de Apoio ao Imigrante
Rua Álvaro Coutinho 14-16, Intendente (808 257 257, from abroad +351 21 810 6100, www.acm.gov.pt). Metro Anjos. **Open** 8.30am-6.30pm Mon-Fri. Legal and other help and advice specifically for foreign residents, run by ACM, the state agency for migration.

LIBRARIES

Specialist libraries are listed in the free council-published *Agenda Cultural* magazine.

Biblioteca Municipal Central
Palácio Galveias, Campo Pequeno (21 780 3020). Metro Campo Pequeno. **Open** 1-7pm Mon, Sat; 10am-7pm Tue-Fri. **Map** p248 M4. The main municipal lending library. Show ID for access, and proof of residency for borrowing.

Biblioteca Nacional
Campo Grande 83, Entrecampos (21 798 2000). Metro Entrecampos. **Open** 9.30am-7.30pm Mon-Fri; 9.30am-5.30pm Sat. **Map** p248 L2. Portugal's national library. Use is restricted to over-18s. Present ID for access.

British Council
Rua de São Marçal 174, Príncipe Real (21 045 6210, www.british council.pt). Metro Rato or bus 758. **Open** 2-8pm Mon, Tue, Thur, Fri; 11am-8pm Wed; 9.30am-6.30pm Sat for language classes. **Map** p246 K8. The longest continuously established British Council office in the world.

Its information centre has a decent collection of novels and poetry, as well as DVDs, music and periodicals. Access for reference purposes (and to use the internet PCs) is free; to borrow items you must join (€30/6mths, €25 reductions).

LOST PROPERTY

For lost or stolen property, try the lost and found section of the **Lisbon police** (*see p230*). Theft should be reported at any police station, in person. For lost or stolen credit cards, contact your bank.

Airport

If your luggage has gone astray, go to the desk in Arrivals set up for this purpose. Items found in the building and handed in go to the PSP police in the airport (21 844 4530).

Public transport

For buses and trams, contact the PSP police station in Olivais (21 853 5403). For the Metro, go to Marquês de Pombal station.

Taxis

If you leave something in a Lisbon taxi, you'll have to phone the company. If you have a receipt with the car's number on it, all the better. If you can't remember the name of the company, and your ride was in central Lisbon, there's a fair chance it will be **Retális** (21 811 9000), the largest taxi company.

MEDIA

Newspapers

A Bola, Record, O Jogo
These three football papers are the country's most popular daily read, respectively biased towards Benfica, Sporting and Porto.

Correio da Manhã
A diet of crime and scandal has made this the country's biggest-selling daily.

Diário de Notícias, Jornal de Notícias
Oporto-based *Jornal de Notícias* is still a big seller; stable-mate *Diário de Notícias* has good classifieds.

Diário Económico, Jornal de Negócios
Rival business dailies.

Expresso
Weekly political analysis.

Público

Comprehensive, quality daily coverage; good on global events.

English-language

The News

This English-language newspaper can be picked up free in pubs in the Cais do Sodré area or read online at www.the-news.net.

The Resident

Algarve-based weekly, also online at http://portugalresident.com.

Foreign newspapers

Delivery of British tabloids is regular, as *The Sun*, *The Daily Mirror*, *The Daily Mail* and *The Daily Express* print in Spain; quality dailies turn up late or even the next day.

Radio

The airwaves are filled with music. Mainstream rock station **Rádio Comercial** (97.4FM) beats the more varied state-run **Antena 3** (100.3FM) at the ratings game, while **Oxigénio** (102.6FM) is wall-to-wall dance music. Church-owned **Rádio Renascença** (103.4FM) has news and talk shows. It and its sister stations have the biggest combined audience. **TSF** (89.5FM) is news radio 24hrs a day. State-run **Antena 1** (95.7 FM) is also a good news and football source. For the **BBC World Service** and other stations you must go online (www.bbc.co.uk/radio).

Television

Privately owned **TVI** and **SIC** have a diet of *telenovelas* – Brazilian and home-grown soaps – docudramas and absurd game shows. The latter's cable offshoot **SIC Notícias** leads in rolling news. State flagship **RTP1** has upped standards lately after a lengthy period of dumbing down, while **RTP2** caters to a discerning (and tiny) audience.

MONEY

Portugal's currency is the **euro** (€). The notes in public circulation are €5, €10, €20, €50, €100, €200, €500, while coins come in €1, €2, 1 cent, 2 cents, 5 cents, 10 cents and 20 cents.

ATMs

You're never far from a Multibanco machine in Lisbon, and locals conduct a vast range of day-to-day transactions on them, from paying bills to buying train and even concert tickets. You can withdraw €200 per day – usually in the form of €20 notes – although you'll probably be charged a handling fee. Terminals are also common in shops, and these and ATMs accept MasterCard, Visa and other major international cards, including Maestro and Cirrus.

Banks

Open from 8.30am to 3pm, though a few branches stay open later. For travellers' cheques, banks charge hefty commission compared with bureaux de change (*see below*) or the large hotels. All major banks have retail branches throughout the city.

Bureaux de change

There are clusters of these around Rossio. As well as tending to offer a better rate of exchange than banks, they also handle a wider range of currencies.

Credit cards

MasterCard and Visa are the most widely accepted, though use is far from universal. Many shops and restaurants don't take American Express.

Tax

Residents of EU member states may not claim back any value-added tax on purchases. Non-EU residents may do so if they buy goods at shops that adhere to the Tax-free scheme; they'll have a sticker displayed in the window. Claims are made by filling in a form available at the Tax-free counter (21 840 8813, 7am-midnight daily) at the airport, near Departures.

NATURAL HAZARDS

There hasn't been a big earthquake in the city since the 1755 disaster. Unlike the Azores, where tremors are relatively common, the very occasional ones that do strike Lisbon are tiny. Otherwise, aside from some fierce Atlantic waves, Portugal is free of natural hazards.

OPENING HOURS

Shops are normally open from 9am to 1pm and 3pm to 6pm or 7pm, although nowadays many high-street shops stay open during lunch. Most supermarkets stay open until 8pm or later. In shopping centres, hours tend to be from 10am until 10pm. Post offices (*correios*) are open from 9am to 6pm, weekdays only (smaller branches may close for lunch). *See also left* **Banks**.

POLICE

Polícia de Segurança Pública (PSP) officers have a relaxed air, but as is typical in former dictatorships, Portugal's law enforcers are only gradually regaining the trust of the population. Their training and image have improved, and you should find them polite and helpful. But don't try to resist or argue if you get into bother. Quiet politeness is definitely the best approach. There is a police station for tourists in Palácio Foz on Praça dos Restauradores (21 342 1634).

POSTAL SERVICES

State postal service **CTT** (whose clunky site is at www.ctt.pt) has a monopoly on letter delivery. First-class mail is *correio azul* (blue mail). Costing a minimum €2.20, it should get anywhere in Europe in under four days and to the US in no more than six. Second-class mail, *correio normal*, to Europe (other than Spain) costs €0.72 for a standard-sized letter under 20g (7oz); to the rest of the world it costs €0.80. Within Portugal, sending a 20g letter costs €0.42, or €0.50 for *correio azul*. An alternative is to buy a pre-paid *correio verde* envelope or box, whose contents may be of any weight; for light packages this works out more expensive, though.

Stamps and envelopes are sold at all post office counters or from nearby machines. Mailing boxes usually have two or more slots to keep *correio azul* apart.

Main post office

Praça dos Restauradores 58, Restauradores (21 326 1370). Metro Restauradores. **Open** 8am-10pm Mon-Fri; 9am-6pm Sat. **Map** p250 L8.

Poste restante

Mail can be addressed to someone by name 'Poste restante' and sent to a particular post office. It costs €0.60 per item to pick up. If no office is specified then mail ends up at the Cabo Ruivo depot in eastern Lisbon (Avenida Marechal Gomes da Costa 13A, 21 831 8470).

RELIGION

Portugal remains a thoroughly Roman Catholic country and you'll never be very far from a church. Check on the doors for mass times.

St George's Church (Anglican)
Rua São Jorge, Estrela (21 390 6248, 21 468 3570, www.lisbonanglicans. org). Tram 25, 28 or bus 709, 720, 738. **Service** 11.30am Sun. **Map** p245 J8.

Igreja Evangélica Baptista da Graça (Baptist)
Rua Capitão Humberto Ataíde 28 (21 813 2889). Metro Santa Apolónia or bus 735. **Services** 10am, 11.30am, 6pm Sun; 3pm Wed. **Map** p247 O8.

Budismo Tibetano Nyingma (Buddhist)
Rua do Salitre 117, Rato (21 314 2038, 92 548 2986). Metro Avenida/ Rato. **Open** *Reception* 10am-3pm, 4.30-7pm Mon-Fri. *Practice* 7.15am, 9.30pm Mon-Fri; 9am, 9.30pm Sat, Sun. **Map** p246 L8.

Basílica da Estrela (Catholic)
Praça da Estrela, Estrela (21 396 0915). Tram 25, 28. **Open** 7.30am-1pm, 3-8pm daily. **Mass** 8am, 12.15pm, 7pm Mon-Fri; 7pm Sat; 9am, noon, 1.15pm (except July-Sept) Sun. **Map** p245 J8.

Sé Catedral (Catholic)
Largo da Sé, Alfama (21 886 6752). Tram 12, 28. **Mass** 6.30pm Tue-Sat; 11.30am, 7pm Sun. **Map** p251 M10.

Comunidade Hindú de Portugal (Hindu)
Alameda Mahatama Gandhi, Lumiar (21 757 6524). Metro Campo Grande then bus 778. **Open** 9am-5pm Mon-Fri.

Centro Ismaelita de Lisboa (Ismaili)
Avendia Lusiada 10, 1500-657 (21 722 9000). Metro Laranjeiras. **Open** 9am-7pm daily. **Map** p248 J3.

Mesquita Central de Lisboa (Islamic)
Avenida José Malhôa, Praça de Espanha (21 387 4142/2220). Metro Praça de Espanha. **Open** 9am-6pm daily. **Map** p248 K4.

Sinagoga Shaaré Tikvá (Jewish)
Rua Alexandre Herculano 59, Rato (21 393 1130). Metro Rato. **Open** 10am-1pm, 2-5pm Mon-Thur; 9am-1pm Fri. **Map** p246 K7.

St Andrew's Church of Scotland (Presbyterian)
Rua da Arriaga 13, Lapa (21 468 0853, www.standrewslisbon.com). Tram 25 or bus 713, 727, 760. **Worship** 11am Sun. **Map** p245 H10.

SAFETY & SECURITY

Lisbon is a relatively safe town, but be aware of pickpockets in crowds, especially on trams. Violent incidents are rare but basic safety rules apply: carry little cash, avoid dark, deserted places, and look after valuables.

Be particularly alert when visiting the Bairro Alto, Cais do Sodré and the lower Alfama. There's heavier drug-related crime in the peripheral shanty towns. Car crime is common and the usual precautions should be taken.

SMOKING

Smoking isn't permitted on public transport or in museums, and few restaurants opt to install the expensive equipment needed to have licensed smoking sections in closed premises. However, terraces abound.

STUDY

Language classes

Aside from the university's well-regarded summer course (*see below*), several local institutions offer Portuguese language classes. Try the **Cambridge School** (21 312 4600, www.cambridge.pt) and **International House** (21 315 1493/4/6, www.ihlisbon.com).

Universities

Universidade de Lisboa
Alameda da Universidade, Cidade Universitária 1649 (21 796 7624, www.ulisboa.pt). Metro Campo Grande.

Portugal's first university, founded around 1288, ended up up in Coimbra. It wasn't until the 19th century that higher education regained a foothold in the capital in the form of this institution. Its Faculdade de Letras has run summer courses in Portuguese language since 1934; for information, visit www.iclp. letras.ulisboa.pt.

TELEPHONES

Dialling & codes

The international access code for Portugal is **351**. Lisbon numbers start with 21 (this forms part of the number). To dial another part of Portugal from Lisbon, simply dial the number, which invariably starts with 2; there are no area codes. (If you have an old number together with an area code starting with zero, try replacing the zero with a 2.) To make an international call from Portugal

dial 00, followed by the country code (Australia **61**, Canada and the US **1**, New Zealand **64**, United Kingdom **44**) then area code (without the zero if dialling the UK) and number.

Operator services

For directory enquiries (national or international) or to reverse charges, dial **1820** (€0.74 plus €0.43/min).

Public phones

Portugal Telecom (PT), now trading mainly under the name MEO, has both coin-operated booths and phonecard kiosks. Various PT and other calling cards are available but deals change constantly; look out for leaflets (invariably in English) at kiosks and in shops. Such cards are a boon when phoning from hotels.

Mobile phones

All three main mobile network operators – **MEO**, **NÓS** and **Vodafone** – have good coverage in the city. Portugal was a pioneer of pre-paid no-strings accounts and all these providers offer a SIM card for under €10 (including calls of that value), and sell products online and from agents across the city.

TIME

Portuguese time is always the same as British time, keeping in line with GMT in winter and moving an hour ahead in summer. The 24-hour clock is normally used, even in everyday speech.

TIPPING

In restaurants and cafés, a tip of anything between two and ten per cent is normal. Tipping in bars is less common, although meagre wages often warrant it. With taxi drivers, it's less common and frankly few deserve it. We would encourage tipping those who take you to your destination without griping.

TOILETS

Lisbon isn't overly endowed with public toilets (*sanitários* or *casas de banho*). Café owners aren't fussy about people wandering in off the street, but it's only polite to ask and the facilities may be less than fragrant; museums, restaurants and shopping centres tend to be a better bet. The men's is usually marked with an H for *homens*, the women's with an S for *senhoras*.

TOURIST INFORMATION

As well as the offices listed below, there are well-stocked **Ask Me** city tourism booths located in Rua Augusta and in front of the Mosteiro dos Jerónimos in Belém (both open 10am-1pm, 2-6pm Tue-Sat).

Lisboa Welcome Center
Praça do Comércio, Baixa (21 031 2810, www.visitlisboa.com or www.askmelisboa.com). Metro Terreiro do Paço or tram 12, 15, 18, 28. **Open** 9am-8pm daily. **Map** p250 M10.
Helpful staff, leaflets, internet PCs and a shop selling local handicrafts and gourmet products (entry on Rua do Arsenal) are found in the Lisbon tourist board's main complex. Here you can buy a **Lisboa Card** offering up to three days' unlimited public transport – including on trains to Cascais and Sintra – plus a range of discounts for museums and entertainment (24hr card €18.50, €11.50 5-11s; 48hr €31.50, €17.50 5-11s; 72hr €39, €20.50 5-11s).

The **Lisboa Restaurant Card**, offering discounts of up to 20 per cent in 36 restaurants, isn't quite such good value. Staff here will also book you a rental car or pricey sightseeing tour, or help find accommodation.

There's now also a **Y Lisboa** tourist office for young people just off Praça dos Restauradores (open 10am-10pm daily), with targeted information and more internet PCs.

Other locations Airport (21 845 0660; open 7am-midnight daily); Y Lisboa, Rua do Jardim do Regedor 50 (21 347 2134).

Turismo Palácio Foz
Praça dos Restauradores, Restauradores (21 346 3314, www.visitportugal.com). Metro Restauradores. **Open** 9am-8pm daily. **Map** p250 L8.
City tourist officials armed with leaflets and Lisboa Cards (*see above*) have a desk in this walk-in space run by the national tourist institute, which can provide information about the whole of Portugal.

VISAS & IMMIGRATION

Standard EU immigration law applies: EU citizens planning to stay more than six months will need to apply for a residence permit, but are otherwise free to come and go. Nationals of the US, Australia and New Zealand are entitled to stay

LOCAL CLIMATE

Average temperatures and monthly rainfall in Lisbon.

	Max temp	Min temp	Rainfall (mm/in)
Jan	14°C (57°F)	8°C (46°F)	110/4.3
Feb	16°C (61°F)	9°C (48°F)	111/4.3
Mar	18°C (64°F)	10°C (50°F)	69/2.7
Apr	19°C (66°F)	11°C (52°F)	64/2.5
May	22°C (72°F)	13°C (55°F)	39/1.5
June	25°C (77°F)	15°C (59°F)	21/0.8
July	27°C (81°F)	17°C (63°F)	5/0.2
Aug	28°C (82°F)	18°C (64°F)	6/0.2
Sept	26°C (79°F)	17°C (63°F)	26/1.0
Oct	22°C (72°F)	14°C (57°F)	80/3.1
Nov	18°C (64°F)	11°C (52°F)	114/4.5
Dec	15°C (59°F)	9°C (48°F)	108/4.3

up to 90 days with just a passport; Canadians for up to 60 days. If you do have a visa and need to extend it, you should apply at least a week before the previous leave expires.

WHEN TO GO

Lisbon has long, dry summers and a mild winter, limited to a period of wetter and cooler weather between December and February. Autumn (October and November) and spring (March to May) are mild but sometimes very wet. May is a particularly lovely month. August is generally the hottest month but temperatures rarely rise to the levels of, say, Madrid. Outside July and August, nights can be cool. On sunny days, suncream is a must.

Public holidays

Most shops close on public holidays, except for shopping malls and big supermarkets. Restaurants, cafés and cinemas tend not to close either, but museums do.

Good Friday (Sexta-feira Santa)
Friday before Easter Sunday (date varies)
Freedom Day (Dia da Liberdade)
25 April
Worker's Day (Dia do Trabalhador)
1 May
Portugal Day (Dia de Portugal, de Camões e das Comunidades)
10 June
St Anthony's Day (Dia de Santo António)
13 June
Assumption (Assunção de Nossa Senhora)
15 August

Immaculate Conception (Imaculada Conceição)
8 December
Christmas Day (Natal)
25 December
New Year's Day (Ano Novo)
1 January

WOMEN

Lisbon is fairly safe, but it's best not to walk alone late at night in some dingier districts. *See also p231* **Safety & security**.

WORKING IN LISBON

EU citizens are free to work in Portugal, although if they intend to stay for more than six months they'll need a residence permit. Permits are issued occasionally to other nationals, but aren't easily arranged. For more information, contact the Portuguese embassy or consulate in your home country.

Serviço de Estrangeiros e Fronteiras
Avenida António Augusto de Aguiar 20, Marquês de Pombal, 1050-017 (808 202 652/21 358 5500, www.sef.pt). Metro Parque. **Open** 8am-4pm Mon-Fri. **Map** p246 L6.
Either you or your *despachante* (agent) must pre-book an appointment at this state immigration office if you intend to get a residence permit.

ERES Relocation Services
Centro Comercial Charneca, Loja 13, Rua das Lapas, Cascais, 2750-772 (21 485 8233, www.ereselocation.com/pt). Train from Cais do Sodré. **Open** 9am-6pm Mon-Fri.
Private outfit with decades of experience handling work-related problems.

Vocabulary

Although the language spoken in Portugal can sound indecipherable even to Brazilians, speakers of other Romance languages are in better shape than they might think, as reading Portuguese is a lot easier than understanding it when spoken. Locals are themselves often good linguists. For decades, millions of them have packed their bags to try their luck elsewhere; of those who return, most speak another language. Youngsters, too, invariably speak some English.

PRONUNCIATION

Pronunciation follows some clear rules. The **s** always takes the **sh** sound at the end of words. Elsewhere, it becomes **sh** only when followed by **t** or **c**. Watch the latter: Cascais is 'Kashkaish', whereas *piscina* is 'pisheena'. Another feature is the **nh** and **lh** consonants, which are similar to the Spanish **ñ** and **ll**. Thus Saldanha is 'Saldanya', and *bacalhau* is 'bakalyow'.

The **c** is soft before **e** and **i**, but hard elsewhere. Note also that **m** takes on a nasal tone at the end of words, as in *sim*, for yes.

Vowels are tricky. Accents denote a stressed syllable, although the tilde (~) and the ^ also give the vowel a more elongated sound. The **ão** is unique to Portuguese. A nasal, truncated 'ow' is the best description. Thus *informação* is 'informasow', with a nasal yelp on the last syllable.

The **e** is silent at the end of the word, unless it has an accent. So *saudade* is 'sowdad', whereas *café* is 'kaffay'. Also:

ç – like the **s** in song
ch and **x** – both like the **sh** in ship
j – like the **s** in treasure
g – is like **j**, except when it comes before an **a**, **o** or **u** when it is hard
q – is like **k** in English, even when twinned with u
ei – like the **ay** in hay
ou – like the English exclamation **oh**

BASICS

yes *sim*; **no** *não*; **maybe** *talvéz/se calhar*
with/without *com/sem*
good *bom* (masc), *boa* (fem);
bad *mau* (masc), *má* (fem)
big *grande*; **small** *pequeno*

very *muito*
hot *quente*; **cold** *frio*
there is/are... *há...*
there isn't/aren't... *não há...*
why *porquê*; **when** *quando*;
who is it? *quem é?*
I'd like... *queria*
where is...? (a fixed thing) *onde fica...?*
where is...? (a movable thing or person) *onde está...?*

USEFUL TERMS AND PHRASES

men's *homens/senhores*
women's *mulheres/senhoras*
open *aberto*; **closed** *fechado*
entrance *entrada*; **exit** *saida*
what is your name? *como se chama?* (formal) *como te chamas?* (informal)
my name is... *chamo-me...*
I am English/American *sou inglês/norte-americano* (masc) *sou inglesa/norte-americana* (fem)
I don't speak Portuguese *não falo Português*
do you speak English? *fala inglês?* (formal) *falas inglês?* (informal)
I don't understand *não entendo*
speak more slowly please *fale mais devagar, por favor*
where is the toilet? *onde fica a casa de banho?*

POLITE CONVERSATION

hello *olá*
good day/evening/night *bom dia/ boa tarde/boa noite*
goodbye *adeus* (formal) *ciao* (informal); **see you later** *até logo*
how are you? *como está?* (formal) *como estás?* (informal) *tudo bem?* (more informal)
I'm fine *estou bem*
thank you *obrigado* (masc) *obrigada* (fem)
you're welcome *de nada/ não tem de quê*
please *por favor/se faz favor*
excuse me *com licença*
sorry *desculpe* (formal) *desculpa* (informal)
that's/it's okay *está bem/ não faz mal*

SHOPS AND HOTELS

is it cheap/expensive? *é barato/caro?*

how much is it/are they? *quanto é/quanto são?*
buy *comprar*; **rent** *alugar*
I like... *gosto de...*; **I don't like...** *não gosto de...*
do you have a single/double room for tonight? *tem um quarto individuo/duplo para hoje?*
bed *cama*
bathroom *casa de banho*; **bath** *banheira*; **shower** *chuveiro/duche*

GETTING AROUND

near *perto*; **far** *longe*
left *esquerda*; **right** *direita*
straight on *sempre em frente*
train station *estacão de comboios*
bus station *rodoviário*
do you know the way to...? *sabe o caminho para...?*
bus stop *paragem de autocarros*
petrol *gasolina*; **diesel** *gasóleo*
ticket office *bilheteira*
single *ida*; **return** *ida e volta*
I'd like to go to... *queria ir à...*
one/two/three o'clock *uma/duas/ três horas*

EMERGENCIES

I feel ill *sinto-me mal*
doctor *médico*
pharmacy *farmácia*
hospital *hospital*
emergency ward *serviço de urgência*
ambulance service *ambulância*
police *polícia*
fire brigade *bombeiros*

DAYS, TIMES AND NUMBERS

today *hoje*; **tomorrow** *amanhã*
now *agora*; **later** *mais tarde*
before *antes*
Sunday *domingo*
Monday *segunda-feira*
Tuesday *terça-feira*
Wednesday *quarta-feira*
Thursday *quinta-feira*
Friday *sexta-feira*
Saturday *sábado*

1 *um/uma*; **2** *dois/duas*; **3** *três*; **4** *quatro*; **5** *cinco*; **6** *seis*; **7** *sete*; **8** *oito*; **9** *nove*; **10** *dez*; **11** *onze*; **12** *doze*; **13** *treze*; **14** *quatorze*; **15** *quinze*; **16** *dezasseis*; **17** *dezassete*; **18** *dezoito*; **19** *dezanove*; **20** *vinte*; **30** *trinta*; **40** *quarenta*; **50** *cinquenta*; **60** *sessenta*; **70** *setenta*; **80** *oitenta*; **90** *noventa*; **100** *cem*; **1,000** *mil*

EATING OUT

Except for very small or very fashionable restaurants, you shouldn't need to book ahead. Where it is advisable, you may even be able to do it on the day. Note that, away from touristy areas, Lisbon restaurants may close for part or all of August. As a rule, bills do not include a service charge (though at fancier establishments it's worth checking). Locals, if they tip at all, might leave a *gorjeta* of five per cent.

Menus of restaurants frequented by foreigners often seek to cater to them, but mistranslations of dishes and spelling mistakes ('sulking pig') may prompt nervous visitors to stick to an unchallenging diet of grilled chicken and omelettes. Of course, some of the restaurants most worth visiting don't translate their menus at all.

However, all is not lost. A typical Portuguese restaurant will store fresh produce in display cases, so diners can see what's available. Those specialising in seafood – *marisqueiras* – often have a fridge built into the window, so you can check the wares before stepping inside, and select before ordering. Restaurants that lack any such display are either very cheap – in which case they're best avoided unless we recommend them – or untypically modern or posh. Even in the latter, you can always ask to see a particular fish or cut of meat before ordering.

Basics

I'd like to book a table… *gostaria de reservar uma mesa* **…for two** *para duas pessoas* **…for noon/1pm/8pm)** *para meio dia/para a uma/para as oito*

alho garlic; **almoço** lunch; **azeite** olive oil; **azeitona** olive; **coentro** coriander; **conta** bill; **dose** portion; **ementa** menu; **entrada** starter; **jantar** dinner; **lanche** snack; **lista da vinhos** wine list; **manteiga** butter; **meia** half; **ovo** egg; **pão** bread; **petisco** nibble; **piri-piri** chilli; **sal** salt; **salsa** parsley; **sandes** sandwich.

Cooking styles & techniques

açorda bread that has been soaked with olive oil, garlic, herbs and egg; **assado** roasted; **bem passado** well done; **caril** curry; **cebolada** cooked with onions; **caseiro** home-made; **churrasco** barbecue; **cozido** boiled; **espetada** skewer; **estufado** braised; **forno** oven; **frito** fried; **gratinado** baked with cheese on top; **grelhado** grilled; **guarnecido** garnished; **guisado** braised; **mal passado** rare; **massa** pastry/pasta; **médio** medium rare; **molho** sauce; **na brasa** charcoal-grilled; **no forno** oven-baked; **picante** spicy; **quente** hot/warm; **recheado** stuffed; **salteado** sautéed.

Sopas/ensopados (soups/stews)

Caldo verde shredded kale in potato broth; **canja** chicken broth; **cozido à portuguesa** stew of meats, sausages and cabbage; **feijoada** bean stew made with meat, seafood or snails.

Marisco (shellfish)

amêijoa clam; **camarão** shrimp; **gamba** prawn; **lagosta/lavagante** spiny/Norway lobster; **mexilhão** mussel; **ostra** oyster; **perceve** goose-necked barnacle; **sapateira** crab; **vieira** scallop.

Peixe (fish)

atum tuna; **bacalhau** salted cod (…**a brás** shredded, fried with potato and scrambled egg; …**a Gomes Sá** shredded, fried with onion, with boiled potato, egg and black olives; …**com natas** shredded, baked with cream and potato; …**cozido com grão** boiled, with chickpeas, potato and greens; **besugo** sea bream; **cação** dogfish; **caldeirada** fish stew; **cantaril** redfish; **carapau** mackerel; **cavala** horse mackerel; **cherne** large grouper; **choco** cuttlefish; **corvina** croaker; **dourada** gilthead bream; **enguia** eel; **espadarte** swordfish; **garoupa** grouper; **imperador** cardinal fish; **joaquinzinho** whitebait; **linguado** sole; **lula** squid; **pargo** sea bream; **pastel de bacalhau** deep-fried cod croquettes; **peixe espada** scabbard fish; **peixe galo** John Dory; **pescada** hake; **polvo** octopus; **pregado** turbot; **raia** skate/ray; **robalo** sea bass; **salmão** salmon; **salmonete** red mullet; **sardinha** sardine; **sargo** white bream; **solha** plaice; **truta** trout.

Carne (meat)

bifana slice of braised pork; **bife** steak (though not necessarily beef); **bitoque** slice of fried beef, served with chips and a fried egg; **borrego** lamb; **cabrito** kid; **caracois** snails; **chouriço** smoked sausage; **costoleta** chop; **dobrada** tripe; **entrecosto** pork rib; **entremeada** pork belly; **febras** boned slices of pork; **fiambre** uncured ham; **figado** liver; **ganso de vitela** topside of veal; **iscas** sliced liver; **leitão** suckling pig; **língua** tongue; **linguiça** spiced sausage; **lombinhos** tender pieces of meat; **lombo** loin; **medalhões** medallions; **mãozinha** trotter/hock; **morcela** blood sausage; **paio** cured sausage; **peito** breast; **perna** leg; **porco** pork; **porco preto** black pig; **prego** slice of beef, grilled; **presunto** cured ham; **posta** thick slice of meat (or fish); **rins** kidneys; **salpicão** spiced sausage; **salsicha** sausage; **toucinho** lard; **tripas** tripe; **vaca** cow/beef; **vazia** prime cut of beef; **veado** venison; **vitela** veal.

Aves e caça (poultry & game)

cabidela chicken with giblets; **codorniz** quail; **coelho** rabbit; **faisão** pheasant; **frango** chicken; **ganso** goose; **javali** wild boar; **pato** duck; **perdiz** partridge; **perú** turkey.

Arroz, massa e feijão (rice, pasta & beans)

arroz rice; **esparguetes** spaghetti; **favas** broad beans; **feijão(ões)** bean(s); **lentilhas** lentils.

Legumes (vegetables)

alface lettuce; **batata (doce)** (sweet) potato; **cebola** onion; **cenoura** carrot; **cogumelo** mushroom; **couve** cabbage; **ervilhas** peas; **espargos** asparagus; **espinafres** spinach; **grelos** tender greens; **hortaliça** mixed vegetables; **pepino** cucumber; **pimenta** pepper.

Fruta (fruit)

ananás pineapple; **laranja** orange; **limão** lemon; **maçã** apple; **maracujá** passion fruit; **melancia** watermelon; **melão** cantaloupe; **meloa** melon; **morango** strawberry; **pêssego** peach; **uva** grape.

Sobremesa (dessert)

arroz doce rice pudding; **baba de camelo** dessert of yolks and sugar; **barriga de freira** dessert of breadcrumbs, sugar, egg and nuts; **bolo** cake; **gelado** ice-cream; **leite creme** custard; **pudim** caramel pudding; **toucinho do céu** dessert of almonds, eggs and sugar.

Drinks

vinho wine; **cerveja** beer; **àgua (com/sem gás)** (sparkling/still) water; **àgua da torneira** tap water; **café** coffee (espresso); **chá** tea.

Further Reference

BOOKS

Non-fiction

David Birmingham *A Concise History of Portugal*
A short, illustrated classic.
CR Boxer *The Portuguese Seaborne Empire (1415-1825)*
Account of Portugal's glory days.
Almeida Garrett *Travels in My Homeland*
Witty account from the 19th-century Liberal-Absolutist wars.
Barry Hatton *The Portuguese: A Modern History*
Analysis and anecdotes from a foreign correspondent.
Marion Kaplan *The Portuguese: The Land and its People*
Updated in 2006, this 1980s classic is a fine single-volume introduction.
Richard Mayson *Portugal's Wine and Wine-Makers: Port, Madeira and Regional Wines*
A coffee-table tome, updated in 2013, on local wine history and regions.
AH de Oliveira Marques *History of Portugal*
Good, accessible reference work.
Fernando Pessoa *Lisbon: What the Tourist Should See*
Guidebook by Lisbon's iconic poet covers the major sights.
Fernão Mendes Pinto *Peregrinations*
No-holds-barred account of 20 years of pillaging and adventure during the Discoveries.
José Hermano Saraiva *Portugal: A Companion History*
A decent, concise history, with chronology, gazetteer and maps.
Edite Vieira *The Taste of Portugal*
Loads of recipes, plus tasty snippets of history and literature.

Literature & fiction

António Lobo Antunes *The Return of the Caravels*
Hallucinatory tale from an author preoccupied with Portugal's tainted historical legacy.
Luís Vaz Camões *The Lusiads*
Epic by Portugal's national poet chronicling the adventures of Vasco da Gama. Hard going in English.
José Cardoso Pires *Ballad of Dog's Beach*
Detective story set in the Salazar years, based on a real-life murder.
Lídia Jorge *The Murmuring Coast*
Draws on the author's experiences in colonial Africa.

Eugénio Lisboa & Helder Macedo (eds.) *The Dedalus Book of Portuguese Fantasy*
Short stories from leading Portuguese writers.
Eugénio Lisboa (ed.) *The Anarchist Banker and Other Portuguese Stories: Volume I*
Professor Pfiglzz and His Strange Companion and Other Portuguese Stories: Volume II
Great primers featuring Fernando Pessoa, Eça de Queirós and others.
Pascal Mercier *Night Train to Lisbon*
Mousy Swiss professor obsesses over a dead Portuguese writer. This novel falls short yet captures something of the essence of Lisbon.
Fernando Pessoa *The Book of Disquietude*
The savagely solipsistic 'factless autobiography' of Bernardo Soares, now available in Richard Zenith's translation.
Fernando Pessoa *A Centenary Pessoa*
Eugénio Lisboa's excellent anthology of Pessoa's poetry and prose with critical commentary, a chronology and two 'posthumous interviews'.
Fernando Pessoa *Selected Poems*
Peruse at one of Pessoa's old haunts, such as Café A Brasileira.
Eça de Queirós *Cousin Bazilio*
From Lisbon's premier 19th-century novelist; recounts an affair between a bored bourgeois Príncipe Real housewife and her dashing cousin.
Eça de Queirós *The Maias*
Sort of a Portuguese version of Mann's *Buddenbrooks*.
Erich Maria Remarque *The Night in Lisbon*
The author of *All Quiet on the Western Front* sets an adventure and love story in neutral Lisbon during World War II.
José Saramago *Baltasar and Blimunda*
This almost magically realist adventure set in Lisbon and Mafra made the name of the 1998 Nobel Prize-winner for literature.
José Saramago *The History of the Siege of Lisbon*
Set both in the present day and the twelfth century (during the Christian Reconquest) and with a printshop drudge as its anti-hero.
José Saramago *The Year of the Death of Ricardo Reis*
One of Pessoa's heteronyms returns from Brazil to Salazar-era Lisbon, and meets the ghost of his creator.

Antonio Tabucchi *Pereira Maintains*
A newspaperman questions his life in the face of state censorship, during the oppressive Salazar years. Alain Tanner's film of this intriguing classic starred Marcello Mastroianni.
Robert Wilson *A Small Death in Lisbon*
Unfolds in 1940s and 1990s Portugal, with an engaging detective as its hero.
Richard Zimler *The Last Cabbalist of Lisbon*
This absorbing story is set during the anti-Jewish riots of 1506.

MUSIC

Zeca Afonso *Cantigas de Maio*
A rousing song on this 1971 album by the great folk singer was the signal for the 1974 coup.
Camané *Sempre de Mim*
The most impressive of the current crop of fado singers.
Carlos do Carmo *Um Homem na Cidade*
A 1977 landmark, mixing traditional fado with Sinatra-style crooning.
Deolinda *Dois Selos e um Carimbo*
This group's music draws on fado, but is livelier and more playful.
Alfredo Marceneiro *The Fabulous Marceneiro*
At the age of 70, the inventor of modern fado was still at his peak.
Mariza *Transparente*
Portugal's most versatile female *fadista*.
OqueStrada *AtlanticBeat Mad'in Portugal*
This south-bank trio's sound is eminently danceable.
Carlos Paredes *Movimento Perpétuo*
The art of *guitarra* playing, raised to unprecedented heights.
Amália Rodrigues *Com que Voz*
The fado diva is said to embody the soul of Portugal.
Buraka Som Sistema *Black Diamond*
Angolan *kuduro*, electronically charged and taken from the Lisbon suburbs to the world.

WEBSITES

www.transporlis.sapo.pt
Handy Lisbon route-finder.
www.timeout.sapo.pt Your critical guide to arts, culture and going out in Lisbon (Portuguese).
www.visitlisboa.com
Official tourist office site.

ESSENTIAL INFORMATION

Index

INDEX

Maps

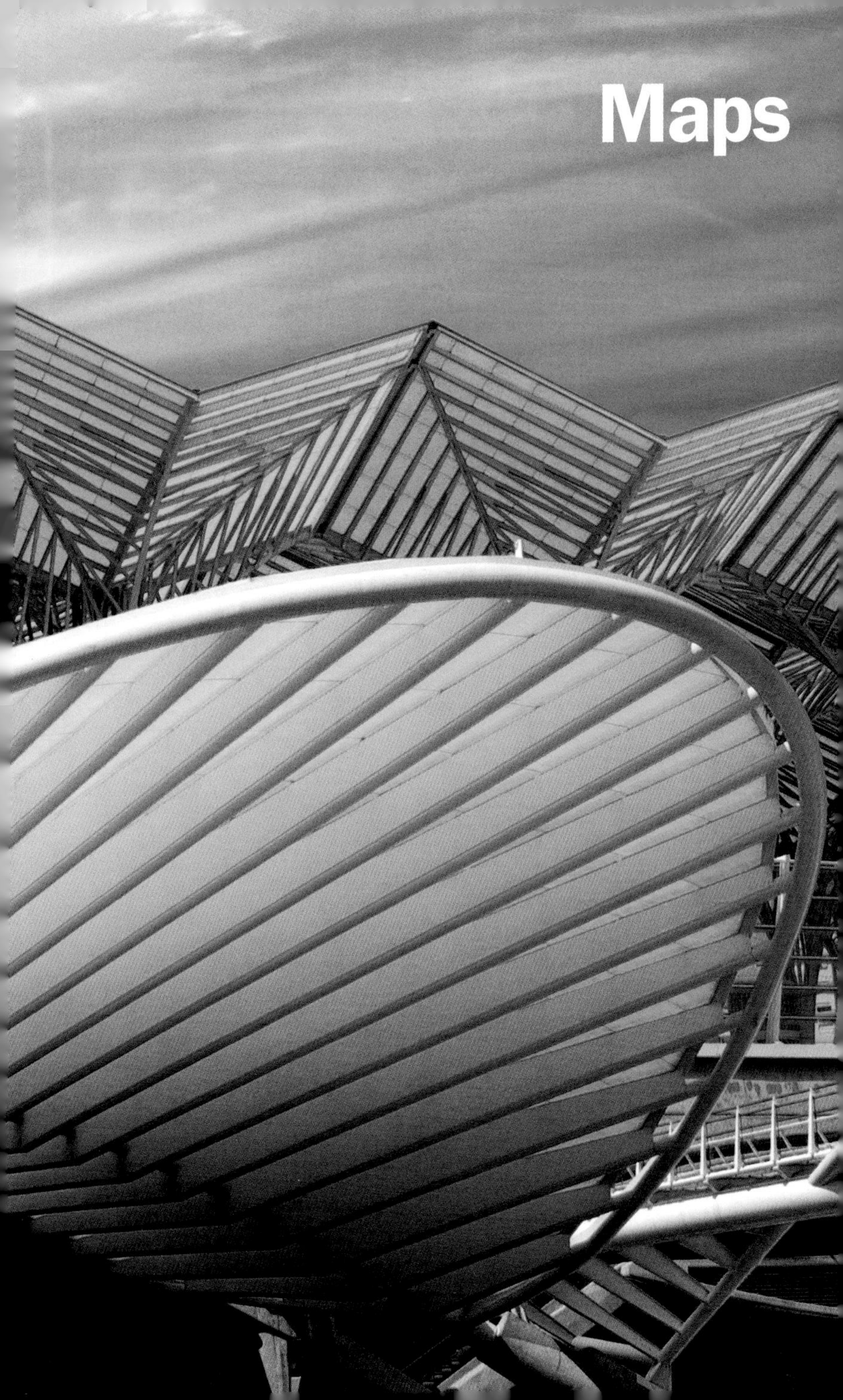

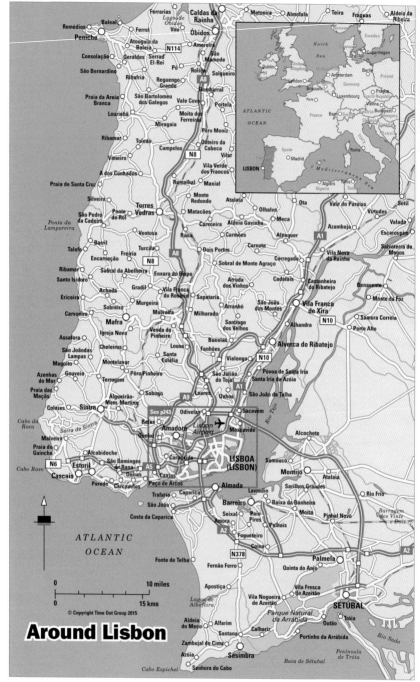

MAPS

Around Lisbon

© Copyright Time Out Group 2015

ATLANTIC
OCEAN

0   10 miles
0   15 kms

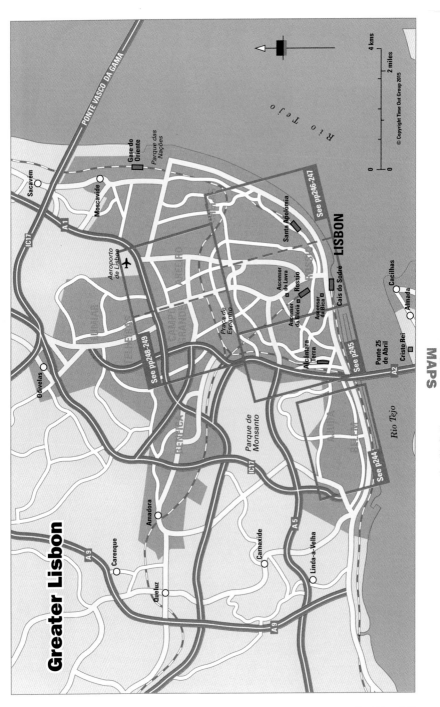

Greater Lisbon

MAPS

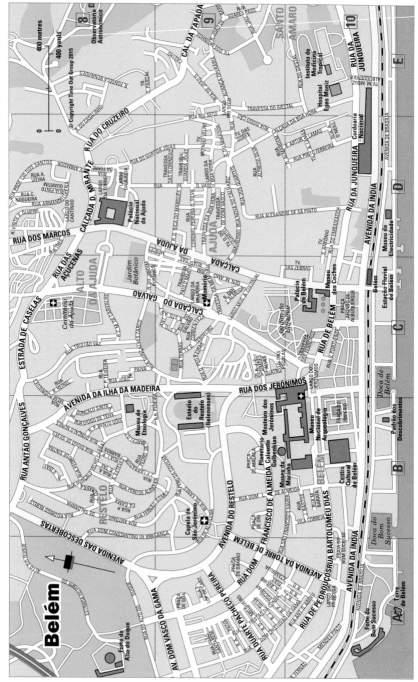

MAPS

Belém

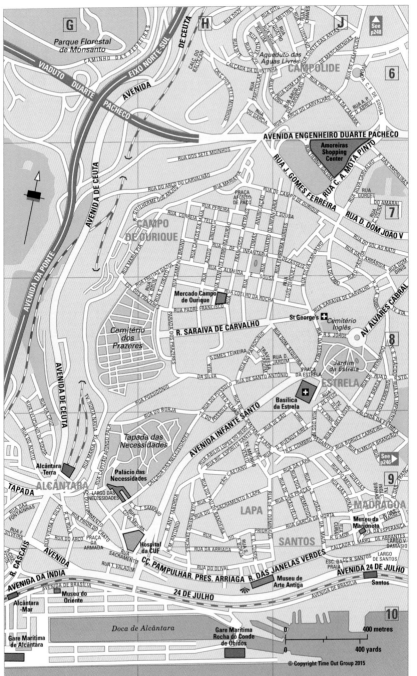

© Copyright Time Out Group 2015

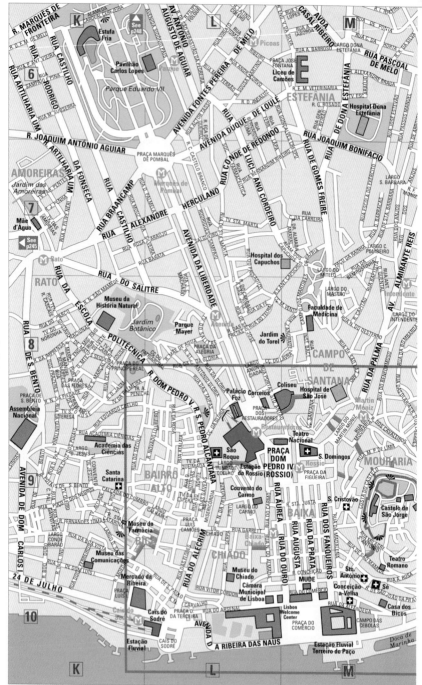

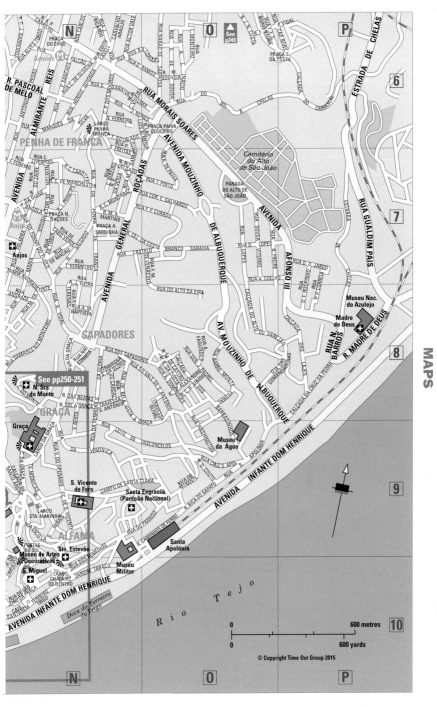

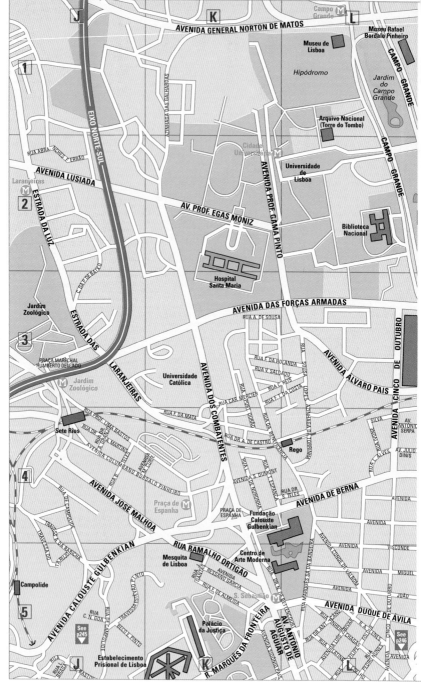

MAPS

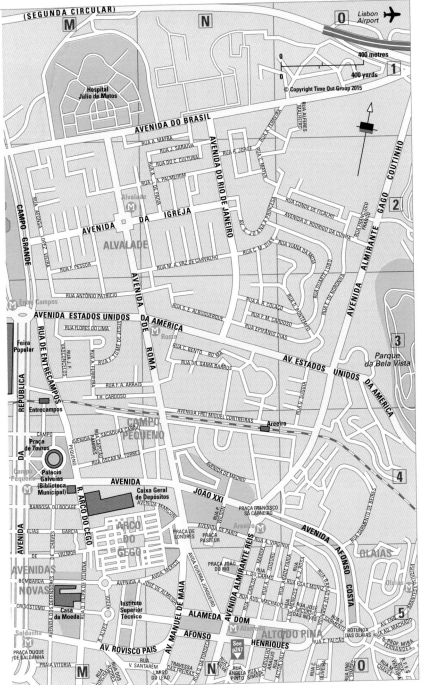

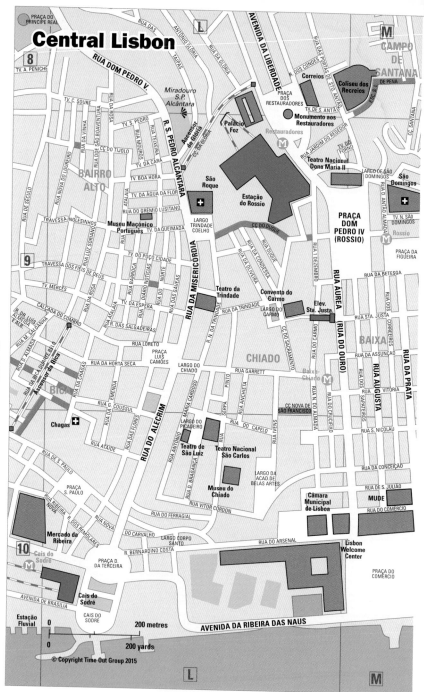

Central Lisbon

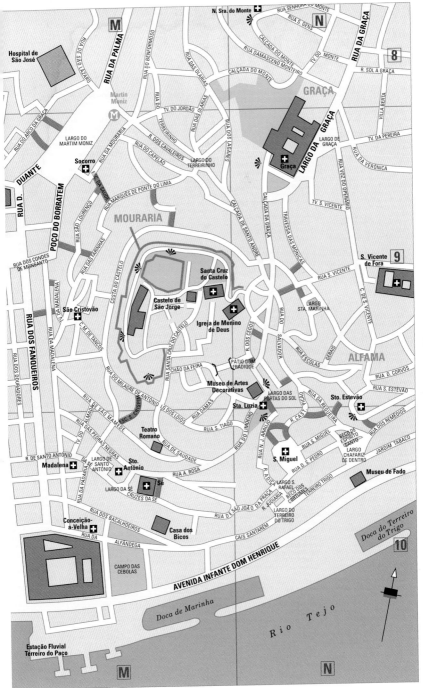

Street Index

STREET INDEX

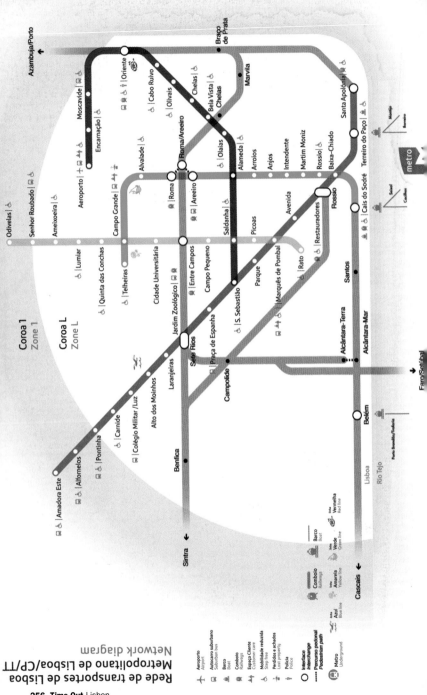